THE LAW
IN AMERICA

The American Heritage History of

THE LAW
IN AMERICA

by
Bernard Schwartz

EDITOR
Alvin M. Josephy, Jr.

Published by American Heritage Publishing Co., Inc., New York
Book Trade Distribution by McGraw-Hill Book Company

The text of this volume, with some variations and without illustrations or feature articles, has been published simultaneously in THE LAW IN AMERICA by Bernard Schwartz.

Staff for this Book

ART DIRECTOR
Mervyn Edward Clay

PICTURE EDITOR
Douglas Tunstell

COPY EDITOR
Brenda Bennerup

ASSISTANT EDITOR
Mary Elizabeth Wise

ADDITIONAL TEXT
Ralph K. Andrist

AMERICAN HERITAGE
PUBLISHING CO., INC.

PRESIDENT AND PUBLISHER
Paul Gottlieb

GENERAL MANAGER, BOOK DIVISION
Kenneth W. Leish

EDITORIAL ART DIRECTOR
Murray Belsky

The editors appreciate the assistance and cooperation of the Centennial Commission of the American Bar Association and its Chairman, Whitney North Seymour, Jr.

Text for Chapters One thru Nine and Important Law Cases in American History (pages 373–376) Copyright © 1974 by Bernard Schwartz. Illustrations, captions, feature articles, and all other materials Copyright © 1974 by American Heritage Publishing Co., Inc., a subsidiary of McGraw-Hill, Inc. All rights reserved. Printed in the United States of America. No part of this publication may be reproduced, stored in a retrieval system, or transmitted, in any form or by any means, electronic, mechanical, photocopying, recording, or otherwise, without the prior written permission of the publisher.

Library of Congress Cataloging in Publication Data

The American heritage history of the law in America.

The text of this volume, with some variations and without illustrations or feature articles, has been published simultaneously by the McGraw-Hill Book Company under title: The Law in America.
   Bibliography: p.
   1. Law—United States—History and criticism.
I. American heritage. II. Title. III. Title: History of the law in America. IV. Title: The law in America.
KF352.S34   340'.0973   74-8264
ISBN 0-07-055749-7
ISBN 0-07-079385-9 (de luxe boxed set with Stories of great crimes and trials)

A Vermont lawyer, 1841, by Horace Bundy

The author dedicates the text

to his wife, Judge Aileen H. Schwartz

Contents

"The Trial," an American courtroom scene painted by Jack Levine, 1953–1954

Introduction

Gilbert and Sullivan's *Iolanthe* notwithstanding, the law is neither the true embodiment of everything that is excellent, nor is it without fault or flaw. American law is no more a perfect product than are other aspects of American life. The test of perfection is, however, scarcely the proper one by which to judge any institution. "An acre in Middlesex," said Macaulay, "is better than a principality in Utopia." A legal system that works to serve the community is better than the academic conceptions of a bevy of Platonic guardians unresponsive to public needs.

The history of American law is a history of the effort to mold legal institutions and doctrines to meet the felt necessities of each period in the nation's development. The effort has not always succeeded; at times there has been an all-too-large gap between the law and public needs. Yet the gap has always ultimately been narrowed, as judges, lawyers, and legislators have worked out new principles and doctrines better adapted to the changed conditions of the day. This volume tells the story of these adaptations, covering the two centuries' evolution of American law. It tells how English law was molded to fit the demands of a new nation of continental extent; altered to meet the requirements of the galloping capitalism of the Gilded Age; and then adjusted to suit the changing social consciousness of the emerging Welfare State. The story ends in our own day, with the law beset by an institutional crisis now endemic in the society as a whole. The widespread doubts about the adequacy of our institutions as the nation approaches its bicentennial are reflected by malaise in the legal world that is all but unique in our experience.

The crucial role of the law in American history has been apparent to all observers, from Alexis de Tocqueville to the present day. The true American contribution to human progress has not been in technology, economics, or culture; it has been the development of the notion of law as a check upon power. American society has been dominated by law as has no other society in history. Struggles over power that in other countries have called forth regiments of troops, in this country call forth battalions of lawyers.

The story of American law is the story of the great lawyers and judges in our past. Inevitably, the emphasis is on those who worked at the apex of the system, particularly in the U.S. Supreme Court. It is, nevertheless, erroneous to assume that those who sit in the marble palace are too remote to affect our immediate lives. The contrary is the case. Most of us may have no formal dealings with the law outside the traffic courts. Yet, so far as the law is concerned, we are all in the position of Molière's *Bourgeois Gentilhomme*, who for forty years had spoken prose without knowing it. In a legally oriented society we speak law more often than we know.

Whenever we buy a car or a home, get a job, travel by auto, train, or plane, turn on an electric light, or even cross the street, we are performing an act that has legal consequences. Our rights and obligations in all these situations are fixed by the law and, if need be, determined by the courts and ultimately by the highest courts of the states and nation. In this sense, we are all consumers of the law, intimately affected in all the details of our lives by the quality of the product consumed.

The noted French historian Fustel de Coulanges is said to have told a lecture audience, "Do not imagine you are listening to me; it is history itself that speaks." The same assertion can scarcely be made of this book. It is a personal, not to say, kaleidoscopic, survey. Above all, it seeks to present the pageant of American legal development and all that it has meant in the history of freedom. When one thinks on this majestic theme, his eyes dazzle. If only a part of this feeling is communicated to the reader, the author will be amply rewarded for his labors.

The Pedestal of Society

Since man's beginnings, rules and laws have given order and security to his ways of life. Among the oldest known formal law codes was that of Hammurabi, Babylonian king of the second millennium B.C. (and a precursor of Moses), shown above receiving the laws (center) from his sun god.

At left is Maat, the Egyptian goddess of justice, wearing her emblematic feather. Civil and legal rule were merged under the king's chief minister who, when judging, wore a collar with her image.

One of Rome's principal legacies to the world was its system of laws, codified about A.D. 550 by the emperor Justinian, seen at right with his ministers in a detail from a mosaic at Ravenna.

In large part, Roman law was based on the ideas of Greek philosophers, one of the greatest of whom, Socrates, is depicted being tried by an Athenian jury, below, in a relief by Antonio Canova.

These drawings of Celtic dispensers of justice, a judge and the king, embellish the manuscript of the Welsh Code, laws compiled by an assembly of bishops, jurists, and chieftains convened by King Howel the Good about A.D. 900.

Hyvreithu Huwel Dda

DETRAHS   DESCELERI

The Fuero Juzgo, left, a code that fused Spanish and Visigothic law, was once used in Spanish possessions in the New World, including the present-day U.S. Southwest.

A law teacher, lecturing to his class at Bologna—medieval Europe's leading school on Roman and canon law—is shown at right in a sculpture on his sarcophagus.

I

The English Heritage

The law, said Supreme Court Justice Oliver Wendell Holmes, is a magic mirror in which we see reflected not only our own lives but also the lives of those who went before us. Thus, a history of American law reflects the history of the United States in all its manifold aspects. Every important development in American life has had its impact on the law, from the founding of the Republic to the internal stresses of the nation's society two centuries later.

At the same time, the law is more than a passive reflection of other aspects of national life. Law is as much a prescription for the establishment of standards as it is a description of those standards: it defines an *ought* as well as an *is*. As the leading instrument of social control, the law influences historical developments no less than it is influenced by them. Justice Holmes tells us that "The rational study of law is . . . to a large extent the study of history." The converse is also true. American history is incomplete and distorted unless it takes account of the development of American law and legal institutions. The history of its law may not be the history of a society; yet, since law is the foundation of every society, the connection between the two is obvious.

A particularly close connection exists in the United States, where the law has always played a crucial part in every facet of life. Over a century ago, Alexis de Tocqueville commented on the primordial place of the law and the legal profession in our society. "Scarcely any political question arises in the United States," he wrote, "that is not resolved, sooner or later, into a judicial question." The American system has always meant legalism—the predominance of lawyers and judges—the prevalence of a spirit of legality among the people. In the words of an informed English observer, A. V. Dicey,

Published 1628–1644, Coke's Institutes on the common law influenced lawyers in the American colonies.

The King's Bench (left) was England's principal court of common law.

Sir Edward Coke was known as a hard prosecutor—he helped doom Sir Walter Raleigh—but after becoming England's chief justice he fought for the supremacy of the common law against the power of the Crown.

author of *The Law of the Constitution,* "the people of the Union are more thoroughly imbued with legal ideas than any other existing nation."

The vital role of the law in America was apparent even before the Revolution. Said Edmund Burke concerning the extent of legal influence in the American colonies: "In no country, perhaps, in the world, is the law so general a study. The profession itself is numerous and powerful, and in most provinces it takes the lead. The greater number of the deputies sent to the [Continental] Congress were lawyers."

In a broad sense, the struggle for American independence was a legal struggle; or, at the least, it was framed in terms of legal issues. The conflict which led to the Revolution was in large part a conflict over differing interpretations of the colonies' status under the British Constitution. "In Britain," wrote the royal governor of Massachusetts, Francis Bernard, in 1765, "the American Governments are considered as Corporations empowered to make by-Laws, existing only during the Pleasure of Parliament. . . . In America they claim . . . to be perfect States, no otherwise dependent upon Great Britain than by having the same King."

The legal nub of the constitutional controversy could scarcely be resolved by compromise between the diametrically opposed English and American viewpoints. While London was willing to appease the colonists by revoking exactions such as the Stamp Act, it could not give way on its constitutional right to legislate for the colonies. The Americans, for their part, could hardly assent to the parliamentary interpretation. The colonists may have faced no great risk of actual impoverishment from the British tax on tea, but they were convinced that their constitutional rights were being violated and that acquiescence on their part would have disastrous consequences.

Framing the controversy between the colonies and the Mother Country in legal terms was possible only because of the widespread influence that law and lawyers had attained in the American system by the time of the Revolution. Such influence was far from confined to members of the legal profession: ". . . all who read, and most do read," noted Edmund Burke, "endeavor to obtain some smattering in that science. I have been told by an eminent bookseller, that in no branch of his business . . . were so many books as those on the law exported to the plantations." In Massachusetts the British governor General Thomas Gage complained, according to Burke, "that all the people in his government are lawyers, or smatterers in law." A similar comment could have been made about the other colonies. By the outbreak of the Revolution, an established legal profession existed throughout the country. This was true despite the fact that the early colonists had attempted to get on without lawyers. Legislation hostile to the practice of law had been continuous from the middle of the seventeenth century to the middle of the eighteenth century. Somewhat typical was a 1658 Virginia statute which provided that no attorney should "pleade in any courte of judicature within this collony, or give councill in any cause, or controvercie whatsoever, for any kind of reward or profitt."

The attempt to administer justice without lawyers is characteristic of both Utopias and revolutions. The cry of Shakespeare's Dick the Butcher in *Henry VI,* "The first thing we do, let's kill all the lawyers," soon gives way, however, to the realization that the legal profession is an essential element of any working society. By Independence Day, 1776, there was a trained Bar in virtually all of the colonies.

The rise of a legal profession accelerated rapidly in the generation before the Revolution. When he was admitted to practice in Massachusetts in the middle of the eighteenth century, John Adams wrote, "Looking about me in the Country, I found the practice of Law was grasped into the hands of Deputy Sheriffs, Pettifoggers, and even Constables, who filled all the Writts upon Bonds, promissory notes, and Accounts, received the Fees established for Lawyers, and stirred up many unnecessary Suits." Typical of the pettifogger lawyers he encountered was a tavern keeper. "In Kibby's Barr Room, in a little Shelf within the Barr, I spied 2 Books. I asked what they were. He said every Man his own Lawyer, and Gilberts Law of Evidence. Upon this I asked some Questions of the People there, and they told me that Kibby was a sort of Lawyer among them — that he pleaded some of their home Cases before Justices and Arbitrators &c." Adams ended by saying that he told Kibby to purchase a copy of Blackstone's *Commentaries on the Law of England*.

But Adams also noted the existence of a flourishing and reputable Bar in the province. "Boston was full of Lawyers and many of them of established Characters for long Experience, great Abilities and extensive Fame," he wrote. Massachusetts, indeed, had had a strong Bar since the beginning of the eighteenth century, when a statute required an oath of office for admission to practice. (By the end of the colonial period, this was also true in the other colonies.) Particularly in the generation before the Revolution, lawyers came to the fore. They were the most influential members of the colonial legislatures and the Continental Congress. They not only led the Revolutionary movement, but also, and perhaps more important, they translated the Revolution into institutions that gave its peculiarly legal cast to the American polity.

Thus, as Chief Justice Harlan Fiske Stone of the U.S. Supreme Court wrote in 1919, "Burke's portrayal of the position and influence of the legal profession in Revolutionary America was not overdrawn. . . . Such names as James Otis, John Adams, Josiah Quincy, Robert Payne of Massachusetts, Peyton Randolph, Patrick Henry, Edmund Pendleton of Virginia, Charles Carroll and Samuel Chase of Maryland, and Alexander Hamilton and James Kent of New York recall vividly to mind . . . the ascendancy of the legal profession in legislation and in the political and social life of the growing nation."

During the earlier colonial period, the leadership may have been furnished by others, for example, the clergy in New England; toward its end the lawyers assumed increasing prominence. Their position is graphically shown by statistics: of the 56 signers of the Declaration of Independence, 25 were lawyers; of the 55 members of the Federal Constitutional Convention, 31 were lawyers; in the first Congress, 10 of the 29 senators and 17 of the 65 representatives were lawyers. If, as David Dudley Field, a great American lawyer of the nineteenth century, asserted in 1844, "the condition of the legal profession is an index of the civilisation of a people," the newly established nation had reached an unusually high level of development.

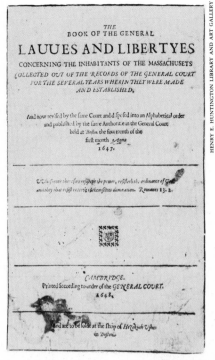

An early concern of settlers in all the American colonies was to establish and codify their systems of law. The Laws and Liberties of Massachusetts of 1648 (above) was one of the most important of these codes.

Nevertheless, a legal profession is only one of the necessary elements of a mature legal system. Even more important is the existence of developed legal institutions which both make and apply law in a society. To the legal historian, particularly one with a common law background, the courts are the pre-eminent institution involved in the legal process. "Who can estimate the sum of the influences of this portion of the social machine, or the variety of the directions in which they are exerted?" asked the *North American Review* in 1843 regarding the courts. "Through the whole country, not a bargain is made, nor an institution founded, nor a marriage contracted, nor a death occurs, but that this powerful and almost unseen agent controls the expectations of the actors or the spectators, and decides what shall be the consequences of the act." From the outset, as this comment makes clear, the courts were recognized as the fulcrum upon which the legal system turned.

By the first part of the eighteenth century, the larger colonies had set up court systems: New York in 1691; Maryland and Massachusetts in 1692; Pennsylvania in 1701; New Jersey, 1704; Virginia, 1705; and South Carolina, 1721. The system set up in New York was typical: Courts of Sessions for each county, a Court of Oyer and Terminer together with other minor courts, and a Supreme Court of Judicature (consisting of a chief justice and four associate judges). The New Jersey system was similar: Justices of the Peace, a Court of Common Pleas, a Court of General Sessions of the Peace, and a Supreme Court of Judicature.

These court systems possessed many of the characteristics of Anglo-American court systems, both before and since independence. Their principal feature was a two-tiered judicial structure, with inferior courts set up on a territorial basis throughout the colony and a central high court to hear appeals from the inferior courts. Of course, the jurisdiction of the different tribunals was not as sharply differentiated as it has become in more modern court systems. Thus, it was common for the highest courts to exercise both original and appellate jurisdiction. The landmark 1761 *Writs of Assistance Case* (in which James Otis made his famous attack on the legality of the writs—general warrants permitting customs officers to search ships, homes, shops, and warehouses for suspected smuggled goods without a specific warrant) arose out of a petition by a customs official filed originally with the Superior Court, then the highest court of Massachusetts.

In the two centuries since independence, American court systems have made important changes in the colonial model. The multiplicity of minor tribunals has been simplified into a more unified court system, with a common three-tiered structure—trial, intermediate appellate, and ultimate appellate. The method of judicial appointment has been substantially modified—and not always in the direction of improvement, since the first great change in the courts of the new nation was widespread provision for the election of judges. The judges themselves have come to be chosen from members (hopefully leaders) of the legal profession, marking a substantial step forward from the colonial situation, when lay judges predominated. But the essentials of the American court system were in existence at the time of the Revolution. Subsequent progress has been accomplished by building upon the early foundation.

Religion and superstition were an inextricable part of colonial law. Judge Samuel Sewall was a presiding justice at the Salem witchcraft trials in 1692, though he later publicly confessed shame for the role he played.

During the Salem trials for witchery, eighteen innocent men and women were put to death on the testimony of hysterical young girls who claimed to be possessed by the devil. Above, the farcical trial of George Jacobs, one of the victims.

What was true of the courts was also true of the other institutions of American law. By the end of the Revolutionary period, the American system had evolved its principal legal institutions. Laws were enacted by elected legislatures, administered by elected Executives, and enforced by an elaborate system of courts. The legal framework was established by written constitutions, and the means of making or amending them had been settled. To be sure, many of these institutions (especially the Executive) were rudimentary compared to their present-day counterparts. But the striking thing is the extent to which they had already developed by the time the nation began its independent existence. The far-reaching changes that have occurred in American law during the last two centuries have been not so much changes in the institutions that make and enforce laws as in the issues with which they have been concerned and the substantive law (that part of the law which defines one's legal rights and obligations, as contrasted with procedural law, which defines the procedure followed in cases) that has developed to deal with those issues.

The history of American substantive law has seen an almost complete transformation in principles, rules, and doctrines. The very subjects of the law today are radically different from the curriculum prevailing at the founding of the Republic. Consider the subjects studied by those seeking to enter the legal profession in 1787. At that time, Thomas Jefferson prepared

"The Golden Metwand and Measure"

To American lawyers of the late colonial period and the early years of the Republic, no legal textbook was more important than the *Commentaries on the Laws of England* by the British jurist Sir William Blackstone (1723–1780). Published in four volumes between 1765 and 1769, it described the essentials of the "common law" of England—the legal system and methods of legal thought that had evolved through the centuries in England and that formed the basis of the law in the thirteen colonies.

The origins of the common law went back to the royal courts established in England after the Norman Conquest. Though many local courts and regional variations in the law continued to exist in Great Britain, even until today, the fundamentally different laws that had governed separate sections of pre-Norman England slowly disappeared. There emerged a general body of principles and rules that were followed in all of the King's courts.

This law was "common," since it applied throughout the realm, and by the thirteenth century it was already being called "the common law." Its outstanding feature was that it was based not on specific laws and statutes or on a code of such laws, but on principles enunciated by judges in their decisions recorded in the reports of decided cases. Judges were appointed to administer the "law and custom of the realm," but in practice they built up their own set of principles and rules, relying on precedents established by decisions in previous cases. The result was a continuous process of legal evolution, founded on general custom as reflected in the decisions of generations of judges, that furnished both stability and flexibility to the developing legal system.

The common law was, thus, judge-made law, and its history was the biography of the great men who sat on the English Bench over the centuries. Most of them are today little

known save to specialists in legal history. The most notable exception is Sir Edward Coke (1552–1634), perhaps the greatest of all common lawyers, who was Chief Justice of Common Pleas and King's Bench from 1606 to 1616 and whose four *Institutes*, published between 1628 and

Sir William Blackstone

1644, were also influential in the legal education of early American lawyers. Coke was the very epitome of the common lawyer, with an almost fanatic reverence for precedent and technicality. "There is no jewel in the world," he declared, comparable to the common law.

Since Chaucer's day, there has been a continuity of English law that is unique. For all the changes that have occurred—hardly a law has survived unaltered—the essentials have remained the same. Most importantly, they have served as the greatest safeguard of the rights of Englishmen. From the earliest times, the diffusion of the "common" law led men to realize the role that law could play in controlling governmental power. When, in 1608, James I claimed that the King himself could decide any case as he chose, Coke delivered his famous answer that the King was

under God and the law—"that the law was the golden metwand and measure to try the causes of the subjects." The gradual development of the common law placed the rights of Englishmen on a firm case-by-case basis, enforceable in the courts of the land. "Even the framers of Magna Carta," wrote Winston Churchill, "did not attempt to lay down new law or proclaim any broad general principles. This was because both sovereign and subject were in practice bound by the Common Law, and the liberties of Englishmen rested not on any enactment of the State, but on immemorial slow-growing custom."

The common law is usually contrasted with systems of law derived from Roman law. During the sixteenth century particularly, Roman law principles spread through Europe, but did not become dominant in England as they did on the Continent. The freedom of English law from the Roman influence was of crucial significance to Britain. As codified under Justinian, the Roman law had become an instrument of imperial absolutism, its key principle that the will of the Prince had the force of law. The common law of England was based on the opposite principle—that the King himself was subject to law. The common law, as noted by an eminent nineteenth-century British jurist and historian, Frederic W. Maitland, was tough law, but its toughness enabled it to survive as the bulwark of English liberty and to resist the Romanizing elements that sought to shape it into an instrument of royal absolutism.

When the English colonists sailed to America, they took the common law with them. Though individual systems and bodies of law evolved in each colony, their bedrock was the common law. And when, in the eighteenth century, the colonists began to assert their own rights, they based their claims in large part on the rights guaranteed by that venerable system of the mother country.

a list of books for "A person who would wish to have a good general idea" of Anglo-American law. They covered the following areas: feudal property, evidence, bills, maritime law, equity, pleas of the Crown (criminal law), wills, uses, tenures, law merchant, civil and Chancery practice.

The subjects studied at the nation's first law school, set up in 1784 in Litchfield, Connecticut, by Judge Tapping Reeve, also illustrate the then narrow range of substantive law. The five notebooks kept by Roger S. Baldwin when he was a Litchfield student dealt with the following: one notebook covered municipal law, master and servant, contracts, baron and feme, parent and child, executors and administrators, and fraudulent conveyances; a second and third were devoted to bailments, forms of action, pleading, and evidence; a fourth defined commercial law (almost entirely bills and notes and insurance), Chancery, and criminal law; and the fifth dealt with real property. Almost half the student's time was spent on real property and forms of action and pleading.

A glance at the curriculum offered by present-day law schools indicates the extent to which both law and legal education have changed during the past two centuries. The simple list of substantive subjects has become a veritable catalogue. Law schools are, of course, still teaching almost all the substantive subjects that filled the Litchfield student's notebooks. But they now occupy only a small portion of the law student's time (as well as that of the lawyer). Most of the important modern law school subjects had not even begun to develop at the time of independence. This was true even of the staples of present-day legal education: torts (civil wrongs), constitutional law, administrative law, international law, trusts, corporations, labor law, trade regulation, taxation, and conflict of laws.

Westminster Hall in London was built by William II in the eleventh century and rebuilt by Richard II in the fourteenth. For six centuries it housed important courts in which English law was developed.

THE NEW-YORK HISTORICAL SOCIETY

In 1735 a jury acquitted publisher John Peter Zenger of seditious libel against the royal governor of New York, on the ground that Zenger had printed the truth. It was the first major victory for freedom of the press in the American colonies.

The Common Law

If substantive law was comparatively elementary at the time of independence, perhaps the more important fact was that a body of *American* law did exist, distinct from the English law from which it was derived. As early as 1704, an *Abridgement of the Laws in Force and Use in Her Majesty's Plantations* was printed in London, devoted to the laws of Virginia, Maryland, and Massachusetts, together with a smattering of items from New York and the Carolinas. This was a clear recognition that American law should be treated separately. Those having dealings with the colonies could no longer rely solely on the English legal authorities.

Of course, the foundation of American law was the English common law — the law developed over the centuries by the English judges. "With us the common law," reads the classic statement in James Kent's *Commentaries on American Law* (1826–1830), "has been recognised and adopted, as one entire system, by the people of this state. It was declared to be a part of the law of the land, by an express provision in the [New York] constitution."

From the time of the first Virginia charter (1606), the colonists were guaranteed the rights and liberties of Englishmen — in the terms of the Virginia charter, "all Liberties, Franchises, and Immunities . . . to all Intents and Purposes, as if they had been abiding and born, within this our Realm of *England*." Foremost among the rights the colonists took with them to the New World was the right to be tried by the common law. As early as 1639, in the Maryland Act for the Liberties of the People, the colonists expressly recognized that the common law was part of the English heritage to which they were entitled.

By the middle of the seventeenth century, the common law tradition had become blurred, in large part because of the scarcity of trained lawyers. But with the growth of a professional Bar, there was a reaction in favor of the common law. As the struggle with the Mother Country intensified, Americans tended increasingly to rely on the common law as the embodiment of their rights. The 1774 Declaration of Rights of the First Continental Congress asserted categorically "That the respective colonies are entitled to the common law of England." More and more the rallying cry was "the common law is our birthright and inheritance."

So strongly implanted had the common law tradition become that it could not be uprooted even by the hostility toward things English which accompanied the Revolution. The bitterness of the divisions among Americans during the struggle for independence is often forgotten. Confiscations, attainders, loyalty oaths and investigations, guilt by association—these were the all-too-common accompaniments of the Revolutionary effort.

Feelings against those who remained loyal to the Mother Country found particular expression in a revived hostility toward the legal profession. "Nothing in legal history is more curious," said Charles Warren, a distinguished historian of the American Bar, "than the sudden revival, after the War of the Revolution, of the old dislike and distrust of lawyers as a class." The popular antipathy is easily explained. In the first place, a large number of lawyers, including many eminent men, were Tories, forced by public opinion either to leave the country or retire from practice. It is not too much to say that the Revolution virtually decimated the profession. The situation in Massachusetts was graphically described by William Sullivan in 1824: "Such effect had the Revolution on the members of the Bar, that the list of 1779 comprised only ten barristers and four attorneys, for the whole State, who were such before the Revolution."

Suspicion continued to be directed against many lawyers who remained in America. Typical of the popular attitude was a 1779 New York statute, which declared that "many Persons who have heretofore been authorised and licenced to plead or practice as Attornies, Solicitors and Counsellors at Law . . . have some of them gone over to, and put themselves under the Protection of the Armies of the . . . King, and others have conducted themselves in such a neutral or equivocal Manner, as has justly rendered them suspected of disaffection to the Freedom and Independence of this State." The statute in question suspended from practice all attorneys licensed before April, 1777. The suspension could be removed only upon application to the supreme court of the state after a jury decision establishing that the applicant had been "a good and zealous Friend to the American cause."

But the revived antipathy toward lawyers was based upon more than the high proportion of Tories among the profession. Equally important was the fact that lawyers were looked upon as instruments of an *English* system of law. Now that the fundamental rights of Americans were guaranteed in indigenous constitutions and bills of rights, reliance upon the common law was no longer necessary. "I deride with you," wrote Jefferson to a federal judge, "the ordinary doctrine that we brought with us from England the Common Law rights. This narrow notion was a favorite in the first moment of rallying to our rights against Great Britain. The truth is that we brought with us the rights of men."

English law was now looked upon as "this last seeming badge and

Philosopher John Locke was called upon to draw up a system of government for the colony of North Carolina. It proved so impracticable that only a faint shadow of it survived into the eventual government—and then only briefly.

23

When Colonists Erred

The law, to be meaningful, must be able to enforce its edicts—and in colonial America the punishments for transgression were many and harsh: ears cropped, noses slit, bodies branded, a multitude of other barbaric punishments. At near right, an offender is being put into bilboes, or ankle shackles. At far right, a man wears a drunkard's cloak, designed for humiliation as well as discomfort.

Laying by the heels in the Bilboes.

The Drunkards Cloak.

The ducking stool was a common punishment for scolds in all the American colonies, save in New England.

A few LINES on

Magnus Mode, Richard Hodges & J. Newington Clark.

Who are Sentenc'd to ſtand one Hour in the

Pillory at Charleſtown;

To have one of their EARS cut off, and to be Whipped 20 Stripes at the public Whipping-Poſt, for making and paſſing Counterfeit DOLLARS, &c.

BEHOLD the villains rais'd on high !
(The *Poſt* they've got attracts the eye :)
Both Jews and Gentiles all appear
To ſee them ſtand exalted here ;
Both rich and poor, both young and old,
The dirty ſlut, the common ſcold :
What multitudes do them ſurround,
Many as bad as can be found.
And to encreaſe their ſad diſgrace,
Throw rotten eggs into their face,
And pelt them ſore with dirt and ſtones,
Nay, if they could wou'd break their bones.
Their malice to ſuch height ariſe,
Who knows but they'll put out their eyes :
But pray conſider what you do
While thus expos'd to public view.
Juſtice has often done its part,
And made the guilty rebels ſmart ;
But they went on did ſtill rebel,
And ſeem'd to ſtorm the gates of hell.
To no good counſel would they hear ;
But now each one muſt looſe an EAR,

And they although againſt their will
Are forc'd to chew this bitter pill ;
And this day brings the villains hence
To ſuffer for their late offence ;
They on th' Pillory ſtand in view :
A warning ſirs to me and you !
The drunkards ſong, the harlots ſcorn,
Reproach of ſome as yet unborn.
But now the *Poſt* they're forc'd to hug,
But loath to take that nauſeous drug
Which brings the blood from out their veins,
And marks their back with purple ſtains.
From their diſgrace, now warning take,
And never do your ruin make
By ſtealing, or unlawful ways ;
(If you would live out all your days)
But keep ſecure from Theft and Pride ;
Strive to have virtue on your ſide.
Deſpiſe the harlot's flattering airs,
And hate her ways, avoid her ſnares ;
Keep clear from Sin of every kind,
And then you'll have true peace of Mind.

The punishment of criminals occasioned public gatherings; this Massachusetts broadside announces such an event.

mortifying memento of . . . dependence." At political dinners and meetings after the Revolution, a common toast proclaimed, "The Common Law of England: may wholesome statutes soon root out this engine of oppression from America."

During the Revolution and in the post-Revolutionary period, the common law itself was in danger of being eliminated as the foundation of American law. "Must we tread always in their steps, go where they go, be what they are, do what they do, and say what they say?" plaintively asked William Sampson, a leader of the New York Bar. Many shared the attitude expressed by a Pennsylvania legislator in 1805: "The Judges ought to follow the spirit of the laws of this State and the spirit of our Constitution, and not of a Constitution hostile to our government, our manners and our customs."

Several states—Delaware, Kentucky, New Jersey, and Pennsylvania, among others—went so far as to pass laws prohibiting the citation of English decisions handed down after independence. Under one of these laws, Henry Clay in 1808 was stopped in the middle of argument by the supreme court of Kentucky while reading from an opinion of Lord Ellenborough. The supreme court of New Hampshire adopted a rule prohibiting English citations. In 1791 Chief Justice Livermore of that Bench stopped a lawyer reading from an English law book with the query, "Do you think we do not understand the principles of justice as well as the old wigged lawyers of the dark ages did?"

Additionally, the earlier feeling revived that law and lawyers were but obstacles in the way of securing justice. According to a contemporary, Justice Dudley, the most prominent member of the New Hampshire Supreme Court in the 1790's, used to charge the jury thus: "They [the lawyers] talk about law—why, gentlemen, it's not law we want, but justice. They want to govern us by the common law of England; trust me for it, common sense is a much safer guide for us. . . . It's our business to do justice between the parties; not by any quirks o' the law out of Coke or Blackstone—books that I never read and never will—but by common sense and common honesty between man and man." Dudley, like so many judges of the day, it might be added, was not a lawyer, but a farmer with almost no formal education.

Once again, the desire to have justice without law and lawyers could not be translated into reality. A nation entering upon the task of the political and economic conquest of a continent needed a legal order that would enable it to cope with the growth of population, commerce, and wealth. Uniformity, equality, and certainty could scarcely be supplied by a system based on the pioneer faith that anyone was competent to administer justice, and the less law there was to hamper the layman's sense of justice, the better.

But if law was plainly necessary to the burgeoning post-Revolutionary society, it was not necessary that it be English law. In his Rede Lecture, Frederic Maitland, an eminent British jurist and legal historian, described how, during the Renaissance, the common law was in danger of being Romanized by an English version of the Reception (the revival of Roman law) that was taking place on the Continent. In the end, the common law survived in England; Roman law, which rushed like a flood over Europe, gave way before the traditional English body of law. An American version

The brutal branks, or scold's bridle, was the Puritans' concept of fitting chastisement for a virago. The head-piece originally had a tongue de-pressor extending from the mask back into the mouth.

of this story took place after the Revolution. This time the Romanizing influence was provided by French law. The post-Revolutionary hostility toward things English was accompanied by what Jefferson termed "the predilection of our citizens for France." Stemming originally from the crucial assistance given the colonists during the Revolution, Francophile feelings were intensified when the French began their own revolution. The field of law, particularly, saw a growing appreciation of the work of the great French civilian jurists and an increasing desire to emulate the movement which culminated in the Napoleonic Code.

As late as 1856, or perhaps as late as 1876 when he reprinted his thesis, Sir Henry Maine, another respected British jurist and author of numerous works on the law, still believed that a reception of French or Roman-French law was taking place in America. It is singular that so perceptive an observer could so misconceive the nature of American law at mid-century. By then, the common law was firmly established as the foundation of the nation's legal system; in fact, all danger of a reception of French law was over by the 1830's. Yet, as Roscoe Pound wrote, at one time it had actually been a very real danger.

The wigs worn by English lawyers became so elaborate as not only to bring ridicule on the lawyers but to cast humor on the courts themselves. This satirical drawing was published in England in 1773.

As it turned out, the movement in favor of French law had a broadening effect on the work of American judges such as James Kent and Joseph Story, as well as on the ambitious attempts at law codification in the pre-Civil War generation. Kent particularly told how he was able to use the civil law as a leavening influence: "I could generally put my brethren to rout and carry my point by my mysterious wand of French and civil law. The judges were Republicans and very kindly disposed to everything that was French, and this enabled me, without exciting any alarm or jealousy, to make free use of such authorities and thereby enrich our commercial law."

Despite the efforts of the Francophiles, American law treated European continental civil law, with its emphasis upon codes rather than case law, much as the Church does the Apocrypha: it is instructive rather than authoritative. The English common law proved too tenacious in the United States to be displaced. The reasons for its continued vitality were various. The most important was contained in Maitland's famous aphorism that taught law is tough law. The common law was taught almost from the beginning. True, no formal legal education was available to the men who molded American law after independence. But what training they had was in the common law, particularly through the great English text writers. Kent found a copy of Blackstone "and the work inspired me . . . with awe," he wrote. Supreme Court Chief Justice John Marshall was given a copy by his father, one of the original subscribers to the American edition, and the common law began its march straight to the Pacific.

All the leaders of the American Bar had similar formative experience. Speaking of English law books, Edmund Burke noted, "The colonists have now fallen into the way of printing them for their own use. I hear that they have sold nearly as many of Blackstone's 'Commentaries' in America as in England." What was true of Blackstone held also for other English text writers, especially Sir Edward Coke of the late sixteenth and early seventeenth centuries. The young John Adams and Thomas Jefferson could com-

Patrick Henry first won fame in 1763 in the case of "the Parson's Cause." When Virginia clergymen obtained a royal veto of a law that had fixed their salaries, Henry (shown pleading) attacked the practice of vetoing laws necessary for the public good and won his case against the ministers.

plain of the drudgery of having to labor through Coke's crabbed medieval style. "I do wish the Devil had old Cooke [Coke]," plaintively wrote Jefferson at the age of nineteen, "for I am sure I never was so tired of an old dull scoundrel in my life." In later life they realized how much their training owed to the masterful Elizabethan—"our juvenile oracle," as Adams was to term him in 1816. Coke's famous *Commentary upon Littleton*, Jefferson eventually conceded, "was the universal elementary book of law students and a sounder Whig never wrote nor of profounder learning in the orthodox doctrines of . . . British liberties." Men trained upon Coke and Blackstone were bound to remain faithful to the common law which those writers synthesized. Moreover, when jurists like Kent and Story began to write the formative textbooks of American law, they would naturally use the system expounded by the English texts that had shaped their base.

In 1817 Jefferson asserted that the issue of the binding force of the common law was "a very plain one, and merely a question of document. If we are under that law, the document which made us so can surely be produced; and as far as this can be produced, so far we are subject to it, and farther we are not." But the great Virginian utterly misconceived the nature of the common law's force. The common law carried the day because it was, practically speaking, the only system that was or could be taught with the books at hand. Jefferson, himself, when suggesting books to be read by young men desirous of studying law, confined his choices to English texts, led by those of Coke and Blackstone.

Fortunately for the common law, most Americans were either unable or unwilling to read legal works in a foreign tongue. As learned a scholar as John Adams related his struggles in studying European continental authorities, concluding plaintively that he was but a novice in their civil law. Very few American lawyers were able to make effective use of the civil law. The average lawyer and judge hardly had the ability or diligence to plow through technical texts written in Latin or French. Many judges may have been Francophile in their outlook, but when it came down to deciding cases they were compelled to rely upon English common law authorities.

The victory of the common law in America was confirmed when Kent and Story wrote their authoritative guides for judges and practitioners in the years between 1826 and 1845. After their texts were published, the cult of the civil law virtually disappeared. They had restated the common law in American form. It was now so clearly presented that the energies of judges could be turned to applying common law principles to concrete cases.

American Modifications

"The common law of England," wrote John Dickinson in his *Letters from a Farmer in Pennsylvania* in 1768, "is generally received . . .; but our courts EXERCISE A SOVEREIGN AUTHORITY, in determining what parts of the common and statute law ought to be extended: For it must be admitted, that the difference of circumstances necessarily requires us, in some cases, to REJECT the determination of both. . . . Some of the English rules are adopted, others rejected."

In other words, the colonists did not adopt the whole body of the common law, but only those portions which their different circumstances did not require them to reject. "The common law of England is not to be taken in all respects to be that of America. Our ancestors brought with them its general principles, and claimed it as their birthright; but they brought with them and adopted only that portion which was applicable to their situation," wrote Story in an 1829 Supreme Court decision. Indeed, a principal task during the formative era of American law was to adapt the common law to the situation that existed on this side of the Atlantic.

Reflection will demonstrate the undesirability of a wholesale transportation of a legal system from one country to another, however alike the two countries in background and tradition. When we compare the England of the mid-eighteenth to mid-nineteenth centuries with the America of that time, it is obvious that the English law had to be remade for Americans. "The English common law, so far as it is reasonable in itself, suitable to the condition and business of our people, and consistent with the letter and spirit of our federal and state constitutions and statutes, has been and is followed by our courts. . . . But wherever it has been found wanting in either of these requisites, our courts have not hesitated to modify it to suit our circumstances," asserted an 1853 Ohio decision.

The modifications made in the common law by American judges may be explained, first of all, by the drastically different physical setting in this country. Geography indeed provided a new frame for our law and directly affected its emphasis and direction. The classic illustration of this was the *Genesee Chief* case of 1851, in which the Supreme Court refused to follow

The painter who made this portrait of Patrick Henry some years after the patriot's death created no likeness, but the words from the "Give me liberty or give me death" speech were sufficient identification.

29

an English rule that confined Admiralty jurisdiction to the high seas and upon rivers only as far as the tide extended. This limitation might have been adequate in a small island like Britain, where practically all streams are tidal. But it could not be applied in a transcontinental America.

The *Genesee Chief* opinion illustrated a need for change in the English law because of different physical conditions. When the first colonies were settled, the English "tidal flow" test may well have sufficed. In the original thirteen states, as in England, almost all navigable waters were tidewaters. The westward movement, and the growth of commerce on the Mississippi River and other inland waterways, revealed the law's inadequacy. Said Chief Justice Roger B. Taney in his decision: "It is evident that a definition that would at this day limit public rivers in this country to tide waters is utterly inadmissible. We have thousands of miles of public navigable waters, including lakes and rivers in which there is no tide. And certainly there can be no reason for admiralty power over a public tide water, which does not apply with equal force to any other public water used for commercial purposes."

The size of the country and the abundance of its natural resources made impossible the importation of the common law exactly as it had been developed in England. Measured by English standards, America had superabundant land, timber, and mineral wealth. American law had to serve the primary need of the new society—to master the vast land areas of the American continent. The decisive facts upon which the law had to be based

The stamp tax of 1765, the first direct tax levied on the colonies by England, aroused bitter opposition and a cry of "no taxation without representation." In the print below, a New Hampshire protest mob hangs a royal stamp master in effigy.

were the seemingly limitless expanses of land and the wealth and variety of natural resources.

The physical setting also worked to free America from restrictive English legal traditions. The land law in England was not only feudal in origin; it still retained much of its feudal character with a labyrinth of primogeniture, fee tail, seisin, attornment, seigniories, reversions, remainders, and the like. Of course, there were attempts to introduce the feudal land law into the colonies. Perhaps the most curious was contained in the 1669 Fundamental Constitutions of Carolina, drafted by John Locke for the proprietors who founded that colony. It was a rare example of the Platonic ideal in operation, a frame of government drawn up by one of the greatest political philosophers. Unfortunately, as all too often happens, Plato-become-Solon produced a fundamental law which—however attractive to the speculative theorist— proved wholly unworkable. In truth, it is amazing that a mind as acute as Locke's should have produced so clumsy a document, with its reliance on feudal conceptions and Graustarkian layers of nobility, and with its palatines, seigniories, baronies, manors, court-leets, landgraves, and caziques. Certainly, the elaborate structure was bizarre in the Carolina colony, which could scarcely be settled as a miniature feudal kingdom based on institutions that had become anachronisms even in the Old World.

The Locke-type efforts to transfer feudal institutions from England (where they may still have had some meaning) were foredoomed to failure, though they lingered on in scattered places, notably the Hudson Valley in New York, until after the Revolution. The need to tame a vast continent demanded substantial alterations in the English land law. Primogeniture, entailed estates, and other common law fundamentals were the worst possible foundations for American property law, for they destroyed the incentive that would induce men to settle and develop the constantly expanding frontier. Tocqueville contrasted the European expectation of passing on to sons land held in a long family line with his observation of the American practice, where the farmer "brings land into tillage in order to sell it again, . . . on the speculation that, as the state of the country will soon be changed by the increase of population, a good price may be obtained for it." In America, the governing policy had to be that stated during the New York constitutional debate on the abolition of feudal tenures in 1846: "There should be no more restrictions placed upon the alienation of real estate than upon personal property. Property was improved by passing from hand to hand."

Feudal land law, like the royal prerogative in government and the navigation acts in commerce, was an obstacle to Americans' ability to utilize their own resources as they saw fit. As vestiges of colonialism, the feudal rules had to go. Thus, as Kent pointed out, "Estates tail were introduced into this country with the other parts of the English jurisprudence. . . . But the doctrine of estates tail, and the complex and multifarious learning connected with it, have become quite obsolete in most parts of the United States." By Kent's day in the early nineteenth century, primogeniture, conveyances by feoffment or fines, and common recoveries also gave way to a system in which land became readily transferable. Feudal land tenure was abolished and the freehold established as the basic type of land title. Freedom of con-

The Stamp Act required that stamps like the one above be affixed to all publications, legal papers, and the like. Ensuing protests were a seedbed of the Revolution. The Pennsylvania Journal used the device below to express its opinion of the tax.

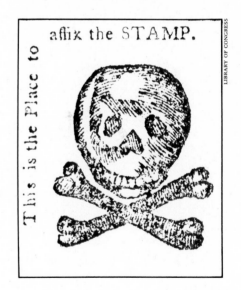

The Boston Massacre: Lawyer for the Defense

In 1770 John Adams of Braintree, Massachusetts, was called a traitor to the patriot cause. Yet thirty-one years later he became the second President of the United States. Adams was the lawyer for the defense of the hated British troops charged with the Boston Massacre. But there was a principle involved, entirely consistent with the goals for which the patriots, including Adams, were struggling. In time, when tempers cooled, his point was perceived.

Numerous lawyers like Adams, trained during the colonial period, were in the forefront of those who resisted British tyranny, made the Revolution, and created the new nation. The most famous of them—fiery spirits and Founding Fathers like James Otis, Patrick Henry, Alexander Hamilton, and Thomas Jefferson—are familiar to every school child. But in almost each colony at the time of independence were many less-celebrated lawyers, some of them brilliant and widely known in their day.

It had not always been so. In the early settlements, matters of law were the province of clergymen and political and civic leaders. Eventually, professional lawyers appeared, most of them arriving from England to assist the agents of the Crown in governing. As their numbers and influence in the colonies swelled, they frequently became the object of distrust and hostility. The general populace identified them with the interests of the wealthy and powerful, while the latter group regarded their special learning and talents with envy and fear. In some colonies they were barred or restrained by legislation. In others, like New Jersey and North Carolina, there were occasions when mobs rose against them as a class.

But the colonies burgeoned, their societies grew more complex, and lawyers became increasingly necessary for the conduct of commerce and personal affairs and to help settle conflicts. Amateurs and part-time lawyers, often untrained and even uneducated, offered their services and

John Adams, counsel for the defense

received fees for legal assistance in drawing up documents and defending people's interests. Side by side with them, however—and eventually becoming strong enough to challenge such unprofessionalism—were growing numbers of full-time attorneys, men of sound education and legal training. A few of them got their legal education by going to England and attending the Inns of Court, but most of them were trained as apprentices under older, established lawyers near their homes.

Adams was typical of the second group. Born in Braintree in 1735 and educated at Harvard, he started as a schoolmaster in Worcester. The drama of courtroom law and the opportunities to enter politics and gain prominence which the law provided attracted him to that profession, and in 1756 he applied for training to a legal friend, James Putnam, a Worcester lawyer considered so expert that "he could get a man hanged for stroking his neighbor's cat." For two years, while he continued to make a living as a teacher, Adams served as an apprentice to Putnam, following court

sessions, doing rudimentary jobs for his mentor, studying the law books in Putnam's library, and generally learning the practical requirements of the profession.

In 1758 he returned to Braintree and, with the support of several leading members of the Boston Bar, was sworn as an attorney, taking substantially the same oath still given to the Massachusetts Bar. Less than two months later, he handled his first case, seeking a "Declaration in Trespass for a Rescue" in a dispute between two Braintree neighbors over a stray horse. The fledgling lawyer drew a defective declaration and lost the case for his client. In his diary, he noted his regret over his "Precipitation" in taking the case and his "fear of having it thought I was incapable of drawing the Writt."

There was plenty of business for lawyers, however, and the initial setback did not prevent him from securing other clients. Drawing up deeds and wills, riding circuit, and defending persons charged with smuggling, bastardy, theft, assault, and other offenses, he steadily built up a practice. Ten years after his admission to the Bar, he appeared in over three hundred cases, and the next year even the great James Otis, older than Adams and at the time a towering figure in the Boston Bar, complained that he was "greatly mortified in looking over the Entries this present term in the Superior Court" to find that he had only four cases while Adams had sixty.

During the next few years, Adams's practice increased to the point where, according to the editors of his papers, he was the busiest lawyer in Massachusetts, handling cases concerned with almost every kind of public and private activity of the time. In this his practice was typical, for every lawyer was still a general practitioner. The majority of his cases arose out of simple financial transactions (suits to recover on notes, bonds, and accounts), but others concerned land, injuries to property, suits for defamation and assault and battery, crimes, and public matters. His clients came from all segments of colonial society and included the leading citizens of the day.

Those formative years of Adams's career were also stormy ones in the colonies. Otis's dramatic legal attack on the arbitrary search warrants known as writs of assistance in 1761 inspired the 26-year-old Adams and swept him into the ranks of the patriots. Otis became his friend and instructor in politics, but Adams's own abilities soon won him a prominence equal to that of his teacher. He gave leadership to the opposition to the Stamp Act in 1765 and thereafter was active in attacking British actions that he felt endangered the liberties of Americans. Nevertheless, in 1770, he confounded the colonists by agreeing to defend Captain Thomas Preston and the British soldiers prosecuted for the killings in the Boston Massacre—in his own words, "hazarding a popularity very general and very hardly earned: and for incurring a Clamour and popular Suspicions and prejudices." When he was told that even the Crown lawyers would not touch the case, he said, "I had no hesitation in answering that Council ought to be the very last thing that an accused person should want in a free Country."

Adams's successful defense of the accused troops (winning acquittal for all save two of the soldiers, who were branded on their thumbs, lectured from Scripture, and dismissed) was a high point in the history of the colonial Bar and in his own legal career. After 1774, his political activities in behalf of the patriot cause took up most of his time. When he retired from the Continental Congress in 1777, he sought to resume practice. His appointment in 1778 as Joint Commissioner to France changed his plans and marked the end of his law career.

To the end of his days, he had to deal with charges that he had turned against the patriot cause in the Boston Massacre case. But he had vindicated the right of even the most unpopular to counsel in America, and in old age wrote that "it has been a great Consolation to me through Life, that I acted in this Business with steady impartiality."

The Boston Massacre, as visualized by a later artist, Alonzo Chappel

tract and the autonomy of private decision making captured the land, as it was soon to capture other areas of American law.

The Ends of Law: 1789

The law moves with the main currents of the society that it regulates. Each society has its own values which are necessarily reflected in the ends that the legal order seeks to further. The ends of law are attained by recognizing certain interests, defining the limits within which they shall be recognized legally, and endeavoring to secure those interests that are within the limits defined. If the Founding Fathers had been asked to define the interests that their legal order should recognize and secure, they would have answered in terms of the natural rights of man. Essentially, they divided these into personal rights and property rights. "The fundamental maxims of a free government," affirmed Justice Story in 1829, "seem to require, that the rights of personal liberty and private property should be held sacred."

Broadly speaking, the history of American law has seen a growing shift in emphasis from property rights to personal rights as the focus of the law's concern. As a generalization this is doubtless true, particularly if we contrast the ends of law two centuries ago with what they have become today. Nevertheless, it is erroneous to assume that America's legal history unfolded in a wholly consistent fashion, one development leading inexorably to its juristic successor. An analysis of the history of American law would surely show a basic stream of development. Within it, however, are inconsistent currents at variance with the underlying drift of the stream.

The American of two centuries ago may have been a prime example of *Homo economicus* in operation. But a major concern in establishing the legal system of the new nation was to draw up an inventory—later to become the classic inventory—of human rights. The adoption of the federal Bill of Rights and its state counterparts will be discussed more fully in the next chapter. It is sufficient to say here that the movement to secure bills of rights indicates the shallowness of the notion that the nation's founders were concerned only with property. They were careful to provide express constitutional guaranties for *life* and *liberty*, as well as *property*. Indeed, their formulation of individual rights has served as the foundation for the progress made in the protection of human rights—and not only in American law.

At the same time, one need not subscribe wholly to historian Charles A. Beard's interpretation of the founding of the Republic to recognize the paramount place held by property rights. If anything is clear from the words and actions of the men who established the nation, it is that property to them was as important as liberty. "The preservation of property . . . ," declared William Paterson, a justice of the first Supreme Court who had been a member of the Philadelphia Convention, "is a primary object of the social compact." Without property rights, as the leaders of the new nation well knew, personal rights would be devoid of practical content. "The moment," said John Adams, "the idea is admitted into society that property is not as sacred as the laws of God . . . anarchy and tyranny commence."

To men who felt this way, perhaps the primary purpose of law was the protection of property rights. Nevertheless, a subtle, albeit vital, difference

James Otis aroused the colonies in 1761 with his fiery attack on writs of assistance in Boston.

existed between that end of law as it was conceived in America and its conception in England and the Continent. Before the French Revolution at least, the role of law on the eastern side of the Atlantic was still essentially what it had been in Roman and medieval times: to maintain the social status quo. The basic approach was still that contained in Justinian's classic statement: "The precepts of law are these: to live honorably, to injure no one, and to give every man his due." What were the interests of the person one was not to injure? And what constituted his due? These were questions left to the traditional social organization. In this view, law exists to maintain those powers of control over things and those powers of action which the society has awarded or attributed to each man.

Law based solely upon the need to preserve the social status quo would scarcely have been sufficient for a people engaged in creating a new society. The law had to shift its goal from one of giving to each his due to one of promoting a maximum of individual self-assertion. Unlike the law on the other side of the Atlantic, American law became expansive rather than defensive in nature, favoring change more than stability. The challenge of the untamed continent required a release of men's innate capacities; the way to such release was to be a conception of property that catered to enlightened self-interest. If men were to be measured by their accomplishments rather than by their social status, the law had to foster individual accomplishment.

In the law of the new nation, as much emphasis had to be placed on the right to acquire property as on the right to secure existing property. This was accomplished by a virtual marriage of property and contract law. Insofar as possible, limits on private freedom of decision were removed. Property itself was defined in terms of a legally assured measure of autonomy for

The First Law Professors

In 1806 a horrifying murder by poisoning claimed the life of George Wythe, a signer of the Declaration of Independence from Virginia, the first law professor in the United States, and a man whom his grieving friend, President Thomas Jefferson, called "the Cato of his country, without the avarice of the Roman."

A kindly and scholarly lawyer and jurist, Wythe had been Jefferson's law instructor and then his associate in the Revolutionary cause and in many of the political affairs of Virginia. Born in 1726, he had little formal schooling himself. But with his mother's help and by continuous reading and self-education, he so mastered Latin, Greek, mathematics, the classics, moral philosophy, and the natural sciences that eventually he

George Wythe

was acknowledged to be the most learned lawyer in Virginia, if not the colonies. A practicing attorney in pre-Revolutionary Williamsburg, noted for his precise, logical manner of reasoning and his many cultural interests (he even studied Hebrew with the aid of a rabbi), he was a member of the House of Burgesses and a close friend of the royal governor. In 1762, Jefferson, then nineteen years old, entered his law office as an apprentice.

Wythe played a leading part in the founding of the new nation, participating with Patrick Henry, George Washington, Jefferson, and other prominent Virginians in the tumultuous events that led to the final break with Great Britain. After he signed the Declaration of Independence, he

private decision makers. Natural rights came to be thought of as the rights of individuals who had entered into a contract, and it was these rights that the law had to maintain. The market became the key legal, as it became the key social, institution—with the role of law confined (in theory at least) to securing its untrammeled functioning.

But we are getting ahead of ourselves. Freedom of contract as the alpha and omega of the legal system was to be the dominant characteristic of nineteenth-century American law. Yet the trend in that direction was already apparent at the time of the founding of the Republic. When the federal Constitution was drafted, the one guaranty of real importance that the framers inserted to protect private rights was the Contract Clause of Article I, section 10, which prohibits states from impairing the obligation of contract. If they did so with surprisingly little interest and discussion, it was because they thought and wrote with near unanimity on the need to curb state infringements upon contract rights.

When the Constitution's framers prohibited the states from impairing the obligation of contracts, they sought to prevent government interference with the autonomy of the individual will. It was through contract that the individual could be given the fullest opportunity to exercise his faculties and to employ his substance. Contract was the primary legal tool for increasing the scope of individual discretion in the utilization of resources. The emphasis on contract thus marked the transition from law as a system designed to maintain the social status quo to law intended to secure a maximum of individual self-assertion. The stage was now set for an overwhelming predominance of the law of contract in all its ramifications that sharply characterized the American legal development in the following century.

became, in 1778, a judge of the Virginia Court of Chancery and, in a case in 1782, was one of the first judges to lay down the principle that a court can review the constitutionality of a law.

In 1779 the board of visitors of the College of William and Mary, headed by Jefferson, then governor of Virginia, established a "professorship of Law and Police" at the Williamsburg institution, and Wythe was appointed to occupy the chair. It was the first law professorship in the United States and was modeled on Sir William Blackstone's chair at Oxford, the first law professorship in England, set up only twenty-one years before. Wythe taught at William and Mary for ten years and numbered John Marshall and James Monroe among his stu-

dents. (Later, in a private law school which he opened in Richmond, he also taught Henry Clay.) He used the lecture method begun by Blackstone, as well as moot courts and moot legislatures which he held in the old capitol building in Williamsburg and which he apparently originated as a method of law instruction.

In 1788 he became chancellor of the state (necessitating his resigning from William and Mary and moving to Richmond). His sudden, tragic death came at the hands of his grandnephew who, seemingly in debt and anxious to receive his legacy, poisoned Wythe's coffee. The testimony of the only witness, a cook, was inadmissible in Virginia because he was black, and the murderer was freed.

In his law lectures, Wythe had been the first to attempt a systematic exposition of American law comparable to what Blackstone had done at Oxford in his *Commentaries*. Unlike Blackstone, however, Wythe did not publish his lectures. It remained for James Kent of New York to publish the first commentaries on American law. Kent (1763–1847), like Wythe, was a law teacher and a judge; he held the second law chair established at an American university, at Columbia in 1793. His academic career was interrupted by twenty-five years service as a judge, but was resumed in 1823. Out of his lectures came his landmark four-volume *Commentaries on American Law* (1826–1830), which contained the classic systematization of U.S. law during its formative period.

SOLON

FIAT JUSTITIA

II

The New Nation

Public Law: 1789–1860

You give me a credit to which I have no claim," wrote James Madison to a correspondent in 1834, "in calling me '*the* writer of the Constitution of the U.S.' This was not, like the fabled Goddess of Wisdom, the offspring of a single brain. It ought to be regarded as the work of many heads and many hands."

Madison's comment could apply as well to all the constitutions and bills of rights adopted during the Revolution and in the post-Revolutionary period. True, many of these basic documents are customarily spoken of as the products of particular authors. We learn, for instance, that John Jay drafted the New York Constitution of 1777, John Adams the Massachusetts Constitution of 1780, George Mason the Virginia Declaration of Rights of 1776—and that Madison wrote the federal Bill of Rights. To assume, however, that these documents were the "offspring of a single brain" is to oversimplify. An attempt to write an organic document on a clean slate may turn out favorably in Greek myth. In actual life, the successful constitution maker must work on an existing political and historical mold. Even a Madison could draw up the Bill of Rights only because of the precedents furnished by centuries of Anglo-American constitutional development.

By the end of the colonial period, Americans had gone far toward creating the constitutional polity that is this country's great contribution to political science and public law. The colonial period had seen develop the concept of a fundamental law to define and limit government and its powers, a concept that flowed naturally from the establishment of the first colonies under Crown charters. The next step was the realization that the colonists could provide their own fundamental laws, a step first taken in the Fundamental Orders of Connecticut in 1639. In the 1641 Massachusetts Body of

An election day scene in Philadelphia in 1815

Chief Justice John Marshall, painted by Rembrandt Peale

FREE LIBRARY OF PHILADELPHIA

George Washington presiding at the Constitutional Convention of 1787

Liberties, protection for individual rights was made a vital part of colonial law. By 1682 and the Pennsylvania Frame of Government, and with the 1701 Pennsylvania Charter of Privileges, the colonists had moved far in the direction of the modern Constitution and Bill of Rights.

When it came time for Americans to set up independent governmental institutions, they did so through written constitutions setting forth both the essential powers of government and the fundamental restrictions on those powers. The drafting of written fundamental laws was the natural response to the May, 1776, resolution of the Continental Congress urging the various colonies to set up governments of their own.

Colonial constitutional experience had been dominated by the concept of fundamental law contained in charters and basic laws. By appeal to such fundamental law the rights of the colonists were first asserted. But they could readily see how weak were claims that were based on documents subject to alteration or repeal by London or on unwritten principles of the British Constitution. The first state constitutions were a direct result of the colonial awareness of the lack of higher laws that were legally, as well as morally, beyond the reach of governmental power. When the time came, the colonists sought to correct the deficiency with binding written directions. By the end of the Revolution, written constitutions had been adopted in all the states, eleven of them being wholly new documents, while two of them, in Connecticut and Rhode Island, were the old royal charters with minor modifications. Drawing up a single constitution for the new nation was a more difficult matter. The Article of Confederation, which went into effect in 1781, proved inadequate. It was not until 1788 that an effective federal Constitution was adopted, and the government instituted under it went into operation on March 4, 1789.

With the ratification of the federal Constitution, American public law completed the first great task of its formative era: to establish frames of government for each of the states, as well as for the nation itself. In its essentials, the constitution-making process was now settled. The constituent power was vested in a convention specially called for the purpose of drafting a Constitution. This was the method used for the federal Constitution as well as that employed by most of the states during the Revolution, and it fixed the pattern for subsequent American organic instruments. Though there has been only one federal Constitutional Convention in America's history, over two hundred state conventions have met to adopt or revise their constitutions since the founding of the nation.

As stressed earlier, the first American constitutions were not the products of single draftsmen. That they could be drawn up in relative haste reflects the existence of a general consensus in American political theory. From the first constitution—that of Virginia in June, 1776—all the state organic documents provided essentially similar three-branched structures of government. This was the consequence not so much of a *stare decisis* (strict adherence to precedent) in the constitution-making process, as of the fact that Americans already took for granted most of the important structural attributes of government. The tie-in between these accepted attributes and the structure of government during the colonial period is seen when comparing the first state constitutions with the more advanced colonial organic instruments, such as the Pennsylvania Frame of Government and Charter of Privileges.

At the same time, it would unduly denigrate the contribution made to public law by the first American constitutions to think of the men who adopted them only as codifiers. Of course, the draftsmen of the Revolutionary and post-Revolutionary constitutions built on earlier theory and practice. But they were truly innovators; they were the first to give full practical effect to the concept of a written constitution as both a charter of government and a check upon its powers.

The contribution of the first constitution makers can be best appreciated through examination of the work of the federal Constitutional Convention of 1787. The document there drawn up was no mere borrowing from colonial experience or past history. However much the framers drew upon the past, their efforts were genuinely creative. As Tocqueville half a century later was to note of the federal system set up in 1787: "The Constitution, which may at first sight be confused with the federal constitutions that have preceded it, rests in truth upon a wholly novel theory, which may be considered as a great discovery in modern political science."

The document drafted by the Founding Fathers in Philadelphia marked a fitting culmination to the classic age of constitution making. The fifty-five men who came to Independence Hall had a background of ability and public service that fitted them admirably for the task they were undertaking: "The assembly . . . contained the finest minds and the noblest characters that had ever appeared in the New World," declared Tocqueville. Most important, to one interested in the history of law, nearly two-thirds of the Constitution's framers were members of the legal profession, of whom ten had been state judges. The training and experience in the law shared by these men enabled the assembled group to draft a document that was no mere product of academic speculation, but a practical charter of government.

Voltaire, in a famous exclamation, demanded the total destruction of all existing laws: "Do you want good laws? Burn yours and make new ones!" Men who were themselves practitioners of the law knew better. They knew that law was reason codified by experience. "Experience must be our only guide," affirmed John Dickinson at Philadelphia. "Reason may mislead us." Hardheaded legal realism enabled the framers of the Constitution both to draw upon the best features of the existing state constitutions and to combine them with truly original contributions of their own—notably in their establishment of the federal system, a strong Executive, and independent federal judicial power.

By now, we have become so accustomed to the federal system that we tend to forget that its creation, as Tocqueville suggested, was a political invention of the highest order. The form of federation offered by the framers was far more than mere refurbishing of the models furnished by the federations of antiquity or contemporary Europe. "In all the confederations that preceded the American Constitution of 1789," Tocqueville said, "the states . . . agreed to obey the injunctions of a federal government; but they reserved to themselves the right of ordaining and enforcing the execution of the laws of the union." This basic defect was eliminated by making federal power operative directly on individuals, as well as states, and giving the nation authority to execute its own enactments, without any need for state implementation. "I know not," said John Lansing in New York's ratifying convention, "that history furnishes an example of a confederated Republic coercing the States composing it, by the mild influence of laws operating on the individuals of those states. This, therefore, I suppose to be a new experiment in politics."

By setting up a federal government with distinct executive and judicial branches, completely separate from the legislative department, the framers were able to ensure that each of the three great powers essential to government would be effectively exercised. This was particularly true in the establishment of an independent Executive, at a time when most state constitutions were based on a popular tradition of distrust of executive power. The composition of the executive department posed a real dilemma to the men of 1787. On the one hand, there was the need for an Executive strong enough to penetrate to the remotest reaches of the Union. Just before the Convention, Shays's Rebellion had underlined how pressing this need was. At the same time, there was the danger of stirring up the popular fears of a new monarchy. Those hostile to the Union, the framers well knew, would be all too ready to picture the new Executive with a diadem on his brow and the purple flowing in his train.

That the problem was resolved by the creation of the Presidency was an act of political boldness of the first magnitude. By rejecting the notion of a plural Executive, the unity essential to effective action was ensured. By discarding the idea of election by the legislature, the independence necessary for presidential power and prestige was established. The state Executives, Madison had said, were but ciphers, with all power absorbed by the legislative vortex. The history of the Presidency has shown that the same

John Dickinson, a delegate to the Constitutional Convention, had been well known in colonial days, arguing in his Letters from a Farmer in Pennsylvania that Parliament had no right to tax the colonists for revenue.

cannot be said of the polity provided for under the federal Constitution.

Even more significant was the establishment of an independent judiciary as one of the three coordinate departments. The primary difficulty confronting the framers was not how to constitute the federal government, but how to provide a method of enforcing its laws. Without an independent judicial department—one with the authority to ascertain and enforce the powers of the Union—the laws, the treaties, and even the Constitution of the United States might well become dead letters. With the setting up of a federal judicial branch, every person having a claim involving a federal question was given a right to submit his case to a court of the nation. The judicial arm of the nation was given the controlling word in the enforcement of its basic instrument and laws. "A more imposing judicial power was never constituted by any people," observed Tocqueville.

The Bill of Rights

The great deficiency of the original federal Constitution was its failure to contain any bill of rights. Its lack in this respect was a serious obstacle to ratification by the states. In 1788 five of the state ratifying conventions—those of Massachusetts, South Carolina, New Hampshire, Virginia, and New

Shays's Rebellion of 1786–1787 was an attempt by impoverished farmers in Massachusetts to prevent courts from acting against debtors. The inability of the government of the Confederation to restore order did much to convince the nation of the need for a new and stronger system.

Artist Benjamin Latrobe enjoyed making candid sketches of life in the young Republic. Here his pen has caught a judge of the Court of Appeals at Richmond, Virginia. The year was 1798.

York—recommended proposed amendments that would add a bill of rights to the Constitution, and compliance with their and other states' recommendations was an urgent task of the first Congress which met in 1789.

The concept of a bill of rights is primarily American in its origins. The existence of the English Bill of Rights of 1689 tends to obscure this fact. Except for the name, however, the 1689 enactment is far from the American conception of a bill of rights. In the first place, it was passed as a statute by Parliament and could thus, legally speaking, be amended or repealed at any time at the discretion of the legislature. The American notion of a bill of rights turns upon inclusion of guaranties of individual right in a constitutional document binding upon the legislature itself. In this sense, the Virginia Declaration of Rights of 1776 was the first true bill of rights, since it was the first protection for the rights of the individual to be contained in an enforceable constitution.

In addition, the English Bill of Rights was a rudimentary document insofar as the individual rights guaranteed by it were concerned. The 1689 enactment was intended primarily to eliminate the methods by which the last two Stuart kings had sought to control Parliament, as well as the abuses of the prerogative committed by James II. The only portions relevant to a bill of rights in the American conception, the prohibitions that dealt with the perversions of justice by the last Stuart kings, were essentially the guaranties later included in the U.S. Constitution's Eighth Amendment.

By the time the English Bill of Rights was adopted, Americans had already enacted far more complete protections for individual rights—notably the Massachusetts Body of Liberties in 1641 (containing at that early date detailed guaranties that anticipated many of the fundamental liberties protected in the federal Bill of Rights), and the Pennsylvania Frame of Government in 1682. The former included guaranties covering the taking of property without just compensation, freedom of speech and petition at public meetings, bail, right to counsel, trial by jury, double jeopardy, and cruel and inhuman punishments. The latter was an organic document issued by William Penn as Proprietor which contained an express series of guaranties of the fundamental rights of Pennsylvania, including religious freedom, jury trial, public trial, right to appear and plead, bail, and moderate fines. When the time came for Americans to set up their own governments in response to the congressional resolution of May, 1776, most of them followed Penn's example. The Virginia Convention of 1776, which drew up the first state constitution, resolved at the outset that it would "prepare a Declaration of Rights." The document drafted to give effect to this resolution was appended to the new constitution and set the pattern for subsequent American constitution making. Eight of the states that framed constitutions during the Revolutionary period adopted fundamental laws which included specific bills of rights. The others adopted constitutions that contained provisions protecting individual rights within the text of the constitution. All the important provisions of the federal Bill of Rights were derived from the state Declarations of Rights.

On June 8, 1789, James Madison rose in the House of Representatives and introduced the amendments that would become the federal Bill of Rights. The Madison proposals covered all the articles eventually included in the first ten amendments, including most of the language ultimately adopted. Madison's draft for the Bill of Rights built on the states' consensus in the matter as expressed in the amendments recommended by the state ratifying conventions, particularly by Virginia.

This June 8 speech by Madison is rightly considered one of the great state papers in American history, for it contains the classic presentation of the case for a bill of rights in a government such as ours. The Constitution itself, Madison conceded, was opposed "because it did not contain effectual provisions against encroachments on particular rights, and those safeguards which they have been long accustomed to have interposed between them and the magistrate who exercises the sovereign power." Madison's amendments were introduced to remedy the deficiency, by providing "securities for liberty" and declaring "the great rights of mankind secured under this constitution."

The purpose of a bill of rights such as that proposed was "To limit and qualify power by excepting from grant cases in which it shall not be exercised or expressed in a particular manner." The basic intent was to guard "against the legislative, for it is the most powerful, and most likely to be abused," as well as to protect against abuses by the Executive and "the body of the people, operating by the majority against the minority." Of particular interest to the legal historian in a system where judicial review has played so crucial a part was Madison's express recognition that a bill of rights would be effective because it would be enforced by the courts: "independent tribunals of justice will consider themselves in a peculiar manner the guardians of those rights."

Four of Madison's original amendments — containing a general declaration of the theory of popular government, a prohibition against state violations of freedom of conscience, the press, and trial by jury, a limitation of appeals,

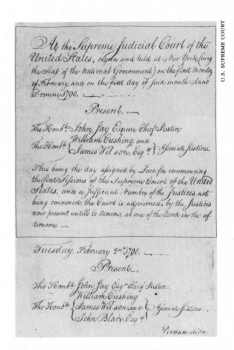

These are the minutes of the first session of the Supreme Court of the United States, February, 1, 1790. It was not a good beginning; the session had to be adjourned because too few justices were present.

and a provision for separation of powers—were eliminated during the congressional debate, and two, dealing with congressional size and compensation, failed of ratification. The others survived substantially in their proposed form as the federal Bill of Rights. The extent of Madison's achievement is not lessened by the fact that he based his draft on the recommendations submitted by state ratifying conventions. It was Madison who chose which of the state proposals Congress should act on. It was he who tightened the constitutional language, substituting an imperative "shall" for the flaccid "ought" and "ought not" of the state proposals. He also drafted his version of Chapter 39 of Magna Carta in terms of "due process of law" rather than "the law of the land"—a change of seminal significance for subsequent constitutional history, since it was the origin of the Due Process Clause of the Fifth, and later, of the Fourteenth Amendment.

From the perspective of two centuries, we can see that Madison chose remarkably well among the pyramid of state proposals; he included all the great rights appropriate for constitutional protection (except for equal protection, not thought of as a basic right at the time). The Bill of Rights contains the classic inventory of individual rights, and it has served as the standard for all subsequent attempts at constitutional government.

The adoption of the federal Bill of Rights on December 15, 1791, represented a suitable climax of the great age of constitution making with which the formative era of American law began. The basic structure of government was now established in written organic instruments at both state and

New York's City Hall was remodeled, renamed Federal Hall, and, with the convening of Congress in 1789, became the nation's first Capitol. Pictured below is the chamber of the House of Representatives.

The Bill of Rights— Madison's Language of Command

When the first Congress convened in the old City Hall in New York in April, 1789, James Madison was at the peak of his powers. He was then thirty-eight, not yet clothed in the habitual black which later ruled his dress. His more likely costume then was ornate blue and buff, with hair powdered and gathered in the beribboned queue of fashion. "He speaks low," said Fisher Ames, a congressional colleague from Massachusetts, "his person is little and ordinary." He was so small that he could not be seen by all the members, and his voice was so weak that he could scarcely be heard throughout the hall. Yet John Marshall said of him that if eloquence included the art of "persuasion by convincing, Mr. Madison was the most eloquent man I ever heard."

Madison was the prime mover in the congressional debate on the federal Bill of Rights. He had originally been lukewarm on the subject; a year earlier he had told Jefferson, "I have never thought the omission [of a Bill of Rights] a material defect [of the Constitution]." Madison's attitude changed, influenced both by Jefferson's enthusiasm for a Bill of Rights and his own need to gain popular support in his closely contested congressional election. In a campaign letter to voters, Madison promised to get Congress "to prepare and recommend to the States for ratification, the most satisfactory provisions for all essential rights."

In the first Congress, Madison acted to make good on his campaign promise, drafting proposed amendments and constantly prodding the House to consider them. He rose several times to urge his colleagues to act on the amendments, but the House was involved in a lengthy debate on import and tonnage duties. Members objected to consideration of Madison's amendments, asserting that even "if gentlemen should think it a subject deserving of attention, they will surely not neglect the more im-

James Madison, by Thomas Sully

portant business which is now unfinished before them." This theme was repeated throughout the debate.

It may seem surprising that members could believe that "there were several matters before them of more importance than the present" or that "the discussion would take up more time than the House could now spare." But as late as 1886, so discerning a legal scholar as Sir Henry Maine could refer to the American Bill of Rights as "a certain number of amendments on comparatively unimportant points." To the Federalist majority in the first Congress, the Madison amendments seemed less pressing than setting up the details of the new government. To get consideration, Madison had to stress how necessary it was to reconcile those who had opposed the ratification of the Constitution and the new governmental system because there had been no Bill of Rights securing the people's liberties. "Is it desirable," he asked, "to keep up a division among the people of the United States to a point in which they consider their most essential rights are concerned?"

The Bill of Rights (the Constitution's

first ten amendments, which became effective in December, 1791) was essentially Madison's handiwork. The congressional debate tightened the language, but the substance was contained in the original Madison draft. The states had submitted over two hundred proposed amendments. Madison not only chose which rights should be safeguarded (he condensed the proposals into sixteen amendments, four of which Congress eliminated and two of which the states ultimately failed to ratify), but also wrote a mandatory imperative into the amendments, substituting the word "shall" for the "oughts" and "ought nots" that had characterized earlier documents guaranteeing similar rights. For example, the English Bill of Rights in 1689, the Virginia Declaration of Rights in 1776, and Virginia's proposed constitutional amendment offered in 1788 had all read: "That excessive bail ought not to be required, nor excessive fines imposed, nor cruel and unusual punishments inflicted." Madison's wording for what became the Eighth Amendment, which he proposed on June 8, 1789, read: "Excessive bail shall not be required, nor excessive fines imposed, nor cruel and unusual punishments inflicted." The difference was significant and substantial.

Wishful normatives, Madison realized, were not enough for a free people. "In Europe," he wrote, "charters of liberty have been granted by power"; in America, "Charters of power granted by liberty." In Magna Carta, where King John spoke as monarch, "We will not" was deemed proper. In the English Bill of Rights, where William and Mary spoke as sovereigns, "ought not" was thought bold enough for the protection of the rights of subjects. Now, however, when the American people prescribed the acts which their new federal government must not do, it was appropriate, said Madison, to say "shall not"—the language of command.

federal levels. Moreover, the fundamental rights of the individual were protected in the state Declarations of Rights and federal Bill of Rights. As finally passed by Congress, the latter was binding only on the federal government. The Senate had eliminated the proposed amendment which Madison had characterized as "the most valuable amendment in the whole lot"— that prohibiting the states from infringing on freedom of conscience, press, and jury trial. The result was that the Bill of Rights, as adopted, did not impose limitations on state power. For protection against state violations of his personal rights, the individual had to rely on the guaranties contained in the particular state constitution or bill of rights. It was not until after the Civil War that significant limitations on state power were added to the federal Constitution.

Judicial Review

Alexis de Tocqueville was the first foreign observer to appreciate the crucial position of the Supreme Court in the American constitutional system. "The Supreme Court," he affirmed, "is placed higher than any known tribunal. . . . The peace, the prosperity, and the very existence of the Union are vested in the hands of the seven Federal judges."

It required acute perception on the part of the young French visitor to see the vital role of judicial power so early in American history, for a less discerning observer might readily have concluded that American courts offered nothing contrary to the usual habits and privileges of judicial tribunals. He might have gone further and pointed to the assertions by men such as Alexander Hamilton on the weakness of judicial power under the Constitution. "The judiciary," wrote Hamilton in the *Federalist*, "is beyond comparison the weakest of the three departments of power." The situation of the Supreme Court during its first decade justified this remark.

When the justices met in their first public session on February 2, 1790, in the Royal Exchange at the foot of Broad Street in New York City, they were splendidly attired in black and scarlet robes, "the elegance, gravity and neatness of which," remarked a Philadelphia newspaper, "were the subject of remark and approbation with every spectator"—though they had discarded what Jefferson termed "the monstrous wig which makes the English judges look like rats peeping through bunches of oakum!" The elegance of the justices' attire could, however, scarcely serve to conceal the relative ineffectiveness of the fledgling Supreme Court. During its first decade, the Court handled few matters; it decided only one important case—a 1793 decision that a state could be sued in a federal court by a citizen of another state—and that decision was speedily overruled by the Eleventh Amendment prohibiting such suits. The weakness of the early Court was demonstrated symbolically in the building of the new Capitol: the august tribunal was completely overlooked, and no chamber was provided for it. When the seat of government was moved to Washington, the High Bench was relegated to an undignified room in the basement beneath the Senate Chamber. "A stranger," wrote a contemporary, "might traverse the dark avenues of the Capitol for a week, without finding the remote corner in which Justice is administered to the American Republic."

The Supreme Court held its first two sessions, in 1790, in this New York building known as the Exchange. Until the Court moved in, the second-story hall had been used for exhibitions, meetings, and sales.

All this changed after John Marshall of Virginia became chief justice in 1801. All history, says Emerson, is subjective; in other words, there is properly no history, only biography. As a wholesale generalization, this may be debatable. But it is surely true of the early history of American public law, which can be stated essentially in terms of Marshall's contribution to it. "Marshall found the Constitution paper; and he made it power," said James A. Garfield. "He found a skeleton, and he clothed it with flesh and blood." Marshall transformed the supreme tribunal into a fully coordinate department endowed with the ultimate authority of safeguarding the ark of the Constitution.

In terms of the history of American public law, Marshall's great contribution was the decision in *Marbury* v. *Madison* in 1803. This opinion laid down the doctrine of judicial review which has since been the keystone of the constitutional arch. *Marbury* v. *Madison* was the first case to establish the Supreme Court's power to review the constitutionality of legislative acts, and it did so in terms so firm and clear that the power has never since been legally doubted. Had Marshall not confirmed review power at the outset in his magisterial manner, it might never have been insisted upon, for it was not until 1857, in the *Dred Scott* decision, that the authority to invalidate a federal statute was next exercised by the Supreme Court. Had the Marshall Court not taken its stand, more than sixty years would have passed without any question arising as to the omnipotence of Congress. After so long a period of judicial acquiescence in congressional supremacy, it is probable that opposition then would have been futile.

Political theorists have long questioned whether the assumption by the Marshall Court of review power was justified by the Constitution or was an act of judicial usurpation. Those who urge the latter position lose sight of the fact that *Marbury* v. *Madison* merely confirmed a doctrine that was part of the legal tradition of the time, derived from both the colonial and

Revolutionary experience. One may go further. Judicial review was the inarticulate major premise upon which the movement to draft constitutions and bills of rights was ultimately based. The doctrine of unconstitutionality had been asserted by Americans even before the first written constitutions, notably by James Otis in his 1761 attack on general writs of assistance and by Patrick Henry in 1763 when he challenged the right of the Privy Council in London to disallow Virginia's Two-penny Act. The Otis-Henry doctrine was a necessary foundation, both for the legal theory underlying the Revolution and the constitutions and bills of rights it produced.

The doctrine could, however, become a principle of positive law only after independence, when written constitutions were adopted that contained binding limitations beyond the reach of governmental power. Of what avail would such limitations be if no legal machinery enforced them?

"Much As the Lord Hit the Chaos"

One of John Adams's last acts as President in early 1801 was his nomination of John Marshall as Chief Justice of the Supreme Court. "My gift of John Marshall to the people of the United States," Adams remarked years later, "was the proudest act of my life." History has confirmed Adams's estimate. Said Justice Oliver Wendell Holmes: "If American law were to be represented by a single figure, sceptic and worshipper alike would agree without dispute that the figure could be one alone, and that one, John Marshall." Indeed, Holmes added, "there fell to Marshall perhaps the greatest place that was ever filled by a judge."

To many of his contemporaries, Marshall—whose decisions established the fundamental principles for the interpretation of the Constitution—seemed ill-equipped for the position to which Adams named him. Born in 1755 in Fauquier County, Virginia, he had had only meager education and training, both generally and in the law. His entire formal schooling consisted of one year under a clergyman and one under a tutor who resided with his family. The rest of his learning was under the superintendence of his father, who, according to Marshall, had himself received only "a very limited" education. His law study was equally rudimentary, amounting to attendance at George Wythe's lectures at William and Mary for a mere six weeks.

His lack of formal schooling, however, was not the deficiency that it might have been in another time. Marshall's was not the ordinary judicial role. As one writer put it, "he hit the Constitution much as the Lord hit the chaos, at a time when everything needed creating." The need in the early days of the Republic was for formative genius—for the transfiguring thought that a judge normally is not called upon to impose on society. Had Marshall—a veteran of the Revolution, a member of the Virginia House of Burgesses and then of the U.S. House of Representatives, and, from 1800 to 1801, U.S. Secretary of State—been more learned in the law, he might not have performed his creative task as well as he did, for his role called for the talent and insight of a statesman capable of looking beyond the confines of strict law to the needs of a new nation.

It is customary to designate a particular Supreme Court by the name of its chief justice. The designation was more than formalism when Marshall presided over the Court. From the time when he first took his judicial place in 1801 until his death thirty-four years later, it was emphatically the Marshall Court that stood at the head of the U.S. judiciary. Marshall's aim was to use the Supreme Court to lay the constitutional foundation of an effective nation. Before this could be realized, the prestige and power of the Court itself had to be increased.

Before Marshall, the Court had followed the English custom of having opinions pronounced by each of the justices. The practice of presenting, instead, one ruling opinion of the Court was begun by Marshall in the very first case after he became Chief Justice. The change was admirably suited to strengthen the prestige of the fledgling Court. To win conclusiveness and fixity for its constrictions, Marshall strove for a Court with a single voice. How well he succeeded was shown by the reception accorded one of the associate justices, William Johnson, who sought to express his dissent from a majority decision of Marshall's Court. "During the rest of the Session," he plaintively wrote Thomas Jefferson, "I heard nothing but Lectures on the Indecency of Judges cutting at each other, and the Loss of Reputation which the Virginia appellate Court had sustained by pursuing such a course."

To the historian, Marshall is the pre-eminent chief justice—the outstanding judge in American legal history. The magisterial character of

Even a constitution is empty words if it cannot be enforced by the courts.

Judicial review started to become a part of the living law during the decade before the adoption of the federal Constitution. During that time American courts first began to assert the power to rule on the constitutionality of legislative acts and to hold unconstitutional statutes void. Cases in at least eight states between 1780 and 1787 involved direct assertions of the power of judicial review. Marshall himself could affirm, in *Marbury* v. *Madison*, not that the Constitution established judicial review, but only that it "confirms and strengthens the principle." Soon after the Constitution went into effect, further assertions of review authority were made by a number of federal judges, including members of the Supreme Court sitting on circuit. As seen earlier, when Madison introduced the proposed amendments that became the federal Bill of Rights, he recognized

John Marshall stops at a tavern during his days as a circuit-riding judge.

sponsibility of appointing the chief justice fell to John Adams, instead of to his successor, Thomas Jefferson, a month later, the seminal expounder of the Constitution would have been anyone but a man of Marshall's views. That Marshall was able to mold his intense convictions on effective national power into positive law at the outset contributed greatly to the ordered development of the nation.

More than that, Marshall's judicial genius enabled him to lay down the foundations of American constitutional law in terms that have endured. It is difficult to read one of his great opinions, even today, without being converted to its views. In his own time, his strongest critics were affected by his logic. "All wrong, all wrong," was the despairing comment of John Randolph of Roanoke, "but no man in the United States can tell why or wherein." But the largest measure of Marshall's greatness, perhaps, lay in the fact that the cases he decided were historic because of what he made of them. Any of them could have been decided in narrow, technical ways that would have left them all but unheard-of outside the courts. If today they are legal landmarks, it is because they were raised to that high plane by Marshall's magnificent transforming touch.

his opinions, marching with measured cadence to their logical conclusions, has never been equaled, much less surpassed. Clarity, conciseness, and eloquence are Marshall hallmarks which, combined with what the constitutional authority Edward S. Corwin termed his "tiger instinct for the jugular vein," his rigorous pursuit of logical consequences, his power of stating a case, his scorn of qualifying language, the pith and balance of his phrasing, and the developing momentum of his argument, made his opinions irresistible.

It is not necessary to endorse the hero theory of history to recognize that great men do make a difference, even in the law. With his decisions in such landmark cases as *Marbury* v. *Madison* and *McCulloch* v. *Maryland*, Marshall alone transformed the Supreme Court into the vital center of the constitutional system and laid down the legal foundation of an effective union. Had he not sat when he did in the central judicial chair, it is unlikely that they would have been accomplished. But for the circumstance that the re-

expressly that the new guaranties would be enforced by the courts. For Madison, as for his compatriots generally, judicial review was an implicit aspect of the constitutional structure.

To one trained in the law, the power upheld in *Marbury* v. *Madison* is the very essence of judicial power. The authority to declare constitutionality flows naturally from the judicial duty to determine the law. As John C. Calhoun—himself no friend of the Court's power—conceded in 1833, "Where there were two or more rules established, one from a higher, and the other from a lower authority, which might come into conflict, in applying them to a particular case, the judge could not avoid pronouncing in favor of the superior against the inferior. It was from this necessity . . . that the power which is now set up to overrule the rights of the States, against an express provision of the constitution, was derived." One may go beyond this and say that judicial review, as declared in *Marbury* v. *Madison*, has become the sine qua non of our constitutional machinery; draw out this particular bolt, and the machinery falls to pieces.

Marshall and National Power

The primary concern of the men who drafted the federal Constitution was to establish an effective national government endowed with vital substantive powers, the lack of which had rendered the Articles of Confederation sterile. It was the task of the Marshall Court to translate this goal into legal reality and to weave the legal fabric of Union in such a way that it was to prove strong enough to withstand even the shock of civil war.

After asserting the power of judicial review, the Marshall Court employed the authority thus asserted to lay down the doctrinal foundations of an effective nation. It did so through a series of landmark decisions that had two principal aims: (1) to ensure that the nation possessed the powers needed to enable it to govern effectively; and (2) to ensure federal supremacy vis-à-vis state powers.

The key decision in the first respect was rendered in the case of *McCulloch* v. *Maryland* in 1819. It elevated the doctrine of implied powers to the constitutional plane, resolving in the process a controversy that raged in the early days of the Republic between those who favored a strict and those who favored a broad construction of the Necessary and Proper Clause at the end of Article I, section 8, of the Constitution ("The Congress shall have Power . . . To make all Laws which shall be necessary and proper for carrying into Execution the foregoing Powers, and all other Powers vested by this Constitution in the Government of the United States, or in any Department or Officer thereof."). The strict view, urged by Jefferson, emphasized the word "necessary" in the clause, arguing that it endowed the federal government only with those powers indispensable for the exercise of its specifically enumerated powers. The broader view, advocated by Hamilton, maintained that to take the word "necessary" in its rigorous sense would be to deprive the clause of real practical effect: "It is essential to the being of the National Government, that so erroneous a conception of the meaning of the word *necessary*, should be exploded," said Hamilton.

In *McCulloch*, Marshall emphatically adopted the broad Hamiltonian

Thomas Gibbons ran a steamboat line between New York and New Jersey. In the complex Gibbons v. Ogden case in 1824 the Supreme Court ruled that a state monopoly that forbade Gibbons from operating conflicted with Congress's power to regulate commerce, and was invalid.

approach. Though the authority of Congress to establish a national bank—the federal power at issue in the case—was not contained among the enumerated powers in the Constitution, that did not end the matter. If the establishment of a national bank would aid the federal government in the exercise of its granted powers, the authority to set up a national bank would be implied. The constitutional clause embraces "all means which are appropriate" to carry out "the legitimate ends" of the Constitution, unless forbidden by "the letter and spirit of the constitution."

In *McCulloch* the Marshall Court construed the basic document in the grand manner, in accordance with its own dictum that we must never forget that "it is a *constitution* we are expounding"—a living instrument that must be interpreted to meet the practical needs of government. As construed by the Court ever since, the Necessary and Proper Clause has been the fount and origin of vast federal authority; practically every power of the national government has been expanded in some degree by the clause. By refusing to bind the nation within the literal confines of its granted powers, the Marshall Court enabled it to grow and meet governmental problems that the framers could never have foreseen.

The same expansive approach to federal authority can be seen in Marshall's opinion on the most important substantive power granted to Congress: to regulate commerce. Marshall's overriding concern to interpret the Constitution so as to make effective national government possible led him to describe "the federal commerce power with a breadth never yet exceeded." He did so in the case of *Gibbons* v. *Ogden* in 1824, in which he defined commerce as all commercial intercourse—a conception comprehensive enough to include within its scope all business dealings. An equally broad view was taken on the extent of congressional power to *regulate*. "What is this power?" Marshall asked. "It is the power . . . to prescribe the rule by which commerce is to be governed. This power, like all others vested in congress, is complete in itself."

So interpreted, the Commerce Clause in the Constitution was to become the source of the most important powers the federal government exercises in time of peace. If in recent years it has become trite to point out how regulation from Washington controls us from the cradle to the grave, that is true only because of the Marshall Court's emphasis at the outset on the embracing and penetrating nature of the commerce power.

To uphold the expansive reach of federal authority was, however, but half the task of the Marshall Court. Equally important was to uphold federal supremacy against state encroachments. The Supremacy Clause of Article VI is the very foundation of the federal system and it was first given full effect by the decisions of the Marshall Court. Under these rulings, all state acts are subordinate to the valid exercise of federal authority, whether expressed in the Constitution, a congressional enactment, or a decision of the Supreme Court. Nor do the states have any power to impede or control the operations of federal laws or the agencies to which they have been entrusted by Congress.

Marshall's principal opinions were summarized by his biographer, Albert Beveridge, as follows: In *Marbury* v. *Madison*, he established the

Aaron Ogden was the loser in his battle with Gibbons. His state monopoly on steamboat travel was thrown out by the Marshall Court, which construed Congress's power to regulate commerce broadly to include "every species of commercial intercourse," and not just trade.

Marshall's Great Decisions—Foundations of the U.S. System

Marbury v. Madison (1803)

This case established the power of the Supreme Court to rule on the constitutionality of a congressional act.

In February, 1801, during the last days of John Adams's Federalist Administration, Congress passed legislation providing for the appointment of a large number of new federal judges. The bills angered the Jeffersonians, who were about to assume office. In the words of the pro-Jefferson Philadelphia *Aurora*, they would allow Adams, in his last days in the Presidency, to provide "sinecure places and pensions for thoroughgoing Federal partisans." That, of course, was the intention of Adams, who wished to fill the judiciary with men who would carry on Federalist principles. He appointed over fifty men—all right-thinking Federalists. Among them, selected as a justice of the peace for the District of Columbia, was a member of a prominent Maryland family, a banker and large landowner named William Marbury.

The Senate confirmed the appointees, and the outgoing President signed their commissions of office. It was now the job of the Secretary of State, John Marshall—who had just been appointed and sworn in as Chief Justice of the Supreme Court—to place the Great Seal of the United States on the commissions and deliver them. Because of the pressure of last-minute duties, Marshall overlooked delivering the commissions of the justices of the peace, and the new President, Thomas Jefferson, ordered his Secretary of State, James Madison, not to deliver them. Marbury then went to court, bringing an action for mandamus (an order directing an official to perform a mandatory duty imposed by law) against Madison, asking the court to order Madison to deliver his commission. Marbury brought the action directly in the Supreme Court under section 13 of the Judiciary Act, which Congress had passed in 1789 and which gave the High Court original jurisdiction (cases could start there) in man-

damus cases against federal officials.

The case appeared only to raise the question of whether the Court could issue a mandamus against the Secretary of State. Seemingly, the Court could either disavow having such power over the executive branch of the federal government and dismiss Marbury's application, or it could order Madison to deliver the commission to him. The first course would have meant abdicating the essentials of "the Judicial Power" conferred on the Court by the Constitution. But the second course would have been no better. While it would have declared the Court's authority to hold the Executive to the law, it would have remained only a "paper declaration," for the Court would have had no power to enforce its mandate.

That Marshall was able to choose neither course was a great tribute to his judicial statesmanship. He escaped from the dilemma by ruling that section 13 of the Judiciary Act was unconstitutional on the ground that, since the original jurisdiction conferred upon the Supreme Court by the Constitution was exclusive (excluded any jurisdiction not specifically stated), it could not be enlarged by congressional law. Thus, the Court could deny Marbury's application, not because the executive branch was above the law (Marshall's opinion, on the contrary, contained a strong repudiation of that claim), but because the Court itself did not possess the original jurisdiction to issue the writ that Marbury requested.

To reach that decision and rule that the congressional law was invalid, the Court was asserting that it had power to review the constitutionality of acts of Congress. From a strategic point of view, the Court could not have chosen a better case through which to declare that power. Since its decision did not rule in favor of Marbury, there was nothing that would bring on a direct conflict with the Jefferson Administration. More than that, the assertion of the greatest of all judicial powers—review of laws—was made

in a case that ruled against certain authority that had been granted to the Court itself (section 13 of the Judiciary Act). The Jeffersonians found it hard to attack the decision, in which the Court declined—even from Congress—a jurisdiction to which it was not entitled by the Constitution.

McCulloch v. Maryland (1819)

This case—involving a clash of conflicting sovereignties which in most other systems of government could be resolved only by force of arms—established the supremacy of federal jurisdiction over that of a state. It ruled on the interest of the government of the United States against that of the state of Maryland and decided for the United States. At the same time, it enunciated a doctrine of implied powers for the federal government which has become a basic part of American constitutional law.

In 1816 the Second Bank of the United States had been established by Congress to serve as a depository for federal funds and to print bank notes. Under pressure from its state banks, Maryland imposed a tax upon the federal bank's Baltimore branch and then brought suit in a state court against James William McCulloch, the branch's cashier, when he refused to pay the Maryland tax. The state won its suit, but the federal government, facing similar taxes in other states, appealed to the Supreme Court.

The immediate issue was whether the Maryland tax law was constitutional. To decide it, the Court had to probe into the very heart of national power under the Constitution and the relation between states and the nation. Marshall's opinion took up first the question of whether Congress had the power to charter a bank. The issue centered on the point of view that believed that the federal government possessed only those powers which were enumerated in the Constitution—and which did not include the power to establish a bank. But, said the Court, there was nothing in the Constitution which "excludes incidental or implied powers; and which requires that everything granted shall be expressly and minutely described." On the contrary, Article I, section 8, after enumerating the specific powers conferred on the government, authorized Congress "To make all Laws which shall be necessary and proper for carrying into Execution the foregoing Powers." If the establishment of a national bank aided the government in the exercise of its granted, or enumerated, powers, then the authority to establish the bank, Marshall said, would be an implied power. Thus, he conclusively put to rest the view that the Necessary and Proper Clause extended only to laws which were indispensably necessary. Aptly termed

Early in the nineteenth century, Fulton and Robert Livingston, American Minister in Paris when the inventor had demonstrated his steamboat in France in 1803, secured from the New York legislature a monopoly of steam navigation on the waters of that state. Under the monopoly, the partners licensed Aaron Ogden to operate ferryboats between New York and New Jersey. When Thomas Gibbons began to run steamboats in competition with Ogden and without New York permission (though he had a coasting license from the federal government),Ogden sued to stop Gibbons.

The case became a sensational battle between the two men and almost wrecked them both. (One man who

Gibbons spared no expense. He hired the top lawyers of the day, including Daniel Webster and Attorney General William Wirt, and made a provision of $40,000 in his will to carry on the case if he died before it was finished. During the litigation, Gibbons went to Ogden's home with a challenge to a duel. Instead of fighting, Ogden sued for trespass and won a $5,000 verdict. It was to prove of slight satisfaction. Before he was through, the case wrecked a fortune that he had accumulated in his legal practice.

The Supreme Court's decision, nullifying Ogden's monopoly and reversing the injunction he had secured from the New York courts to restrain Gibbons from operating in New York

The Gibbons v. Ogden decision opened the waters to free competition; this is the New York waterfront in 1839.

the "sweeping clause" at the time of the adoption of the Constitution, its enfolding of implied as well as enumerated powers made it, after Marshall's decision, the foundation stone of federal power.

As to the validity of Maryland's tax law, Marshall went on to decide against it. The federal government needed the bank, but "The power to tax involves the power to destroy," he ruled, and "the power to destroy may defeat and render useless the power to create."

Gibbons v. Ogden (1824)

This dramatic case, resulting directly from Robert Fulton's invention of the steamboat, established the broad scope of Congress's power to regulate the economic affairs of the nation.

prospered was young Cornelius Van Derbilt, Gibbons's skipper, who got his start by running his craft in defiance of Ogden's attempts to halt him.) Gibbons was a southern planter, noted for his belligerence. He had once been a campaign manager in a congressional election where there were more votes than voters. When the loser, James Jackson, attacked Gibbons in Congress, excoriating him as "this person . . . whose soul is faction, and whose life has been a scene of political corruption," Congress nullified the election result. Gibbons challenged Jackson to a duel in which shots were exchanged, though neither man was injured. His litigation with Ogden, a former governor of New Jersey and U.S. senator, became a personal vendetta in which

waters, was far more than the settling of a quarrel between two combative men. In his ruling, Marshall seized the opportunity to deliver an opinion on the breadth of Congress's authority under the Constitution's Commerce Clause, which had vested in the national legislature the power "to regulate Commerce." According to Marshall, commerce covered all intercourse—a conception comprehensive enough to include within its scope all business dealings. As Marshall construed the power to regulate commerce, the Commerce Clause thus became as broad as the economic life of the nation, and the federal government thereafter was able increasingly to exercise an authority, by legislation and judicial decision, over that area of the country's affairs.

fundamental principle that a permanent written Constitution controls a temporary Congress; in *McCulloch* v. *Maryland*, he made the government of the American people a living thing; in *Gibbons* v. *Ogden*, he welded that people into a unit by the force of their commercial interests.

To the legal historian, even more important is what Marshall did for the authority and prestige of the Supreme Court. When John Jay (who had resigned in 1795 as the first chief justice to become governor of New York) declined reappointment to the Court in 1800, he wrote President Adams that he had "left the bench, perfectly convinced that under a system so defective, it would not obtain the energy, weight and dignity, which were essential." No such statement could be made at the end of Marshall's tenure in 1835. In thirty years, wrote historian Charles Warren, he "had transformed the Supreme Court from a weak and uncertain body, hesitating to measure its strength against the prevailing jealousy of the Federal power, into an acknowledged supreme authority."

Taney and Economic Expansion

The Marshall Court transformed the Supreme Court into the vital center of the constitutional system and laid down the legal foundation of an effective national government. Under Marshall, the emphasis was strongly in favor of federal power. Constitutional principles were molded to meet the expansionist demands of the new nation.

There was an almost inevitable reaction after Marshall's death in 1835. Yet the change was not so great as is generally supposed. Some historians, wrote Felix Frankfurter in 1937, "stage a dramatic conflict between Darkness and Light: Marshall, the architect of a nation; Taney, the bigoted provincial and protector of slavery." The actual contrast between Marshall and his successor, Roger B. Taney of Maryland, was by no means so dramatic. Marshall's death may have given President Andrew Jackson—who was to appoint six justices, more than any president between Washington and Franklin D. Roosevelt—the opportunity to remold the Supreme Court in the radical Locofoco image. Yet it is erroneous to assume that the Court under Taney worked a wholesale reversal of all that the Marshall Court had accomplished. That is not the manner in which a tribunal such as the Supreme Court functions; it is certainly not the manner in which the Taney Court functioned.

To be sure, Taney and the justices appointed by Jackson and his successors inevitably had a different outlook than their predecessors, themselves products of an earlier day. Taney was the first chief justice to wear trousers rather than knee breeches; and there was something of a portent in his wearing democratic garb beneath his judicial robe. For, under Taney, the Supreme Court for the first time mirrored the Jacksonian emphasis on public power as a counterweight to the property rights stressed by the Federalists and then the Whigs.

In the Taney Court, the focus of concern shifted from federal to state power. It did so not because the justices were extreme exponents of states' rights, but because they saw state authority as the instrument for redressing the balance of constitutional protection which they felt the Marshall Court

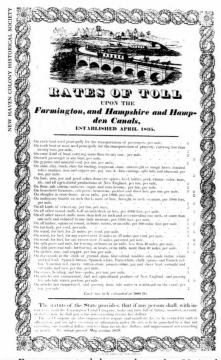

Powers not delegated to the United States are, by the Tenth Amendment, reserved to the several states; this includes the power to regulate commerce between points within a state. Pictured is the 1835 toll schedule of a Connecticut canal.

had tipped unduly against the public interest and in favor of property. Relying on the fundamental notion that property and the rights derived from it owe their existence to "the sovereign power of the political body, organized in such mode or exerted in such way as the community or State may have thought proper to ordain," the Taney Court developed the police power as the basic instrument through which property might be controlled in the public interest. Community rights were thus ruled "paramount to all private rights. . . , and these last are, by necessary implication, held in subordination to this power, and must yield in every instance to its proper exercise."

In the Taney Court's conception, the police power of the states included all powers necessary to their internal government which were not prohibited to them by the federal Constitution. Taney's opinion in the *License Cases* in 1847 gave currency to the phrase "police power," and by the time of the Civil War the term was in common use in both federal and state courts.

The Taney Court's articulation of the police power concept was a necessary complement to the period of expansion prior to the Civil War that characterized the westward march of the national center of gravity. During that time, people demanded internal improvements, for public construction of roads, canals, and free schools, and for laws regulating the professions and the sale of liquor. In the police power concept, the law developed the constitutional theory needed to enable the states to meet the public demand. Government was given the "power of accomplishing the end for which it was created." Through the police power, said the *License Cases* decision, a

This 1848 daguerreotype is one of a series showing the Cincinnati riverfront lined with steamboats. It is graphic evidence of the growth of trade that made necessary broad reinterpretation of the power of the federal government over commerce.

state might "for the safety or convenience of trade, or for the protection of the health of its citizens" regulate private rights. Thenceforth, a principal task of American public law was to be determination of the proper balance between individual rights and the police power.

In developing the police power, the Taney Court was giving effect to the prevailing desire to make the law serve as an instrument for creative change. Though the nineteenth century is identified in our minds with the judicial protection of "vested rights," it emphatically did not seek to preserve in American law anything like the Old World reign of the dead hand. On the contrary. In his important opinion, in *Charles River Bridge* v. *Warren Bridge,* in 1837, Chief Justice Taney spoke out vigorously in favor of freedom for creative change as against unyielding protection for existing commitments. He did so by holding that the grant of a charter to operate a toll bridge did not give the grantee an exclusive franchise; hence it did not prohibit the building of a nearby competing bridge under a later charter. Taney refused to hold that the first charter granted a monopoly. Instead, such a public grant should be construed narrowly to preserve the rights of the community. The community's power may not be transferred, by mere implication, "to the hands of privileged corporations."

Though in form the *Charles River Bridge* decision was a blow to economic rights, it actually facilitated economic development. The case itself arose when the corporate form was coming into widespread use as an instrument of capitalist expansion. In the famous *Dartmouth College* case in 1819, the Marshall Court had ruled the grants of privileges in corporate charters to be contracts and, as such, beyond impairment by government. In the *Charles River Bridge* case, the Marshall approach would have meant the upholding

John Marshall's Successor

In 1865 an anonymous pamphlet was published entitled *The Unjust Judge—A Memorial of Roger Brooke Taney, Late Chief Justice of the United States.* It excoriated the man who had succeeded John Marshall, calling him, "next to Pontius Pilate, perhaps the worst that ever occupied the seat of judgment." Undoubtedly, the attack on Taney, who had just died, was the result of his identification with the verdict in the *Dred Scott* case which had preceded the Civil War. Prior to that decision, Taney had been acclaimed as a worthy successor to Marshall, destined to rank almost on the same level with him in the judicial pantheon. "No man in the United States," said Henry Clay to Taney himself, "could have been selected, more abundantly able to wear the

ermine which Chief Justice Marshall honored."

Born in Maryland in 1777, Taney headed the Supreme Court from 1836 until his death in 1864, a tenure second only to that of Marshall. Before his appointment, he had been a leading Jacksonian politician, serving President Andrew Jackson both as Attorney General and Secretary of the Treasury. In 1832 he had drafted the key portions of Jackson's famous veto message on the bill to renew the Bank of the United States, and the following year had carried out the President's plan for the removal of government deposits from the Bank. His years on the Court were marked by a growing judicial concern for the safeguarding of the rights of the community as op-

posed to property rights—of the public welfare as opposed to private interests. "While the rights of property are sacredly guarded," declared the first important Taney opinion, "we must not forget that the community also have rights, and that the happiness and well being of every citizen depends on their faithful preservation."

The Taney Court shifted the constitutional emphasis from the federal level to the power that states possessed—particularly the power reserved to them by the Constitution to regulate business and other activities within the state, known also as the police power. Through this power, the states might take whatever measures they deemed necessary to protect public

of the first bridge company's monopoly, a result that would have most undesirable consequences, for it would have meant that every existing bridge or turnpike company had an exclusive franchise which could not be impaired by newer forms of transportation. To read monopoly rights into existing charters would be to place modern improvements at the mercy of existing corporations and defeat the right of the community to avail itself of the benefits of scientific progress.

Justice Joseph Story, who dissented, bitterly attacked the *Charles River Bridge* decision. "A case of grosser injustice . . . ," he wrote to his wife, "never existed." Those who agreed with Story refused to see the beneficial effects of Taney's decision. "I stand upon the old law . . . ," plaintively affirmed the Story dissent, "not . . . any speculative niceties or novelties." To men like Story, Taney and the majority had virtually "overturned . . . one great provision of the Constitution."

The truth is that the Taney Court had changed the interpretation of the Contract Clause in a manner that coincided with the felt needs of the new era of economic expansion. Because of the Taney decision, that expansion could proceed unencumbered by inappropriate legal excrescences. Paradoxically perhaps, Taney, the erstwhile Jacksonian politician, did as much as Marshall to promote economic development and the concentrations of wealth and power that were its inevitable concomitants.

New State Constitutions

"It is one of the happy incidents of the federal system," said Justice Louis D. Brandeis in an often-quoted passage, "that a single state may, if its citizens choose, serve as a laboratory; and try novel social and economic

Roger B. Taney served with distinction for twenty-eight years as chief justice, but he remains most identified with the Dred Scott decision. In that ruling he broadened the issues to try to defend the culture of his own South, but only succeeded in hastening its downfall.

health, safety, and morals within their respective borders. The police power, in Taney's period, became the basic instrument through which property might be controlled in the public interest.

Despite his contribution to the law, Taney has come down in history as a remote, somewhat forbidding figure. In part, it is due to the shadow cast on him by his association with the *Dred Scott* decision in 1857. But it also results from his cold, aloof character, so different from that of his straightforward predecessor. Taney's own autobiography emphasized what he termed his "morbid sensibility," which was apparently exaggerated by his delicate health and by an inhibition at being a Catholic in the xenophobic Know-Nothing era. "I do not

exactly understand why *Friday* has become the fashionable day for dinners, here," he once complained plaintively to his son-in-law, reflecting his acute susceptibility to supposed slights to his religion in the nation's capital.

Admirers of the Marshall constitutional edifice sometimes looked on Taney as Jackson's chosen instrument for its destruction ("Judge Story thinks the Supreme Court is *gone*," wrote Daniel Webster after Taney's appointment, "and I think so too.") Furthermore, the *Dred Scott* decision, with its link to the cause of slavery and the Confederacy, long cast a pall over Taney's judicial stature. But if one avoids trying to compare his accomplishments with those of his pred-

ecessor, his contributions are seen as having been far from mean—and as not having been as much of a reaction to the direction of Marshall's Court as has often been supposed. Taney was not as nationalistic as his predecessor, but his greater emphasis on states' rights continued the formulation of principles needed to ensure the effective operation of the Constitution. "The devastation of the Civil War," said Felix Frankfurter, "for a long time obliterated the truth about Taney. . . . But the intellectual power of his opinions and their enduring contribution to a workable adjustment of the theoretical distribution of authority between two governments for a single people, place Taney second only to Marshall in the constitutional history of our country."

experiments without risk to the rest of the country.'' The concept of the states as laboratories is as valid in public law as in other fields, though it is too often obscured by the U.S. Supreme Court's dominant role in public law cases. Many important constitutional principles have first been developed in the states and then been adapted for use in federal law. This was true of the very concept of a written constitution and bill of rights. Twelve states had written constitutions, and eight of them had bills of rights, before the federal Constitution and the first ten amendments were written.

There has, of course, been only one federal Constitutional Convention, and the Constitution drawn up by it has remained virtually unaltered as the nation's basic document; after ratification of the Bill of Rights, no important amendments were added until after the Civil War. The same has not been true of the state constitutions. The classical age of constitution making, which began America's history as an independent nation, was only the first stage in the constitution-making process at the state level.

Between the Revolutionary constitutions and the Civil War, all of the original states except Massachusetts and North Carolina adopted new constitutions—though, in one case, it took a mini-revolution (the so-called Dorr Rebellion in Rhode Island) to accomplish the result. In addition, each new state admitted to the Union during this period drew up its own constitution. As was the case during the Revolution, the new constitutions were framed by conventions elected for the purpose (except in Nebraska, whose first constitution was drawn up, in 1866, by its territorial legislature).

Attempts by disenfranchised voters to change a state constitution limiting suffrage to a few property owners led to the Dorr Rebellion in Rhode Island in the early 1840's. The revolt was crushed by state militia, and leader Thomas Dorr was imprisoned. A more liberal constitution was soon adopted. Below: a pro-Dorr cartoon.

The mechanics of the constitution-making process continued to be that fixed at the end of the eighteenth century: conventions were used to prepare an original constitution or revise an existing one, though ordinary amendments could be prepared by the legislature.

The constitutions drafted in the states after the Revolutionary period marked substantial changes, particularly as compared with the federal Constitution. The original framers of the national document avoided a cardinal error common among draftsmen of fundamental laws. Men who write constitutions all too often seek to provide expressly for every foreseeable contingency. The result is that most constitutions are political codes. The federal Constitution embodied only the fundamentals of government: the great outlines were marked, the important objects designated; but the detailed particulars were left to be deduced. The same was also generally true of the first state constitutions.

The newer state constitutions, especially those drafted after the 1830's, usually did not conform to the early models. They began to include more and more procedural details and specific legislative provisions. In addition, detailed amendments on relatively minor matters were increasingly added to the state organic documents. The trend toward the overly detailed constitution may be traced to the New York Constitution of 1846, which replaced the simpler constitutions of 1777 and 1821. The 1777 document had 42 short sections; the 1846 constitution contained 14 articles and 136 sections. They dealt with such matters as the composition of the electorate and legislative districts, provision for a number of executive officers other than the Governor and Lieutenant-Governor (including State Engineer and Surveyor, Canal Commissioners, Inspectors of State Prisons, and Commissioners of the Canal Fund), revenues and finance, corporations, sheriffs, county clerks, coroners, district attorneys, and the militia. These details belong in statutes; they only clutter up a constitution and make it unduly cumbersome. It was of the New York-type of document that James Bryce was to speak when he complained in *The American Commonwealth* in 1888 that "the later State Constitutions are so full and precise that they need little in the way of expansive construction, and leave comparatively little room for the action of custom." Not only do such documents detract from the dignity of a constitution; worse, they freeze details of policy into a form hard to change.

But in another respect the new state constitutions marked a substantial step forward. Almost all of them moved in the direction of broader democracy. During the early history of the nation, the right to participate in the political process was substantially restricted. At the time the federal Constitution was adopted, a majority of the state constitutions expressly limited the franchise to males who possessed a stated amount of property. The elimination of property qualifications was among the primary objectives of the egalitarian movements that dominated much of nineteenth-century politics.

As Chief Justice Earl Warren pointed out in 1964, "history has seen a continuing expansion of the scope of the right of suffrage in this country." The trend toward the removal of suffrage restrictions began even before the end of the eighteenth century, when, in 1792, the New Hampshire Constitu-

The Pennsylvania State Assembly used a unique way in 1775 to finance the Walnut Street Jail in Philadelphia: it simply authorized the printing of a special issue of currency. The bills (above) carry a picture of the jail and a warning against counterfeiting.

PENN MUTUAL LIFE INSURANCE COMPANY, PHILADELPHIA

When Virginia held a Constitutional Convention in 1829, George Catlin made a group portrait of the delegates and called it "Last Meeting of the Giants." Among "the giants" are James Monroe, James Madison, John Randolph, and John Marshall.
VIRGINIA HISTORICAL SOCIETY

tion provided for universal male suffrage, the Delaware Constitution provided that adult white taxpayers might vote (thus substituting payment of taxes for the property qualification), and the new state of Kentucky's Constitution provided that all free males over twenty-one would have the right to vote. The next year the new Vermont Constitution provided for the vote for "the freemen of each town."

The movement toward universal male suffrage was renewed in the next century when Maryland adopted an 1810 amendment abolishing all property qualifications for voting, and gathered momentum as other new states entered the Union during the next decade with constitutions that provided for manhood suffrage. The trend toward universal male suffrage heightened when property restrictions were eliminated from the constitutions of Massachusetts and New York. The debates in the New York Convention of 1821, in particular, marked a constitutional watershed in the movement for unrestricted suffrage. Here the conservatives, led by Chancellor James Kent, were "stationed in the straits of Thermopylae." Kent luridly described the dangers of universal suffrage: "The tendency of universal suffrage, is to jeopardize the rights of property, and the principles of liberty." Pointing to the growth of New York City, he said it "is enough to startle and awaken those who are pursuing the *ignis fatuus* of universal suffrage. . . . The radicals . . . with the force of that mighty engine, would at once sweep away the property, the laws, and the liberties . . . like a deluge." But the sweep of democracy could not be restrained. The New York Constitution of 1821 granted the franchise to male taxpayers and, five years later, in 1826, an amendment extended the vote to all adult males. In both of these cases,

however, a property qualification was imposed upon "persons of color."

Only in the South was the tide temporarily held. In the Virginia Convention of 1829–1830, the conservatives, led by the aged John Marshall, were able to ensure the retention of property qualifications. A determining element was southern resistance to reforms imported from the North: "if any plague originate in the North, it is sure to spread to the South and to invade us sooner or later: the influenza — the smallpox — the varioloid — the Hessian fly — the Circuit Court system — Universal Suffrage." Yet even the Virginia Constitution of 1850 was to provide for universal white male suffrage. By that date, all the states except North Carolina had abandoned property qualifications, and that state did so in 1856.

Restrictions on the right to vote were, of course, the principal casualty of the movement we know as Jacksonian Democracy. At the beginning of the Jacksonian era, Tocqueville could still note the existence of property qualifications in some states. By the time of the Civil War, virtually all adult white males possessed the right to vote. Yet the Jacksonian concept of equality was, by present-day standards, quite limited. Though the Jacksonians went farther than the Founders in the direction of both political and economic equality, their notion of the democratic ideal must be sharply distinguished from the modern one. The Jacksonians, like the framers of the Constitution before them, did not carry their concept of equality to the point of extending the rights and privileges of citizenship to *all* members of the community. They did not understand the ideal of liberty and equality *for all men* to require the abolition of slavery, the emancipation of women from legal and political subjection, or the eradication of all constitutional

George Caleb Bingham painted the rough-and-ready American frontier, reflecting, among other aspects of life, the extension of suffrage. Above and below are two of his sketches of the stump-speaking politician that rose with Jacksonian Democracy. At right his "Verdict of the People" shows an election day in early America.

discriminations based on wealth, race, or previous condition of servitude.

All the same, one should not minimize the significance of the Jacksonian conception. Under Jackson the nation achieved its first great egalitarian revolution. Even if we realize that Jacksonian Democracy was scarcely intended to be as radically democratic as its contemporaries feared, we must still recognize that it made substantial contributions to both the theory and practice of equality. The achievement of universal suffrage (though only for white males) was a substantial step forward, without which subsequent progress in the area of individual rights would hardly have been possible.

Police Power and Due Process

During the formative era, important doctrines were also developing in the work of the state courts. State judges were quick to make use of the police power concept, which had been given currency by the Taney Court. In 1851 the first case in a state court to speak of the police power was decided — the now-classic Massachusetts case of *Commonwealth* v. *Alger*, with an often-cited definition of the term by Chief Justice Lemuel Shaw. Only four years later, a Missouri court could say of this power that it was "known familiarly as the police power," for by then the concept was firmly embedded in state public law.

Nevertheless, it should be recognized that, in an age in which freedom of

Charles River Bridge

In 1785 John Hancock and others received a charter permitting them to set up a Massachusetts corporation to operate a toll bridge across the Charles River in Boston. With no competition, the bridge became immensely profitable, its shares of stock increasing tenfold in value. The large income fed by the tolls eventually succeeded in arousing the antagonism of the public, especially since the bridge's stock was held by some of Boston's leading citizens and by Harvard College, which received £200 a year from the profits.

By the mid-1820's the Charles River Bridge had become a popular symbol of monopoly. In 1828 the Massachusetts legislature incorporated a rival group, the Warren Bridge Company, to build and operate another span near the Charles River Bridge. Under its charter, the new bridge was to be free to the public after a short period of time. Such competition posed an immediate threat to the owners of the Charles River Bridge, who sued to enjoin construction of the new span, alleging that the contractual obligation contained in its own charter had been impaired.

The case, *Charles River Bridge* v. *Warren Bridge*, was the first important one to be decided by the Taney Court. It became a *cause célèbre* because it brought the Federalist and Jacksonian views on property into sharp conflict and involved Harvard and notable Bostonians. The case was argued before the Supreme Court on January 24, 1837, with Daniel Webster appearing for the Charles River Bridge. At an early hour, according to a newspaper account, "all the seats within and without the bar . . . were filled with ladies, whose beauty and splendid attire and waving plumes gave to the Court-room an animated and brilliant appearance such as it seldom wears."

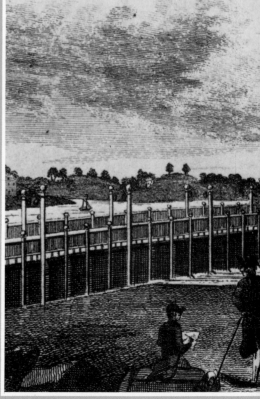

The Charles River Bridge, above, was not a grand

contract was coming to be the primary policy, the police power was developed in what would be considered today essentially negative terms. In Chief Justice Shaw's definition, the police power was stated as "the power vested in the legislature . . . to make, ordain and establish all manner of wholesome and reasonable laws . . . as they shall judge to be for the good and welfare of the commonwealth." Though this was tantamount to the power to govern, its scope was not as far reaching as one might imagine. This was true because the power to govern was itself, until the present century, conceived of mainly as a negative concept. The basically negative aspect of the police power in its early development may be seen from the definition of another state judge: "This police power of the state extends to the protection of the lives, limbs, health, comfort, and quiet of all persons and the protection of all property within the state."

As first developed in the state courts, the police power was firmly anchored in the limitations that the pre-existing law had imposed upon property rights. These limitations were embodied essentially in the common law maxim: *sic utere tuo ut alienum non laedas* ("use your own property in such a manner as not to injure that of another"). "According to the maxim . . . it must, of course, be within the range of legislative action to define the mode and manner in which every one may so use his own as not to injure others," read one decision in Vermont in 1854. The police power was seen

structure, but it was the subject of one of the Supreme Court's landmark decisions.

The Court's decision, rendered on February 12, was in favor of the new bridge, holding that there had been no valid infringement on the Charles River Bridge Company's charter rights. Taney's opinion declined to support the argument that the charter to operate a toll bridge had granted the Charles River Bridge owners a monopoly, but stated, instead, that the charter should be construed narrowly to preserve the rights of the community: where the rights of private property conflict with those of the community, the latter must be paramount. "The object and end of all government," declared Taney, virtually setting forth the theme of Jacksonian Democracy in economic affairs, "is to promote the happiness and prosperity of the community by which it is established, and it can never be assumed that the government intended to diminish its power of accomplishing the end for which it was created."

The ultimate defender of the public safety is the policeman, and in this daguerreotype (perhaps posed for public education) Sheriff Frederick Warren of Worcester, Massachusetts, is putting the collar on a prisoner.
AMERICAN ANTIQUARIAN SOCIETY

to stem from the right of society to be free from noxious exercises of private rights. The basic interests to be protected were the social interest in the general security and that in the general morals. The public law of the first half of the nineteenth century recognized these social interests by putting "public health, safety, and morals" in the police power as a ground of governmental restraint to which private rights must give way.

Today, to be sure, the original limitations of the police power — expressed in the traditional formula of public health, safety, and morals as the ends to be served — seem unduly narrow. The short list of 125 years ago has become a veritable catalogue. But we should not underestimate the importance of the cases that first developed the police power concept. Rudimentary by present-day standards, the original concept was, nevertheless, to serve throughout the nineteenth century as a reminder that, however far the doctrines of contract and vested rights might be pushed, government still possessed a residual power to ensure that the public interest was not completely overlooked. When, toward the end of the century, men began to realize that private rights might have to be restricted in the public interest, the police power furnished the instrument for the exertion of governmental authority.

Apart from the further development of the police power, the most important public law contribution of the state courts during the pre-Civil War period was their virtual transformation of the concept of due process. To today's public lawyer, the Due Process Clause so plainly imposes the most important substantive limitation upon governmental power that he may forget how limited due process was in its original connotation. When Madison wrote the Due Process Clause into his first draft of the Bill of Rights, he thought of due process only as a procedural guaranty. His view was doubtless that expressed by Hamilton in 1787 on a New York law which contained provisions guaranteeing that no one should be deprived of specified rights except by "due process of law." This apparently was the first American enactment (save a 1692 Massachusetts statute) to substitute "due process of law" for "the law of the land" phraseology originally derived from Magna Carta. "The words 'due process' have a precise technical import, and are only applicable to the process and proceedings of the courts of justice; they can never be referred to an act of the legislature," said Hamilton.

This does not mean that no substantive restraints upon governmental power existed before the broadening of the due process concept. The early American judges, both federal and state, appealed to natural rights and the social compact as limiting governmental powers, even aside from any express constitutional restrictions such as the Contract Clause. In this sense, the different constitutions were treated as declaratory of natural law, and hence as embodiments of universal precepts that were the root of all constitutions. "Though there may be no prohibition in the constitution," argued Daniel Webster in 1829, "the legislature is restrained from committing flagrant acts, from acts subverting the great principles of republican liberty, and of the social compact." The very "nature of society and of government" prescribed essential limits upon legislative power. Those limits, according to a New York State decision in 1849, rested "upon the broader and more solid ground of natural rights, and [were] not wholly dependent upon these negatives . . . contained in the constitution."

With the discrediting of natural law that followed the work of philosopher Immanuel Kant, natural rights and the social compact could not have served long as the basis for substantive restrictions upon governmental power. But the constitutional focus was soon to shift from natural law theories to the express limitations contained in the Due Process Clause. This was primarily the result of several state court decisions during the pre-Civil War period, notably those of the New York Court of Appeals. The New York cases reflected a steady development of the notion that the rights of the individual were protected by due process from a substantive, as well as a procedural, point of view. That development culminated in the celebrated case of *Wynehamer* v. *People* in 1856.

The case arose out of a New York law that prohibited the sale of intoxicating liquors except for medicinal purposes, and the storage of liquors not intended for sale in any place but a dwelling house. The law further provided for the immediate summary destruction of all liquor held in violation of its provisions, and made any violation a misdemeanor. The New York court ruled that the law operated to "annihilate and destroy the rights of property which the citizens of this state possessed, at the time it took effect, in intoxicating liquors." This might not be done consistently with the Due Process Clause in the New York Constitution. In so holding, the court was clearly giving due process a substantive connotation. Such a deprivation, providing for the destruction of property already in the possession of its owner, was beyond the power of government, "even by the forms which belong to 'due process of law.'" The statute at issue, though it contained no procedural defects, fell "certainly within the spirit of a constitutional provision intended expressly to shield private rights from the exercise of arbitrary power."

Of particular significance was the New York court's use of substantive due process as a substitute for the natural law approach. Although the court was not urged to invalidate the law at issue because it violated an express organic provision, but because it was contrary to "the nature and form of our government," it said that inquiry into that question was not really necessary: "There is no process of reasoning by which it can be dem-

The Dred Scott Case

The plaintiff of record—though he was the passive instrument of the real plaintiffs—was a slave living in St. Louis and somewhat bewildered by all the "fuss" being made over him. The defendant of record was his legal owner, John F. A. Sanford, a man of antislavery sentiment who lived in New York. The litigation—a test case that began obscurely with a different defendant—was one of the most complicated and confused ever to come before the Supreme Court (even Sanford's name got incorrectly spelled, so that the case was officially known as *Dred Scott v. Sandford*), and no case ever had graver consequences for the Court and the nation.

Born in Virginia about 1795, Scott (originally known only as Sam) was taken to St. Louis when his owner, Peter Blow, moved to that city. After Blow's death, Scott had a series of owners, including Dr. John Emerson, an army surgeon, who took him to

MISSOURI HISTORICAL SOCIETY

Dred Scott

Illinois and Wisconsin Territory, so that for approximately five years before returning to St. Louis the slave—by then known as Dred Scott—lived on free soil. In time, Emerson died, and his widow moved to New York. Scott was left behind and came

under the care of one of Peter Blow's sons, Henry, a Missouri businessman and ardent abolitionist. In 1846, Blow, with the approval of Mrs. Emerson, helped institute a suit in the Missouri courts to declare Scott free.

Mrs. Emerson could have signed papers giving Scott his freedom, but *Scott, a Man of Color, v. Emerson*, as the litigation was first known, was a deliberate test case in the fight against slavery, designed to prove that a slave's bondage ended when his master took him into free territory. The case dragged on for years in the Missouri courts. Meanwhile, with the acquisition of western territories and the heightening of conflict between pro- and anti-slavery partisans over whether those new lands should be free or slave, the issue in the case steadily gained importance. By the time it reached the Supreme Court in 1856, the case (now defended by

onstrated that the 'Act for the prevention of intemperance, pauperism and crime' is void, upon principles and theories outside of the constitution, which will not also, and by an easier induction, bring it in direct conflict with the constitution itself."

The *Wynehamer* decision was recognized as epoch making almost as soon as it was rendered. This was true even though it was soon seen that the immediate holding in *Wynehamer* went too far, because of the well-nigh complete power of the states over intoxicating liquors, which even the New York courts came to recognize. The reasoning of the *Wynehamer* court, particularly its substitution of substantive due process as a check upon arbitrary governmental power for the prior natural law approach, was to be that ultimately adopted by American courts, including the highest bench in the land after ratification of the Fourteenth Amendment.

Constitutional Crucible

The immediate effect of *Wynehamer* on American public law was, nevertheless, little short of disastrous, for it helped lead to the self-inflicted wound of the *Dred Scott* decision in 1857. It was essentially the *Wynehamer* approach that Chief Justice Taney followed when he held that Congress lacked the power to deal with slavery in the territories by enactment of the Missouri Compromise of 1820. According to Taney, congressional authority to regulate the territories was restricted by the protection given property rights

Sanford, Mrs. Emerson's brother to whom she had transferred title to Scott) commanded national attention. It had also grown more complicated with additional issues: Was Scott, the slave, a citizen of Missouri and thus entitled to sue in a federal court? Did Congress have the power to prohibit slavery in a territory? Was the Missouri Compromise of 1820 unconstitutional?

Chief Justice Roger B. Taney's stunning decision, rendered for the Court on March 6, 1857, ruled that Negroes were not and could not become citizens within the meaning of the Constitution. Moreover, Taney rejected the claim that Scott had become a free man by virtue of his residence in Wisconsin, a territory from which slavery had been excluded by the Missouri Compromise, because "the act of Congress which prohibited a citizen from holding and owning property of this kind in the territory of the United States north of the line therein mentioned, is not warranted by the Constitution, and is therefore void."

There was more in the Chief Justice's opinion and in seven others rendered by the associate justices. But what burst with dramatic impact on the nation was the fact that the Court had denied both the right of Negroes to be citizens and the power of Congress to interfere with slaveholding in the territories. It meant that slavery was a national institution which could not be abolished without a constitutional amendment.

The slavery question, President James Buchanan had told the country in his inaugural address only two days before the Supreme Court decision, "is a judicial question, which legitimately belongs to the Supreme Court of the United States, before whom it is now pending, and will, it is understood, be speedily and finally settled." Buchanan could not have been more wrong. A storm of abuse burst over the majority decision, casting a dark and enduring shadow over Taney and the High Bench itself. For more than a century, *Dred Scott* has stood as a monument of judicial indiscretion. Even more important was the case's immediate effect in accelerating the polarization of the nation over slavery. Far from quelling the sectional strife, it proved a catalyst that helped precipitate the civil conflict that soon followed.

Dred Scott himself was freed by his owners a few weeks after the decision and worked as a hotel porter in St. Louis until his death from tuberculosis the next year. It took the Civil War and the Thirteenth and Fourteenth amendments after the war to settle the "fuss" that people had raised in his name.

by the Due Process Clause of the Fifth Amendment. "And an act of Congress which deprives a citizen . . . of his liberty or property, merely because he . . . brought his property into a particular Territory of the United States, and who had committed no offence against the laws, could hardly be dignified with the name of due process of law." Hence the Missouri Compromise prohibition against the holding of property in slaves was unconstitutional.

The *Dred Scott* use of the *Wynehamer* approach was, of course, calamitous in its consequences. Acquiescence in the Supreme Court decision was fatal alike to the Republicans and the advocates of popular sovereignty. It meant slavery was a national institution that Congress could not confine to a section that would become an ever-smaller minority in an expanding nation. Regardless of legal logic, the opponents of slavery could scarcely accept the Court's decision as final. A concurring justice stated that the issues involved in *Dred Scott* had become so controversial "that the peace and harmony of the country required the settlement of them by judicial decision." Seldom has wishful thinking been so spectacularly wrong. Whatever *Dred Scott* brought about, it was not peace and harmony—either for the Court or for the country.

Dred Scott was, however, only the most spectacular manifestation of the failure of American public law to resolve the slavery issue—a failure that was to result in its ultimate resolution by force of arms, itself the very negation of all that public law was intended to accomplish. By mid-century, the slavery controversy had become a distorting element with direful consequences throughout the law; it exercised a kind of hydraulic pressure which made what was previously clear seem doubtful and before which even settled principles had to bend. How else are we to explain such legal heresies as the congressional Gag Rule, with its utter prostration of the constitutional right of petition; the suppression of antislavery material from the mail; and the complete abrogation of the Bill of Rights safeguards in the Fugitive Slave Law of 1850? Or the contemporary assumption expressed in an 1850 congressional debate that the law was clear "in putting horses and negroes together as property," or even that blacks were not legally as well off, since there was no "clause in the Constitution . . . which provides for the restitution of fugitive horses by the Government"?

To be sure, as the *Dred Scott* case dramatically demonstrated, it was a fundamental error to assume that the law could resolve the basic controversy over slavery. A question that was to result in a civil war was hardly a proper one for a judicial forum.

In many ways, the Civil War was the test of fire of the American system of public law. In an 1862 article, Lord Acton referred to it as the Second American Revolution—a characterization that has since been made often. Like the Revolution, the Civil War represented an extralegal appeal to force to settle the ultimate legal issue of the nature of the polity. And the issue itself was decided, not by the tribunal to which the resolution of such questions was confided by the Constitution, but by the victorious Union armies. When the Supreme Court in 1869 decided that secession was illegal, since "The Constitution in all its provisions, looks to an indestructible Union," it only confirmed the decision made at Appomattox Courthouse.

CAUTION!!
COLORED PEOPLE
OF BOSTON, ONE & ALL,
You are hereby respectfully CAUTIONED and advised, to avoid conversing with the
Watchmen and Police Officers of Boston,
For since the recent ORDER OF THE MAYOR & ALDERMEN, they are empowered to act as
KIDNAPPERS
AND
Slave Catchers,
And they have already been actually employed in KIDNAPPING, CATCHING, AND KEEPING SLAVES. Therefore, if you value your LIBERTY, and the Welfare of the Fugitives among you, Shun them in every possible manner, as so many HOUNDS on the track of the most unfortunate of your race.
Keep a Sharp Look Out for KIDNAPPERS, and have TOP EYE open.
APRIL 24, 1851.

The Fugitive Slave Law of 1850 not only made the North responsible for the return of escaped slaves, but sometimes led to the kidnapping of freed slaves and their shipment to the South. This warning was posted in Boston by abolitionists.

Yet, if our public law broke down in the face of the nation's most serious crisis, that was not so much the fault of the law itself. The men of the day expected too much of both the law and the courts. In particular, the power and prestige that had been built up under John Marshall, and continued under Roger B. Taney, had led to these too-great expectations. And the justices themselves had succumbed to the lure of seeking to save the country from the Bench, losing sight the while of the limitations inherent in judicial power.

If the Civil War represented an appeal from law to the sword, that was true because the opposing extremes no longer accepted the underlying premises of the legal order. Americans too often forget that the rule of law draws only limited strength from judicial guaranties; it must have roots far deeper than a formal fundamental document and decisions of the judges enforcing it. Our public law depends for its efficacy on popular acceptance of its basic presuppositions. Acceptance, rather than formal legal machinery, is the decisive force in the law's implementation. With the late great jurist Learned Hand, in one of his famous passages from *The Spirit of Liberty*, we may "wonder whether we do not rest our hopes too much upon constitutions, upon laws and upon courts. These are false hopes, believe me, these are false hopes."

Northern moral indignation against slavery gave birth to the so-called Underground Railroad, by which an estimated fifty thousand slaves escaped to freedom between about 1830 and 1860. A network of changing, secret routes and hiding places, it was without formal organization.

III

The Golden Age

Private Law and Institutions 1789–1860

The period before the Civil War appears today as the Golden Age of American Law. Those were the years that followed the classical era of constitution making, when the basic political and legal institutions of the nation had been fixed. Now the details of the marriage between English common law and the people and conditions of the new country had to be worked out. It was a period of remarkable legal development, when Crèvecoeur's "new man" was making law in the grand manner. This was the age of legal giants, both at the Bench and Bar. When Roscoe Pound in 1938 drew up his list of the ten judges who must be ranked most highly in American judicial history, he included six who had done their enduring work before the Civil War—John Marshall, James Kent, Joseph Story, John B. Gibson, Lemuel Shaw, and Thomas Ruffin. With the exception of Marshall, all were acknowledged masters of the common law and equity. The Bar, we are told, has been particularly anonymous in the sight of history. But this was surely not true of the lawyers of the formative era. The leading lawyers of the period—Daniel Webster, Luther Martin, William Wirt, William Pinkney, Jeremiah Mason, to name but a few—have remained heroic figures, to recall to the Bar a standard of advocacy seldom attained in any system. Tocqueville's famous description of the United States as a lawyer-dominated society, with the legal profession its only aristocratic element, reflects how well the practitioner and judge of the early Republic built their legal superstructure.

To be sure, the present-day reader tends to look with suspicion on any account that emphasizes anything but the mote in the historical eye. Laudatory history today seems as out of date as the flamboyant rhetoric of a century and a half ago. Yet, no longer looking on the past with veneration does

Virginia lawyer and writer William Wirt was an eminent U.S. attorney general for twelve years.
VIRGINIA STATE LIBRARY

The lawyer, by David Blythe—corrupt and dreaming of political fame

Ignored by the dog, a rural justice conducts court informally, probably in his own home, in early America.

not mean that we must go to the opposite extreme. Twentieth-century denigration cannot change the fact that the formative era of American law was a time of prodigious accomplishment.

Essentially, the task of the pre-Civil War period was to construct upon the constitutional foundation a legal system adapted to the needs of the new nation and the new era into which it was entering. The law, said Justice Oliver Wendell Holmes, "is forever adopting new principles from life at one end, and it always retains old ones from history at the other." This was the precise situation of American law during the years from independence to the Civil War. According to Roscoe Pound, "It was the task of our formative era . . . to work out from our inherited legal materials a general body of law for what was to be a politically and economically unified land." As indicated in Chapter I, the job was done by receiving the common law and reshaping it into a law for America. The basic starting points were retained from English history; but new principles were constantly adopted from American life, molding and reshaping the common law. The period was thus one of growth through adaptation, in which received materials were worked over and developed into a consistent legal system.

What distinguishes the law of the nation's formative era so sharply from that of a century and more later was its self-sufficient character — or at least the Bench and Bar that made it, deemed it self-sufficient. Its growing point was analysis rather than philosophy. The disciples of Coke had taken over from those of Bacon and sought to construct a legal system complete within itself, that laid down the rules required by the new society.

The prime agency in the shaping of American law during the last century was judicial decision. Judges received and reshaped the common law. For the better part of a century, the growing point of American law was case

The Ten Greatest American Judges

Who were the ten greatest judges in American history? In 1938, Roscoe Pound, the nation's foremost legal scholar, and from 1916 to 1936 Dean of Harvard Law School, proposed such a list. In chronological order his selections included:

John Marshall, Chief Justice of the United States, 1801–1835.

James Kent, Justice of the Supreme Court of New York, 1798–1804; Chief Justice of that court, 1804–1814; Chancellor of New York, 1814–1823.

Joseph Story, Justice of the U.S. Supreme Court, 1811–1845.

John Bannister Gibson, Justice of the Supreme Court of Pennsylvania, 1816–1830; Chief Justice of that court, 1830–1853.

Lemuel Shaw, Chief Justice of Massachusetts, 1830–1860.

Thomas Ruffin, Judge of the Superior Court of North Carolina, 1818–1827; Justice of the Supreme Court of that state, 1827–1834; Chief Justice of North Carolina, 1834–1853.

Thomas McIntyre Cooley, Judge of the Supreme Court of Michigan, 1864–1885; chairman of the Interstate Commerce Commission, 1887–1891.

Charles Doe, Justice of the Supreme Court of New Hampshire, 1861–1876; Chief Justice of that court, 1876–1896.

Oliver Wendell Holmes, Justice of the Supreme Judicial Court of Massachusetts, 1882–1899; Chief Justice of that court, 1899–1902; Justice of

the U.S. Supreme Court, 1902–1932.

Benjamin Nathan Cardozo, Justice of the Supreme Court of New York, 1914–1917; Judge of the New York Court of Appeals, 1917–1932; Justice of the U.S. Supreme Court, 1932–1938.

Marshall, Story, and Holmes, according to Pound, were "obvious" choices for his list from among the greatest jurists who had served on the U.S. Supreme Court. The others he selected for the caliber of their service on the highest courts of their states — a consideration that held true also for Cardozo, who made his principal contributions to American law as a New York judge, rather than as a

law (law made by decisions of judges, rather than by legislative acts), and the chief energies of the courts were turned toward that development of law by judicial decision. In particular, this was the chief function of the highest state courts. "For a time it was meet that John Doe suffer for the commonwealth's sake. Often it was less important to decide the particular cause justly than to work out a sound and just rule for the future," observed Pound in his work *The Spirit of the Common Law.*

Pound has characterized the process of judicial lawmaking as one of "Juristic Chemistry": "The chemist does not make the materials which go into his test tube: He selects them and combines them for some purpose and his purpose gives form to the result." During the formative era, the process went on when common law rules and doctrines were selected under the criterion of applicability to American conditions. If, later, the judicial process became a force for obstruction to change, during the pre-Civil War period it was primarily a progressive process.

As emphasized in Chapter I, the job of the American courts was a creative one, far more than the mechanical reception of common law principles. American judges recast the common law into an American mold. In doing so, they performed a legislative role in its broadest sense. Rarely articulated considerations were the secret root from which the law drew its life. These were, of course, considerations of what was advantageous for the community. The felt necessities of the time, the prevalent philosophical and political theories, intuitions of what best served the public interest, even the prejudices that the judges shared with their fellow men — all had at least as much to do with the American version of the common law as the analytical jurisprudence the judges professed to be applying. The principles and rules developed were the result of the judges' view of public policy, even where

justice of the U.S. Supreme Court.

The state judges had all been leaders in molding the English common law to meet American needs. Perhaps the greatest among them in this respect were Gibson, Shaw, and Ruffin — jurists of completely different backgrounds and temperaments. Gibson was a Jacksonian Democrat brought up in a frontier community; Shaw was a staunch Federalist trained at Harvard, who practiced law in the stable Boston commercial environment; and Ruffin was a conservative Democrat, born and reared as a southern aristocrat, who lived on his own plantation among fellow gentlemen planters. Shaw was the son of a Congregational minister, Ruffin a zealous Episcopalian, while Gibson had evaded baptism by going hunting at the time of the ceremony.

Each of these men had long dominated the highest court of an important state, from which newer states had taken their legal traditions and whose decisions they had followed as precedents. The differences in their upbringing, social and political affiliations, environment, and economic surroundings, according to economic and psychological determinism, should have led to three different judicial approaches. Yet each had contributed to the same body of American law based on the common law tradition, shaping the technique in which they had been trained to the demands of American conditions.

In the more than thirty years since Pound compiled his list — years that have seen American law enter a period of creative activity comparable to that of the post-Revolutionary period — it is doubtful that any judges have appeared greater than those whom Pound named. In recent years, the nation has seen outstanding judges, including Earl Warren and Hugo L. Black on the Supreme Court and Roger Traynor and Arthur T. Vanderbilt in state courts. But their contributions to American law, in the opinion of most contemporary jurists, do not surpass those of any of the men on Roscoe Pound's 1938 list.

they were the unconscious consequence of instinctive preferences and inarticulate convictions. The judges knew too much to sacrifice good sense to syllogisms and the common law could thus receive a new content in its transplanted ground.

Aiding the Businessman

The writer who would fit the early development of American private law to his logical analytical scheme must proceed after the manner of Procrustes. The method of the common law has never been to evolve according to philosophical theory. "The law did not begin with a theory. It has never worked one out." These words were written by Holmes with reference to the law of torts, or civil wrongs. In that branch of the law particularly, we find significant changes in the common law. Those changes were not based on any general theories of offenses, but on responses (almost always inarticulate) to the needs of the expanding society. The opinions of the judges abounded in moral phraseology; but it was not so much ethical conceptions that determined the way in which the law of torts was developed by American judges. More important was the overriding need to erect a system of liability that would encourage men to venture for productive ends.

Before 1800, negligence was not a separate tort: "under the common law a man *acts* at his peril." From this point of view, English law was still characterized by absolute liability; it did not differentiate between varying degrees of the same type of conduct, but branded all equally, meting out similar consequences to those concerned. Liability was attached indiscriminately to acts causing injury, regardless of the actor's degree of culpability. The defendant who committed a trespass was liable, regardless of how innocent his crossing of the plaintiff's boundary may have been. It was only in the nineteenth century that actions for negligence supplanted actions for trespass (where negligence need not be proved) and the rule developed that the law determined liability by blameworthiness.

The changing law in this respect marked a natural response of the judges in a society that placed great stress upon individual initiative. American law soon came to emphasize the social desirability of free individual action and decision. The burden was imposed upon the injured person to show why the law should shift the loss onto the one who caused the injury. Liability became a corollary of fault instead of being attached indiscriminately to all acts causing injury. What James Barr Ames was to call the "unmoral standard of acting at one's peril" was replaced by the question, "Was the act blameworthy?"

By 1850, Chief Justice Lemuel Shaw of Massachusetts could declare, in *Brown* v. *Kendall,* that "the plaintiff must come prepared with evidence to show either that the intention was unlawful, or that the defendant was *in fault;* for if the injury was unavoidable, and the conduct of the defendant was free from blame, he will not be liable." In such a matter, commented Holmes years later, no authority is more deserving of respect than that of Chief Justice Shaw. *Brown* v. *Kendall* was speedily followed in other states, and the U.S. Supreme Court was also to give the sanction of its approval to the Shaw doctrine. By the end of the formative era, American law

Father-in-law of Herman Melville, Lemuel Shaw was chief justice of Massachusetts, 1830–1860. His powerful, enduring influence on U.S. commercial and constitutional law landed him on Roscoe Pound's list of the ten greatest American judges.

had virtually completed the shift from trespass to negligence, with "no liability without culpability" already considered the basic maxim of tort law. "No case or principle can be found, or if found can be maintained, subjecting an individual to liability for an act done without fault on his part . . .," read a New York decision in 1843. "All the cases concede that an injury arising from inevitable accident, or, which in law or reason is the same thing, from an act that ordinary care and foresight are unable to guard against, is but the misfortune of the sufferer, and lays no foundation for legal responsibility."

What was true of fault also came to be true of causation. In 1773 an English court had held that "Everyone who does an unlawful act is considered as the doer of all that follows." In American law this gave way to a rule stated by Simon Greenleaf of the Harvard Law School in 1846 that damages "must be the natural and proximate consequences of the wrongful act." The American law of damages was based on the need to encourage men to take risks in the interest of productivity. The law should, insofar as possible, not add risks to those inherent in the business situation. If the businessman were to be responsible for all damages flowing from his acts, however remote, he could not operate "in the market with any safety. The result of such responsibility," said the Wisconsin Supreme Court, "would necessarily be to embarrass and check an important business, and greatly to injure an important industry of the state." To encourage entrepreneurs, risks were reduced by the doctrine of proximate cause. "The reasonable inquiry . . .," said a Massachusetts judge in 1855, "is not which is nearest in place or time,

This accident on the Providence and Worcester Railroad in Rhode Island in 1853 took a number of lives. Only after a law governing legal responsibility for accidents had become fixed were businessmen willing to take the risks necessary for meaningful commercial and industrial expansion.

but whether one is not the efficient producing cause, and the others but incidental." Liability would be imposed only for those damages of which the defendant's act was "the efficient producing cause."

It is of interest that the American development just summarized was paralleled in English law. Although negligence was not an independent tort before 1800, it became one during the nineteenth century in England as well as in the United States. The reasons were largely the same. The acceleration of the Industrial Revolution led the English judges to be as receptive as their American confreres to legal doctrines that would encourage enterprise by eliminating indefinite risks of liability. The raising of capital for industrial expansion could not be subjected to the undue financial burdens involved in too-broad tort liability. Liability, said an English case in 1854, should be limited to the damages that may reasonably be supposed to have been in the contemplation of the parties concerned.

For the businessman to rely on the rules of liability, they had to be certain in character: "The known certainty of the law is the safety of all," wrote Daniel Chipman, author of the first American book on contracts in 1822. Hence, the emphasis in nineteenth-century law on "objective" measures of liability. The standard developed was that of the conduct of "the average man, the man of ordinary intelligence and prudence," not a measure tailored to individual peculiarities. Such objective measures had a special importance in American society a century and a half ago, when the market was the key institution and belief in maximum individual self-assertion the prime article of faith. Only within a framework of objective consequences

Courts for 1,500,000 (and More) Cases

One of the first laws enacted by the first Congress was the Judiciary Act of 1789, which established a federal court system for the new nation. It provided for a virtual duplication of the state judiciaries, with a three-tiered system of federal courts — thirteen district courts, three circuit courts, and one Supreme Court. At the same time, all of the state court systems were left untouched. Each of the states had — and has continued to have — its own judges and courts, whose functioning was not affected by the federal courts.

There was sound reason for this duplication of court systems. The experience during the period of the Confederation after the Revolution heightened fear that prejudice by the citizens of one state toward those of another would result in unjust treatment of out-of-state citizens within the individual state courts. Federal courts were provided to assure out-of-state litigants courts that would be free from local bias. "The whole purpose . . . ," explained Justice Robert H. Jackson in recent years, "is to give one of the parties a better break in federal court than he would expect in state court." And, indeed, the principal business of the federal courts under the 1789 act arose out of "diversity cases," involving suits between citizens of different states.

In addition, there was a need to ensure the supremacy of federal law. The Supreme Court was authorized to review state court decisions that involved questions arising under the Constitution, treaties, or laws of the United States. In 1875, Congress authorized all cases arising under federal law to be brought in the lower federal courts. The vindication of federal claims has since become the main function of those courts, though they still entertain actions between citizens of different states, even where they involve purely issues of state law.

The parallel structure of federal and state courts which was set up in 1789 has continued to the present time (comprising today fifty-one separate judicial systems). It became too onerous for Supreme Court judges to travel and sit in circuit courts, and that practice was ended in the 1870's, so that today the federal system includes eighty-nine district courts, eleven courts of appeals, and the Supreme Court. There are four hundred district judges, ninety-seven court of appeals judges, and nine members of the High Court. (The

were men likely to act with the boldness and energy that were required.

The feature that most characterized nineteenth-century American law was this stress upon individualism and self-reliance. "In other words," declared Pound, "it held that every man of mature age must take care of himself. He need not expect to be saved from himself by legal paternalism. . . . When he acted, he was held to have acted at his own risk with his eyes open, and he must abide the appointed consequences." This statement, according to Pound, epitomized the spirit of the common law. It manifested itself most plainly in the American tort law of the last century, particularly in the development of the doctrine of contributory negligence and the fellow-servant rule.

"In its essence," states a leading torts text, *The Handbook of the Law of Torts*, by William Prosser, the contributory negligence doctrine "is an expression of the highly individualistic attitude of the common law, and its policy of making the personal interests of each party depend upon his own care and prudence." Between two wrongdoers, the law let the consequences rest where they chanced to fall. Hence, a misstep, however slight, from the objective ideal of conduct placed upon the injured party the whole burden of his loss, even though the defendant was far more at fault. There was actually some question of whether American law would adopt contributory negligence in all its rigor. Though the doctrine appears first to have been accepted in an 1824 Massachusetts decision, as late as 1858 an Illinois court urged a different doctrine: "the degrees of negligence must be measured and considered and whenever it shall be considered that plaintiff's negli-

A courthouse, visible presence of the law

last figure was changed from time to time in the past. Originally, there were six Supreme Court justices. For various reasons, Congress increased the number to as high as ten, but has kept it at nine since 1869. Only Congress may change the figure.) All federal judges are appointed by the President, subject to senatorial confirmation. In addition, there are five federal courts with specialized jurisdictions: the Court of Claims, Tax Court, Customs Court, Court of Customs and Patent Appeals, and Court of Military Appeals.

Most states have their own three-tiered systems of courts (some have only two tiers). Generally, they are courts of general jurisdiction with various names, including District or Superior courts; intermediate appellate courts (Court of Appeals); and highest court (Supreme Court). The court names often differ from state to state. In New York, for instance, the court of general jurisdiction is the Supreme Court, the intermediate court is the Appellate Division, and the highest court is the Court of Appeals. There are also state specialized courts, such as the New York Court of Claims, and many separate local courts like the Traffic Court, Small Claims courts, Magistrates courts, and courts of Justices of the Peace in individual communities.

More than ten thousand judges preside over these different state and local courts.

The bulk of the nation's judicial business is done outside the federal courts. In 1972 the latter decided over 150,000 cases, but at least ten times that number were disposed of in state and local courts.

The first great era of railroad expansion, reflected by the passenger tickets of some of the many new American lines, above, resulted from the development of sympathetic corporation law by the courts.

gence was comparatively slight . . . he shall not be deprived of his action.'' The move in the direction of comparative negligence was to prove abortive, however. Under the leadership of judges such as Chief Justice Shaw of Massachusetts, contributory negligence was to take over the field.

The influence of Shaw was also responsible for the adoption of the fellow-servant rule. The rule that an employer was not liable for injuries caused by the negligence of a fellow servant had first appeared in England in 1837 and in this country immediately afterward. But it was not until Shaw's elaborate opinion in the case of *Farwell* v. *Boston and Worcester Rail Road* in 1842 that the rule was firmly implanted in Anglo-American law. The fellow-servant rule, more than any other principle, was an expression of the rigorous individualism of nineteenth-century law. The individual was free to pursue the calling of his choice; as such, he assumed the risks of his chosen occupation, including any harm that might befall him from the negligence of his fellow workers. The law would not protect him from the consequences of his own choice. Harsh though it seems over a century later, the fellow-servant rule fitted the needs of the nascent industrial society by making the legal burden on economic development as light as possible. As industrialism expanded, factory and railroad accidents proliferated. The fellow-servant rule relieved employers of a critical financial burden: "The encouragement of 'infant industries,'" according to Leonard W. Levy in *The Law of the Commonwealth and Chief Justice Shaw*, "had no greater social cost."

Securing Contracts and Property

The nineteenth century was the century of contract. Americans of the formative period were a people going places in a hurry. Contract was the legal instrument that helped them to get there. The freedom of action allowed by the expansion of contract law enabled Americans to meet the challenge of the unexploited continent; it gave private decision makers the autonomy needed to commit the necessary resources and energy.

Holmes began his analysis of contract in his *Common Law* by declaring that "The doctrine of contract has been so thoroughly remodelled to meet the needs of modern times, that there is less necessity here than elsewhere for historical research." Before the Industrial Revolution, the common law of contracts was narrow in scope and technical in application. This was to change completely during the nineteenth century. The law of contracts in all its ramifications overwhelmingly predominated in the legal growth that took place during the century. The expansion of contract is revealed dramatically in the legal texts. The situation when Blackstone wrote was pointed out by the leading treatise of the pre-Civil War period, Theophilus Parsons's *The Law of Contract:* "The title of the thirtieth chapter [some forty-five pages] of the Second Book of Blackstone's Commentaries is, 'Of title by gift, grant, and *contract.*' And in no other chapter does he treat of the law of contracts." When Blackstone's American counterpart, James Kent's *Commentaries on American Law,* was published in 1826–1830, contract and its related commercial subjects covered one out of four large volumes. By then, too, texts devoted solely to the law of contracts had appeared. When Parsons published his classic volumes on contracts in 1853, he could state that many treatises on the subject had already been published: "some of them are large volumes, and the latest are the largest. . . . This volume is larger than any of its predecessors."

The nineteenth-century development of contract law was a direct response to the needs of the burgeoning American society. The law, like the society, put individual conscience and judgment first. If men were to be willing to act, legal consequences must be attached to their free exertions of will. Everyone must abide by the consequences of his free choice; the law must impose liability whenever a man agreed to do something and did not do it.

To nineteenth-century American law, wrote Parsons, "The Law of Contracts . . . may be regarded as including nearly all the law which regulates the relations of human life." Contract became the solving idea for the law's response to the needs of the expanding society. The courts enlarged the array of procedures and instruments to promote commercial dealings and gave a contract cast to relations between men. The key social interest became the security of transactions freely entered into, the basic legal principle that promises be kept and undertakings be carried out in good faith. The interest

In 1857 hardware manufacturer Thomas Douglass was able to advertise both his Vermont factory and his New York outlet (below). But only in 1839 had the Supreme Court (in Bank of Augusta v. Earle) confirmed the right of an enterprise incorporated in one state to conduct its business in other states as well.

SMITHSONIAN INSTITUTION, HARRY T. PETERS COLLECTION

Above is a view of Philadelphia's Fairmount waterworks in 1840. Because of the developing nation's almost insatiable need for new services and industries, court-made law during the period overwhelmingly favored corporation growth.

of the promisee—his claim to be assured in the expectation created—became the interest primarily protected by the law.

Contract was the growing point of nineteenth-century private law. "All social life presumes it, and rests upon it; for out of contracts, express or implied, declared or understood, grow all rights, all duties, all obligations, and all law," Parsons observed in 1853. Legal relations were more and more controlled by the autonomy of the individual will. To be sure, the evolution had not yet progressed to the extremes it would take during the latter part of the century. But the starting point for those developments was the freedom of contract doctrine laid down during the pre-Civil War period, as well as the ever-increasing expansion of contract into areas previously governed by status relationships. In addition, it was in the field of contract that the judges exercised their invention, developing virtual new branches of law to serve the new industrial era. New legal tools were developed throughout the law, particularly in the law of negotiable instruments, of sales, of factors, of agency, of insurance, and of banking. The entire field of commercial law, later to be governed primarily by statute, was the creative domain of the common law during the nation's formative era. Judges built up a doctrine about day-to-day transactions that may have originated in Elizabeth I's day, but was completely remodeled as the nineteenth century began to foreshadow modern conditions.

The conquest of private law by contract during the formative period may be seen dramatically in the victory of contract over the land. The main development in this respect was noted in Chapter I. The English theme until well into the nineteenth century was how dangerous it was to meddle with as old a structure as the land law, almost untouched for centuries. If, in England, improving the land law was beyond the power of mortal man, that plainly was not the case in America. "It is a matter of curious history," declared a New York court in 1835, "to trace the successive inroads upon the common law which have been made during the last half century, by more than fifty prominent acts of the legislature." Old common law abuses fell like autumn leaves. Primogeniture and entails (the limiting of the inheritance, usually of property, to a specified, unalterable succession of heirs) were not saved by their antiquity, nor the rules of descent by their incongruity, nor fines, recoveries, and real actions by their absurdity and costliness. A decent oblivion was provided for most of the "monarchial machinery of landed tenures. . . . This ancient, complicated and barbarous system . . . is entirely abrogated in relation to the tenure, the acquistion, the enjoyment and the transmission of property," noted the 1835 New York decision. The result was to make all tenure allodial (held in absolute ownership, without obligation to any overlord), with the freehold established as the normal type of land title. Land could now be dealt with according to the will of the owner on virtually the same basis as other types of property.

Support for Corporations

The ability of American courts to adapt the common law to their requirements is nowhere better seen than in the development of corporation law. The American law of corporations, more than most branches of our judge-made law, was an indigenous product. The English courts had for centuries been deciding cases relating to corporate problems, but the law developed by them dealt almost entirely with nonprofit corporations and was of limited value in solving the problems confronting business enterprises in the United States. The development of the business corporation (formed to carry on business for profit) and resolution of the legal issues connected with it were almost entirely the handiwork of American law.

Before independence, only a handful of business corporations had been chartered in this country. By the close of the eighteenth century, no less than 310 such bodies had been created, mostly banking, insurance, canal, tollbridge, turnpike, and water supply companies. After the turn of the century, the chartering process went on even more rapidly; by 1830, New England alone had chartered nearly 1,300 business corporations, including almost 600 manufacturing and mining companies.

In the business corporation, the law developed an instrument particularly appropriate to the demands of the expanding American economy. The industrial growth which so strikingly altered the nature of the society during the last century could scarcely have been possible had it depended solely upon the initiative and resources of the individual entrepreneur. It was the corporate device that enabled men to establish the pools of wealth and talent needed for the economic conquest of the continent.

The corporation is, however, entirely a creation of the law; its existence and legal personality have their origins in some act of the law. The corporation as a legal person may go back to precolonial English Law, but English law, as stated, dealt primarily with nonprofit corporations. The rapid growth

This factory, photographed about 1850, was typical of hundreds that once flourished in New England. Textile mills, especially, became notorious for labor exploitation, particularly of women and children, but the courts of the time were more interested in promoting industry than in protecting social welfare.

The "God-Like Daniel" and His Contemporaries

The lawyer has spoiled the statesman," Disraeli once wrote critically of a contemporary. In the case of Daniel Webster, it might have been said that the politician spoiled the lawyer. "I have given my life to law and politics. Law is uncertain and politics are utterly vain," Webster stated just before his death. But although he was the most famous lawyer of his day, with an ability for courtroom oratory that was legendary, his pursuit of political power and ambition to be President prevented his making the significant contribution to American law that his great talents might have made possible. Even so, the "God-like Daniel, the Defender of the Constitution," as admirers called him, stood at the head of the Supreme Court Bar. He first appeared before the High Court in 1814 and until his death in 1852 rarely missed a term of the Court, frequently arguing a dozen or more cases a year.

Webster was born in Salisbury, New Hampshire, in 1782, graduated from Dartmouth College, and after clerking in two law offices, opened practice in Portsmouth in his home state. By 1816, when he moved to Boston, his outstanding abilities were already carrying him to the pinnacle of the American Bar, both as the leading constitutional advocate before the Supreme Court and in the fees he received. His income from his practice was soon ranging from $15,000 to $21,000 a year, far more than that of other lawyers. For his most famous Supreme Court arguments, he was paid $1,000 each in the *Dartmouth College* case in 1819 (representing Dartmouth) and the *Gibbons* v. *Ogden* case in 1824 (representing Gibbons), and in the *McCulloch* v. *Maryland* case in 1819 he received a $1,500 bonus to supplement his $500 retainer fee from the Bank of the United States. Despite his income, his extravagance kept him in constant financial difficulties. He was the best example of one of his own observa-

Daniel Webster, by Francis Alexander

tions: "I can give it as the condensed history of most, if not all, good lawyers that they lived well and died poor."

Perhaps his most famous legal plea —and the one which first brought him national recognition—was made for his alma mater, Dartmouth, in 1819. Under its founding charter in 1769, the college was to be governed by a board of trustees with power to fill vacancies in their number and to choose and remove the college president. Factionalism, first personal, then political, arose within the college, and in 1816 a newly elected governor and legislature in New Hampshire took sides against the board of trustees. A state law was passed increasing the number of trustees, and empowering the governor and his council to appoint the overseers and new trustees and to inspect Dartmouth and report to the legislature concerning it. In effect, the law annulled Dartmouth's original charter and brought the college under the state's control. The old trustees resisted the change, and when William H. Woodward, secretary and treasurer of the college, sided with the state government and new appointees against them, they sued Woodward to make him surrender to them the col-

lege's various records and accounts.

Woodward won in the New Hampshire state courts, and the case went to John Marshall's Supreme Court, with Webster pleading for the original trustees. His words, "It is, Sir, as I have said, a small College. And yet, there are those who love it!" made him known throughout the country and, it was said, caused Chief Justice Marshall to be filled with emotion, his eyes "suffused with tears." Marshall's decision, ruling for Webster and the old trustees, held that the New Hampshire law violated the Contract Clause of the Constitution which prohibited the states from passing any "law impairing the obligation of contracts." Asserting that Dartmouth's original charter was a contract, he established, with his decision, an assurance for all investors in American corporate enterprises that the terms upon which they had committed their capital could not be unilaterally altered by a state. At a time when corporations were first being widely used, it thus encouraged the expansion of American business enterprise.

In the long run, Webster's political career eclipsed his record as a lawyer. He served in the U.S. House of Representatives from New Hampshire, 1813–1817, and from Massachusetts, 1823–1827. In the Senate, 1827–1841, and again, 1845–1850, his statesmanship and oratory made him one of the all-time giants of that body. He was twice secretary of state, and in 1852, just before his death, was an unsuccessful candidate for the Whig nomination for the Presidency.

At the opposite extreme from successful Eastern lawyers like Webster were those who, at the same time in the nation's history, were attempting to earn a living in the country's less populated back country. George W. Strong wrote of his father's attempts to set up practice in upstate New York: "The account books . . . bear abundant evidence of his early struggle. . . . Most of the charges were insignificant amounts, such as 50¢ for drawing a deed, $2.50 for drawing a deed, bond, mortgage and agreement, $1.00 for advice . . . and from $3.00 to $5.00 for going to some neighboring township to attend the trial of a case in a Justice's court. . . . His aggregate fees amounted during his first year—from January 14, 1826, to January 18, 1827—to $217.00." Even a successful Western lawyer like Abraham Lincoln in Illinois could not come close to matching Webster's income. In most of his cases, Lincoln's fees were only five to ten dollars. For his legal services to Menard County, including ten court appearances, he collected twenty dollars; for taking care of at least fifteen cases for the Illinois Central Railroad in a single year he charged $150; and for arguing before the Illinois Supreme Court he often received as little as five dollars.

The back-country lawyer's practice differed drastically from that of a Webster, not only in the inexorable need for what Webster called "money-catching," but in its predominantly itinerant nature. Thomas Ruffin, later a great chief justice of North Carolina, spent about forty-three weeks each year "on the circuit." What this meant was graphically illustrated in Lincoln's career—the gaunt figure riding along trails on horseback for hundreds of miles, with saddlebags containing a spare coat, a clean shirt, a lawbook or two, and some paper. William Herndon, Lincoln's last law partner, later said, "No human being would now endure what we used to do on the circuit. I have slept with 20 men in the same room . . . and oh—such victuals."

The frontier Bar did produce great men like Lincoln, Ruffin, and Alphonso Taft (founder of the Taft dy-nasty in Cincinnati). But the rigor of the life and its meager reward kept the level of the profession, in general, all too low. "Attorneys came in great numbers almost by every stage-coach," reported an account of the Bar in the American interior. If some were "men of learning and worth," most others were "of a different description"—uneducated, meddlesome fomentors of quarrels, on a level with land speculators, moneylenders, and swindlers. The low character of the frontier Bar explained the dwindling esteem for lawyers as one moved westward. "Lawyers," noted the Jefferson City, Missouri, *Inquirer* in 1847, "were never buried in the city where they lived. They were simply laid out at night in a room with the window open and the door locked, and next morning they were always gone . . . there was a strong smell of brimstone in the room."

As A. Wighe's 1849 "Rural Court Scene" indicates, informal frontier justice could be dispensed even in a barn.

William Woodward was named the defendant in the famed Dartmouth College case in 1819. Though he was only one of a group trying to change the college charter, his position as secretary and treasurer gave him custody of the original charter, seal, and records that his opponents were seeking to recover.
DARTMOUTH COLLEGE

of business corporations in nineteenth-century America was followed by judicial decisions on the nature of those bodies, their rights and duties, and the rights and duties of their stockholders. The law made by American legislators and judges in this area was itself a powerful stimulus to the use of the corporate device to help meet the economic challenges of the day.

The first important development was the legal recognition of the business corporation as a legitimate instrument for the accomplishment of economic ends. At the outset American corporations could be created only through the method used in English law: a special act of the legislature. The need for special legislative authorization, however, gave way during the first half of the nineteenth century. In 1811 New York enacted a general corporation law permitting incorporation of companies formed for manufacturing textiles, glass, or metal products for a period of twenty years, with a maximum capital of $100,000. Incorporation was accomplished by signing articles of agreement and filing a certificate. Other states soon followed New York's example. By 1860, the normal method of setting up a corporation was under a general corporation law, rather than by a charter granted by special legislation.

Equally important was the benevolent attitude displayed by the courts. From the beginning, American judges looked with favor upon the corporate device as a method of doing business. It was during the formative era that the first steps were taken in what one court noted was "The constant tendency of judicial decisions in modern times . . . in the direction of putting corporations upon the same footing as natural persons." The key decisions were those of the U.S. Supreme Court. Corporations may, in Coke's famous phrase, "have no souls," but they gained the essentials of legal personality by the decisions of the Marshall and Taney courts.

The Marshall Court laid down the first essential prerequisite to corporate expansion in the *Dartmouth College* case in 1819. This decision vested the corporation with indestructible contract rights by holding that a corporate charter was a contract within the protection of the Contract Clause of the Constitution. The corporate creature of the law—"invisible, intangible, and existing only in contemplation of law"—was endowed with basic legal rights, even against its creator.

Sir Henry Maine, writing in 1885, characterized the *Dartmouth College* decision as "the basis of the credit of many of the great American Railway Incorporations." It was, he went on, its principle "which has in reality secured full play to the economical forces by which the achievement of cultivating the soil of the North American Continent has been performed." At a time when no other constitutional provision would serve the purpose, corporate property rights were brought under the fostering guardianship of the Contract Clause. Those who were called upon to pool their wealth and talents in the vast corporate enterprises needed for the nation's development were thus ensured that their contributions would not remain at the mercy of what Justice Story termed "the passions or popular doctrines of the day." Before the *Dartmouth College* case there were still relatively few manufacturing corporations in the country. Under the new-found confidence brought about by Marshall's decision, such corporate enterprises began to proliferate to such an extent that they soon transformed the face of the nation.

Even more important were the decisions furthering corporate expansion rendered by the Taney Court. What makes the Taney decisions of particular interest was the fact that Taney and most of his colleagues on the Bench shared the Jacksonian distrust of corporations as aggregations of wealth and power—the "would-be lordlings of the Paper Dynasty"—which posed a direct danger to the democratic system. But in practice, even the Jacksonian justices recognized that the corporate device had a necessary place in the legal and economic systems.

It was not until the Taney Court's decision in *Bank of Augusta* v. *Earle* in 1839 that the corporation could really be made to serve the needs of the expanding American economy. The question presented in that case was characterized by Charles Warren, the Supreme Court's historian, as "of immense consequence to the commercial development of the country—the power of a corporation to make a contract outside of the State in which it was chartered." The case arose out of the purchase in Alabama of bills of exchange by three out-of-state corporations. They brought an action in the federal court in Alabama when the makers refused to pay on the ground that the corporations had no power to do business in Alabama, or indeed, outside their own states. Their contention was upheld by Supreme Court Justice John McKinley, sitting on circuit. As explained in an often-quoted letter of Justice Story to Charles Sumner, "He has held that a corporation created in one State has no power to contract (or, it would seem, even to act) in any other State, directly or by an agent."

The McKinley ruling was characterized by Story as "a most sweeping decision . . . which has frightened half the lawyers and all the corporations of the country out of their proprieties." Its practical effect was to limit corporations to doing business only in the states in which they were chartered, which would have rendered the growth of interstate business enterprises all but impossible. Well might Daniel Webster, in his argument, characterize McKinley's decision as "anti-commercial and anti-social . . . and calculated to break up the harmony which has so long prevailed among the States and people of this Union."

The full Supreme Court overruled McKinley and rejected the notion that a corporation had no existence outside the state in which it was chartered. On the contrary, it held that a corporation, like a natural person, might act in states where it did not reside. Comity among the states provides a warrant for the operation throughout the Union of corporations chartered in any of the states.

By permitting corporations to operate nationwide, the *Bank of Augusta* decision provided a powerful stimulus to economic expansion; business and commercial interests now possessed the legal authority needed for the interstate conduct of their affairs. The view of the rising capitalist class was expressed by Story, when he wrote to Taney, "Your opinion in the corporation cases has given very general satisfaction to the public; . . . it does great honor to yourself as well as to the Court." Because of the Taney decision, said Webster, "we breathe freer and deeper."

One further legal development was necessary to transform the corporation

John Wheelock, president of Dartmouth College, set off the chain of events leading to the Dartmouth College case by feuding with the trustees and finally getting himself ousted by them. Both he and Woodward (opposite) died before the Supreme Court decision, unfavorable to them, was handed down.
DARTMOUTH COLLEGE

The New York State Capitol at Albany exemplified the political power centers of pre-Civil War days. The Executives of the states, and even of the nation, were often subservient to the legislatures, and the courts themselves were not entirely independent of such control.

from a device of mercantilist policy to the principal instrument of American enterprise. That was the recognition of the principle of limited liability. The privilege of limited liability was not granted to all English corporations until after the middle of the nineteenth century. In this country limited liability came earlier, as a positive aid by law to the enlistment of capital. As early as 1792, an article on the first New Jersey business corporation stated that "The subscribers, to avoid risquing more than their subscriptions, were, of course, to apply for an incorporation." The notion that incorporation implied limited liability was confirmed in leading early cases. Legislative attempts to impose unlimited liability on shareholders merely delayed the inevitable. The basic consideration was noted by a Massachusetts writer in 1829, after an attempt by that state's legislature to make shareholders liable for corporate debts: "this personal responsibility has, in fact, drawn manufacturing capital from Massachusetts . . . and it has been frequently asserted that the injurious consequences resulting from it are very great." An 1830 law abolished unlimited shareholder liability in Massachusetts. By that time, the principle of limited liability had also been accepted in most other states.

The recognition of limited liability was another development that came during the period of Jacksonian dominance. Jacksonians such as Governor Marcus Morton of Massachusetts, who opposed limited liability as a vestige of special privilege, could not in the nature of things hope to do so successfully. The America satirized in Charles Dickens's *Martin Chuzzlewit* was one in which a chance to buy shares with a minimum of risk had strong appeal. Even those who regarded themselves as Democrats (with a large as well as a small *d*) would not long support unlimited liability provisions in incorporation acts.

The Power of Legislatures

The dominant theme at the outset of the nation's formative era was legislative hegemony. The period began with every advantage possessed by the legislative department. To their natural position as the heirs of the British Parliament, American legislatures added the legitimacy acquired by their roles during the colonial and Revolutionary struggles. Colonial history in this respect had been but a chapter torn from the constitutional history of Stuart England. The battles between Crown and Parliament were all fought out, on a smaller scale, on the western side of the Atlantic. And in America, too, the representative assembly gradually triumphed. The other branches were mere creatures of the Crown and could scarcely compete with the legislature in popular esteem. Legislative primacy received its test of fire in the Revolutionary crisis. Legislative assemblies took charge of both the movement for independence and the war itself. The successful outcome of the legislative-led struggle gave an imprimatur to the notion that legislators were peculiarly the delegates of the sovereign people, with all the powers of the sovereign devolved upon them.

Throughout the formative era, American legislatures acted on the assumption that they were the vital organ in the polity. "The period from the Revolution to the Civil War was clearly the heyday of the legislative arm of government in both the states and the nation," wrote Arthur T. Vanderbilt, the American jurist, in *The Doctrine of the Separation of Powers and Its Present-Day Significance*. In an 1835 Senate speech, Webster referred to the division of powers as a leading constitutional principle; but he had no doubt where the primacy lay: "As first in importance and dignity, it begins with the legislative department." As late as Andrew Johnson's impeachment, the Executive was considered accountable to the legislature, even for the exercise of those powers committed to the Executive by the Constitution.

At the outset, Madison had complained that all power had been drawn into the legislative vortex, and this continued despite the separation of powers formally provided by the different constitutions. In the first part of the nineteenth century, legislatures assumed that even the courts were accountable to them for the way in which they decided cases. Starting with the famous Rhode Island case of *Trevett* v. *Weeden* in 1786, state legislatures summoned judges before them to be interrogated on particular decisions exactly on the model of the celebrated colloquy between James I and the judges of England. Sometimes they took more drastic action, as when the legislature of one state reduced the salary of the state's supreme court

OVERLEAF: *In his memorable 1822 painting of an evening session of the House of Representatives, Samuel F. B. Morse—who later invented the telegraph—included the presence of the members of the Supreme Court (grouped on dais at the left).*
CORCORAN GALLERY OF ART

Congressional primacy was exerted by strong senators like Calhoun, Webster, Benton, and Clay (shown speaking in 1850).

justices to twenty-five cents, after a decision at which the legislators took strong offense.

In addition, the early legislatures did not hesitate to exercise judicial power directly, both of an original and appellate kind. State legislatures passed statutes annulling or reversing judgments; granted new trials after judgment; gave the right to appeal after the time to do so had expired; admitted to probate wills rejected by the courts; dictated details of administration of particular estates; validated otherwise invalid marriages; suspended the statute of limitations for individual litigants; designated the particular cases to be heard at the next term; empowered the sale of particular estates; foreclosed mortgages; awarded dower to particular widows; and exempted a particular wrongdoer from liability for a wrong for which his neighbors would be held by the general law.

Among the more striking exercises of judicial power by legislatures were laws in the different states granting divorces. As late as 1888, legislative divorces were upheld by the Supreme Court and the power to pass private divorce acts was widely exercised through most of the century. Other direct exercises of judicial power also continued later than is generally realized. Appellate jurisdiction was exercised by the New York Senate until 1846, and by the Rhode Island legislature until 1857; the Pennsylvania legislature could grant equitable relief until 1874.

Legislative primacy was also apparent in the relations between the legislative and executive branches. The early state constitutions gave substance to Madison's complaint that the state Executives were mere ciphers. In all the original states but two (Massachusetts and New York), the legislature even appointed the governor. Common tradition favored legislative participation in executive functions, with the situation under the Confederation Congress the best-known example. The exception was, of course, the Executive set up under the federal Constitution, and the growth of presidential power stands in marked contrast to the position in the states. Yet, even here, the strength of the early Presidency should not be exaggerated. Except for the strong tenure of Andrew Jackson, the early Presidency was primarily a passive office—dominated by the Jeffersonian notion of subordination to "the supreme legislative power."

For the better part of the formative era, even the federal Executive was characterized by the weakness and indecision that continued as the dominant theme in the states, despite the later state constitutions which moved toward the presidential model in their Executives. If, as Webster put it in another Senate speech, executive power must be "regarded as a lion which must be caged," such caging was the peculiar province of the legislature during the pre-Civil War period.

Despite the dominant legislative role, however, the story of the legislature in the history of American law during the formative era becomes largely negative in the telling: potential promise remained unfulfilled. Compare the permanent results of legislative leadership with those of judicial decision during the same period and it is apparent that the former did relatively little. Aside from the early constitutions and bills of rights, little creative legislation had enduring impact. Certainly, in the whole field of private

English visitor Mrs. Frances Trollope approved of little that she saw during her travels in the United States, 1827–1831. This unflattering sketch of a congressman in her book Domestic Manners of the Americans reflected her low opinion of the people's representatives.

law, American legislatures produced nothing even remotely comparable to the Code Napoleon. The failure of the codification movement (to be discussed next) dramatically points up the fact that the history of the legislature during the early development of American law was essentially an account of lost opportunities.

What is clear is that the legislatures of the formative era were increasingly ill suited to play the leadership role in the growth of American law. The aggressive confidence of the nation's early legislators, and the popular trust that accompanied it, gave way to increasing disillusionment and distrust. Here, as in other areas of American life, Jacksonian Democracy was not entirely beneficial. What it produced was anything but the natural nobility of Rousseau's *Émile* or the vision of Jefferson: the quality of popular representation seemed to sink as the full effects of manhood suffrage were felt.

Virtually all contemporary observers concurred in their estimate of what Tocqueville termed the "slender abilities" of the men who sat in legislatures of the day. Visiting the Capitol in the 1840's, Charles Dickens asked, "Where sat the many legislators of coarse threats; of words and blows such as coal heavers deal upon each other, when they forget breeding? On every side . . . Dishonest Faction in its most depraved and unblushing form, stared out from every corner of the crowded hall."

And yet, as every schoolboy knows, this was also the age of giants, when men such as Clay, Calhoun, Benton, and above all, Webster — no man was ever as great as Webster looked! — trod the legislative scene. Rarely have Capitol Hill leaders compared in caliber with those who dominated the congressional scene in the first part of the nineteenth century. Legislators of ability sat in the statehouses as well — men such as the young Joseph Story, Lemuel Shaw, and James Kent.

Nevertheless, the giants were only the apex of the legislative iceberg. Below them was a mass of more than mediocre members, who fully justified Tocqueville's description: "On entering the House of Representatives, one is struck by the vulgar demeanor of that great assembly. . . . Its members are almost all obscure individuals." If this was the age of Clay and John Quincy Adams, it was equally the age of "Sausage" Sawyer, House member from Ohio, who earned his sobriquet by happily munching sausages at the Speaker's rostrum.

Over all hung the cloud of corruption: "in the ratio of our mechanical triumphs has been the decline of our moral superiority," complained the *North American Review* in 1855. This was the period when lobbyists first appeared and a Sam Ward could be widely known as "King of the Lobby." In 1858 Francis Wharton could assert that politicans were publicly bought and sold "at the Washington brokers' board . . . like fancy railroad stock or copper-mine shares." The situation in the states was, if anything, worse. Special-interest legislation and the grant of corporate privilege were often the quid pro quo for payments made to leading legislators. The bribes paid to virtually every member of the Georgia legislature for the law granting the so-called Yazoo lands in 1795 were merely an extreme example of an all-too-common practice. "The legislation of the whole winter," wrote a

New York Democratic leader to Martin Van Buren in 1836, "has been a matter of bargain and sale; . . . it is not to be disguised that their conduct is more under the regulation of pecuniary considerations than motives of a higher origin and character."

And so the legislature lost its major inheritance, its title of legitimacy based upon the people's trust. The enthusiasm for legislation with which the century began gave way to growing distrust. The 1840's saw a spreading movement to write into state constitutions various substantive and procedural limits on legislative power. The legislator as statesman gave way in the public mind to the legislator as the butt of popular humor.

The Movement for Law Codification

Nothing pointed up the failure of the legislature during the formative era better than the abortive codification movement. Proposals to codify the common law went back at least to Francis Bacon's 1614 "proposition . . . Touching the Compiling and Amendment of the Laws of England." It was not, however, until the first part of the nineteenth century that Anglo-American law saw a serious movement for codification. In this country various factors influenced the movement's growth. In the first place, there was Jeremy Bentham, whose practical influence on legislation (in British

An unruly House of Representatives in 1841, below, debates the gag rule that prevented consideration of petitions against slavery. Although clearly unconstitutional, the gag on the right of petition was continued for eight years until it was rescinded in December, 1844, largely through the efforts of Congressman (and former President) John Quincy Adams.

Though David Dudley Field is known mainly for his work in codifying law, he also had a checkered career as a lawyer, serving in some cases with distinction, but at other times being criticized for exhibiting unprofessional conduct in defending such unsavory characters as James Fisk, Boss Tweed, and Jay Gould.

jurist Sir James Fitzjames Stephen's famous characterization) can only be compared "to those of Adam Smith and his successors upon commerce." Bentham, the famed English legal philosopher and expounder of utilitarianism, shifted the growing point of the law from the judge to the legislator; for the first time, statute law, rather than case law, became the instrument of advance. Above all, Bentham sought to frame the law in codified form, readily accessible to all. He advocated codification as a means of complete remaking of the legal system and clearing away of unduly technical and arbitrary precepts. Between 1811 and 1817, he addressed a series of letters to President Madison, state governors, and the "Citizens of the several American United States," offering to draw up a complete code for the United States, and cautioning them "to shut our ports against the Common Law, as we would against the plague."

Bentham was, nevertheless, more the theorist than the legislator; for all his influence, he never had to try his hand at the much more difficult task of actually drafting a comprehensive code. It has, indeed, been said that to draw up a civil code required a much better lawyer than Bentham. Just such lawyers sat on the commissions which wrote the Code Napoleon at the outset of the century. The French Civil Code showed that Bentham's dream could be given practical effect. More than that, its example pointed the way to the means by which the new nation could draw up its own strictly American system of law, freed at last from its "colonial acquiescence" to English law, "too often without probation or fitness."

Steps toward codification were taken in several states during the 1820's. It was then that Louisiana promulgated her Civil Code (based largely on the Code Napoleon), as well as the Penal Code drafted by Edward Livingston (a highly original work), and New York enacted her revised statutes, with their complete reconstruction of the law of real property. The New York model was followed in the statutory revisions enacted during the following decade in Pennsylvania and Massachusetts.

Then, in 1836, Massachusetts took the further step of appointing a commission headed by Justice Story "to take into consideration the practicability and expediency of reducing to a written and systematic code the common law of Massachusetts or any part thereof." Story wrote after his appointment that the commission's "report will be very qualified and limited in its objects. We have not yet become votaries to the notions of Jeremy Bentham." The commission recommended against "a Code of the entire body of the Common Law of Massachusetts," though it did favor codification of selected parts of the law, notably crimes, evidence, property, and contracts. Even this more limited recommendation was not carried out, and a proposed criminal code put forward by a later commission, in 1844, was also rejected by the legislature.

The prime mover in the nineteenth-century codification movement was David Dudley Field, a distinguished New York City lawyer, and it is with his name that the movement remains inseparably associated. For half a century, Field led the effort to codify the common law and, several times during that period, he came within a step of having New York adopt a comprehensive code of substantive law. His failure to achieve more than a

The Influential Field Brothers

Cyrus W. Field, who laid the Atlantic cable, had five brothers. Two of them, David Dudley Field and Stephen J. Field, were among the most influential members of the American legal profession in the nineteenth century. Their father was a Congregational minister in Connecticut. David, born in 1805, went to Williams College and after reading law in an Albany law office, entered practice in New York City, where Stephen, born in 1816, eventually joined him.

David rose to become one of the most commanding figures at the American Bar, arguing many important Supreme Court cases, including those of the Reconstruction period, and serving as counsel to numerous leading men of the time. But his greatest fame stemmed from his efforts to codify American laws.

Such a code implies 1) a compilation and systematic arrangement of existing laws according to logical principles, and 2) a thorough revision in order to harmonize conflicts, supply omissions, and clarify and make complete the body of laws designed to govern the subjects to which they relate. Thus, more than a compilation (which only rearranges existing laws into logical order), a code is an act of positive legislation, proclaimed as one new, all-embracing law, encompassing the whole field covered by its title and replacing pre-existing laws in that field.

The two most famous legal codes in history were those proclaimed by Justinian in A.D. 533–534 and by Napoleon in 1804. The former, a systematic restatement of the whole body of Roman law in statutory form, has served as the basis for modern civil-law (as distinguished from judge-made common-law) systems. The Code Napoléon, drawn up by commissions appointed in 1800 by Napoleon, who was then First Consul, abrogated the law of the old French monarchy and substituted a coherent code, logically arranged and precise. Outside of the English-speaking world, it has been used as a model for similar

codes in many countries, including Italy, Japan, and Egypt.

Following the example of the Code Napoléon, David Dudley Field proposed to replace the common law in the United States by "a written and systematic code of the whole body of the law." Though he personally drafted codes that covered the different branches of the law, and even attempted an international code, he did not succeed in his ultimate goal of reducing all American law to a "Code American." But his influence was far-reaching, and before he died in 1894, he had spread the notion of law reform throughout the English-speaking world.

Above, Judge Terry is shot by a marshal after assaulting Justice Stephen Field.

Stephen lived a more flamboyant life. In 1849 he joined the gold rush to California, becoming a frontier lawyer and carrying a pistol and bowie knife. He became involved in a quarrel with a judge, during which he was disbarred, sent to jail, fined, and embroiled in a duel. His lengthy feud with another judge, David Terry (chief justice of the California Supreme Court when Field won election to that body in 1857), led to a threat to shoot Field. Years later, in 1889, when Field had long been an associate justice of the U.S. Supreme Court, Terry assaulted him in a restaurant and was shot by a federal marshal assigned to guard Field. The marshal was indicted for murder, but the Su-

preme Court held the killing justified.

Field was appointed to the High Court by President Lincoln in 1863. His years on the Court saw the law responding to the demands of the galloping capitalism of the post-Civil War period by insulating business from governmental interference. Field was the leader in inducing the Court to employ the Due Process clauses of the Fifth and Fourteenth amendments to protect property rights. He served in an influential capacity for thirty-four years, eight months, and twenty days on the Court—the longest tenure save that of Justice William O. Douglas. Toward the end, Field's mind began to falter. In 1896, Justice John

Marshall Harlan was deputed to suggest that Field resign. He reminded the aged justice that Field had done the same years earlier in suggesting that another justice step down. "Yes!" replied Field. "And a dirtier day's work I never did in my life!" In April, 1897, however, he sent a letter of resignation to take effect December 1 —the postponement enabling him to stretch the length of his tenure beyond that of John Marshall, the longest up to that time. While on the Court, Field wrote 640 opinions, a record for any justice. He died in 1899, but the impact of his opinions, placing property above personal rights, was felt in the United States for years to come.

part of his goal prevented Field from becoming the American Justinian; more important, it settled decisively the relative roles of legislator and judge in nineteenth-century law, ensuring that American law would continue to develop primarily by common law methods.

Field began writing on the need for codification as early as 1837. But his great opportunity came when, largely as a result of his agitation, the New York Constitution of 1846 provided for the appointment of commissioners "to reduce into a written and systematic code the whole body of the law of this State." Field was the most important member of the different commissions appointed under this provision and the principal draftsman of the codes reported by them.

The first of the Field codes was the Code of Civil Procedure enacted in New York in 1848. It was a landmark in the movement for law reform, since it substituted the modern system of code pleading for the pleadings run riot, which had made common law procedure one (in the characterization of Lord Chief Justice Coleridge) "so carefully framed to exclude falsehood, that very often truth was quite unable to force its way through the barriers." The Field Procedure Code "In one section . . . struck out of existence all of that law" and put in its place one simplified form of action. At one stroke this eliminated the common law forms of action and the distinction between actions at law (generally involving claims for damages) and actions in equity (seeking injunctions), which had to be brought in separate English courts. The dualized system of justice that had become the incubus of English law was replaced by one unified system administered by one court of general jurisdiction. A similar reform was not to occur in England itself until 1873.

To Field, procedure codification was only a small part of his task. The major job was still ahead—that of codifying the substantive law. "What we wanted," Field asserted, "was a codification of the Common Law," so that "we shall have a book of our own laws, a CODE AMERICAN." A second code commission, headed by Field, drafted three new codes—a Penal Code, a Political Code, and a Civil Code. The latter two were almost entirely Field's work. The Civil Code constituted Field's attempt to codify the common law: it contained 2,034 sections and was separated into four divisions, dealing with Persons, Property, Obligations, and General Provisions.

Field's efforts to codify the law occupied the major portion of his time for eighteen years. With the final text of the code submitted in 1865, he spent twenty years more in the struggle to have the codes enacted into law. Here Field was less successful; of the substantive codes, only the Penal Code was ultimately enacted in New York. The most important of them, the Civil Code, passed one or the other house of the state legislature several times and both houses twice; but the bills were not signed by "the Governor, who," said Field's biographer brother, "shrank from the responsibility of putting his name to a Reform which reconstructed the very substance of the Law." Even though five other states, led by California, adopted the Civil and Political codes, the Field effort to secure a codification of American law must be accounted an overall failure.

Various reasons must be assigned for the failure of the codification move-

A Boston policeman of 1840 is shown above in civilian clothes. Not until the 1850's were American prejudices against any citizens wearing special garb overcome, and the first police forces put into uniform (in New York, Philadelphia, and Boston). The need for quick identification won out over democratic scruples.

ment. First must be listed the inadequacies of the nineteenth-century legislature as an instrument for the remaking of substantive law. Sir Courtenay Ilbert, in *The Mechanics of Law Making* in 1914, observed that Parliament was not interested in "lawyers' law." This was even more true of the American legislature of the formative era. It had not the interest nor the ability to undertake the rigorous and technical task of codifying the law.

Yet the failure of the codification effort was more than legislative inadequacy. It was Field's fate to arrive at his task both too late and too early. Had he been born in 1770 instead of 1805, he would have reached maturity while the reception of the common law was still an issue. As it was, he came to his life work as the American common law was ceasing to be formative, but before it was sufficiently systematized to be codified. The great legal text writers, notably Kent and Story, had presented American law in usable doctrinal form, and the cult of the code had passed its peak.

In a broader sense, however, the movement led by Field was also premature. Field's overpowering aim was to frame "the whole of the Common Law . . . into distinct Codes, which should be so plain and simple that they could be read and 'understood of the people.' " As applied to America's formative era, the notion, as expressed by Justice Benjamin R. Curtis, "that the whole body of the law may be reduced to a pocket volume, so that every man may carry about his own lawyer" was at best quixotic. The American law of the day was not yet ripe enough. When a leading advocate of codification, in an 1836 speech, condemned the common law as "subversive of the fundamental principles of free government" and declared that "All American law must be statute law," he was stating an impossible objective for the law of his day. The important codes, like those of Justinian and Napoleon, came at the end of long periods of juristic development, after the growing point of the law had shifted to legislation. In the America of the

Before city policemen were put into uniform, their only distinguishing marks were the copper badges that dangled from their buttonholes. Shown above is an early badge of a New York City police chief.
BETTMANN ARCHIVE

Actions at Law and Actions in Equity

One feature of the English system of law which the Americans inherited from the mother country was separate courts for actions at law and actions in equity. The distinction between them was based on the remedies that were available in each court. In general, the common law courts awarded only money damages, while equity courts issued injunctions — ordering, for example, the specific performance of a contract that had been breached.

This dual system had roots in England's history. After a few centuries of the existence of the common law, it had become a rigid and inflexible system that denied court relief in cases that did not precisely meet technical rules. Eventually, disappointed litigants petitioned the king for extraordinary relief, and in time, through his Chancellor, he set up a special court, the Court of Chancery, to deal with those petitions. That court developed the law of equity which became part of the law of the land, alongside the common law. But the two systems remained separate in England, each with its own courts and distinctive rules. A litigant had to know whether a particular rule was one of law or of equity and had to be careful to proceed in the right court.

The Civil Procedure Code drafted by David Dudley Field in New York in 1848 abolished this two-court system, substituting a unified court in which all actions could be brought. A litigant no longer had to worry whether his action was one at law or in equity, since both types could be brought in the same court. It was not until 1873 that England followed suit, finally abolishing the old common law courts and Court of Chancery and in their place establishing a single Supreme Court of Judicature. The same reform has since been followed in every American state save a handful, which still have separate law and equity courts. Elsewhere, throughout the English-speaking world, the system inaugurated by Field now prevails.

early nineteenth century, these conditions did not exist. The great need was to shape the common law into an American mold — something for which the Anglo-American method of lawmaking by judicial empiricism has proved peculiarly appropriate. From this perspective, the American Benthamites were a century too early. James Fenimore Cooper's Dunscomb, in *The Ways of the Hour*, spoke the common sentiment in preferring "the perfection of human reason" embodied in the common law to the "great innovation" in "the new and much-talked-of code."

Bench and Bar

"The opinion prevails pretty generally . . . that the Bar of this country is deteriorating in learning, eloquence and character." This comment from an 1851 article on the American Bar echoed a common theme of the period. David Dudley Field, writing a decade earlier, had affirmed that "They who can recollect the men of the last generation, will recall very different figures from those which now occupy the courts." And, describing one of the older lawyers whose portrait hung in the supreme court room at Albany, as if it "scarcely knew what to make of . . . the new spectacle," Field had asked, "Was he the last of his race?"

Extralegal justice was sometimes meted out by private groups usurping the authority of the courts. Artist David Blythe portrayed a "trial" (below) by one such group, the secret, and often violent, Molly Maguires, Pennsylvania miners who combined to fight unfair labor practices of the mine operators.

MEMORIAL ART GALLERY OF THE UNIVERSITY OF ROCHESTER

The plaint of professional deterioration strikes a responsive chord in every generation of lawyers. Yet it may have been more justified than usual in the middle of the nineteenth century. A roll call of the leaders of the Bar in the first part of the century is a list of men who have become legends in the profession: William Pickney, Luther Martin, William Wirt, Jeremiah Mason, Daniel Webster. Bentham once said that law is really made by "Judge & Company"—meaning that counsel, by their argument, have a large part to play in the judicial shaping of the law. It is not "exaggeration to say, that no Bar was ever more capable of aiding the mind of the Bench, than the Bar . . . in the time of Chief Justice Marshall," said Charles Warren in *A History of the American Bar.* As Supreme Court Justice James Moore Wayne was later to affirm of the "eminence of the American bar of that day. . . . There were giants in those days."

But the picture of professional decay toward the end of the formative era should not be overdrawn. It is hard to equate deterioration with a Bar that produced Judah P. Benjamin, Horace Binney, William M. Evarts, Rufus Choate, Reverdy Johnson, Benjamin R. Curtis, and Abraham Lincoln. Still, even these men were not up to the forensic measure of Marshall's day. And the level of competence below the professional apex declined sharply, under the pressure both of increasing numbers and the Jacksonian movement to deprofessionalize the practice of law. More and more, the age of the legendary founders of the Bar gave way to that of the "bustling and restless men," in which, said Field in 1844, "A feverish restlessness, and an overtasked mind, are the present concomitants of . . . the profession." Even a leading defender of the profession, Timothy Walker, had to concede in 1837 that "Lawyers are said to delight in tricks, strategems, and chicanery; to argue as strenuously for the wrong as for the right . . . ; and to hire out their conscience, as well as their skill, to any client, who will pay the fee."

As Walker stressed, the truth of the charge was not the fault of the Bar alone: "Our profession . . . does but adapt itself to circumstances; and it depends upon the community, whether it shall be elevated or degraded." If the level of the profession declined, it also reflected developments in the society as a whole. Here, too, Jacksonian Democracy had an ambivalent effect. The Age of Jackson opened more doors to the common man, giving American society the egalitarian cast which Tocqueville noted as its outstanding feature. But it had a leveling effect upon the Bar which resulted in a virtual deprofessionalization in most parts of the country. Egalitarianism was perverted into the notion that every man had a natural right to practice any lawful calling he chose, and the requirement of professional qualifications violated that right.

It should be remembered that, in the early part of the nineteenth century, the law was the only profession that restricted entry; even medicine and divinity were open to all without qualification requirements. Proponents of legal deprofessionalization in Michigan in 1850 declared they wanted "the lawyers to stand upon the same platform with the priests and the doctors. . . . We allow a man to tamper with soul and body, but not with property." The hostility toward a trained Bar, described by Dickens in his Jefferson

William M. Evarts was one of many eminent lawyers in an era when there were complaints that the profession was in decline. Evarts's career alternated between the law and statesmanship; a high point in his life was his defense of President Andrew Johnson during the impeachment trial.
History of the Bench and Bar of New York, NEW YORK, 1897

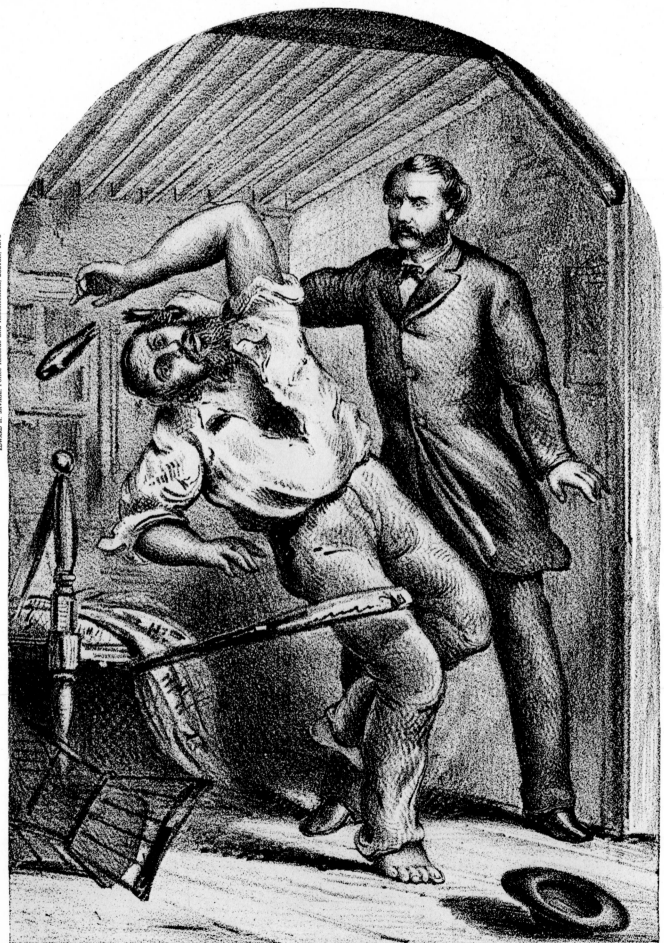

The Law
in the City

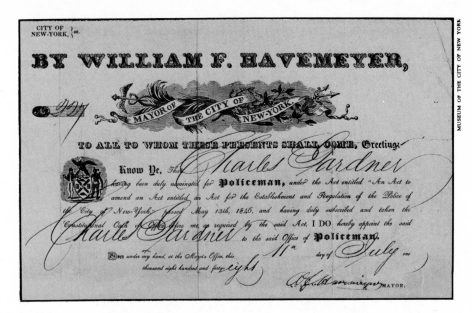

At left, a wifebeater is subdued—an illustration from the memoirs of a Boston policeman. At right is an 1848 certificate of appointment of a New York policeman. Below is a line of New York patrolmen in 1864 and, at bottom, a graphic depiction of the New York Police Court in 1853: crowded, hectic, and sordid.

Brick frontier community, was more common than is generally realized.

A widespread legislative and constitutional elimination of professional qualifications followed. What better way to remove the Bar as "A privileged order or class, to whom the administration of justice is given as a support," than to open the practice of law to all? In 1800 a definite period of preparation for admission to the Bar was required in fifteen of the nineteen states and organized territories which then made up the Union. By 1840, only eleven out of thirty jurisdictions insisted on such a requirement. By 1860, the number had fallen to nine of the then thirty-nine jurisdictions. North Carolina was the only southern state and Ohio the only state or territory west of the Alleghenies that retained the requirement even nominally.

In a number of states, legislation was passed giving every citizen or resident the right to practice law. Such laws were enacted in New Hampshire in 1842, Maine in 1843, and Wisconsin in 1849. In some states, the elimination of professional qualifications was contained in constitutional provisions. The best-known example was a provision in the Indiana Constitution of 1851 that "Every person of good moral character who is a voter is entitled to practice law in any of the courts of this state"—a right that stood in the state's constitution until 1932. In most of the country, by 1860, the only requirement for the practice of law was "good moral character"—which, as one wit put it, was the one qualification most practitioners plainly lacked.

In addition, the period saw a virtual breakdown of professional organizations. Even in Massachusetts, which had the strongly organized Bar described by John Adams before independence, with regular meetings and direct control over education and admissions, the organized Bar largely disbanded. The Bar of Suffolk, to which Adams had belonged, dissolved in 1836 and was replaced by a loose fraternal organization. The same thing happened in other counties of the state. An attempt in 1849 to set up a Massachusetts State Bar Association proved abortive. Similar conditions of bar association disintegration prevailed in other states, most of which did not have strongly organized Bars to begin with. Deprived of control over professional training, admission, or misconduct, the remaining bar associations degenerated into moribund social organizations, with little to do but adopt resolutions on the retirement or death of judges.

The Jacksonian notion, stated by one partisan in 1830, that the legal profession was "genius putting itself to sale . . . offering itself a loose prostitute to the capricious use of all men alike, for gold!" resulted in gearing the profession toward mediocrity. The practice of law became a trade, more than a profession; the belief that it was simply one more means of livelihood turned it ironically in that direction. Opening the profession to all led to an influx of untrained lawyers and depressed professional standards to levels unheard of since the Revolution. "Imagine," wrote a member of the California Supreme Court in 1858 of his early days in practice in Alabama, "thirty or forty young men collected together in a new country, armed with fresh licenses which they had got gratuitously, and a plentiful stock of brass which they had got in the natural way; and standing ready to supply any distressed citizen who wanted law, with their wares counterfeiting the article." The leaders of the early formative era had given way to a mass of jobbers and pettifoggers, veritable pharisees in "anise, mint and cummin," but without knowledge or judgment in weightier matters.

What was true of the Bar was also, in the main, true of the Bench. Justice Story's lament on John Marshall's death, that the old race of judges was gone, may have been too extreme; a Bench that included Roger B. Taney, Lemuel Shaw, John B. Gibson, and Thomas Ruffin, as well as Story himself, could scarcely be considered lacking in judicial giants. Yet most of the outstanding judges toward mid-century were, like Story, holdovers from an earlier period. As they left the Bench, they were replaced by men plainly not of the same caliber, for example, the replacement of Story himself by Levi Woodbury in 1845. Except for Taney, almost no one elevated to the Bench between Marshall's death and the Civil War comes to mind as having made any real contribution to legal history.

With the Bench, as with the Bar, the leveling effect was a result of the new democratic spirit swept into national power with Andrew Jackson. Fundamental Jacksonian notions were applied to the selection of judges and resulted in a movement for popular election. At the beginning of the nineteenth century, all judges above the rank of justices of the peace were appointed by the Executive or the legislature. Before 1846, deviations from this situation occurred in only four states. Once again, New York set the new pattern. The change in its 1846 constitution to elected judges heralded

The merry scene, below, of judges, lawyers, and clients—with an Indian and a fiddler—on their way through the woods to the holding of a frontier court, was drawn by Augustus L. Mason in 1884, long after the early period it depicts.

107

FRANCES TROLLOPE, *Domestic Manners of the Americans,* LONDON, 1832

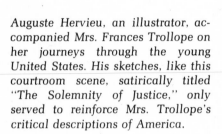

Auguste Hervieu, an illustrator, accompanied Mrs. Frances Trollope on her journeys through the young United States. His sketches, like this courtroom scene, satirically titled "The Solemnity of Justice," only served to reinforce Mrs. Trollope's critical descriptions of America.

the change to the popular election of most judges. Within ten years, fifteen of the twenty-nine states existing in 1846 had changed their constitutions to provide for the popular election of judges; in addition, the six states admitted to the Union between 1846 and the Civil War stipulated popular election of all or most judges. Only the then relative unimportance of the federal trial courts and the difficulty of amending the federal Constitution saved the nation from an elective federal judiciary.

Here, too, the picture was not entirely unfavorable, however. In the pre-Civil War period as at the outset, the crucial role played by law and lawyers continued as an outstanding feature of the society. Sampson Brass (himself the most repulsive of Dickens's legal characters) referred to the English legal profession in *The Old Curiosity Shop* as "the first profession in this country, sir, or any other country, or in any of the planets that shine above us at night and are supposed to be inhabited." If this was true in the England of the 1840's, how much more so was it in a system where, according to Justice Story, "The discussion of constitutional questions throws a lustre round the bar, and gives a dignity to its functions, which can rarely belong to the profession in any other country." The limits and injunctions of the constitutional charter gave law and lawyers an ascendancy attained in no other system. "The *Constitution* with Captain Hull in her, did not come down upon the *Guerriere* in a spirit of more daring and triumphant energy than the Philadelphia or New York lawyers will sometimes do upon a statute that happens to run a little amiss!" intoned Richard Rush, an attorney general of the United States.

Rush, writing early in the century, could sum up the situation by saying, "Here the law is every thing." The law, according to a later commentator in 1851, was still "the highway to official distinction." Tocqueville could place the American aristocracy among the Bar because the lawyers of the day "are naturally called upon to occupy most of the public stations." In particular, as Timothy Walker put it in 1837, "In the halls of legislation, he must ever occupy a conspicuous place." More than half of the Senate and half of the House of Representatives were lawyers. The legal profession also contributed between half and two-thirds of all state governors. Legislatures in the southern states in particular had a noticeably high percentage of lawyer members. The tradition was becoming blurred toward the end of the period, but the law was still considered the path to public service, as much as that to private gain. "If a lawyer," affirmed Horace Binney, "confines himself to the profession, and refuses public life, though it is best . . . for his own happiness, it makes sad work with his biography. You might almost as well undertake to write the biography of a millhorse. . . . The biography of lawyers, however eminent, *qua* lawyers, is nothing." Leadership had not yet passed from the lawyer to the entrepreneur.

Within the profession, encouraging trends might ultimately counter the deterioration. First, a unified profession developed, rather than the truncated Bar that existed in England: "the profession here is not subdivided in any of the states, in the ways that it is in England," noted Richard Rush. Although some of the colonies had had the English division, it disappeared soon after the Revolution. The unified American Bar was in a much better position to assert its leadership role, unhampered by the formal dignities and etiquette of the barrister-solicitor distinction. Later in the century, Bryce was to testify to the broader opportunities available to the American Bar, concluding that the American example "seems to show that the balance of advantage is in favor of uniting barristers and attorneys in one body."

Even more important for the profession was the emergence of legal education in the modern sense. At the time of independence, training for the Bar was entirely through the apprentice system; well past 1850, indeed, the chief method of legal education was apprenticeship. Many lawyers had not even had the benefits of journeyman training; like Abraham Lincoln, they prepared for the profession almost entirely by self-directed reading. But there were also the beginnings of more formal legal education, first in proprietary law schools, of which the most important was the Litchfield Law School in Connecticut. Established in 1784 by Judge Tapping Reeve, the Litchfield School operated until 1833. Among its graduates were many leaders of the pre-Civil War profession: "Probably no law school has had — perhaps . . . never will have — so great a proportion of distinguished men on its catalogue," observed one writer. Litchfield saw the beginning of the teaching of law in schools. In fourteen months, students covered the law in "all its important branches . . . divided into forty-eight Titles." Instruction was by lectures, supplemented by moot courts. Similar private law schools were set up in other parts of the country, and were the chief source of formal instruction in the first quarter of the century.

In the meantime, the next step in legal education had been taken in the establishment of law professorships at different universities. The first professorship was set up at William and Mary as early as 1779, with the chair occupied by George Wythe, perhaps the leading American jurist of his day. Law professorships were soon established in other universities as

America's first law school, which Judge Tapping Reeve established in Litchfield, Connecticut, in 1784, was housed in this one-room building, seen above in restored state.

well, notably at Columbia in 1793, at Yale in 1801, and at Harvard in 1815.

The first incumbent of the Harvard chair, Chief Justice Isaac Parker of Massachusetts's High Court, suggested the establishment by the university of a separate law school, which was founded in 1817. Combining the English Inns of Court idea of professional training with the continental concept of academic law teaching, the Harvard Law School was the first example of what was to become the distinctive type of American law school—the academic-professional school.

The success of the new Law School was assured when a second chair in law was occupied in 1829 by Justice Story, who capped his career on the Bench with his decision "to take a general superintendence of the Law School, that is to visit it and examine the students occasionally, and to direct their studies, and to lecture to them." The method of instruction was a combination of lecture and textbook instruction, as well as moot court sessions. The lectures covered the different branches of the law. "In treating most of those branches," reported the Overseers in 1850, "the Professors adopted certain text-books . . . as the basis of their remarks. They also examined the students in these books."

The success of Harvard under the Story regime was largely responsible for the growth of American law schools after 1830. By the Civil War almost a score of schools existed in different parts of the country. A further step in the method of law teaching was taken when Benjamin F. Butler organized the Law School at the University of the City of New York (now New York University) in 1835, using the course method. When William Kent (the chancellor's son) was invited to leave his post at New York University to join the Harvard staff in 1846, he brought with him the *course* as it had been established by Butler. The form of teaching by subject courses has

"The Last of the Old Race"

HARVARD LAW SCHOOL COLLECTION

Justice Joseph Story

Joseph Story, considered perhaps the most learned scholar ever to sit on any American court, was also the youngest man ever named to the Supreme Court. He was thirty-two when President James Madison appointed him in 1811. He had been born in Marblehead, Massachusetts, in 1779, and had become well known in state and national politics, serving in the House of Representatives in 1808–1809. Madison chose him for the High Court because, according to the President, he had "a character of firmness enough to preserve his independence on the same Bench with Marshall." But Story was soon the Court's leading supporter of Marshall's nationalistic views and became a virtual second in doctrine to Marshall himself.

In his opinions supporting Marshall, Story supplied the one thing the great Chief Justice lacked—legal scholarship. "Brother Story here . . . can give us the cases from the Twelve Tables down to the latest reports," Marshall is reputed to have once said. If Marshall disliked the labor of investigating legal authorities to support his decisions, Story reveled in legal research. His opinions were usually long and learned and relied heavily on prior cases and writers. When he joined the Court, it was entering upon its historic period of constitutional construction, and Story participated in the landmark de-

continued as the basis of the law school curriculum until the present day.

Another significant development, itself the fruit of law school teaching, must also be mentioned: the publication of the great texts of the formative era. The most important of them were produced by law teachers—Kent, Story, Greenleaf, Parsons, and Washburn—and they served both practitioner and teacher. The work of the text writers was of prime importance in the development of American law. Without Kent and Story, it is doubtful that the common law could have been received as readily as it was or that judicial decision could have taken over as the law's growing point. At a critical period, the doctrinal writers gave the courts authoritative statements of the received common law and so gave judges something from which to make needed new starts. Above all, the text writers and their affiliated law schools were a great unifying influence in American law. The Harvard *Catalogue* in 1841 proudly proclaimed its "national" tradition: "No public instruction is given in the local or peculiar municipal jurisprudence of any particular state." The text writers wrote in the same tradition. What Story the judge could not do, Story the text writer accomplished.

The Ends of Law: 1860

In 1815 Richard Rush, then U.S. Attorney General, published a little book titled *American Jurisprudence.* Aware that in literature and art "it ought not to be expected of us to produce a Lord Byron or a Walter Scott," Rush sought consolation in asserting that, amid these "other great excitements of the mind" only "In the department of jurisprudence" did the United States "approach . . . nearer to a par with the old nations."

The law of the formative era developed as an aggressively self-assured system, secure in the knowledge that its fundamental purpose was to pro-

James Kent won renown as an innovative judge and as a professor of law. Though he disliked classroom teaching, his lectures, published as Commentaries on American Law, still comprise an important legal treatise.

cisions of the next two and a half decades.

On Marshall's death in 1835, Story's admirers hoped that he would become the new chief justice. ("The Supreme Court . . . ," Harvard President Josiah Quincy toasted, "may it be raised one Story higher.") President Andrew Jackson, however, could scarcely appoint one so opposed to his views and, instead, named Roger B. Taney, a leading Jacksonian, to the position. In the Taney Court, Story became a vigorous dissenter, delivering caustic dissents like his 35,000-word opinion in the *Charles River Bridge* case. Several weeks after it was delivered, he declared, "I am the last of the old race of judges."

In 1829, while he was still on the Court, Story became the first Dane Professor of Law at Harvard. His appointment signaled the reorganization of Harvard Law School and its emergence as the first modern school of law. Despite his heavy judicial duties, he taught two of the three yearly terms at the school and found time to publish a number of significant works that constituted the first great specialized treatises on American law. As a judge, he was overshadowed by Marshall, but as a law teacher and writer on the subject, he had no peer.

This was not all. During most of his years on the Supreme Court, he served as president of one bank and

vice-president of another. He was also president of the American Unitarian Society and enjoyed a reputation as a minor poet, having published a volume of poetry, *The Power of Solitude,* before his High Court appointment.

In 1845 he wrote to an old friend: "I am the last member, now living, of the old Court, and I cannot consent to remain where I can no longer hope to see those doctrines [of Marshall] recognized." He planned to resign and devote his life to teaching and writing. But before he could send his letter of resignation from the Court, he suddenly became ill and died at his Cambridge home just prior to his sixty-seventh birthday.

The Harvard Law School, pictured here about 1860, was founded in 1817 by Isaac Parker. The school enjoyed its finest era under Christopher Columbus Langdell, who became its head in 1870 and introduced the case method of teaching.

vide the legal instruments needed to fulfill the nation's manifest destiny. The lawyer could mold the legal system to the needs of the new nation confident, said a writer in 1849, that he "has entrusted to him the social life of man. This is his function, to preserve the social life in security and soundness; and by his preservative care secure its full and complete development."

As emphasized at the close of Chapter I, Americans at first thought of the law as designed primarily to protect personal and property rights, with the emphasis in their scale of values placed upon what Story, in his 1829 Harvard inaugural address, called "the sacred rights of property. . . . I call them sacred because, if they are unprotected, all other rights become worthless or visionary." If anything, this emphasis increased during the latter part of the pre-Civil War period. Wrote Theodore Sedgwick in a pioneer 1857 treatise on statutory interpretation, "All government, indeed, resolves itself into the protection of life, liberty, and property. Life and liberty in our fortunate condition are, however, little likely to be injuriously affected by the action of the body politic. Property is very differently situated. It is therefore of the highest moment . . . to obtain a clear idea of the nature and extent of the protections which guard our rights of property."

Emerson, in *Politics* (1844), might express "doubts . . . whether too much weight had not been allowed in the laws to property." The vast majority of his compatriots had no such doubts. With Noah Webster, they believed that "property is . . . the basis of the freedom of the American." The major end

of law to them was to protect property rights. "The sense of property," declared Kent (never fully able to shed his educational origins in Connecticut Calvinism), "is inherent in the human breast, and the gradual enlargement and cultivation of that sense" was necessary for the society's progress. The law had to stress the right to acquire property even more than the right to secure existing property.

This meant, as already noted, a tremendous expansion of the law of contracts, which "may be looked upon as the basis of human society." Will became the central point in every legal situation. The domain in which the individual was referred to his own will grew throughout the period, burgeoning in the latter part of the century into a vast no-man's land of private right from which government was virtually barred. The law existed to secure the right to contract freely and the right to exact performance freely promised. The natural rights that early Americans considered the measure of the law became the rights of individuals who had entered into a contract. If the object of law was to protect the *suum cuique*, meaning "to give to each his own," and since, paraphrasing Hobbes, where there is no "own" there is neither property nor justice, the "own" was more and more thought of in terms of rights secured by contract. The nature of justice itself consisted in the keeping of valid contracts.

We err seriously if we look at our early contract-dominated law as a restrictive system. On the contrary, contract was the great liberating instrument that not only conquered a continent, but also, and more important, opened up the expanding economy to men of all social strata and enabled them to share its fruits. Individualism, fostered by the power to make contracts freely, supplied the motive force for the needed mobilization and release of energy. If in the end it turned into an ultraindividualism that made attempts to correct abuses futile, that did not occur until the latter part of the century. In the beginning at least, contract enabled the society to manage the resources available to it and, at the same time, afforded the average man freedom of opportunity and mobility (both physical and social) such as he had never had before.

To the men of the formative era, the end of law was practical, not abstract, justice. The law was a tool to further ambition and energy; in particular, its job was to furnish the legal tools needed for effective mobilization of the community's resources. The instrumentalist emphasis culminated in the development of the business corporation. In the corporation in all its manifold aspects, the businessman's inventiveness joined that of the lawyer: the product was a vehicle admirably suited to the uses to which it was soon put. The corporation has been well characterized as the most potent single instrument which the law put at the disposal of private decision makers. By 1860, it had transformed both the face of the nation and the society itself; as an 1830 article had prophesied, the corporation had already gone far to "absorb the greatest part of the substance of the commonwealth."

Yet, if the primary aim of law in the first half of the nineteenth century was to serve as the vehicle by which a maximum of individual self-assertion might be secured, the end of the period gave indications of a more static conception of the legal role. What William Wirt termed "the principle of restraint" was to become a dominant theme as the century progressed. By 1857, Theodore Sedgwick was to describe that principle as the fundamental purpose of all law: "the law of nature, the moral law, the municipal law, and the law of nations, form a system of restraints before which the most consummate genius, the most vehement will, the angriest passions, and the fiercest desires are compelled to bend." The purposive vision of law as an expansive instrument was giving way to a more restrictive conception of the law as a negative tool. The new theme was set in an 1845 address by Rufus Choate, a Massachusetts lawyer and senator, on "the Bar, as an Element of Conservatism." Choate used the word "conservatism" in something like its modern sense, and set up the law as the great conservative bulwark against the evolution of the country.

The changing concept of law was a direct response to changes in the society itself. Today we find only hyperbole in Story's characterization of Jacksonian Democracy as "the reign of King 'Mob.'" As the century went on, however, leaders of the profession came increasingly to feel, with Kent, the danger of "the evil effects of sudden and strong excitement, and of precipitate measures springing from passion, caprice, prejudice." The *Communist Manifesto* in 1848 might well be the precursor of a future in which— using the words of a judge in 1834 — "a portion of the people could wage war, equally against political liberty, the sacred rights of property, and religious charity."

But the publication of another nonlegal work was to be the determining influence on American law during the remainder of the century. Before the close of the formative era, American jurisprudence had already begun to move toward an organic conception of legal development. Historical thinking was in the air; Burke had insisted on historical continuity, and Friedrich Karl von Savigny, a Prussian jurist and statesman, had founded the historical school of jurists. Savigny's doctrine was taught at Harvard by Luther S. Cushing from 1848 to 1852. In England, Sir Henry Maine was delivering the lectures that were to make his reputation when they were printed in 1861 as a book titled *Ancient Law*. In 1859 came the publication of Charles Darwin's masterpiece, *On the Origin of Species*. Evolution would soon become the school in which the law itself was to be learned; natural selection would justify the growing conservatism of the heirs of Jefferson and Jackson. If, as Maine himself was to say of the American system a generation later, there had never been a society in which the weak had been pushed so pitilessly to the wall and success given so uniformly to the strong, that was only the way things had to be according to the Abraham of scientific men, as the British physicist John Tyndall characterized Darwin.

The blessings of the American way of life, secured by a system of justice that allowed maximum freedom to attain one's own prosperity, was reflected in prints like this popular Currier scene of 1855, showing a happy family amid its property and possessions, the fruits of enterprise protected by U.S. law.

IV

Years of Laissez Faire

Public Law: 1860–1910

The year 1868 marked a turning point in American public law: the Fourteenth Amendment, designed originally to protect the freed slaves after the Civil War from coercive actions by the southern states, was added to the federal Constitution. "No state shall make or enforce any law which shall abridge the privileges or immunities of citizens of the United States," read its first section, "nor shall any state deprive any person of life, liberty, or property, without due process of law; nor deny to any person within its jurisdiction the equal protection of the laws." Nationalizing civil rights, the amendment made the great guarantees for life, liberty, and property binding on governments throughout the land. In the years since its passage, it has served as the principal legal instrument for the egalitarian revolution that continues even today in American society. In many ways, indeed, present-day constitutional law is merely a gloss on the Fourteenth Amendment's key provisions.

During the first part of its history, however, the impact of the amendment was almost entirely economic. As such, it supplied the constitutional text for the laissez-faire capitalism of the post-Civil War period. In 1868, too, laissez faire received its legal ideology with the publication of *Constitutional Limitations* by Thomas M. Cooley, an eminent judge and professor of law at the University of Michigan. Perhaps the most influential public law book ever written, the Cooley work furnished the doctrinal foundation for the conversion of the Fourteenth Amendment into a virtual Magna Carta for business.

Despite these developments, the framers of the Fourteenth Amendment intended it as a Great Charter for personal rights, which would serve as the shield of individual liberties throughout the nation. In particular,

Congressman John A. Bingham of Ohio was the draftsman of the important first section of the Fourteenth Amendment.

Trusts rise above the people's liberties: an 1889 Thomas Nast cartoon

The slaves of Confederate President Jefferson Davis are seen in this photograph taken after the fall of Vicksburg. Freedom soon followed, but the subsequent promise of equal rights contained in the Fourteenth Amendment was to prove largely illusory; while the amendment would be a boon to corporations, freed slaves would see little of its guarantees of equality.

the sponsors of the amendment (as well as the other post-bellum amendments) sought to raise the concept of equality to the constitutional plane. To understand their accomplishment, we must first inquire into the place of equality in American public law.

"All history," wrote Teilhard de Chardin in *The Future of Man*, "bears witness to the fact that nothing has ever been able to prevent an idea from growing and spreading and finally becoming universal." So it was with the idea of equality. Equality has been the underlying concept of the American system since it was proclaimed as self-evident truth in the Declaration of Independence—in what Lincoln called "the electric cord in that Declaration that links the hearts of patriotic and liberty-loving men together." The effort to realize the Declaration's great theme of the equality of man has dominated American history. This is true despite the failure of the Constitution's framers to repeat the unqualified assertion of the Declaration in their instrument. Nowhere in the document drafted in 1787 was there any guaranty of equality—or even any mention of the concept.

Whatever may have been the intent of the Founders, the triumphant march of the concept of equality became all but inevitable when they established what some of them were already calling a "representative democracy." Democratic communities, concluded Tocqueville after his observation of the American system, may "have a natural taste for freedom. . . . But for equality their passion is ardent, insatiable, incessant, invincible." If, at the beginning, the political, economic, and legal systems were permeated with inequalities, only a century later Bryce could declare, "The United States are deemed all the world over to be preeminently the land of equality."

The early egalitarian movement reached its climax in Jacksonian Democracy, which made substantial contributions to the theory and practice of equality. Jackson himself first gave currency to the term *equal protection*. His 1832 veto of the bill rechartering the Bank of the United States contains a positive statement of the equal right of all persons to the equal protection of equal laws in terms that anticipate the negative version adopted in the Fourteenth Amendment thirty-six years later.

However far-reaching the Jacksonian notion of equality might have seemed to its contemporary opponents, it was by present-day conceptions rather limited: the Jacksonian emphasis on the democratic ideal as providing liberty and equality for all must be sharply distinguished from the twentieth-century concept. To Jacksonians, and to most of their contemporaries, "all" did not include blacks or women; their concept was basically governed by the Aristotelian notion of the inherent inequality of persons outside the select circle of full citizenship.

It was primarily the protection of slavery by the Constitution that made impossible any legal doctrine of equality in the modern sense. "Liberty and Slavery—opposite as Heaven and Hell—are both in the Constitution," said the black leader Frederick Douglass. The Constitution itself, he observed, was "a compromise with Slavery—a bargain between the North and the South." While that bargain persisted, an express guaranty of equality would have been hypocritical hyperbole.

With the Civil War, the situation changed completely. "The bond of Union being dissolved," Jefferson Davis conceded, "the obligation of the U.S. Govt. to recognize property in slaves, as denominated in the compact, might be recognized as thereby no longer binding." William Lloyd Garrison, the abolitionist (who had earlier committed the Constitution to the flames but now supported the Union), could reply to a charge of inconsistency: "When I said I would not sustain the Constitution, because it was a 'covenant with death and an agreement with hell,' I had no idea that I would live to see death and hell secede."

The abolition of slavery repudiated the heresy, put into words by Lincoln, that "all men are created equal, except Negroes." It was no longer inconsistent with reality for the Constitution to contain an express guaranty of equality. The Fourteenth Amendment and the other post-bellum additions to the Constitution made equality regardless of race a fundamental constitutional principle.

The historian who considers the Reconstruction period must balance its constitutional excesses by the commitment of the Republican leaders to the cause of equal rights and the lasting contributions they made to that cause. "What is Liberty without Equality?" asked Senator Charles Sumner in 1866, "One is the complement of the other. . . . They are the two vital principles of republican government." However vindictive and partisan men such as Sumner and Congressman Thaddeus Stevens could be, they and their followers first made equality an express constitutional principle. The history of civil rights in America truly begins with the amendments added under the post-Civil War Republican congressional leadership.

Before Fort Sumter, the great theme in American public law was the nation-state problem. Nation and states all too often confronted each other

Harper's Weekly, NOVEMBER 16, 1867

"The First Vote," an 1867 Harper's illustration, celebrated the granting of suffrage to former slaves. This happy state of affairs continued only as long as federal troops were stationed in the southern states.

and threatened to tear the nation apart. Appomattox put an end to that danger. From then on, the Union was, as the Supreme Court put it in 1869, "indestructible," and the supremacy of federal power was ensured. The law could now turn to the constitutional issues posed by the new amendments. The focus of public law could be transferred from the protection of federal power to the safeguarding of individual rights.

Intent of the Fourteenth Amendment

The Fourteenth Amendment, which became law on July 28, 1868, was the constitutional heart of the congressional Reconstruction program. The Thirteenth Amendment, ratified on December 18, 1865, had outlawed all forms of slavery and involuntary servitude; the Fifteenth Amendment, added to the Constitution on March 30, 1870, guaranteed racial equality in voting. But the Fourteenth Amendment was the epochal provision. It had two effects: (1) the express constitutional guaranty of a right of equality and (2) as previously noted, the federalizing of civil rights. In the history of American public law, the second of these was crucial.

Cartoonist Thomas Nast favored the hard line in Reconstruction; here he depicted President Andrew Johnson as Shakespeare's Iago, with a freed slave playing Othello. The attacks on southern blacks he attributed to Johnson's policy of conciliating the former rebel states.

Until the end of the Civil War, the states were the guardians of their citizens' civil rights, and the states alone could determine the character and extent of such rights. The Bill of Rights itself, the Supreme Court had held in the case of *Barron v. Mayor of Baltimore* in 1833, was binding on the federal government alone—not on the states. As far as the federal Constitution was concerned, except for the minor limitations contained in Article I, section 10, the states were free to encroach upon individual rights as they chose.

The Fourteenth Amendment changed all this. The very language of the amendment indicates the intent of its framers to provide federal protection for personal rights. But more difficult was the question of how far they intended to go. Specifically (in terms of the subsequent legal controversy in the matter), did they intend to make the federal Bill of Rights binding on the states?

If this was their intent, it must have been through the amendment's guaranties, against the states, of "privileges or immunities of citizens of the United States" and of "due process of law." As far as the Privileges and Immunities Clause is concerned, the legislative history is at best ambiguous. Congressman John A. Bingham, who has been called "the Madison of the first section of the Fourteenth Amendment," indicated an intent to make the Bill of Rights binding, but the force of his statement was blurred by his apparent misconception that the Bill of Rights had always been binding on the states. In the Senate, Jacob Howard of Michigan, who made the introductory speech on the amendment, stated specifically that the privileges and immunities guaranteed by the amendment included the privileges and immunities spoken of in the Constitution's Article IV, section 2 ("The citizens of each state shall be entitled to all privileges and immunities of citizens in the several states. . . ."), as well as "the personal rights guaranteed and secured by the first eight amendments."

Against the Howard statement should be set the fact that no other participant in the lengthy Senate debate (or in the House either, for that matter) supported the assertion that the amendment would make the Bill of Rights binding on the states. On the contrary, most senators, particularly those with impressive legal backgrounds, such as Luke Poland (former chief justice of Vermont), Reverdy Johnson of Maryland, and John B. Henderson of Missouri, took positions inconsistent with Howard's view. They asserted either that the new Privileges and Immunities Clause secured nothing beyond what was intended by Article IV, section 2, or that its effect was uncertain. In addition, the Howard view was definitely repudiated by the Supreme Court five years after the amendment was ratified. In 1873 the *Slaughter-House Cases* ruled that a state violation of the rights guaranteed in the federal Bill of Rights did not contravene the Privileges and Immunities Clause of the Fourteenth Amendment.

The *Slaughter-House* decision failed to prevent the Fourteenth Amendment from eventually reviving the constitutional question supposedly laid to rest in *Barron v. Mayor of Baltimore*—whether the Bill of Rights was binding on the states as well as the federal government. After *Slaughter-House*, the claim that the Fourteenth Amendment made the Bill of Rights

Some years after the event, a magazine illustrator drew this view of the predominantly black South Carolina legislature voting on a bill in 1873. After protesting troops were withdrawn from the South, black lawmakers abruptly disappeared; only in recent years have a few begun reappearing in southern statehouses.

Little was omitted by the artist of this 1867 visual glorification of Reconstruction. The exultant symbolism focuses on the setting up of missing pillars (the returning southern states) to form a rotunda of the reunited Republic. To accentuate the point, clasped hands above the national bird are explained with the legend "Union and Liberty Forever." From heaven, apparently, the country's departed leaders look down approvingly—Washington, Lincoln, Jefferson, Webster, Calhoun, and a host of others. Among additional touches: black and white babes (bottom, center), reposing innocently in baskets, remind the viewer that "All men are born free and equal."

"The Banded Butchers Are Busted"

Section 1 of the Fourteenth Amendment defined U.S. citizenship so as to include the newly freed Negro, and it prohibited states from making laws abridging the "privileges or immunities" of that citizenship or denying "due process of law" or the equal protection of the laws. Yet the *Slaughter-House Cases* in 1873, the first cases involving the interpretation of the Fourteenth Amendment, had nothing to do with the rights of freedmen. They arose out of an 1869 statute passed by the "carpetbag" legislature of Louisiana. The law, secured by widespread bribery (the governor, legislators, various state officials, and two newspapers had all been paid for their support), had incorporated the Crescent City Live Stock Landing and Slaughter House Company and had given it the exclusive right to slaughter livestock in New Orleans. It had driven from business all the other butchers in the city, and the Butchers' Benevolent Association had brought an action challenging "the Monopoly," as the new corporation was called, for operating in violation of the Fourteenth Amendment.

The case was argued by legal giants of the day, John A. Campbell (leader of the Southern Bar, who had resigned from the U.S. Supreme Court when his state had seceded) for the butchers, and former U.S. Senator Matthew H. Carpenter (who had helped draft the Fourteenth Amendment) for the Monopoly. The Court ruled for the Monopoly, adopting the view that the provisions of the Fourteenth Amendment were intended only to protect the Negro in his newly acquired freedom, and that the Due Process Clause of the amendment was irrelevant to the case: "under no construction of that provision that we have ever seen, or any that we deem admissible, can the restraint imposed by the state of Louisiana upon the exercise of their trade by the butchers of New Orleans be held to be a deprivation of property within the meaning of that provision."

"The banded butchers are busted," Carpenter announced exultingly after the decision. But, for the moment, it looked as if more than the plaintiff butchers had been "busted." The *Slaughter-House* ruling had virtually emasculated section 1 of the Fourteenth Amendment. The entire Court, however, had not been in favor of the restrictive interpretation of due process. Four justices had dissented. Foremost among them were Justices Stephen J. Field and Joseph P. Bradley, who had urged the pertinency of due process to the Louisiana monopoly law. In their view, the Fourteenth Amendment "was intended to give practical effect to the declaration of 1776 of inalienable rights, rights which are the gift of the Creator; which the law does not confer, but only recognizes."

Their concern was primarily over the protection of property rights, and a transition from the rights guaranteed in the Declaration of Independence to substantive due process for the protection of property was an easy development in the Field-Bradley approach. As Bradley put it, "Rights to life, liberty, and the pursuit of happiness are equivalent to the rights of life, liberty, and property. These are fundamental rights which can only be taken away by due process of law." The Fourteenth Amendment failed to help the freed Negro, but within a quarter of a century the direction taken in the *Slaughter-House Cases* had been reversed, the Field-Bradley approach had been accepted, and the Supreme Court was using the Due Process Clause of the Fourteenth Amendment as the instrument with which to make laissez faire constitutional doctrine.

Cattle for the New Orleans market being loaded on a Mississippi River boat

applicable to the states was based on the amendment's Due Process Clause. The legislative history, however, lends no support to this more recent claim. No participant in either House so much as hinted that the Due Process Clause of the proposed amendment would have the drastic impact that has since been claimed for it.

Civil Rights Acts

The post-bellum amendments provided for legislative as well as judicial enforcement of their provisions. Each one contained an express grant to Congress of authority to enforce its provisions "by appropriate legislation." These Enforcement Clauses have been the constitutional source of the civil rights statutes enacted by Congress since Reconstruction days.

The legislative effort to protect civil rights started with the Civil Rights Act of 1866. According to its sponsor, Senator Lyman Trumbull of Illinois, "the basis of the whole bill" was its first section, which provided that citizens of every race and color shall have the same right "as is enjoyed by white citizens" to contract, sue, take and dispose of property, bring actions and give evidence, and to equal benefit of all laws for the security of person and property. This provision, Trumbull said, was intended to "secure to all persons within the United States practical freedom."

A century later, the 1866 statute acquired particular significance from the Supreme Court decision in *Jones v. Alfred H. Mayer Co.* in 1968. In that case, the Court held that section 1 of the act contains a broad prohibition of any racial discrimination in the sale or rental of property and, as such, forbids a private development company from refusing to rent to someone because he is a Negro. The goal sought by the High Court in *Jones*—elimination of racial discrimination which "herds men into ghettos and makes their ability to buy property turn on the color of their skin"— is so desirable that it may seem mere caviling to question whether it can be attained by judicial reliance on a half-hidden statute that had never before been invoked to accomplish the wholesale result attributed to it by the Court. If it was intended to have this effect, it is astounding that no effort was made to use it to eliminate housing discrimination when that purpose was fresh in the minds of those who had passed the law a century ago.

Both the legislative history of the 1866 Civil Rights Act and the situation with which it was intended to deal indicate the act's two main purposes: (1) to make citizens of the emancipated race and (2) to endow them with the citizens' capacity to make contracts, bring actions, and own property. Before the Thirteenth Amendment, slaves could not own property. After emancipation, the southern states enacted Black Codes to perpetuate this disability. The 1866 law sought to give blacks the same property ownership rights as whites. This was the "incident of slavery" at which the 1866 statute aimed, relying on the Thirteenth Amendment's Enforcement Clause.

In an unpublished 1866 letter, Rutherford B. Hayes, then a congressman from Ohio, dealt with a misconception similar to that upon which the *Jones* decision is based. Writing to a newspaper publisher in his home state, Hayes declared: "I know it [the 1866 act] is grossly misrepresented and greatly misunderstood in Ohio. *The Commercial* speaks of it as if it gives

Massachusetts Senator Charles Sumner, stern foe of slavery, advocate of a harsh policy toward the conquered South, and a leader in the impeachment of President Andrew Johnson, was the principal sponsor of the ill-fated 1875 Civil Rights Act.

125

increased and unheard of rights as privileges to negroes—as if it would compel the schools to receive negro children, the hotels negro guests &c &c &c now please to note what I say. It undertakes to secure to the negro no right which he has not enjoyed in Ohio since the repeal of the Black Laws in 1848–9."

The act's wording of "same right . . . as is enjoyed by white citizens to . . . purchase property" was intended to mean only the same legal right, the same capacity granted by law. It was not contemplated that the ex-slave had a legal right to compel an unwilling seller to convey something no citizen could compel in 1866—a right that was completely alien to the individualist law of that day.

Through civil rights statutes enacted in 1870, 1871, and 1875, Congress sought further to ensure possession by the emancipated race of the civil rights vested in other citizens. These laws had three main goals: (1) to secure Negro voting, both by criminal prohibitions and by setting up independent federal enforcement machinery; (2) to provide sanctions to deter infringements upon other civil rights; and (3) to provide affirmatively for equality in public accommodations.

The civil rights laws of the 1870's are of special interest because they rely on a theory of congressional power rejected by the courts in their own day but received more favorably a century later. The theory in question concerns an extension of congressional authority from official to private action. It was first asserted in Senate amendments extending the reach of the Enforcement Act of 1870 to "any person" who sought to prevent or obstruct any citizen from the exercise of his right to vote or of any other right or privilege guaranteed by the Constitution or federal laws.

According to Senator John Pool, the sponsor of the amendments, the rights secured by the Fourteenth and Fifteenth amendments could be abridged either by positive legislation or by acts of omission. The former was rectified directly by the constitutional provisions; the latter was not. If a state omitted to act to prevent private individuals from contravening the rights of citizens under the amendments, it was the congressional duty "to supply that omission, and by its own laws and by its own courts to go into the States for the purpose of giving the amendment vitality there."

In this approach, the state omission or failure to act may be treated as "state action" for purposes of congressional power to enforce the Fourteenth and Fifteenth amendments. Congress might thus act directly against private individuals who were able to violate constitutional rights because of the failure of state officials to protect those rights. What gives the Pool theory such significance is the recent tendency of the Supreme Court drastically to expand the "state action" which the Fourteenth and Fifteenth amendments alone may reach—a trend that may culminate one day in the acceptance of the extreme Pool view.

The most far-reaching attempt to prevent private discrimination was contained in the Civil Rights Act of 1875. That law is of particular significance to the present-day observer, for it provides the historical nexus between the Fourteenth Amendment and the Civil Rights Act of 1964. The goal of equality in public accommodations, which Congress sought to attain by

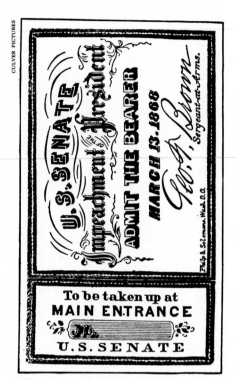

The impeachment trial of President Andrew Johnson in 1868 was a major sensation, and tickets for seats in the Senate gallery were at a premium.

The Trial of a President

One of the most dramatic events in American constitutional history, the impeachment of President Andrew Johnson in 1868, was a striking example of the tendency in the United States to frame political issues in legal terms. In Great Britain, impeachment was entirely a political process, developed to secure the removal of officials who became unacceptable to the legislature. In the U.S., impeachment was more a legal instrument: a President may be removed from office only for "Treason, Bribery, or other high Crimes and Misdemeanors," and only after a trial in the Senate presided over by the chief justice.

Andrew Johnson's impeachment by the House of Representatives climaxed an increasingly bitter conflict between the President and Congress over Reconstruction policy. The congressional leaders, feuding with the President over his lenient treatment of the defeated South, secured the enactment of laws that severely limited presidential power, particularly the Tenure of Office Act of 1867. That act, requiring senatorial consent for removals as well as appointments to office, made it impossible for the President to control his own administration. Johnson resisted enforcement of the new law, convinced that it was an unconstitutional encroachment upon his removal power (a view later affirmed by the Supreme Court in the 1926 case of *Myers v. United States*), and attempted to remove Secretary of War Edwin Stanton from office, even though the Senate had refused its consent. Stanton blockaded himself in his office, and soon thereafter the House resolved that Johnson be impeached, with the attempt to remove Stanton the principal charge against him.

As the future French Premier Georges Clemenceau, then a young reporter in the United States, wrote at the time: "The black cloud has finally broken. The President called upon the lightning and the lightning came." The Senate leaders had hoped to dispose

An unfriendly cartoon has Johnson parroting the Constitution at his defense.

of the matter in a short time. But the Senate acted as a court, allowing a full trial that lasted from March 5 to May 26. In the end, Johnson was acquitted, but only by one vote. The congressional leaders had insisted that the impeachment was, in Senator Charles Sumner's words, "a political proceeding before a political body with a political purpose." Throughout, the prosecutors addressed the chief justice as "Mr. President." Johnson's counsel, to the contrary, insisted on the judicial nature of the proceeding. "Mr. Chief Justice," began former justice Benjamin R. Curtis in his presentation for the defense, "I am here to speak to the Senate . . . sitting in its judicial capacity as a court of impeachment, presided over by the Chief Justice for the trial of the President." The insistence upon judicial procedure enabled Johnson's counsel to demonstrate the legal weakness of the prosecution.

The failure of the Senate to vote Johnson guilty was of major constitutional importance. He may have escaped by only a single vote, but the decisive fact was that he did escape. Had the impeachment succeeded, it would have destroyed presidential independence. "Once set the example of impeaching a President . . .," declared Senator Lyman Trumbull of Illinois in explaining his vote for Johnson, "and no future President will be safe who happens to differ with a majority of the House and two-thirds of the Senate on any measure deemed by them important, particularly if of a political character." Impeachment, as Trumbull warned, would have become a political process, and something like the executive dependence that prevails in a parliamentary system might well have been established in the United States.

The latest news of the impeachment trial reaches a Washington hotel lobby.

enactment of the 1964 statute, was the same intended by the 1875 law. The legislative history of the 1875 act demonstrated that legislators of the post-Civil War period were intimately concerned with many key problems that still exist in the field of civil rights: integration, segregation (particularly in education), legal versus social equality, and the crucial question of whether an ideal such as racial equality can be achieved by legislative action in a society opposed to the practical implementation of that ideal.

The sharpest congressional controversy in the debate on the 1875 act arose over elimination of a provision in the original bill prohibiting racial discrimination in all "common schools and public institutions of learning or benevolence." The debate was directly relevant to the intent of those who wrote the Fourteenth Amendment with regard to segregation in education. One who has read the 1875 debate cannot help but conclude that the Congress that sat less than a decade after the Fourteenth Amendment was sent to the states for ratification did not think the amendment had the effect of prohibiting school segregation which the Supreme Court was to attribute to it in *Brown* v. *Board of Education* in 1954. If that effect had been considered to flow from the amendment, the whole debate on the proposed school provision in 1875 would have been constitutionally irrelevant, since integration would have been constitutionally required, regardless of any congressional provision. Yet, no participant in the debate took such a view (which was, of course, to be that ultimately taken in the *Brown* case).

This does not necessarily mean that the decision in *Brown* was wrong. The Court there was interpreting the Constitution to meet society's needs in 1954 — needs that were not the same as those which existed in 1875. Only those who seek the unattainable — to make the Constitution as inflexible as the laws of the Medes and Persians — can object to constitutional construction not cast in a rigid mold. Stability and change are the twin sisters of the law. To yield slavishly only to the demands of stability would scarcely enable the Constitution to endure as a serviceable document.

The Road to Jim Crow

It has become all but constitutional cliché that the Reconstruction statutes did not succeed in securing equality in civil rights for blacks. In the first

This Thomas Nast drawing expressed the feelings of supporters of the Civil Rights Act of 1875, but the Supreme Court in 1883 ruled that the act was unconstitutional.

Harper's Weekly, APRIL 24, 1875

place, civil rights measures, notably the 1875 Civil Rights Act, were invalidated by the Supreme Court. That statute's prohibition against racial discrimination in inns, public conveyances, theaters, and other places of public amusement was ruled unconstitutional in 1883. In the *Civil Rights Cases* of that year, the Court held that the Enforcement Clause of the Fourteenth Amendment, like its substantive provisions, was limited to actions by states. Hence Congress could not (as it had sought to do in the 1875 act) effect discriminatory action that was purely private in character: "Individual invasion of individual rights is not the subject matter of the amendment," said the Court.

The decision in the *Civil Rights Cases* eventually led to a chorus of criticism, which has grown sharply in intensity in recent years. The High Court has been condemned for emasculating the broad remedial intent of the framers of the post-bellum amendments and civil rights laws. Nevertheless, contemporary observers did not consider the *Civil Rights Cases* decision as unwarranted as have its more recent critics. The legislative history of the 1875 act shows that a substantial number of legislators considered the statute unconstitutional, and for the very reason stated in the decision. More important, the Supreme Court decision in 1883 was met with widespread approval by most of the country. Two decades after Appomattox, the nation was all too willing to forgive and forget. The general consensus was expressed by as liberal a journal as the *Nation*, which declared that the country's approval of the decision showed "how completely the extravagant expectations as well as the fierce passions of the war have died out." The other civil rights laws not invalidated by the Court were either repealed by Congress or became dead letters on the statute book.

But it was not only the civil rights statutes of the period that proved helpless in achieving their aim. One of the ironies of legal history is that although the Fourteenth Amendment turned out to be an excellent shield for the excesses of expanding capital from governmental restraints, it proved of little practical help for the emancipated slaves. By the turn of the century, "equal protection" had been reduced to a mere slogan for the blacks.

The key decision for them was *Plessy* v. *Ferguson* (1896), in which the Court rejected the contention that a Louisiana statute requiring separate railroad accommodations for Negro and white passengers violated the Fourteenth Amendment. The Court refused to accept "the assumption that the enforced separation of the two races stamps the colored race with a badge of inferiority." On the contrary, racial segregation alone was held not unconstitutional.

The *Plessy* decision gave the lie to the American ideal, so eloquently stated by Justice John Marshall Harlan in his dissent: "Our Constitution is color-blind." Upon a "separate but equal" doctrine approved by the Court was built a whole structure of racial discrimination. Jim Crow replaced equal protection, and legally enforced segregation became the dominant fact in southern life.

Corporations Are "Persons"

Paradoxically, although the Fourteenth Amendment, as seen, had little im-

Justice Henry B. Brown, above, wrote the majority opinion in the Plessy v. Ferguson *case. Its "separate but equal" doctrine drew bitter dissent from Justice John M. Harlan, below.*

mediate impact on civil rights, it worked a veritable constitutional revolution in other areas. When, toward the end of the nineteenth century, the Supreme Court came over to the view that the amendment (and especially its Due Process Clause) was intended as an essential change in the organic framework, its decisions limited the change to the area of property rights. The limitation was understandable during the explosive industrial expansion, which so drastically altered the whole social and economic fabric of the nation. In such an era, it was not unnatural for the dominant emphasis to be placed on the proper relationship between government and business. To ensure such relationship, the Fourteenth Amendment was converted into a Magna Carta for business. Before this could happen, two developments were necessary: (1) the inclusion of corporations within the "persons" protected by the amendment; and (2) the judicial broadening of due process to include substantive, as well as procedural, limitations on governmental power.

Legal historians have differed on whether the framers of the Fourteenth Amendment intended to include corporations as "persons." A decade and a half after the adoption of the amendment, Roscoe Conkling, who had been a member of the congressional drafting committee, but was then in private practice, stated in argument before the Supreme Court that he and his colleagues had deliberately used "person" in order to include corporations. "At the time the Fourteenth Amendment was ratified," he averred, ". . . individuals and stock companies were appealing for congressional and administrative protection against invidious and discriminating State and local taxes." The implication was that the committee had taken cognizance of the appeals and had drafted its text to extend the constitutional protection to corporations.

Most historians reject the Conkling insinuation. From a historical point of view, it is clear that Conkling, influenced by the advocate's zeal, over-

"Our Constitution Is Color Blind"

Homer Plessy, a Louisiana resident, was one-eighth Negro. In 1892, while riding on a train out of New Orleans, he was ejected by the conductor from a car for whites and directed to a coach assigned to nonwhites. The conductor acted under a Louisiana statute that provided for separate railway carriages for whites and blacks. Plessy claimed that the statute was contrary to the Fourteenth Amendment's requirement of equal protection of the laws and took his case to court. In 1896 the U.S. Supreme Court ruled — rejecting Plessy's contention and holding that segregation alone did not violate the Constitution. Its view

was that "Laws permitting, and even requiring their separation in places where they are liable to be brought into contact do not necessarily imply the inferiority of either race to the other." If the Negro felt discriminated against, said the Court, it was "not by reason of anything found in the act, but solely because the colored race chooses to put that construction upon it."

"Our Constitution is color blind," objected the first Justice John Marshall Harlan. But he wrote in dissent; by its decision in the famed case, known as *Plessy* v. *Ferguson*, the Court's majority approved a "separate but equal"

A Nast comment on southern white supremacy
Harper's Weekly, OCTOBER 24, 1874

stated his case. Yet, even if his argument on the real intent of the draftsmen was correct, that alone would not have justified the inclusion of corporations within the word "person." After all, what was adopted was the Fourteenth Amendment and not what Roscoe Conkling or any other member of the drafting committee thought about it.

What stands out is the Fourteenth Amendment's deliberate use of the same language employed by the framers of the Fifth Amendment (". . . nor [shall any person] be deprived of life, liberty, or property, without due process of law. . . ."). Congressman Bingham, the primary draftsman of section 1 of the Fourteenth Amendment, specifically indicated that he sought to protect person and property from state power by using the phraseology of the earlier amendment. It is surely reasonable to assume that, in so doing, he intended to follow the same approach as his predecessors with regard to applicability of the new safeguard. If corporate "persons" were to be excluded from the new constitutional protections, it is difficult to see why the term "persons" was again employed.

Clearly the Supreme Court has consistently assumed that corporations come within the class of "persons" protected by the Fourteenth Amendment. In *Santa Clara County* v. *Southern Pacific Railroad* in 1886, less than two decades after the amendment had been ratified, the question of whether corporations were "persons" within its meaning was extensively briefed by counsel. At the beginning of oral argument in the case, however, Chief Justice Morrison R. Waite tersely announced: "The court does not wish to hear argument on the question whether the provision in the Fourteenth Amendment to the Constitution, which forbids a State to deny to any person within its jurisdiction the equal protection of the laws, applies to these corporations. We are all of the opinion that it does."

The Court in the *Santa Clara* case was apparently so sure of its ground that it wrote no opinion on the point. The Waite oral pronouncement settled

Roscoe Conkling of New York, who helped draft the Fourteenth Amendment, was an ambitious politician, an able orator, and a vigorous Republican leader. He left the Senate in 1881 after a long and losing fight against civil service reform.

doctrine which for more than half a century all but nullified the Constitution's Equal Protection Clause as an instrument of racial equality. "Under that doctrine," the Court explained in 1954, "equality of treatment is accorded when the races are provided substantially equal facilities, even though these facilities be separate." That view, however, was inconsistent with reality. The device of holding a group of people separate — whether by confinement of Jews to a ghetto, by exclusion of untouchables from a temple, or by segregation of blacks — is a basic tool of discrimination. "The thin disguise of 'equal' accommodations for passengers in railroad coaches," declared Justice Harlan in his 1896 dissent, "will not mislead anyone, nor atone for the wrong this day done."

Plessy v. *Ferguson* became the constitutional cornerstone of racial discrimination in the United States. On the decision was built the whole system of Jim Crow. Although, strictly speaking, the case upheld only segregated facilities in railroads, the widespread assumption was that the Supreme Court had upheld segregation as such, regardless of the field in which it was applied. "The result," declared the President's Committee on Civil Rights in 1947, "has been the familiar system of racial segregation in both public and private institutions which cuts across the daily lives of Southern citizens from the cradle to the grave."

Within the context of American history, the case has been viewed as reflecting its own time and place. Mirroring a less tolerant society, which was not dominated by the egalitarian ideal, the Supreme Court did not lift itself above the ingrained prejudices of its day. By the mid-twentieth century, when the society had changed, the Supreme Court, too, would change.

the law on the matter. As Justice William O. Douglas observed in 1949, "It has been implicit in all of our decisions since 1886 that a corporation is a 'person' within the meaning of the . . . Fourteenth Amendment." Countless cases since *Santa Clara* have proceeded on the same assumption.

The recognition of corporations as persons under the Fourteenth Amendment may be explained as a merger of legal and economic theories. When the amendment transferred the ultimate protection of person and property from the states to the nation, the judicial trend in favor of the corporation also became a national one. The role of the corporate person in post-Civil War economic development made the use of the Fourteenth Amendment to safeguard such persons well-nigh inevitable, whatever may have been the subjective goals of the framers.

Due Process and Property

If corporations had not been included by the courts within the safeguards of the Fourteenth Amendment, the latter could hardly have developed as the basic charter of the new American economy. Nor could that charter have fostered the galloping industrialism of the post-Civil War period if the due process guaranteed by the amendment had been confined to its literal import of *proper procedure*. It was the judicial importation of a substantive side into due process that made it of such significance as a restriction on governmental power.

Substantive due process received its doctrinal foundation with the publication in 1868 of Thomas M. Cooley's *Constitutional Limitations*. The

With their leader, Chief Justice Morrison R. Waite (seated center), who during his tenure from 1874 to 1888 rendered the Court's opinion in more than a thousand cases, the justices pose for a group portrait in Waite's last year on the Bench. It was a time, Roscoe Pound noted, when both the courts and the Bar were reaching a low point of effectiveness.

very title of the work indicates its author's purpose: to set forth the constitutional limitations imposed on state powers. In his preface Cooley stated that he had "endeavored to point out that there are on all sides definite limitations which circumscribe the legislative authority, aside from the specific restrictions which the people impose by their constitutions." The core of the Cooley doctrine was contained in his eleventh chapter, "Protection to Property by the 'Law of the Land.'" "Law of the land" was, of course, the term originally used in Chapter 39 of Magna Carta, from which American due process clauses are derived. As early as Edward III's time, in 1354, "law of the land" was rendered as "due process of law" and, two and a half centuries later, Coke treated the two terms as equivalent—an approach Cooley expressly followed. American constitutions continued to use the earlier phrase until Madison wrote the Due Process Clause into his draft of the Fifth Amendment. The older terminology, nevertheless, persisted and, when Cooley wrote his book, a majority of state Constitutions still retained the "law of the land" phrase. Hence the title of Cooley's chapter.

Cooley identified due process with the doctrine of vested rights drawn from natural law, which had been developed to protect property rights. This meant that due process itself was the great substantive safeguard of property; its protective umbrella now included all the constitutional limitations, express and implied, upon governmental interference with the rights of property.

What Cooley was doing was what the New York court had done twelve years earlier in *Wynehamer* v. *People,* and what Chief Justice Taney had done in the *Dred Scott* case in 1857. The widespread obloquy attached to the *Dred Scott* decision had made it impossible for any part of the Court's opinion to leave enduring roots. Cooley's great contribution was to give widespread currency to the *Wynehamer* approach and thus rescue substantive due process from the constitutional cul-de-sac in which *Dred Scott* had left it. Cooley was the first text writer to make a broad analysis of due process as a substantive limitation. The popularity of his treatise among lawyers and judges soon made Cooley the most frequently quoted authority on American constitutional law. Almost single-handed, Cooley prepared the way for the virtual takeover of American public law by the Due Process Clause of the Fourteenth Amendment and the shift in constitutional emphasis from personal to property rights that it entailed.

All the same, it should not be thought that the development of due process as a substantive restraint occurred in Supreme Court jurisprudence immediately upon the ratification of the Fourteenth Amendment. The first decisions under the amendment manifested a most restricted attitude toward its Due Process Clause. The early theme was set in 1873 in the *Slaughter-House Cases,* which adopted the limited view that the amendment was intended only to protect the Negro in his newly acquired freedom. Under that view, the Due Process Clause could not be used to strike down state restrictions on property rights. For over a decade after it was decided, *Slaughter-House* sharply confined the reach of the Fourteenth Amendment and its Due Process Clause. "When this generation of mine opened the reports," said a federal judge who came to the Bar at that time, "the chill

Toward the end of the nineteenth century big business and trusts became a political issue. This cartoon of 1888 caricatures Senator James G. Blaine as a champion of trusts, who are shown robbing the taxpayer.

Puck, AUGUST 29, 1888

of the Slaughter House decision was on the bar. . . . appeals to due process were rare, and (barring the negro cases) never successful except on the procedural side."

Freedom for Business

The law at issue in the *Slaughter-House Cases* gave one company the exclusive right to slaughter livestock in New Orleans. This law, voted amid charges of widespread bribery, put one thousand butchers out of business. But it was held constitutional despite the Fourteenth Amendment. Four justices, however, strongly disputed the Court's casual dismissal of the Due Process Clause. Foremost among them were Justices Stephen J. Field and Joseph P. Bradley, who delivered vigorous dissents urging the pertinency of due process to the challenged law. In the dissenting view, the monopoly law did violate due process: ". . . a law which prohibits a large class of citizens from adopting a lawful employment, or from following a lawful employment previously adopted, does deprive them of liberty as well as property, without due process of law."

Much of the substance of public law history in the next quarter century involved the elevation of the Field-Bradley dissents into the law of the land. The judicial development starts with cases involving railroad regulation. In the *Granger Cases* in 1877, the Court followed the strict *Slaughter-House* approach, ruling that the Due Process Clause did not subject the legislative judgment in fixing rates to judicial review: "For protection against abuses by Legislatures, the people must resort to the polls, not to the courts."

The extreme *Granger* approach, however, was abandoned during the next decade. The Court soon held that the power to regulate was not the power

Father of Gilded Age Law

Thomas M. Cooley was a leading lawyer, law professor, and judge, and the initial chairman of the first modern administrative agency, the Interstate Commerce Commission. But he made his main mark as a legal writer. His 1868 treatise, *Constitutional Limitations*, was the most influential lawbook ever published.

Cooley, the son of a farmer, was born in 1824 near Attica, New York. Like many other nineteenth-century lawyers, he was largely self-taught, his schooling consisting of irregular attendance at a rather crude upstate academy. At eighteen he began studying law with a country practitioner, and a year later moved west and resumed his studies in a law office in Adrian, Michigan. In 1846 he was

admitted to the Bar in that state. For ten years he was a typical country lawyer, working hard to build up a practice and engaging in local politics. In 1857 the state legislature chose him to compile the Michigan statutes. His work was widely praised and led to his appointment the next year as reporter for the Michigan Supreme Court. A year later, a law department was established at the University of Michigan, and Cooley was selected to be one of its three professors. He served until 1884, most of the time as dean and the only resident law professor. In 1865, meanwhile, he was elected to the Michigan Supreme Court where he sat until his defeat for re-election in 1885. He then became involved in railroad affairs as an

arbitrator in disputes and as receiver of the Wabash Railway. From the years 1887 to 1891 he served as head of the newly created Interstate Commerce Commission, and capped his career in 1893 by being elected president of the American Bar Association. He died in 1898.

Cooley was one of the greatest state judges, his contributions to American law while he was on the Michigan Supreme Court gaining him a place on Roscoe Pound's list of America's top ten judges of all time. He built up the Michigan Law School to a position of national eminence, and he was largely responsible for shaping the ICC as the model modern administrative agency. But his *Constitutional Limitations*

to confiscate; whether rates fixed were unreasonable "is eminently a question for judicial investigation, requiring due process of law." The rule laid down was that the Due Process Clause permitted the courts to review the substance of rate fixing legislation—at least to determine whether particular rates were so low as to be confiscatory.

During the same period, state courts were also further developing substantive due process. Once again, the New York courts took the lead. In the *Tenement House Cigar Case* in 1885, New York's highest court used the Due Process Clause to strike down a statute prohibiting the manufacture of cigars on floors where tenants lived in tenements housing more than three families. This law "arbitrarily deprives him of his property and of some portion of his personal liberty," the court ruled. Anticipating the language of the Supreme Court in cases such as *Allgeyer v. Louisiana* (1897) and *Lochner v. New York* (1905), the New York judges declared that the "liberty" protected by due process meant one's right to live and work where and how he will; laws that limit his choice or place of work "are infringements upon the fundamental rights of liberty, which are under constitutional protection." Other state courts followed a similar due process approach during the next few years, particularly the courts in Illinois and Pennsylvania. The state decisions had a direct influence on the Supreme Court's adoption of the substantive due process concept: "all that happened," wrote Judge Charles M. Hough in 1919, "was that the Supreme Court joined hands with most of the appellate tribunals of the older states."

The joining of hands occurred in *Allgeyer v. Louisiana*, where, according to Felix Frankfurter, "Mr. Justice Peckham wrote Mr. Justice Field's dissents into the opinions of the Court." In *Allgeyer*, for the first time, a state law was

laid the legal foundation for the Gilded Age and played a principal part in influencing post-Civil War public law. The book originated from the need for a constitutional law course at Michigan. Cooley undertook the course reluctantly, only after the other two professors had refused to give it. The text was written as a basis for his lectures, and Cooley was at first unable to find a publisher for it (the senior member of the firm to which it was first submitted later said that he would regret the mistake till his dying day).

The volume's importance was quickly apparent. It showed judges how they could use the Due Process Clause of the Constitution to review the reasonableness of laws and to

Thomas M. Cooley

AMERICAN HERITAGE

strike down as unreasonable those which interfered with business operations. Laissez faire could thus be imported into the Constitution and the support of contract and property be given the widest scope. With Cooley's book as a foundation, public law enlisted for decades in behalf of the fullest freedoms for the American businessman.

Despite his national stature, Cooley remained the epitome of the nineteenth-century country lawyer. He looked and acted like a rural justice of the peace, with a thin beard, faint voice, and shy manner. His many-sidedness, shrewdness, and passion for reading, however, helped to lift him to the heights of American law.

set aside by the Supreme Court on the ground that it infringed upon the "liberty" guaranteed by due process. The statute in question prohibited an individual from contracting with an out-of-state marine insurance company for the insurance of property within the state. Such a law, it was held, "deprives the defendants of their liberty without due process of law." The "liberty" referred to in the Due Process Clause, said Justice Rufus W. Peckham's opinion, embraces property rights, including that to pursue any lawful calling: "In the privilege of pursuing an ordinary calling or trade, and of acquiring, holding, and selling property, must be embraced the right to make all proper contracts in relation thereto." A state law that takes from its citizens the right to contract outside the state for insurance on their property deprives them of their "liberty" without due process.

Between the 1877 dictum of the *Granger Cases*, that, for protection against legislative abuses, "the people must resort to the polls, not to the courts," and *Allgeyer* v. *Louisiana* and its progeny lies the history of the emergence of modern large-scale industry, of the consequent public efforts at control of business, and of judicial review of such regulation. Thenceforth, all governmental action—whether federal or state—would have to run the gantlet of substantive due process; the substantive as well as the procedural aspect of such action would be subject to the scrutiny of the High Court: "the legislatures had not only domestic censors, but another far away in Washington, to pass on their handiwork," said Hough.

The triumph of substantive due process marked a substantial shift in

Cigar makers are seen at work in a New York tenement. An act put forth by the New York State legislature to alleviate such sweatshop conditions was struck down in 1885 by the state's highest court, which ruled that the act would deprive persons of liberty and property without due process of law.

Procedural and Substantive Due Process

The U.S. Constitution contains two clauses—in the Fifth and Fourteenth amendments—prohibiting the federal government and the states from depriving any person of life, liberty, or property without due process of law. When James Madison included the clause in the Fifth Amendment—part of the Bill of Rights—the meaning of the words "due process" was considered in its literal sense as guaranteeing only that government would follow fair and proper *procedure* in its dealings with private individuals. This became known in law as procedural due process—essentially a requirement that those who were adversely affected by particular government action had to be given fair notice, as well as proper opportunity to be heard, before the government could take action against them. Observance of procedural due process, or fair procedure, was actually as old as Magna Carta, if not older. As an English judge noted in 1723: "Even God himself did not pass sentence upon Adam, before he [Adam] was called upon to make his defence. Adam (says God) where art thou? Hast thou not eaten of the tree, whereof I commanded thee that thou shouldst not eat?"

In the years prior to the Civil War, state courts also began to interpret due process as a protection against arbitrary or unjust laws. In other words, even where the fairest procedure was followed, legislation could deprive a person of life, liberty, or property unless he were protected by limitations imposed by due process on the *substance* of that legislation. As Supreme Court Justice John Marshall Harlan defined this aspect of due process at a later time, substantive due process "includes a freedom from all substantial arbitrary impositions."

Since arbitrary action is synonymous with unreasonable action, due process requires a determination of reasonableness. Substantive due process thus allowed courts to decide

Justice Stephen J. Field, whose touchstone was the "reasonableness" of a law

on the reasonableness of challenged governmental action in relation to the ends which may be legitimately furthered by government, a procedure that permitted judges to substitute their own opinions for those of legislatures on the question of what constituted reasonable governmental acts. This, in fact, is what occurred toward the close of the nineteenth century when the Supreme Court, at the urging of Justices Stephen J. Field and Joseph P. Bradley, adopted the substantive due process approach in its decisions. Particularly after the turn of the century, in cases following that of *Lochner* v. *New York* in 1905, the Court relied on its independent judgment to determine the reasonableness of challenged statutes. In those cases, the Court came close to exercising the functions of what dissenting Justice Louis D. Brandeis called a "super-legislature," setting itself up as virtual supreme censor of the wisdom of legislation.

Under the *Lochner* approach, substantive due process became the great instrument of judicially imposed laissez faire and was employed to invalidate a host of laws, particularly those seeking to regulate economic abuses. As the twentieth century went on, the justices themselves came to see that *Lochner* went too far and that due process was not intended to make them judges of the wisdom or desirability of governmental measures. Eventually, they adopted a view urged by Justice Oliver Wendell Holmes on the proper judicial role in due process cases. The Holmes test was whether a reasonable legislator—the legislative version of the "reasonable man"—could have adopted the law at issue. The legislative judgment might well be debatable. But that was the whole point about the Holmes approach. Under it, the courts left debatable issues, as respects business, economic, and social affairs, to legislative decision.

While courts and legislatures were emphasizing the rights of business, workers had to fight for a share of the good things. Among the worst of many episodes of violence was a confrontation in 1886 in Chicago's Haymarket Square during a mass meeting called to protest an earlier slaying of striking workers by police. A bomb was thrown into the ranks of a police squad by an unknown person, and several were killed. Anarchists were blamed and four of the accused were hanged, although their connection with the crime was never proved. Above, a bilingual poster announcing the Haymarket meeting; at right, an artist's version of the explosion.

public law emphasis that mirrored the change taking place in the society at large. "The memories of the War are fading fast," lamented General Sherman in 1871 to an old comrade in arms. The glory of the war years—the sincere, if often ruthless, idealism of Reconstruction—these were replaced by purely economic concerns. The era of Gettysburg and Appomattox gave way to that of the Crédit Mobilier and the Whiskey Ring.

"I once heard a man say," affirmed Justice Holmes, "'Where Vanderbilt sits, there is the head of the table. I teach my son to be rich.' He said what many think . . . Commerce is the great power." Concern with the vindication of civil rights, which had dominated the Reconstruction era, now receded. In its place, legal stress was placed almost exclusively upon property rights —especially those possessed by corporations.

Lochner and Laissez Faire

How the Supreme Court would use substantive due process to protect corporate enterprise from governmental restraints was foreshadowed in the *Income Tax Case* in 1895. The Court there ruled invalid the federal income tax law of 1894, even though a similar statute had previously been upheld. The decision can be explained less in legal terms than in terms of the personal antipathies of the justices. In opposing the statute, Joseph H. Choate, a noted and powerful attorney, depicted the income tax as "a doctrine worthy of a Jacobin Club," the "new doctrine of this army of 60,000,000 — this triumphant and tyrannical majority—who want to punish men who are rich and confiscate their property."

Such an attack upon the income tax (though, technically speaking, it was an irrelevant one) found a receptive ear. "The present assault upon capital," declared Justice Field, "is but the beginning. It will be but the stepping-stone to others, larger and more sweeping, till our political contests will become a war of the poor against the rich; a war constantly growing in intensity and bitterness." If the Court were to sanction the income tax law, "it will mark the hour when the sure decadence of our present government will commence."

The judges who felt this way about a tax of 2 percent on annual incomes above $4,000 now had at their disposal the newly fashioned tool of substantive due process. *Lochner* v. *New York* was the classic case. The constitutionality of a state regulatory statute furnished the *Lochner* issue. According to the Court, the question to be determined in cases involving challenges to legislation on due process grounds was: "Is this a fair, reasonable and appropriate exercise of the police power of the State, or is it an unreasonable, unnecessary and arbitrary interference with the right of the individual?"

In its *Lochner* opinion, the Court indicated that the reasonableness of a challenged statute, under the Due Process Clause, must be determined as an objective fact by the judge upon his own independent judgment. In *Lochner* the state statute prescribed maximum hours for bakers. In holding the law invalid, the Court substituted its judgment for that of the legislature and decided for itself that the statute was not reasonably related to any of the social ends for which govermental power might validly be exercised. "This

Justice Rufus Peckham, a zealous defender of property rights, wrote the majority opinion in the 1905 case of Lochner v. New York.

Puck, JANUARY 23, 1887

case," asserted the dissent of Justice Holmes, "is decided upon an economic theory which a large part of the country does not entertain." The *Lochner* Court struck down the statute as unreasonable because a majority of the justices disagreed with the economic theory on which the state legislature had acted.

Judicial utilization of the *Lochner* approach to substantive due process was not mere control of state legislation in the abstract. Court control was directed to a particular purpose, namely, the invalidation of state legislation that conflicted with the doctrine of laissez faire which dominated thinking at the turn of the century. What Justice Frankfurter has termed "the shibboleths of a pre-machine age . . . were reflected in juridical assumptions that survived the facts on which they were based. . . . Basic human rights expressed by the constitutional conception of 'liberty' were equated with theories of *laissez-faire*." The result was that due process became the rallying point for judicial resistance to the efforts of the states to control the excesses and relieve the oppressions of the rising industrial economy.

"The paternal theory of government," declared Justice David J. Brewer, one of the principal architects of the post-1890 doctrine of due process, "is to me odious. The utmost possible liberty to the individual, and the fullest possible protection to him and his property, is both the limitation and duty of government." To courts that adopted the Brewer philosophy, the "liberty" protected by due process became synonymous with governmental hands-off in the field of private economic relations. "For years," noted Justice William O. Douglas in 1961, "the Court struck down social legisla-

Public outrage against trusts increased as they became stronger and more arrogant, this 1887 cartoon even picturing them as the bosses of the Senate. The Sherman Antitrust Act of 1890 was an answer to public indignation, but it was ignored until Theodore Roosevelt's administration.

tion when a particular law did not fit the notions of a majority of Justices as to legislation appropriate for a free enterprise system."

The *Lochner* case set a pattern, both as to doctrine and method, that prevailed for a generation. The pattern was not always adhered to; but it constituted the prevailing current in Supreme Court jurisprudence. In truth, had not that current been altered and, as Justice Frankfurter put it, "Had not Mr. Justice Holmes' awareness of the impermanence of legislation as against the permanence of the Constitution gradually prevailed, there might indeed have been 'hardly any limit but the sky' to the embodiment of 'our economic or moral beliefs' in that Amendment's 'prohibitions.' "

Legal Darwinism

On November 9, 1882, Delmonico's in New York City was the scene of a dinner in honor of the English social philosopher Herbert Spencer, then ending a visit to the United States. William M. Evarts, popularly known as "the Prince of the American Bar," made a speech honoring the guest. In all areas of social life, declared Evarts, "we acknowledge your labors, Mr. Spencer, as surpassing those of any of our kind. . . . The faculty of laying on a dissecting board an entire nation or an entire age and finding out all the arteries and veins and pulsations of their life is an extension beyond any that our medical schools afford."

In his *Lochner* dissent, Justice Holmes protested that "The Fourteenth Amendment does not enact Mr. Herbert Spencer's Social Statics." But the Evarts tribute was closer to the truth. Justice Peckham (himself the author of the *Lochner* opinion and hence the architect, in large part, of the due process approach of the day) once pointed out that a judge was "naturally and necessarily affected by the atmosphere of the times in which he lived." His views on the propriety of governmental interferences with private rights were bound to be "colored by the general ideas as to the proper function of government then existing." Judges whose formative years occurred when Spencer's application of Charles Darwin's theory of evolution to human society was the accepted Social Gospel found it difficult not to read the Constitution itself through Spencerean spectacles. Despite the Holmes stricture, Social Darwinism became the dominant legal philosophy. Temporary theories were translated into legal absolutes; abstract conceptions concerning Liberty and Justice were erected into constitutional dogmas. The Fourteenth Amendment was treated as a legal sanction to the Survival of the Fittest.

The theme of the society had been set in Mark Twain's *The Gilded Age* (co-authored by C. D. Warner), with its Colonel Beriah Sellers—he of the magical tongue, grandiose dreams, and flexible ethics. The Twain book stamped its title on much of the post-Civil War period.

The American of the day is described by Henry Adams: "The American thought of himself as a restless, pushing, energetic, ingenious person, always awake and trying to get ahead of his neighbors." All his energies "were oriented in one direction"—the making of money. "It is the desire to earn money," asserted a member of the Supreme Court in 1893, "which lies at the bottom of the greatest efforts of genius. . . . The motive which

Horatio Alger's The Western Boy *of 1878 was later reissued as the well-known* Tom the Bootblack. *Alger wrote many rags-to-riches books, each one bringing to American youth the Legal Darwinism philosophy of the period, that hard work and the right contacts were the recommended steppingstones to success.*

prompted Angelo to paint . . . the frescoes of the Sistine Chapel was essentially the same as that which induces a common laborer to lay brick or dig sewers." Even Herbert Spencer was shocked at the "sole interest—the interest in business" that he found in the United States of 1882.

Yet it was Spencer who furnished the philosophical foundation for the American devotion to material ends. To Americans, Spencer appeared as Saturn returned, who brought back the freedom of contract which the politicians had banished. The Golden Age was to be the reign of Justice, governed by the first principle as enunciated in Spencer's book *Social Statics*: "Every man has freedom to do all that he wills, provided he infringes not the equal freedom of any other man." The essential function of government was to administer this principle and, in doing so, it must keep hands off the economic system. "In putting a veto upon any commercial intercourse, or in putting obstacles in the way of any such intercourse, a government . . . directly reverses its function." In regulating commerce, "the State is transformed from a maintainer of rights into a violator of rights." It was, indeed, "criminal in it to deprive men, in any way, of liberty to pursue the objects they desire."

This simplistic laissez faire received what its contemporaries considered an unshakable scientific base when it was merged with Darwinism. *Social Statics* had originally been published in 1851. But it was not until Darwin provided the scientific justification in his *Origin of Species* that Spencerean sociology took over the field. The concept that species evolved by adapting to the environment was seen as applicable to social, as well as natural, life. There, too, the struggle for existence was similar to that which Darwin had shown existed among plants and animals, and progress resulted from the "survival of the fittest" (Spencer's term originally). The corollary was a strong bias against human interference with the operation of Darwin's natural laws. When Spencer proclaimed that "Progress . . . is not an accident, but a necessity," the implication—especially to his American disciples— was that tampering with the balance set by nature would only impair progressive evolution.

To the American lawyer, as one member of the profession put it in 1900, "the law in all its aspects and evolution presents so many analogies to the biological world" that "translation of it into post-Darwinian language" became appropriate. The judges who decided cases like *Lochner* v. *New York* and the *Tenement House Cigar Case* virtually elevated what Joseph H. Choate called "Darwin's great theory of the survival of the fittest" into the law of the land.

Legal Darwinism permeated the New York *Cigar Case*. The opinion stressed "the unceasing struggle for success and existence which pervades all societies of men." Through it, a man "may be deprived of that which will enable him to maintain his hold, and to survive." But the operation of the evolutionary struggle must not be interfered with by government. "Such governmental interferences disturb the normal adjustments of the social fabric, and usually derange the delicate and complicated machinery of industry and cause a score of ills while attempting the removal of one."

Justice Peckham followed a similar approach as a member of the New

In the late nineteenth century, successful business and industrial leaders were often highly celebrated. Above is the cover of a piece of sheet music of a composition honoring the steel magnate Andrew Carnegie.

143

York court before his elevation to Olympus. As he saw it in 1888, the "liberty" protected by due process "is deemed to embrace the right of man to be free in the enjoyment of the faculties with which he has been endowed by his Creator, subject only to such restraints as are necessary"—plainly a paraphrase of Spencer's first principle. That principle is violated by "legislation . . . of that kind which has been so frequent of late, a kind which is meant to protect some class in the community against the fair, free and full competition of some other class, the members of the former class thinking it impossible to hold their own against such competition, and therefore flying to the legislature."

Lochner v. *New York* reflected the same Spencerean philosophy. Noted Justice Holmes in dissent: "The liberty of the citizen to do as he likes so long as he does not interfere with the liberty of others to do the same, which has been a shibboleth for some well-known writers," was the true basis for the *Lochner* decision. Laws regulating occupations such as that of bakers, in the opinion of the Court, violated "the liberty of the individual in adopting and pursuing such calling as he may choose. . . . Statutes of the nature of that under review, limiting the hours in which grown and intelligent men may labor to earn their living, are mere meddlesome interferences with the rights of the individual."

The judges who wrote these opinions echoed the common view of the legal profession, itself a manifestation of the dominant philosophy of the day. Legal writings and addresses toward the turn of the century were replete with applications of Spencerean Darwinism. Christopher G. Tiedeman, second only to Cooley in his influence on Bench and Bar, virtually wrote Spencer's doctrines into his *Unwritten Constitution of the United States*, published in 1890. Tiedeman states the natural rights doctrine that underlies American law in Spencerean terms, as "a freedom from all legal restraint that is not needed to prevent injury to others." The law, like nature itself, must proceed on the natural selection principle: ". . . society, collectively and individually, can attain its highest development by being left free from governmental control." The notion "that government has the power to banish evil from the earth" is nothing but the revival of an "old superstition."

The prevalence of this view may be seen from the speeches made at bar meetings, particularly those of the newly organized American Bar Association. As the ABA president James M. Woolworth put it in 1897, "Under our system, the gates and avenues . . . are open to all who will run the course . . .; there is no favor for any, and the best wins." To the profession, according to Henry Adams, "Natural Selection seemed a dogma to be put in the place of the Athanasian creed; it was a form of religious hope; a promise of ultimate perfection." Spencerean doctrine was elevated to what Woolworth spoke of as "the vital and mighty fact of modern Christian civilization; the integrity of every human soul and its right to the possession, exercise and enjoyment of all its faculties, capacities and activities as to it seems good and in such full measure as is consistent with the same right of others."

The result was, Louis D. Brandeis was later to say, that the law of the day was based upon "eighteenth century conceptions of the liberty of the individual and of the sacredness of private property. Early nineteenth century scientific half-truths, like 'The survival of the fittest,' which translated into practice meant 'The devil take the hindmost,' were erected by judicial sanction into a moral law.''

Of course, Legal Darwinism had its most striking influence in public law. But its impact was far more pervasive, permeating as it did all aspects of the legal order. Laissez faire became the touchstone in all branches of the law, including those governing the relationships between private individuals. Spencerean doctrine dominated contracts, property, torts, and the other private law subjects. The fundamental principle in all these areas was "that the less the law-making power has to do with controlling [man] in his business methods, the better." Nor was this type of assertion put forth defensively. The prosperity and growth of the country appeared to demonstrate the potential in an environment free of legal controls; the frontier experience had been a veritable proving ground for Darwinist arguments. "Experience," said one lawyer at the 1895 annual meeting of the ABA, "seems to justify the reckless American confidence, which has decided that the forces which make for growth shall be absolutely free to act."

English philosopher Herbert Spencer interpreted all manner of phenomena in terms of evolution. His disciples in America welcomed his teachings as sanction for a survival-of-the-fittest philosophy in a dog-eat-dog laissez-faire world.

V

Excess of Freedom

Private Law and Institutions 1860–1910

In Charles Dickens's *Hard Times*, a striking scene takes place between the factory worker, Stephen Blackpool, and his employer. Blackpool seeks advice on how he can end his unhappy marriage and is told that there is no legal way in which the law can assist him.

> "If I do her any hurt, sir, there's a law to punish me?"
> "Of course there is."
> "If I flee from her, there's a law to punish me?"
> "Of course there is."
> "If I marry T'oother dear lass, there's a law to punish me?"
> "Of course there is. . . ."
> "Now, a'God's name," said Stephen Blackpool, "show me the law to help me!"

The epitome of the perfect corporation lawyer, Standard Oil's counsel, Samuel C. T. Dodd, was expert at finding legal loopholes to justify the actions of a trust.

Blackpool's plaint echoed the popular attitude toward the law. "From my own experience," wrote Jane Addams at the beginning of this century, "I should say, perhaps, that the one symptom among workingmen which most definitely indicates a class feeling is a growing distrust of the courts."

In large part, this could be said because of the extremes to which the law of the day carried the doctrine of freedom of contract. The judges had begun with an unpretentious assertion of the freedom to follow one's calling. By the turn of the century, according to Justice Holmes, "that innocuous generality was expanded into the dogma, Liberty of Contract."

Now contract reached its climacteric in the law. A paper delivered at the 1900 meeting of the American Bar Association proclaimed, "there is . . . complete freedom of contract; competition is now universal, and as merciless as nature and natural selection."

The expansion of contract, which had already given private law its American cast, flowered into a broadside freedom of contract that was

A 1900 attack on John D. Rockefeller as the overlord of government

IT TAKES TWO TO MAKE A CONTRACT.

HOW TO WRITE A CONTRACT.

Rule :—1. The parties to a Contract are taken in the order in which they are written and referred to as " the party of the first part," " the party of the second part," without repeating their names. It matters not which name is written first.

2. After writing the date, names of the parties and their places of residence, state fully all that the first party agrees to do, and then state all that the second party agrees to do.

3. Next state the penalties or forfeitures in case either party does not faithfully and fully perform, or offer to perform, his part of the agreement.

4. Finally, the closing clause, the signatures and seals, the signatures of witnesses are written. (A seal is simply the mark of a pen around the word " seal," written after the signature.)

One of the underpinnings of American society has been the knowledge that the law is committed to the enforcement of contracts. Even the average citizen could draw a contract if he followed simple instructions like these published in the 1890's.

considered the basic part of the liberty safeguarded by the Due Process Clause. The result was an unprecedented accent on the autonomy of private decision makers; the law was devoted to providing legal tools, procedures, and compulsions to create the framework of reasonable expectations within which economic growth could take place.

The right of free contract as a fundamental natural right first appears, in its late-nineteenth-century sense, in Herbert Spencer's *Justice*, written in 1891. Spencer stressed the unrestricted right to make promises, rather than the natural force of promises when made, as emphasized by Grotius. Justice required that each individual be at liberty to make free use of his natural powers in bargains, exchanges, and promises. Contract law was conceived of negatively, a system of hands-off while men did things. Freedom of contract became a chief article in the creed of those who sought to minimize the functions of the state; to their way of thinking, the only legitimate governmental function was to enforce obligations created by private contract. "Men in industrial societies," said James M. Woolworth in 1896, "must have intercourse and commerce by means of the contrivance of contract; the State surrenders its control over them more and more, and they outgrow legal lines until they come to the full stature of free men."

To Spencer, freedom of contract was a prime instrument of social progress. He adopted it as a means; his American disciples made it an end. Contract, they said, "gives to liberty its content and its interpretation." The right to contract was regarded, not as a phase of freedom, but as the essence of liberty, posited as permanent and absolute. Impairment was not to be suffered, except within the most rigorous limits. Conceptions were fixed; basic premises were no longer to be examined. The system became a closed circle; the slightest dent was a subtraction from its essence.

Freedom of contract became the point of fusion between public and private law. In time of crisis, it is said, everything becomes public law. The century since the Civil War has seen a virtual publicization of American law. More and more areas of private law have been infused with public law principles. The result is that public law and private law no longer form what Tocqueville characterized as two separate worlds. Freedom of contract, which dominated the public law concept of due process, virtually took over the private law of contracts as well.

"The Constitution," said Chief Justice Charles Evans Hughes in 1937, "does not speak of freedom of contract. It speaks of liberty and prohibits the deprivation of liberty without due process of law." It was, nevertheless, settled by the end of the last century that liberty of contract was included within the "liberty" guaranteed by the Constitution. "At present," wrote Judge Learned Hand in 1908, "the construction which includes within it the 'liberty' to make such contracts as one wishes has become too well settled to admit of question without overturning the fixed principles of the Supreme Court."

Freedom of contract was first declared a fundamental constitutional right by the High Bench in *Allgeyer* v. *Louisiana* in 1897, where the concept of substantive due process itself was raised to the status of accepted doctrine. In *Allgeyer* the Supreme Court stated specifically that the liberty mentioned in the Fourteenth Amendment embraced "the right of the citizen to . . . enter into all contracts which may be proper, necessary and essential."

The principle of freedom of contract thus articulated was by then dominant throughout the law. Wealth in the commercial and industrial society was largely made up of promises. In such a society, the social interest in the freedom to make promises became of the first importance. Will, rather than relation, became the controlling force; elements contributed by the parties' agreements loomed ever larger in situations where rights and duties had been almost wholly determined by relation. Contract became both a realization of the idea of liberty and a means of promoting the maximum of individual self-assertion. The basic goal was that of unshackling men and allowing them to act as freely as possible. "If there is one thing more than another which public policy requires it is that men of full age and competent understanding shall have the utmost liberty of contracting," a New Jersey court had said in 1875. The law existed to secure the right to contract freely, not merely against aggression by other individuals, but even more against invasion by society. Whatever the state might do in other areas, it might not limit contractual capacity, because this was derived from nature itself.

Today it is hard to comprehend a system grounded upon all but inexorable adherence to freedom of contract. Yet, in order to obtain a true picture of the developing law, it is necessary at least to appreciate the extent to which such freedom dominated thought and writing at the turn of the century. The noted English observer Sir Henry Maine, giving his impression of the American system just before that time, could state, "It all reposes on the sacredness of contract and the stability of private property, the first the implement, and the last the reward, of success in the universal competition."

Maine himself had all but crowned the position of freedom of contract in the post-Civil War society by his celebrated generalization of the progress from status to contract. In as famous an epigram as appears in legal literature, Maine summarized the course of legal progress: "we may say that the movement of the progressive societies has hitherto been a movement *from Status to Contract.*" In other words, legal progress goes from institutions where rights, duties, and liabilities flow from a condition in which the individual finds himself without reference to his will to those where they flow from exertion of the individual will. Looked at this way, the movement stated by Maine is one from subjection to freedom — and the instrument of freedom is the right of contract.

This theory of the course of legal development fitted in so well with the dominant Spencerean philosophy that it soon gained possession of the field. "Contracts," said the Supreme Court in 1878, "mark the progress of communities in civilization and prosperity." Maine's generalization was almost universally accepted in this country. "American civilization," Brooks Adams asserted, "is based upon the theory of freedom of contract." It was taken for gospel that law was moving and must move in the direction of individual self-determination by free contract. "The juridical history of every people," declared the American Bar Association president-elect in 1896, "which has passed from a rude state to an enlightened one begins with laws referable to status, and ends with laws explained by contract." Any limitation on abstract freedom of contract was a step backward and hence arbitrary and unreasonable. To judges imbued with a genuine faith in the progress from status to contract, the strongest presumption existed against any and all restrictions on the freest possible bargaining. Since social progress itself was intimately connected with the extension of contractual liberty, the Maine dictum could be violated only at the peril of social retrogression. Due process itself was violated by legislative attempts to restore status and restrict the contractual powers of free men by enacting that men of full age and sound mind in particular callings should not be able to make agreements which other men might make freely.

Labor and the Law

As the law stood at the end of the last century, the American workingman might well have echoed Stephen Blackpool's plea to be shown how the law could help him. Labor's legal grievances at the time were numerous and real. The law took little account of the inequality of bargaining power that had come to exist between capital and labor. Traditional jealousy of organizations stood in the way of effective employment of collective action through

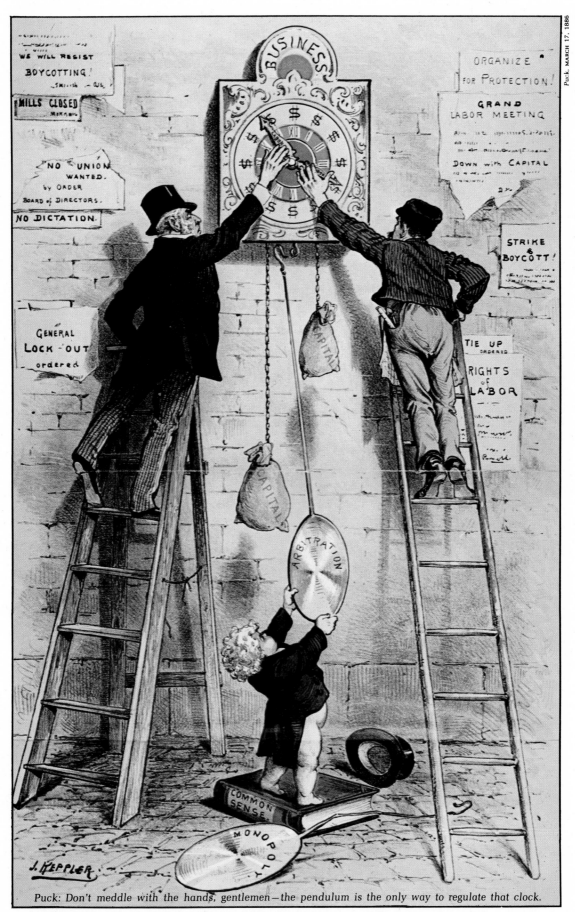

Puck, MARCH 17, 1886

Puck: *Don't meddle with the hands, gentlemen—the pendulum is the only way to regulate that clock.*

An 1886 cartoon suggests that arbitration was the best way to settle a management-labor dispute.

The first eight-hour day came early — in 1868 — but affected only federal employees. This poster was printed by the Mechanics' State Council of California to celebrate the event.

LIBRARY OF CONGRESS

unions. Enormously increased danger to life and limb in industrial employment was inadequately secured against by the common law, as administered by courts hampered by the traditional law of master and servant. The legal situation put the worker in an intolerable condition.

Reaction was inevitable. The abuses inherent in the post-Civil War galloping industrialism led to legislative attempts to protect the worker by laying down minimum standards governing the conditions of employment. Such laws could not, however, successfully run the freedom-of-contract gantlet, for, in the words of the president of the ABA in 1890, they "illustrate the exercise of the 'police power,' so strongly denounced by the . . . disciples of Herbert Spencer and the *laissez-faire* school." As Judge Learned Hand pointed out, they could not be squared with the theory of freedom of contract, "for they indubitably 'deprived' the worker of his 'liberty' to work under such conditions as he saw fit. The only process of law accorded him was the fiat of the legislature which forbade him and his employer to contract as they pleased."

In a 1909 article, Roscoe Pound summarized the decisions employing freedom of contract to strike down legislative intervention in the relations between employer and employee. Legislation thus invalidated included: laws forbidding employers from interfering with union membership; laws prohibiting imposition of fines upon employees; laws providing for the mode of weighing coal in fixing miners' compensation; laws requiring payment of wages in money; laws regulating hours of labor; and laws prohibiting contracts by railway employees releasing their employers in advance from liability for personal injuries.

The Pound list conformed closely to Herbert Spencer's enumeration in his work *New Toryism* of legislation found objectionable because it "tended continually to narrow the liberties of individuals." The American judges agreed with Spencer that "the real issue" posed by such laws "is whether the lives of citizens are more interfered with than they were." In the Spencerean calculus, "the liberty which a citizen enjoys is to be measured . . . by the relative paucity of the restraints [government] imposes on him." Laws that "increase such restraints beyond those which are needful . . . for maintaining the liberties of his fellows against his invasions of them" must inevitably fail the test.

The decisions that so strictly employed the freedom of contract doctrine to strike down laws regulating the relations between employer and employee seem incomprehensible today. In an age of pervasive regulation designed to ensure minimum standards and fair dealing for workers, cases that upheld the right to contract above all else appear mere aberrations. The basic question, affirmed the Supreme Court in 1905, was that "of which of two powers or rights shall prevail—the power of the State to legislate or the right of the individual to liberty of person and freedom of contract." A society controlled by regulation from cradle to grave may look back with nostalgia, but scarcely with understanding, upon an era that opted in favor of freedom of contract.

True, the same judges who applied freedom of contract to invalidate laws regulating labor conditions acknowledged situations where contractual liberty might properly be restricted. Thus, the courts recognized that usury laws might be enacted, even though they contravened the theoretical freedom to contract of those affected. Usury laws were reconciled with freedom of contract, said an Illinois court decision in 1892, "upon the theory that the lender and the borrower of money do not occupy towards each other the same relations of equality that parties do in contracting with each other in regard to the loan or sale of other kinds of property, and that the borrower's necessities deprive him of freedom in contracting, and place him at the mercy of the lender."

In other words, freedom of contract depended upon the position of basic equality that existed between the parties to ordinary private contracts. "Free contract," asserted the economist Richard T. Ely in 1914, "presupposes equals behind the contract in order that it may produce equality." Equality makes it proper to give full effect to agreements arrived at through the free will of the parties. When the condition of the parties is not equality, it cannot truly be said that an agreement between them is the result of a free meeting

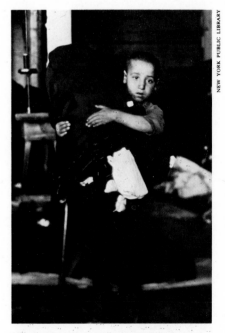

Though there was nationwide concern over child labor by the turn of the century, court protection of the right of contract hindered legislative redress. This boy leaving a New York garment factory with a bundle of homework was photographed in 1920; effective federal regulation of child labor came only in 1938, with the Fair Labor Standards Act.

Women workers, often laboring long hours for low pay, were among the unprotected victims of the legal philosophy of freedom of contract. In 1908 the Supreme Court finally upheld for the first time a law limiting hours for women workers. This scene is of an Oregon salmon cannery.

of the minds. The mind of the inferior may be overborne as much as if actual duress had been used. To restore the balance, society may intervene.

Yet, if the judges at the turn of the century could concede this protection, why did they fail to recognize the legitimate interest of society in protecting the worker? The answer that would have been given was that the community had no legitimate interest in the regulation of labor, because the condition of inequality between the parties which justified infringement of freedom of contract did not exist. Declared the Supreme Court in 1908: "The right of a person to sell his labor upon such terms as he deems proper is, in its essence, the same as the right of the purchaser of labor to prescribe the conditions upon which he will accept such labor from the person offering to sell it. So the right of the employé to quit the service of the employer, for whatever reason, is the same as the right of the employer, for whatever reason, to dispense with the services of such employé. . . . In all such particulars the employer and the employé have equality of right, and any legislation that disturbs that equality is an arbitrary interference with the liberty of contract."

Assuming equality between employer and employee, the conclusion with regard to legislative interference with that equality follows without too much difficulty. "As between persons sui juris," asked an 1899 opinion, "what right has the legislature to assume that one class has the need of protection against another?" To the courts of the time, laws regulating the conditions of employment were portrayed as putting laborers under guardianship, as making them wards of the state, as stamping them as imbeciles, and as "an insulting attempt to put the laborer under a legislative tutelage . . . degrading to his manhood."

These characterizations now seem quaintly ludicrous, for the theory upon

Pennsylvania coal mine "breaker boys," about 1900. The law of the times gave these children almost no protection.

which they were based was wholly out of line with reality. The Supreme Court in 1909 could be described as dealing with the relation between employer and employee in railway transportation, as if the parties were individual farmers haggling over the sale of a horse. Such an approach was rendered obsolete by the modern industrial society. The helplessness of the individual employee, unaided by government or collective action with his fellows, has been a dominant fact since the Industrial Revolution.

"Men are not free while financially dependent," said Justice Brandeis. Such dependence, in the words of a writer in the *Harvard Law Review* in 1915, made "freedom of contract . . . a misnomer as applied to a contract between an employer and an ordinary individual employee." As an English judge had stated almost two centuries before, "necessitous men are not, truly speaking, free men, but, to answer a present exigency, will submit to any terms that the crafty may impose upon them." This remark is particularly relevant in considering the industrial employee's position: he is compelled to bargain, alone and unaided, for whatever terms of employment he can secure. "There is grim irony," declared Justice Harlan Fiske Stone in 1936, "in speaking of the freedom of contract of those who, because of their economic necessities, give their services for less than is needful to keep body and soul together."

Liability and Privacy

The law of torts continued to emphasize the individualist thrust noted in Chapter III. With the stress on the social desirability of free individual action and decision, the rule that liability should rest on a showing of fault

An artist's concept — about the turn of the century — of a mining accident. At that period the mine operator would have had little legal responsibility for safety in the mine prior to the accident, and almost none for any injuries or deaths of the miners.

Leslie's Illustrated Weekly

completed its conquest of tort law. The business of the law of torts is to fix the dividing line between those cases in which there is liability for harm done and those in which there is not. At the turn of the century, the line was fixed almost entirely by the notion of blameworthiness. Unless there was fault, Justice Holmes had pointed out in 1881, "it is no more justifiable to make me indemnify my neighbor . . . than to make me do the same thing if I had fallen upon him in a fit, or to compel me to insure him against lightning."

By 1900 the rule that liability was a corollary of fault had virtually been converted from a rule of common law to one of natural law. So strong had the feeling in favor of "no liability without culpability" become that argument could be made in the Supreme Court "for the general proposition that immunity from liability when not in fault is a right inherent in free government." As late as 1919, four justices could vote to strike down a workmen's compensation law that abolished the need to prove negligence as a prerequisite to recovery. This led to the following animadversion by Sir Frederick Pollock, an eminent British author of legal texts: "It is amazing to my English mind that four judges of your Court should be found to assert a constitutional right not to be held liable *in a civil action* without actual fault."

A law that considered the rule of no liability without fault a legal absolute bore most heavily on the industrial worker; the cost of the pain and mutilation incident to production was borne by him rather than by the enterprise that employed him. Not only did the worker injured on the job have to prove negligence on the part of his employer, he also had to overcome the fellow-servant rule and the doctrine of assumption of risk. "In virtue of the contract of service the servant presumptively assumes the ordinary risks of the service," noted Melville M. Bigelow's *The Law of Torts* at the turn of the century. In addition, "the servant is deemed to have assumed the extraordinary as well as the ordinary risks of negligence on the part of his fellow-servants."

The combined requirement that the injured worker prove negligence on the part of the employer, no negligence on the part of any fellow employee, and that the injury was not due to a voluntarily assumed risk made the worker's right to recover in industrial accident cases more a matter of theory than practice. Yet the law fitted in precisely with the ethic of the day. The employee was a free man; he chose to work in an employment where he ran the risk of being injured. The employee must stand or fall by the consequences of his own conduct.

The judges who rigorously applied the common law of torts in the face of rampant industrialization could scarcely be expected to be receptive to new tort doctrines that modified the individualist emphasis of the common law. Absolute liability had been given a new field by a House of Lords decision in the case of *Rylands* v. *Fletcher* in England in 1868. But American judges were most reluctant to accept the English imposition of absolute liability upon the landowner who brought on his land anything likely to do mischief if it escaped. (For example, water running wild, a machine damaging neighboring property, and so forth.) By the turn of the century, *Rylands* v. *Fletcher* was followed in only a handful of American courts; it had been rejected by most American judges, including the outstanding state judge of

No provision was made for the medical care or pensioning of workers who were maimed on the job, like this man who was crippled while employed in a steel plant near Pittsburgh.

his day, Chief Justice Charles Doe of New Hampshire. A leading tort text headed its discussion: "Rylands v. Fletcher Not Generally Approved in America." Yet, even then, a farsighted observer could predict a "tendency . . . towards the English doctrine—making the keeper of certain things naturally dangerous a virtual insurer." But that was to come later, as judges saw the need to restrain the use of land in the interest of the general security in a crowded country. It was received reluctantly while pioneer ideas, appropriate to a less crowded agricultural country, still lingered.

The judges' restrictive attitude toward new tort doctrines may also be seen from their initial reception of the newly advocated right of privacy. The starting point of the law on that matter was an 1890 article, *"The Right to Privacy,"* by Samuel D. Warren and Louis D. Brandeis. The article, appearing in the *Harvard Law Review*, virtually added a chapter to the law—one in which the individual gained a legally enforceable right in his privacy, a right to be vindicated by the private law of torts. The law of the day, oriented as it was toward the protection of tangible property rights, was not, however, ready to recognize the new personal right. It was put to a judicial test and found wanting by the highest court of New York in 1902.

In the New York case, the defendant, the Rochester Folding Box Company, had used a photograph of the plaintiff without her consent to advertise its brand of flour, along with the legend "The Flour of the Family." The feebleness of the pun alone might have been enough to predispose the court in favor of recovery. But the New York court held otherwise and, rejecting

Three Mile Point on Otsego Lake in New York (below) was inherited by author James Fenimore Cooper, and though it had long been a picnic place, he closed it to the public in 1837 because of vandalism. The villagers ignored his prohibition, something that would later become unthinkable as the enforcement of property laws became stricter.

the Warren-Brandeis approach, ruled flatly that the right of privacy did not exist as a legally protected right.

Even in 1902, the holding that no legal protection existed against the unauthorized use of one's photograph in an advertisement went too far for the community. "There was a natural and widespread feeling," New York's highest court later pointed out, "that such use . . . in the absence of consent was indefensible in morals and ought to be prevented by law." The very next session of the New York legislature enacted a law giving statutory protection to the right of privacy.

Heyday of Property Rights

Early in this century the rights of property, like those of contract, reached their apogee. It was then that an article could be written on the relationship between property and sovereignty, showing that "our property laws do confer sovereign power" on those who control property. Of course, the comparison with the sovereign power of the state was hyperbolic, intended to serve the purpose of a leading social critic. Property has always rested upon governmental power; property unprotected by the state remains only an academic norm. In the America of the early 1900's, the role of the law vis-à-vis private property was largely to secure it from encroachment by others. Within the legal principles of what Kant, in *The Science of Right*, called the conception of external mine and thine, the owner had virtually uncontrolled dominion over the use and disposition of property.

The American courts of the day spoke of property in terms of "that sole and despotic dominion" of which Blackstone had written. A leading writer stated that, though the Blackstone definition tended "to exaggerate somewhat . . . undoubtedly it is correct in the main." The same approach was taken by the judges; the Blackstone definition, said one court, "states the essential characteristic of property." The very word property meant the unrestricted right of possessing, enjoying, and disposing of a thing.

To the law of the period, property, like contract, depended upon a theory of will. "Property, then, is the realization of the free will of a person, the external sphere of his freedom," a prominent text had stated in 1889. As such, the will of the property owner had to be given its fullest expression, both as an aspect of liberty and as a means of promoting social progress. "The infraction of my personal freedom," the same text had added, "is precisely the same if a limitation is put upon my power to alienate property as if I were prevented from acquiring, or from holding or using it. The limitation would in either case . . . destroy my liberty."

The law of the day recognized and dealt with property exclusively through the will of the owner. His right to acquire, use, and dispose of property was protected as never before, or since, in American law, for the all-inclusiveness of property rights was considered an essential aspect of the free society. "Liberty means the power of a man to make the most and the best of himself . . .," said another text. "Private property is realised liberty." Property became a corollary of liberty; law itself was unthinkable without it. From this point of view, the fundamental object of the law, according to Joseph H. Choate, became "preservation of the rights of private property."

The Frontier—Where the Law Was Less "Tight"

I have come, old man, into these districts, because I found the law sitting too tight upon me," one of the characters in James Fenimore Cooper's *The Prairie* says. As a person moved westward in nineteenth-century America, the law, like the society itself, grew less "tight." Legal rules and institutions became more crude, adapted to conditions in the frontier community. "The judges ...," Governor Thomas Ford wrote of the early days in his state of Illinois, "held their courts mostly in log-houses, or in the barrooms of taverns, fitted up with a temporary bench for the judge, and chairs or benches for the lawyers and jurors." The first courthouse in Springfield, destined to become the Illinois capital, was a single-room log cabin that cost $42.50 to construct. In other frontier regions, the situation was even more primitive. As late as 1841, the court in Springfield, Missouri, convened under a tree. A Tennessee judge, after failing to hold court, explained that his "courthouse," which served as a pigpen during vacations, was infested with vermin and was hence unusable.

Within the courtrooms, the procedure, compared to the standards and decorum of courts in places like Boston, was often ludicrous. In an Illinois court presided over by Judge John Reynolds, the sheriff's opening cry was, "Boys, come in, our John is going to hold court!" The frontier ideal was one of popular, individualized justice; it was intolerant of legal refinements and hair-splitting lawyers who drew fine distinctions. When one Indiana lawyer referred several times to "the great English common law," his opponent scored heavily with the jury by declaiming, "If we are to be guided by English law, we want their best law, not their common law. We want as good a law as Queen Victoria herself makes use of."

In many parts of the West, even the crude law of the frontier was tenuous and the system of justice inadequate.

(Continued on page 163)

Tompkins H. Matteson's painting, "Justice's Court in the Backwoods," depicts a rural lawyer

pleading his case, with a cobbler's shop, probably in upstate New York, as the informal courtroom.

Where the Law Was Less "Tight"

Justice on the frontier was often summary, without benefit of judge or jury. At left, a Wyoming "bad man," hanged in Laramie by vigilantes. The medallion above and the certificate below signified membership in the San Francisco Vigilance Committee of 1856.

(Continued from page 160)

Outlaws often intimidated, by bullying and boldness, an entire legal structure and paralyzed law enforcement. The answer was a widespread tradition of vigilantism. To the frontiersman, reliance on the rifle and bowie knife rather than the law was a natural reaction, and the vigilante movement often seemed the most logical way to deal with lawlessness. In *The American Commonwealth*, James Bryce noted that "Many crimes would go unpunished if some more speedy and efficient method of dealing with them were not adopted....the people have concluded that it is cheaper and simpler to take the law into their own hands." Or, as a Denver vigilante of the 1860's reminisced, "When they were proved guilty, they were always hanged. . . . there were no appeals in those days; no writs of errors; no attorneys' fees; no pardon in six months. Punishment was swift, sure and certain." Indiana vigilantes marched to an execution under the banner, "No expense to the country."

Altogether, more than five hundred vigilante movements might have flourished during the course of America's westward expansion. Few states west of the Appalachians did not experience them at one time or another, and often they were supported by prominent citizens. Andrew Jackson, while President, advised Iowa settlers to deal with a murderer by vigilante action, and Theodore Roosevelt, as a cattle rancher in North Dakota, tried to join a vigilante movement but was turned down. In 1915, T.R. wrote about the Far West: "Before there was law in California and Montana, and indeed as a requisite for bringing the law there, the Vigilantes had to . . . hang people. Technically this was murder; practically it was the removal of murderers." Even the U.S. Supreme Court once implied that vigilantism might be justified on the frontier, noting in an 1882 decision that "excuse . . . may exist for the execution of lynch-law in savage or sparsely-settled districts, in order to oppose the ruffian elements which the ordinary administration of law is powerless to control." The Court was doing little more than reflecting what was accepted on the frontier, where the elite, or leading, citizens of a community, far from scorning the vigilante groups, usually headed them. In 1890, for example, four ex-vigilantes were members of the U.S. Senate.

In a sense, vigilantism resulted from the doctrine of popular sovereignty carried to its extreme. "The right of the people to take care of themselves, if the law does not," asserted the Johnson County, Missouri, vigilantes in 1867, "is an indisputable right." The rule of the people was thus declared superior to all else—including the law. The idea was expressed in a jingle pinned to the body of a man hanged by vigilantes in Casper, Wyoming, in 1902:

Process of law is a little slow
So this is the road you'll have to go.
Murderers and thieves, Beware!
PEOPLE'S VERDICT.

UNIVERSITY OF OKLAHOMA LIBRARY

The 1889 Oklahoma land rush came at noon; here, only hours later, a frontier lawyer is ready to take care of clients.

"By private property," one of the texts further explained, "we mean the exclusive right of a private person to control an economic good." The law stressed the rights of the property owner to the exclusion of virtually everything else. Here, too, Legal Darwinism had its effect. Inequalities were assumed to be due, as Roscoe Pound stated, to "greater strength, greater ingenuity, or greater application." Interference with one's consuming the fruits of his greater strength, ingenuity, or application would defeat the progressive evolution of the social order. A complete *jus utendi* and *jus disponendi* (right to use and to dispose) were necessary elements in the concept of property.

Various aspects of the law of property illustrated the extent to which the will theory had come to dominate. In the field of trusts, the courts increasingly emphasized the idea that the will of the settlor (the person who established the trust) should be controlling in all matters relating to the trust. The spendthrift trust (placing the interest of the beneficiary beyond the reach of his creditors) was upheld on the theory that, even here, the intention of the settlor was to be carried out. The same stress on the will of the owner could be seen in the laws passed in a majority of states abolishing the Rule in Shelley's Case (a technical rule derived from feudal law which limited the right to convey of many landowners). As a paper delivered at the 1900 American Bar Association meeting put it, "Ownership and responsibility are now individual, there is complete power to alienate property and almost complete freedom to mold the incidents of property."

A 1914 treatise referred to a Roman law definition of property: *Dominium est jus utendi et abutendi re* ("Property is the right to use and consume a thing"). "Some have said that it means that the right of property carries with it the right to use or to abuse a thing, and so it has been actually claimed that . . . the right of property carries with it the right to make a bad use of things." But the claim rested on more than poor translation. Jurists have for years debated the validity of the so-called abuse of rights doctrine, under which the law may intervene where property is used for the purpose of injuring another. The classic case in American law was that of the "spite fence" built by a landowner near his boundary, not for any advantage of his own, but solely to cut off his neighbor's light or obstruct his view.

American judges generally denied relief in the spite-fence cases, holding, in Justice Holmes's words, that "a man has a right to build a fence on his own land as high as he pleases, however much it may obstruct his neighbor's light and air." Nor was the right to use one's land as he chooses affected by malicious motive. "The doctrine of personal liberty and personal dominium of one over his property enables him to do things to the annoyance of others . . . for which there is no punishment, except loss of that respect which every right-thinking man desires from his neighbors," said a Wisconsin case in 1900. To most courts at the time, even "the right to use one's property for the sole purpose of injuring others . . . is . . . a more or less necessary incident of rights which are established for very different ends." The fact that Justice Holmes could refer to the "*quasi* accidental character of the defendant's right to put up a fence for malevolent purposes" did not change the existence of the right under American common law.

"Laying the Fences," an illustration of the 1880's. So important did the courts consider the right of a person to the free use of his property that they hesitated even to enjoin a landowner from erecting a "spite" fence that would injure a neighbor.

But even during the heyday of property rights in the law, the Supreme Court pointed out that the notion that they "are exempt from legislative modification required from time to time in civilized life is contradicted . . . by the doctrine of eminent domain." Eminent domain cut directly into the idea of property; under that doctrine, the conflict between the interest of the property owner and that of the community is resolved in favor of the latter. "It runs highways and railroads through old family places in spite of the owner's protest sacrificing his will and his welfare to that of the rest," said Justice Holmes.

Yet the eminent domain power, too, fell under the influence of the law's expansive attitude toward private property. "What we have reason to complain of," wrote a rare contemporary critic, "is an undue restriction of the right of eminent domain . . .; this restriction is due to a too narrow interpretation of public purpose, an interpretation which in turn is due to an excess of individualism in the law." The restriction referred to resulted from the rule laid down in *Loan Association* v. *Topeka* in 1875, that a tax was not lawful if "not laid for a *public* purpose," and that use of a city's taxing power to make a grant to a company so that it would locate its factory in the city was not a valid public purpose. The eminent domain power is also limited by the public-purpose requirement, and the courts treated the two powers (taxation and eminent domain) interchangeably so far as the requirement was concerned. Hence, eminent domain was subject to the *Loan Association* limitation. The cases held that condemnation power might not be employed to aid private enterprises, as by the acquisition of land for the site of a private factory or warehouse, even though it meant enlargement of the industrial activity upon which the community's economic life depended. (The one exception was the use of eminent domain to help railroads and public utilities. Since they served public purposes, takings to aid them were not deemed private.)

Nor, under the restricted view of public power that prevailed, could eminent domain or the police power be employed to accomplish aesthetic objectives. "Aesthetic considerations," declared a leading 1905 case, "are a matter of luxury and indulgence rather than of necessity, and it is necessity alone which justifies the exercise of the police power." The critic already quoted could refer to European uses of governmental authority to make cities "beautiful and attractive in the interest of rich and poor" and plaintively ask, "Why should we struggle so long to secure the recognition of beauty as a public concern?" But the law had been summed up in an 1897 article by Sir Frederick Pollock which categorically denied that Anglo-American law took cognizance of aesthetic considerations: "Robust good sense is the merit of our common law, but the fine taste—the aesthetic sensibility which is the birthright of the Frenchman, as it was of the Greek, is denied to the Anglo-Saxon." In support of this assertion, he quoted Thomas Hood's famous lines: "Nature which gave them the goût/Only gave us the gout."

Corporations and Trusts

The last quarter of the nineteenth century saw a phenomenal flowering of the corporate person. "No other country," asserted a paper read to the 1895

American Bar Association meeting, "knows such unchecked corporate powers." To many observers, it was the era of the corporation. In 1878 only 520 of the 10,000 or so manufacturing concerns in Massachusetts were corporations; two-thirds of the state's manufactures were still produced by nonincorporated firms. Before the end of the century the picture had changed completely. A tremendous expansion occurred in the use of the corporate form—so great, indeed, that Edward Bellamy's *Looking Backward* gave the corporation a vital role in his preview of the twentieth-century economy. Justice Brewer was correct when he stated, in 1892, "*Looking Backward* is nearer than a dream."

Not only the increase in the number of corporations was significant. More important was a virtual transformation in the nature of the corporation, caused primarily by a marked growth in the individual corporation's size. The business corporation at the turn of the century bore witness to the validity of Engel's law asserting the passage of quantity into quality. In the corporation of the day, the change of quantity *was* simultaneously a change of quality. The incorporated corner grocery store and the Standard Oil Company could be considered similar business entities only by an act of faith that ignored the extent to which economic reality had diverged from legal form.

The large corporation first developed to meet the needs of the railroads, "the nation's first big business," in the view of many business historians.

The Very Model of a Wall Street Law Firm: "Up-or-Out"

Of all the law firms that became institutionalized—particularly in the early part of the twentieth century—to serve the legal needs of American business and finance, none has been better known than "the Cravath firm" of Wall Street. Cravath, Swaine & Moore, its formal name, goes back to 1819 through various associations of lawyers in practice together. But the modern firm began in 1906, when Paul D. Cravath became head of what was then known as Cravath, Henderson, and de Gersdorff. According to Robert T. Swaine, Cravath's successor, "Cravath had a definite philosophy about the organization of his law firm, its partners, its practice and its relation to its associates." His ideas resulted in what has ever since been considered the model for the organization and operation of a large Wall Street law firm.

Cravath's first principle was that of strong leadership. He believed, said Swaine, "that a law firm, like any

other successful organization, must have strong executive direction, and until the mid-1930's his firm was under a dictatorship in his person." Secondly, he established the policies—since followed by every major law firm—of recruitment of lawyers just out of law school and of promotion through the ranks. A staff trained within the firm, he held, would be better adapted to its work than one recruited from among older lawyers who might have acquired habits inconsistent with the Cravath method. Cravath inaugurated the process of drawing from the top level of eastern Ivy League law school graduates for what were then called "law clerks." He paid these lawyers a salary (itself an innovation at the time) and expected them to devote their entire careers to the firm.

Swaine described the Cravath method in which all new men were indoctrinated: "At the outset of their practice, Cravath men are not thrown

into deep water and told to swim; rather, they are taken into shallow water and carefully taught strokes." They were not allowed to specialize until they attained a general experience over several years, he explained. Their responsibilities increased as their growing competency permitted.

Related to this policy was what Cravath called "the office policy of filling advanced positions from the ranks of the young men who enter the office as beginners." In refusing to allow a former associate to return to the firm, Cravath declared, "If our office has been successful, it is very largely because of our adherence to this plan, which has enabled young men to feel that if they remain with us during the years of preparation, they will have the first chance when opportunities for responsible positions from time to time develop."

A corollary principle was that of discarding lawyers who did not merit

"The power of the railway system" was what Henry Adams termed the "one active interest, to which all others were subservient, and which absorbed the energies of some sixty million people to the exclusion of every other force." Even before the Civil War, ten railroads had been capitalized at $10 million or more apiece; by 1883, over forty fell into this class, with eight possessing assets of above $135 million each. "As [a] spur and stimulus . . . ," said one commentator in 1893, "the railroads have done for this century that which the discovery of America did for the sixteenth century."

The railroads were soon rivaled in size by industrial corporations. Before the 1890's, only three nonrailroad companies (and one of them was a railroad construction company) were chartered in New Jersey with a capital stock of more than $20 million. In the single year 1899, 47 were chartered. By 1902, 101 had been chartered in the state, ranging upward in size to the Northern Securities Co., capitalized at $400 million. The first billion-dollar corporation came into existence when United States Steel, capitalized at $1.4 billion, was formed in 1901.

More than size characterized the new corporations. Their very names stir memories of corporate combines that dominated the economic life of the day. A financial journal reported, when some of the New Jersey companies were chartered at the turn of the century, that one would "control 95 percent of the bicycle-making industry in this country," another "controls about 85 percent of the total upper-leather output of the country," while a third

Paul D. Cravath

promotion. "Every lawyer who enters the Cravath office," said Swaine, "has a right to aspire to find his life career there—but only by attaining partnership." In the words of Paul Hoffman, author of *Lions in the Street*, "It was 'up-or-out.' If a clerk—later called an associate—couldn't navigate the deeper channels, he was sent elsewhere."

Cravath also demanded complete devotion to the firm. "Probably the most rigid feature of the 'Cravath system,'" Swaine noted, "has been insistence that for every man in the office . . . the practice of law must be the primary interest and that that practice shall be solely as a member of the Cravath team."

The Cravath system became the pattern for large American law firms. As their size grew, they copied the Cravath model, particularly its methods of recruitment and promotion, which have since become standard throughout the country. The Cravath firm itself—which has listed many of the most prestigious companies in the United States among its clients, and which by 1973 comprised 179 lawyers (48 partners and 131 associates) —has continued to follow the tradition set by the founding partner. That tradition, observed Francis T. P. Plimpton, a former president of the Association of the Bar of the City of New York, "was very strong. Swaine kept it up. Swaine couldn't have been nicer if you got him away from Wall Street, but in the office he was the apotheosis of the tough corporate lawyer."

The same was said of Swaine's successor, Hoyt Moore—the third member in the firm's name. Once, a colleague is said to have told him that the firm should hire more associates because the staff was overworked. "That's silly," Moore is reported to have replied. "No one is under pressure. There wasn't a light on when I left at two o'clock this morning."

1900: "The Cleansing of New York"

Symbolizing the Law

By the turn of the century, American cartoonists were personifying the law and its attributes with human, easy-to-grasp symbols. These examples from the popular weekly magazine Puck used "the long arm of the law" to make a point against yellow journalism, above, and the female figure of justice, as well as that of a robed Chief Justice, opposite, to editorialize on contemporary national issues.

Puck, July 22, 1903

1903: Mob violence threatens law and order.

Puck, April 5, 1893

1893: Justice is blind to maudlin sentiment.

Puck, June 12, 1901

1901: "Young America's Dilemma, 'Shall I be wise and Great, or Rich and Powerful?'"

brings "under control all the leading ice companies of the country." The corporate device that had been nurtured by the fostering law of the formative era had mutated into giant trusts and monopolies.

An influential text, published in 1898, asserted that corporation law was "somewhat behind the practice of the business community" and that the courts must "continually change the law by endeavoring to keep it abreast of the people's life." In particular, the author felt that corporate personality no longer served its purpose as the central concept in corporation law. As he put it, "the rule of fiction that a corporation is a legal person . . . is dead as a principle"; it was "no longer . . . in logical connection with the great mass of legal rules which have been called forth by controversies relating to railroad and other business corporations."

Nevertheless, it is erroneous to assume that the law of the day lagged behind the needs of business life. On the contrary. From the point of view of corporate enterprise, the law toward the end of the nineteenth century was going through a particularly creative period. Legal "invention was most fertile in relation to business. . . ," wrote the legal historian J. Willard Hurst. "Lawyers contrived or adapted institutions (the corporation), tools (the . . . trust certificate), and patterns of action (the reorganization of corporate financial structure)." If anything, the law was too inventive in the service of economic enterprise, at the same time unduly neglecting the social interest in the control of corporate abuses. "Up to the present time," asserted Louis D. Brandeis in 1905, "the legal ability of a high order which

This Puck cartoon, from an 1890 issue, was titled, "And he asks for More." It was an attack on the monopolies of the period and on their insatiable appetite for profits.

Puck, MAY 7, 1890

The Seneca Oil Company of Connecticut, whose stock certificate is reproduced here, was organized in 1858 in a move of complete legality but of dubious morality. It deprived two oil pioneers of their holdings.

has been expended on [public interest] questions has been almost wholly in opposition to the contentions of the people."

The legal inventiveness in favor of corporate enterprise was seen in the adaptation of the law of trusts and the creation of the holding company. The trust was a legal device created by Samuel C. T. Dodd to enable John D. Rockefeller to establish and consolidate his petroleum empire, which controlled over 90 percent of the country's petroleum capacity. The stock of the forty corporations held by the Standard Oil group was assigned to nine trustees, headed by Rockefeller. In place of the stock the former owners received "trust certificates." The trust proved a most effective instrument for securing control of an industry, enabling the managers to run the business with minimal stock control. It was soon widely imitated, with the manufacturers of tobacco, sugar, whiskey, cottonseed oil, and other products following Rockefeller's example.

The trust had a basic defect: its governing agreements were a matter of public record. As open combinations in restraint of trade, they could be proceeded against at common law and, after 1890, under the Sherman Antitrust Act. The holding company was a more effective controlling device. From 1888 to 1893, New Jersey revised its general incorporation laws to allow corporations to purchase and hold the stock of other corporations. The effect of the changed New Jersey law, enacted after the New York courts had held combinations in restraint of competition illegal, was described in a paper read before the American Bar Association in 1899: "The 'Trusts' having been declared illegal in New York . . . transferred their property to corporations organized under the laws of New Jersey, and during the last ten years companies have been formed under the laws of that state under which the properties and business of corporations in all parts of the country have been united under one management with capital stock of many millions, and the combinations thus formed have accomplished all the purposes of those that had been declared illegal in New York." In the six months before this statement was made, sixty-one corporations (most of them holding companies), each with a capital of over $10 million, had been organized under New Jersey law, as against sixty in all other states.

According to the same paper delivered in 1899, "It is certain that the tendency in the United States toward combination and consolidation has not been seriously checked either by public opinion or by adverse legislation and judicial decision." This statement was made nine years after enactment of the Sherman Antitrust Act. For over a decade after its passage, that law had little practical effect, both because of the paucity of cases (only twenty-three of them from 1890 to 1903) brought by the government and a restrictive interpretation by the courts, particularly in the *Sugar Trust Case* in 1895, which the Supreme Court itself in 1948 conceded had "made the statute a dead letter." This was to change under important decisions, starting with that in the *Northern Securities* case in 1904. But, during the period covered by this chapter, the Sherman Antitrust Act had little more than symbolic value. James Bryce, returning to this country two decades after publishing his *American Commonwealth*, could note that, "Twenty-two years ago there were no Trusts. . . . Today [trusts] have become one of the most salient phenomena of the country."

Gilded Age Legislatures

The Gilded Age saw American governmental institutions sink to the lowest point in their history. Both the executive and legislative branches were, as stated by a contemporary historian, "unequal to their duty; they prove incapable of ensuring the protection of the general interest." Woodrow Wilson said in 1885, "The conditions of public life are not what they were in the early years of the federal government; they are not what they were even twenty years ago. [We] are perplexed at finding ourselves denied a new order of statesmanship to suit the altered conditions of government."

Instead of the needed new order, the country received the Grant Administration and its successors. "The progress of evolution from President Washington to President Grant," declared Henry Adams, "was alone evidence enough to upset Darwin." Certainly Grant in the highest office can only be compared with Harding as the personification of all that a president should not be. The successors to the Grant nadir were bound to be an improvement. But they were scarcely the men to restore the Presidency to the position it had held under Jackson and Lincoln. These were the years when the young Wilson was characterizing the American system as *Congressional Government*, and Bryce was explaining "Why Great Men Are Not Chosen Presidents." Not until Theodore Roosevelt would the White House be occupied by a president of more than limited vision.

The decline of the Executive meant a reassertion of legislative primacy. Less than ten years after it was issued, the conception of executive power urged in the Wade-Davis Manifesto of 1864—that the duty of the President is to obey and execute, not to make, the law—had all but taken over the field. Capitol Hill had once again become the crucial seat of action. And the same was true in the different state legislatures. In the words of a 1907 treatise, "The general law under which we live is entirely under the control of the state legislatures."

An 1868 woodcut pokes fun at apathy in the House of Representatives. Historians generally agree that the caliber of both Congress and the Presidency reached an extreme low point in the years following the Civil War.

Even more than during the nation's formative era, however, the legislature proved unable to realize its potential as the vital center of American law. To be sure, Wilson could write of Congress as the central and predominant power, with the Presidency reduced to an ineffectual office, and Henry Adams could assert that the United States had a "government of the people, by the people, for the benefit of Senators." But in operation neither House was effective enough to give substance to Adams's remark, except in the pejorative sense. Neither Congress nor the state legislatures could recover the inheritance with which American legislatures had begun their history.

The Gilded Age was the age of Senator Abner Dilworthy, Mark Twain's golden-tongued legislative counterpart of his Colonel Sellers. Senator Dilworthy's corruption was generally believed representative of the level of legislative ethics. "It could," wrote Mark Twain in *Pudd'nhead Wilson's New Calendar*, "probably be shown by facts and figures that there is no distinctly American criminal class except Congress."

Almost every account of the legislatures of the day reached the same dreary conclusion. "It is unnecessary," said Sir Henry Maine, "to appeal on this point to satire or fiction; the truth is, that too many Englishmen have been of late years concerned with Congressional business for there to be any want of evidence that much money is spent in forwarding it which is not legitimately expended." "Admitted corruption," to use the 1873 term of the scientist Simon Newcomb, with its inevitable counterpart of "loss of public confidence . . . which should alarm every thinking man," cast a gloomy pall over the American legislature. This was particularly true in the states, where corruption was even "more common" than in Congress. "The public know or believe the legislatures of one third of the States of the Union, perhaps we might say one half, to be more or less corrupt, many of them thoroughly corrupt," said Newcomb. Legislatures whose leaders "were more grotesque than ridicule could make them," in the words of Henry Adams, could scarcely be expected to play a positive part in molding the law. During the latter part of the century even the codification movement finally petered out, despite the continuing efforts of David Dudley Field. It was not until 1886, indeed, that Field's struggle to have his Civil Code enacted in New York was finally lost. By then, Field plainly appeared, in Roscoe Pound's phrase, only "a magnificent battler for a lost cause."

"A Dismal Stench of Fraud and Guile"

Throughout American history, the law has had its villains—corrupt and venal lawyers and judges who twisted, perverted, and broke the law for their own gain. Supreme Court Justice Benjamin N. Cardozo was one of the nation's greatest members of the Bench, the very epitome of an outstanding and upright jurist, and was included by Roscoe Pound in his list of the top ten judges in all of U.S. history. Yet his father, Justice Albert Cardozo of the New York State Supreme Court in post-Civil War days, was the opposite—a corrupt henchman of the notorious New York City political boss, William Marcy Tweed.

The elder Cardozo was far from unique. Since the early days of the Republic, individual judges have been for sale, sometimes taking bribes for decisions or light sentences in particular cases, but more often serving political or business interests that helped them attain their position on the Bench. From time to time, moral rot, ensnaring members of the judiciary, has characterized various cities and even the nation as a whole.

Among the worst of such periods was the Gilded Age, after the Civil War, when corruption was nationwide. The era, observed historian Allan Nevins, stood unique in the comprehensiveness of its rascality. The federal government was rocked by scandals like that of the Whiskey Ring and the Crédit Mobilier, but the Shame of Pennsylvania Avenue during President Ulysses S. Grant's Administration was paralleled by what Lincoln Steffens called The Shame of the Cities. Of these the worst was New York, then under the control of the Tweed Ring.

From 1866 to 1871, Boss Tweed and his cohorts plundered New York with a precision, thoroughness, and arrogance never seen before or since. To accomplish its ends, the Tweed Ring had to capture not only Tammany Hall and City Hall in New York but also the judiciary. Its effectiveness in doing this was acknowledged in 1869 in a satiric doggerel written by Louis S. Robbins and addressed "To the Sachems of Tammany and the Other Grand Magnorums of Manhattan":

> The kind of justice is queer
> and low,
> And comes, like the temple
> building, slow;
> And ever there lingers a
> dismal stench
> Of fraud and guile around
> every bench.

The most notorious of Tweed's judges were the elder Cardozo and George Barnard. The latter was a colorful figure who looked and dressed like a gambler, with expensive frilled shirts and a tall white hat, which, according to The Tweed Ring by Alexander B. Callow, Jr., "more often than not, remained at a rakish tilt throughout the session." When he was finally brought to trial, Tweed recounted how he had originally secured the state supreme court nomination for Barnard at a political convention of which Tweed was the presiding officer: "I saw, as the roll call proceeded, that Doyle [Barnard's opponent] had the majority of the

The successful fight against the Field Code in the 1880's was led by James C. Carter, the outstanding legal philosopher of the American Bar. Carter was the great American apostle of nineteenth-century historical jurisprudence. Like the Prussian Savigny, whose disciple he was, he preached—"for he had all the fervor of a preacher," said Pound—that codification was an exercise in futility. Law must be found, not made, by courts and jurists discovering and applying principles which spring from and rest upon the "character and actual condition of the people." Law was less a product of will than of experience. "I dismiss the topic of codification with the conviction that . . . it is entirely inconsistent with the fundamental principles of law."

Two aspects of the successful opposition to codification are of particular interest. One is the extent to which the opposition by men such as Carter was based on the dominant Darwinian philosophy. Carter, like Herbert Spencer, believed that government should let nature take its course. "To leave each man to work out in freedom his own happiness or misery, to stand or fall by the consequences of his own conduct, is the true method of human discipline," he wrote. Governmental interference in law, as in other areas, was bound to be an example of "demonstrated futility": "hu-

A slap at Tweed: "The Upright Bench."

delegates. Said I to a secretary, 'Have a motion made to dispense with calling the roll!' It was done. 'All in favor of Mr. Barnard as the nominee of this body say aye. Carried! The meeting is adjourned!'" Barnard thereafter faithfully served the Tweed Ring, though his own brother, reported Callow, once asserted that "George knows

about as much law as a yellow dog." Throughout court sessions, Barnard would prop his feet on the desk, make bawdy jokes, and take conspicuous gulps from a brandy bottle.

Cardozo was a striking contrast to the vulgar and ignorant Barnard. He was well-bred and industrious—a gentleman in every respect save for his penchant for corruption. He had one of the best legal minds of his day, but his ambition (he dreamed of an appointment to the U.S. Supreme Court) made him place it at Tweed's service. Both Barnard and Cardozo saw that Ring henchmen were appointed as street commissioners, receivers, and referees. More important, they served as escape hatches for criminals associated with the Ring. In any criminal case tried by Barnard, wrote Denis T. Lynch in *Boss Tweed*, "Tweed's intercession was equivalent to a dismissal of the case." The Tweed judges were particularly useful at election time. If repeaters (men who voted more than once for the Ring) were caught, the judges released them. Barnard and

Cardozo were amply rewarded for their services. Though he never went to the U.S. Supreme Court, Cardozo was bribed hundreds of times for releasing criminals. When Barnard died, more than one million dollars in cash and bonds was found among his effects.

Yet if corruption on the Bench and the Bar made the Tweed Ring possible, it was also the legal profession that ultimately played an important role in destroying the Ring. Prominent members of the local Bar, led by Samuel J. Tilden and the newly organized Association of the Bar of the City of New York, were the prime movers in a reform movement that secured the Tweed Ring's defeat in the 1871 election and the imprisonment of the Boss himself. Judge Barnard was impeached and removed from office, and Cardozo resigned. If the latter's name is no longer remembered as the embodiment of corruption, it is only due to his son, whose integrity and achievements eclipsed the memory of his father's misdeeds.

man conduct is in a very large degree self-regulating, and . . . the extent to which it can be affected by the conscious interference of man is much narrower than is commonly supposed."

Even more relevant was the relation of the Carter triumph over Field to the legislative role in lawmaking. Had the legislative confidence of the early formative era still prevailed, the Carter campaign might not have succeeded. The unarticulated major premise of the opposition to codification of the common law was the inability of the legislature to perform its required role. "Two Legislatures," asserted Carter in an 1884 pamphlet, "have been found so insensible of the magnitude of the trust confided to them as to give their assent to the passage of a scheme of legislation called a 'Civil Code,' which, confessedly, few of them had even read, none had intelligently understood, . . . proceeding from ignorance or design." Toward the end of the pamphlet, Carter referred directly to "the still more marked decline in the character of our legislators." The legislative efforts of the day to mold the law were consequently "ill conceived and pernicious."

What happened at the end of the century to the Field Code of Procedure indicates that the Carter strictures were well founded. The simple 391 sections originally drafted by Field were expanded into a cumbersome collec-

In a 1912 cartoon, Puck leveled its lance at jackass, nit-picking legal officials who impeded justice in her pursuit of evildoers by hampering her with technicalities and their own inertia and stupid quibbling.

tion of procedural and substantive provisions in excess of 3,400 sections. Later, the legislature burdened the procedure code with an even greater mass of detailed, unsystematic amendments, until it took some 50,000 sections of written law, and about 2,000 printed pages, to set forth the whole.

With the legislature unable to carry forward the effort to reduce the law to written form, the emphasis shifted to other institutions. The American Bar Association, formed in 1878, had as one of its major objectives the "promotion" of "uniformity of legislation throughout the Union." The ABA served as "generous godfather" in the organization in 1892 of the National Conference of Commissioners on Uniform State Laws. This body, composed of representatives appointed by the different states, has drafted uniform laws for adoption by state legislatures. From the beginning the work of the commissioners amounted to a peculiarly American type of codification, through legislative restatement of particular fields of the law. Some of the most important uniform laws were drawn up during the early history of the Conference. These included the Negotiable Instruments Law (1896), adopted in all the states, and the Uniform Sales Act (1906), enacted in thirty-seven jurisdictions. The latter has been characterized as "the first thoroughgoing bit of common-law codification in the United States."

Interstate Commerce Commission

"One might," said Henry Adams, "search the whole list of Congress, Judiciary, and Executive during the twenty-five years 1870 to 1895, and find little but damaged reputation. The period was poor in purpose and barren in results." One important result of the period, the consequences of which the contemporary skeptic could not possibly estimate, was the rise of the modern administrative agency. The basic institutions of American law — Executives, legislatures, and courts — had been fixed in form and function at the outset of the nation's history. The one important exception was the administrative agency, which first took form during the last half of the nineteenth century.

The archetype of the modern administrative agency, the Interstate Commerce Commission, was established by Congress in 1887. The history of its creation presents in capsule form the difference between the beneficent aims of Legal Darwinism and its rigor in actual practice. It was quixotic to assume that laissez faire would prove adequate to restrain the abuses that developed in railroading. Stimulated by a policy of benevolent promotion and subsidization on the part of both the states and the federal government, the railroad industry expanded rapidly, especially during the post-Civil War period of industrial growth. Governmental generosity, unaccompanied by effective restrictions, inevitably generated serious abuses. Freedom from public interference led to highly speculative railroad building, irresponsible financial manipulation, destructive competitive warfare resulting in monopolies, fluctuating and discriminating rates — and to the inevitable public reaction.

"The first puff of the engine on the iron road announced a revolution in the law," said a Massachusetts judge in 1867. More than that, it announced the inadequacy of laissez faire and Legal Darwinism in a burgeoning indus-

James C. Carter, best remembered for his fight against codification of laws, was as well or better known in his day for opposing the Tweed Ring and corruption in the entire court system.

History of the Bench and Bar of New York, NEW YORK, 1897

trial economy. Adam Smith's "invisible hand" was not only invisible but also nonexistent to the farmer dependent on the railroad to move his crops. Freedom of contract was merely a euphemism to those who were, practically speaking, at the mercy of the railroads. "He stands there alone, weak and poor and ignorant though he may be, with a ten-dollar case or a one-hundred dollar case. He must make his own case against a wealthy corporation," said one congressman. As stated in a debate in the House on the remedies then afforded by the law, "Pygmies do not invite giants to combat."

The resentment of the farmer led to the Granger movement, which swept the Midwest in the early 1870's. The Grangers became a powerful political force that sought to correct railroad abuses by state regulation. They secured laws in Illinois, Wisconsin, Minnesota, and Iowa regulating railroads, including limitations on railroad rates. These laws were upheld in the landmark *Granger Cases* in 1877, where the Court recognized the essential public power to regulate "businesses affected with a public interest," such as railroads. Even during the apotheosis of Spencerean doctrine, this ruling remained as a potential restraint upon abusive business activity.

The *Granger Cases* sustained state regulation, yet the railroad problem transcended state boundaries; by its very nature, it was an interstate problem and called for federal control. Nevertheless, congressional legislation appeared remote—railroad regulation had been before both Houses for almost two decades, but little had been done—when the Supreme Court, by its *Wabash* decision in 1886, injected a categorical congressional imperative.

"Uncle Sim" Baldwin and the Founding of the ABA

By 1860 in the United States, the once-flourishing bar associations of the type to which John Adams had belonged had either disappeared or become ineffective. Adams's old Suffolk Bar itself had changed into the Fraternity of the Suffolk Bar, whose purpose was simply "to cultivate a spirit of friendship, kindness and good will toward each other." After the Civil War, effective professional organizations of lawyers again began to emerge. The first of them was the Association of the Bar of the City of New York, founded in 1870 by 235 of the city's four thousand lawyers. The initial president of the organization—which is still the most prestigious bar association in the nation—was William M. Evarts, then leader of the American Bar. Founded in the heyday of the notorious Tweed Ring, its principal objective, according to Evarts, was to "restore the honor, in-

tegrity, and fame of the profession."

Associating the new group with the struggle to curb corruption in the courts, the press gave it great publicity. The result was to inspire lawyers generally to the need for professional organizations, so that in the next seven years fourteen similar bar associations, directly stimulated by the New York City example, were established in other cities and states. In 1878 the revival culminated in the founding of a national group, the American Bar Association.

The moving spirit in its creation was Simeon E. Baldwin (1840–1927) of Connecticut, a slight, erect figure with flowing hair and a full beard. "Uncle Sim," as he was known to the Bar of his state, was a professor at Yale Law School, who later revitalized that institution. He was also a prolific legal writer who became chief justice and governor of Con-

necticut and was even mentioned for the Presidency. In January, 1878, he induced the Connecticut State Bar Association to pass a resolution for the appointment of three men "to consider the propriety of organizing an association of American lawyers." He was the only active member of the committee, and on July 1, 1878, he mailed a printed letter signed by fourteen eminent lawyers from twelve states, mentioning himself as corresponding secretary. The letter proposed "an informal meeting at Saratoga, N.Y. . . . to consider the feasibility and expediency of establishing an American Bar Association." The invitation went to 607 lawyers. When the meeting convened in Saratoga on August 21, seventy-five men signed the roll, and twenty-five more signed the second day.

Prior to the gathering, Baldwin drafted a constitution and by-laws.

The *Wabash* ruling denied state power to regulate railroad transportation when the origin or destination went beyond state boundaries, even to regulate that part of the transportation that was entirely within the state. Since some three-fourths of the country's railroad tonnage was interstate in character, Congress was put on warning to act under its commerce power if railroads were to be regulated at all. Within a few months of the *Wabash* decision, the Interstate Commerce Act of 1887 was enacted.

The 1887 act did two main things: (1) it prohibited certain railroad practices that were deemed objectionable, such as rate discrimination, rebating, and the charging of unjust and unreasonable rates; and (2) it set up the Interstate Commerce Commission to aid in the enforcement of these prohibitions.

The ICC of 1887 was a far cry from the powerful regulatory agency of today. Its orders became effective only if they were obeyed voluntarily; otherwise, they had to be enforced through application by the commission to the federal courts for an injunction. More important, the restrictive attitude of the courts, in the words of political scientist Robert E. Cushman, "showed a steady and increasing disposition to do over again the commission's job of finding facts, thereby undermining the prestige of the commission and the effectiveness of its orders." Although the ICC had acted on the assumption that the statute authorized it to fix rates, the Supreme Court held in 1897 that it had no such power. The decisions limiting the commission's authority, declared the first Justice Harlan in a dissenting

These were adopted during the two-day session. In addition, Baldwin's nominee, James O. Broadhead of Missouri, was chosen as the first president (Baldwin himself served as president in 1890). The first printed report of the ABA, issued before the end of 1878, listed 284 members from twenty-seven states and territories. Louisiana had the largest number of members, but the other southern states were also strongly represented.

Some of the nation's best-known lawyers participated in the first ABA meeting. They set the tone for the association's early years, during which it was a select group of lawyers, almost a club of intimates. Each year the members gathered on the porch of one of the three big hotels in Saratoga and, over liquid refreshments, decided on the officers for the next year. The South was always well

BROWN BROTHERS

Simeon E. Baldwin

represented, in part because the cool air and sporting atmosphere of Saratoga were attractive to the Southerners. The century was over before the ABA finally lost its character as a small, exclusive group. Even then, for years, it maintained restricted membership rolls. Not until 1918 did it admit its first woman, Mary F. Lathrop. In 1912 a bitter floor battle was fought over the accidental election of three black lawyers by the Executive Committee, which had been unaware of their race. According to a 1937 account, "since that day a statement of race is required on the application card, and a veto power given any five councilmen, inserted at the request of southern members in the constitution of 1878, has effectively prevented election of colored lawyers." This changed in the 1940's when blacks were at last admitted to this national group of lawyers.

opinion, go "far to make that Commission a useless body for all practical purposes. . . . It has been left, it is true, with power to make reports, and to issue protests. But it has been shorn, by judicial interpretation, of authority to do anything of an effective character."

Looking back at the 1887 act, however, "more important," as one observer put it, "than the immediate powers that in 1887 were vested in the Interstate Commerce Commission was the creation of the Commission itself." For the first time, Congress had set up an independent regulatory agency, which was to serve as the model for later, similar bodies. Testifying before Congress in 1885, Charles Francis Adams had stated that "Congress would provide for a commission of men who were at once honest, intelligent and experienced, whose business it should be to observe this question very much as a physician would observe the progress of disease." Now, with the 1887 act, the instrument of administrative regulation had been created. What was of basic significance was the deliberate organization of a governmental unit (located outside the traditional departments) whose single concern was the regulation of a vital national industry.

During the next century the ICC was the model for a host of similar administrative agencies. The need for specialization to deal with specialized problems of economic regulation was met in the same way as it had been in

New York's Grand Central Terminal in 1909. With several interstate lines using the big terminal, it was one of many reasons why a regulatory body like the Interstate Commerce Commission was needed.

METROPOLITAN MUSEUM OF ART. GIFT IN MEMORY OF THE ARTIST AND HIS WIFE BY MEMBERS OF HIS FAMILY, 1941

Harper's Weekly, APRIL 9, 1887

In 1887, the year the Interstate Commerce Commission was created, Puck printed this cartoon of the new commissioners moving in to tame the unruly railroads. It did not work out quite that way; not until some years later was the ICC given the power to issue enforceable rulings.

1887. By the turn of the century, the movement toward the administrative process had only begun. Before that movement could become a major theme in American legal history, dominant conceptions on the proper scope of governmental authority themselves had to be altered drastically.

Bench and Bar

"We hear sometimes," declared Joseph H. Choate in an 1898 address, "that the American Bar has degenerated, that it does not equal its predecessors in power and character and influence, but this I utterly deny. . . . For skill, efficiency, utility and power, the service which our profession lends to the community today has not been surpassed in any former generation."

The Bar in Choate's day continued to play a crucial role in the American system. "The lawyer," said Justice Brewer in 1895, "is evermore the leader in society"; from the beginning, "the lawyers had always been the rulers of this nation." How could it be otherwise, as a speech to the ABA in 1892 observed, when "the American Bar is and should be . . . that priestly tribe to whose hands are confided the support and defense of this Ark of the Covenant of our fathers, the security of which against the profane touch of open and covert foes is the noblest function and the most patriotic purpose of our great profession?"

Governmental institutions were still dominated by the legal profession. "In our country," affirmed James C. Carter in his American Bar Association presidential address in 1895, "the members of our profession are not . . . mere lawyers. They are everywhere relied upon as the principal legislators." In Washington, D.C., and in the states, lawyers remained the prime managers of the legislative process. "Turning from legislative to other fields," said a book on the American lawyer in 1906, "we find that the lawyers occupy almost the entire horizon, of the official world." Particularly significant was the fashioning of the new administrative process in the lawyer's image. The five men appointed to the first Interstate Commerce Commission were all lawyers—setting a precedent of lawyer dominance that has been followed almost uniformly in American administrative agencies.

Crucial in the molding of the administrative process was the appointment of Thomas M. Cooley, the noted Michigan jurist, law professor, and author of the influential *Constitutional Limitations*, as first chairman of the ICC. Cooley impressed upon the commission its basic pattern of judicial procedure and thus began the trend toward judicialization that has been the outstanding feature of American administrative procedure. "You have organized the National Commission," wrote a commissioner to Cooley when the latter retired from the ICC, "laid its foundations broad and strong and made it what its creators never contemplated, a tribunal of justice, in a field and for a class of questions where all was chaos before." A commission thus set in the mold of the courtroom was, almost by definition, bound to be run by lawyers.

Crucial though the lawyer's role remained in society, a change can be noted after the formative period of the country. It was signaled by Bryce in his *American Commonwealth*. Bryce referred to the high place of the Bar in America, then said, "I am bound to add that some judicious American observers hold that since the Civil War there has been a certain decadence in the Bar of the great cities. They say that the growth of enormously rich and powerful corporations, willing to pay vast sums for questionable services, has seduced the virtue of some counsel whose eminence makes their example important." The Bar had evolved from an independent profession, whose client was the society, into an adjunct of the business community. As a study of the lawyer's role put it early in the century, the period was "an era of professional change—perhaps I am justified in saying, an intellectual decadence—in the Bar. There certainly was a transformation, from a profession to a business."

The lawyer of the pre-Civil War period had "been superseded . . ., said another observer, "by a business lawyer who is suspicious of political affairs, . . . less vocative, less individual and even timid in public causes. The new lawyer had traded for security some of the opportunities of the barrister's position." The result, as Bryce described it on his return visit in 1905, was that "Lawyers are now to a greater extent than formerly business men, a part of the great organized system of industrial and financial enterprise." Even at the Bar, "Business is King."

The inevitable consequence, said Brandeis in the same year, was "that at the present time the lawyer does not hold as high a position with the people as he held seventy-five or indeed fifty years ago." Bar association meetings could resound with self-laudatory addresses and resolutions. But the profession was no longer recognized as the aristocracy of the nation. It still commanded respect, but the respect now accorded was that for an intellectual jobber and contractor, rather than for any moral force. The lawyers, Brandeis went on, "have . . . allowed themselves to become adjuncts of great corporations and have neglected the obligation to use their powers for the protection of the people." The lawyer had evolved from the public-spirited advocate, practicing in Matthew Arnold's "grand style," into the business adviser, specializing in corporate practice. Social leadership in the

Louis D. Brandeis was one of the great justices of the Supreme Court. As a lawyer he was known as the "people's attorney" for his defense of public causes; much later, as an opponent of bigness—in government or business—he was consulted by President Wilson who in 1916 appointed him to the Supreme Court over the opposition of the conservative Bar.

United States had definitely passed from the lawyer to the entrepreneur.

The latter part of the nineteenth century also saw a decline in respect for the courts. As William Howard Taft, then a U.S. Circuit Court judge, pointed out in 1895, the public generally believed that the courts "have flagrantly usurped jurisdiction, first, to protect corporations and perpetuate their many abuses, and second, to oppress and destroy the power of organized labor." More important was the poorer caliber of the Bench. Bryce noted the lowering in quality of state judges with emphasis on the "low standard of learning and capacity among the State judges." Tracing the judicial decline to the popular election of judges, he declared that corruption on the Bench "has arisen only in States where popular election prevails." Bryce recognized the motives behind the movement for election but, referring to the New York Convention of 1846, which started the trend, asserted that "the quest of a more perfect freedom and equality on which the Convention started the people gave them in twenty-five years Judge Barnard [a notoriously corrupt judge employed by the Tweed Ring] instead of Chancellor Kent."

By 1905, the trend toward judicial election had reached its climax. Judges were elected by popular vote in thirty-six states; appointment by the governor or legislature prevailed in only ten. What popular election meant in practice is shown in Michigan in 1885. Thomas M. Cooley, who had served with such distinction on the state's supreme court for twenty-one years that he is considered one of the greatest judges in American history, had to retire when he lost the election to a graduate of an agricultural college.

Bryce did not include the federal Bench in his assessment of low judicial quality. Even the "minor Federal judges," he conceded, "are usually persons of ability and experience," while the Supreme Court was filled with "first-rate men." Compared to the state judges, this may well have been true. Nevertheless, within the federal judiciary, too, one cannot also help noting a decline in the caliber of the judges appointed in the latter part of the century. This was true even of the High Court.

To be sure, the sharp drop in the Supreme Court's prestige until almost the turn of the century must be laid primarily to the disastrous *Dred Scott* decision in 1857 and the subdued role of the Court during the post-Civil War period. But the lesser men appointed to the Court also contributed, particularly those selected as the successors of Marshall and Taney.

When Chief Justice Taney died toward the end of 1864, the age of Supreme Court giants ended. Taney's place went to Salmon P. Chase, the leading political jobber in Lincoln's Cabinet, who never ceased trying to use the Court's central chair as a stepping-stone to the Presidency. Chief Justice Chase "loved power as though he were still a Senator," said Henry Adams. Throughout his judicial career, his colleagues on the Bench — and most of his countrymen — felt that Chase's actions were governed primarily by political considerations. As Chief Justice Morrison R. Waite, Chase's successor, wrote, "My predecessor detracted from his fame by permitting himself to think he wanted the Presidency. Whether true or not it was *said* that he permitted his ambitions in that direction to influence his judicial opinions." As for Chase's legal ability, when he applied to Judge William Cranch in 1829 for admission to the District of Columbia Bar, the latter was so skeptical of

Chase's professional attainments that he agreed to admit him only after Chase explained that he did not intend to practice in Washington, but expected to go to the western country. An advertising circular sent out by Chase in 1839 indicated that his practice in Cincinnati was largely that of a glorified debt collector.

At Chase's death in 1873, Charles Sumner declared, "We stand at an epoch in the country's life . . . and I long for a Chief Justice like John Marshall, who shall pilot the country through the rocks and rapids in which we are." Instead, the country got Morrison R. Waite in 1873 and Melville W. Fuller in 1888. Each may be characterized as the luckiest of all persons in the law—the innocent third party without notice. Both were pedestrian mediocrities who did not have the remotest reason to expect the judicial lightning to strike. If both proved more competent than had been feared, they scarcely possessed the spark that had made giants of Marshall and Taney. "I can't," wrote Justice Samuel F. Miller of the High Court a year after Waite's appointment, "make a silk purse out of a sow's ear. I can't make a great Chief Justice out of a small man."

Of course, there were outstanding judges during the period—Justice Miller on the Supreme Court and Chief Justices Charles Doe of New Hampshire and Oliver Wendell Holmes of Massachusetts in the state courts. Still, they were less common than at any other time in the nation's history. More typical was Justice Rufus W. Peckham, who delivered the already discussed *Allgeyer* and *Lochner* opinions. Peckham, the judicial type of the day, has nowhere been better summed up than in Holmes's pithy comment: "I used to say his major premise was God damn it. Meaning thereby that emotional predilections . . . governed him on social themes."

Yet, if the Gilded Age saw the nadir of Bench and Bar, as of other American institutions, there were indications toward the end of the century of efforts to improve the situation. Roscoe Pound fixed 1890 as the low point in professional standards, particularly those of admission and control. After that date, a movement to raise standards began, gathering strength during the present century. In large part, this was due to the organization of the American Bar Association in 1878. It was founded by legal leaders— men such as William M. Evarts, Simeon E. Baldwin, and James O. Broadhead, its first president. For twenty-five years the ABA was a small and select organization (having only 1,718 members by 1902), which held elegant and innocuous annual meetings at Saratoga Springs.

Despite its restricted cast, the establishment of the ABA had an important impact upon the legal profession. It inaugurated a new era of professional activity. The ABA led to active bar associations in each state and almost every locality, thus reviving the tradition of professional organization that had virtually died out before the Civil War. These associations were to spearhead the movement to improve professional standards.

Perhaps the most important accomplishment of the early ABA was its sponsorship of the meetings that led in 1900 to the organization of the Association of American Law Schools. Founded by thirty-five of the existing ninety-six law schools (and the founders included all the better law schools of the day), the AALS from its beginnings struggled for the im-

Jurist George Sharswood lectures in the University of Pennsylvania Law School.

Christopher Columbus Langdell became dean of the Harvard Law School in 1870 and instituted the case method of teaching—now almost universal but then revolutionary—which holds that the way to study law is to dissect actual cases, not attend lectures and read treatises.

provement of legal education. The requirements they laid down for admission to the new association included a minimum of high school graduation for admission to law school, two years as the minimum period of law school study (to be increased to three years after 1905), written examinations for the law school degree, and minimum library requirements. The original AALS requirements reflect the low legal education standards of the day; even the requirement of high school graduation was far beyond that of most law schools. Membership in the AALS became the goal for law schools throughout the country. "The effect of these requirements . . . is incalculable. They have standardized legal education at a high level," wrote Harvard law professor Joseph H. Beale in 1937.

Another development, perhaps of even greater consequence, was the virtual revolution in the method of legal education. In the 1870's Christopher Columbus Langdell, no less than his namesake, discovered a whole new world—this time in the case method of teaching law, a method that has become so engrained in the American law school that it is easy to forget how innovative it was. When Langdell made his celebrated assertion, "First, that law is a science; secondly that all the available materials of that science are contained in printed books," he struck a responsive chord in an age dominated by Darwinism. President Eliot, who appointed the then unknown lawyer dean of Harvard Law School, was himself a chemist "quite prepared to believe" the Langdell assertion. As a scientist, he also knew that "the way to study a science was to go to the original sources." In the law, the "original sources" were the reports of decided cases. The law was to be learned through critical analysis of selected opinions of courts, a radical change in law teaching.

As President Eliot pointed out in his annual report for 1870–1871, the traditional phrase "reading law" had been rendered obsolete. "The idea conveyed by this phrase is that Law is to be learned by reading treatises and reports." The case method relies not on lectures and readings, but on intensive class discussion, designed to train the student in "the power of legal reasoning." As a leading exponent stated in 1894, "The object of the Case System is not to have students memorize cases, but to analyze them."

Langdell instituted other important changes in legal education. If law was a science worthy of inclusion in the university curriculum, it deserved study in depth. During Langdell's deanship, the number of year-hours of instruction offered at Harvard almost doubled. In addition, annual written examinations, covering the work of each year, were instituted and, at the end of Langdell's tenure, admission to the Law School was limited to college graduates. In 1873 another precedent was set when James Barr Ames was appointed as assistant professor. "Thus far, Law School has taken its Professors . . . from the ranks of the active profession," President Eliot noted. But Ames was only twenty-seven, just out of law school, with no experience in practice. His appointment inaugurated the career of the scholar-teacher who devoted his professional life to law teaching.

The Langdell innovations transformed legal education. His successor, Dean Ames, was able to speak of "the revolution effected by him in the matter of teaching and studying law, a revolution that has spread and is spreading so rapidly to other schools that in a few years his views may be expected to dominate legal education." The Ames prophecy was soon borne out. Langdell had established the first modern law school, which set the pattern for legal education for the better part of a century. By 1910, the case method of teaching had become dominant throughout the country.

The Ends of Law: 1900

The law of the nation's formative era had been marked by self-confidence; by 1900, this had degenerated into almost Hegelian arrogance. In lectures prepared for delivery at Harvard Law School in 1905, James C. Carter traced the different stages of legal development to "the last stage. . . . This is the stage of full enlightenment, such as is exhibited in . . . the United States at the present day." In a similar self-congratulatory vein, Joseph H. Choate referred to the American Bar as "the happiest illustration of Darwin's great theory of survival of the fittest." Its leaders were "eliminated by a process of natural selection, for merit and fitness, from the whole body of the Bar."

Judges and lawyers of this ilk would scarcely make the law an instrument of transforming innovation. The dominant jurisprudence of the day was that of the historical school. Its fundamental tenet was that the law was found, not made; in law, as in nature, the process was an evolutionary one, whose progress could only be impeded by outside intervention. "The popular estimate of the possibilities for good which may be realised through the

Large law offices like the one below, pictured in 1901, often looked like business offices. In truth, their bigness required that if they were to operate effectively, they had to operate as a business.

enactment of law is, in my opinion, greatly exaggerated," said Carter. In law, as in economics, hands-off became the rule. "The Written Law is victorious upon paper and powerless elsewhere," Carter announced.

The ends of law at the turn of the century may be summarized in the watchwords *equality* and *opportunity*. As shown in Chapter IV, equality became a constitutional principle with the ratification of the Fourteenth Amendment. But the civil rights emphasis of Reconstruction soon gave way to the Gilded Age stress on property rights. The concept of equality had shifted to one of equality of economic opportunity. From this point of view, the purpose of law was to ensure equality of opportunity to exercise one's faculties and to employ one's substance.

The dominant tone in the law was, however, becoming defensive rather than expansive, favoring stability instead of change, and emphasizing the security of acquired interests more than the freedom of the individual. The desired security was to be attained by insisting upon will as the dominant factor. The security to be achieved by law included two essential ideas: (1) everyone is to be secured in his acquired interests against aggression by others; and (2) others are to be permitted to acquire from him only through his will that they do so, or through his breach of legal rules designed to secure others in like interests.

To ensure both opportunity and security, the law insisted upon property and contract as its fundamental rights. A paper read at the 1900 American Bar Association meeting referred to "the foundations on which [our law] is bottomed:—individual ownership, free contract and free competition." Property and contract were the all-important institutions by which the free competition necessary for economic and social progress was to be secured.

As already stressed, this was the period when contract completed its conquest of the law. Yet it was also the time when contract itself came to be treated from a proprietary standpoint. The right of the individual to make contracts freely was thought of primarily as a sort of asset. As a leading state case put it, "The privilege of contracting is both a liberty and a property right, and if A is denied the right to contract . . . it is clear that he is deprived of both liberty and property to the extent that he is denied the right to contract." Even personality acquired a property aspect. The New York court refused to recognize the right of privacy because it was not an incident of "possession or enjoyment of property." Other courts adhered to the doctrine that interests of personality might not be protected except where they could be subsumed under some interest of substance.

Without a doubt, the law of the late nineteenth century provided a new balance for the trilogy of rights protected by the Constitution. The Due Process Clause, declared John F. Dillon in his 1892 American Bar Association presidential address, "puts property upon precisely the same footing of security that it puts life and liberty. It binds them each and all indissolubly together." What is striking today, almost a century later, is not the treatment of property as an equal member of the constitutional triad, but its elevation to a position of all-dominance. Brandeis gave contemporaneous expression to this development: "Property is only a means. It has been a frequent error of our courts that they have made the means an end."

Looking back, it can be seen that the emphasis on the rights of the property owner and his virtually unlimited freedom from public interference with his will went too far. "Nothing, it has been said," declared a 1942 judicial opinion, "exceeds like excess. Laissez-faire went too far." By the turn of the century, V. L. Parrington noted in his *Main Currents in American Thought,* "Freedom had become individualism, and individualism had become the inalienable right to preempt, to exploit, to squander." In the law as elsewhere, utterly unrestrained individualism becomes self-devouring. If unlimited freedom of contract alone is to prevail, the individual may be forced to part, by the very contract he is allowed to make, with all real freedom. "One law for the Lion & Ox," said William Blake, "is Oppression." The same is true of one law for the mammoth corporation and its employee. Survival of the Fittest had turned the Gilded Age into brass.

Even at the time, there were those who saw the tarnish. In a law school lecture early in this century, Brooks Adams stated that "freedom of contract is an effect of unrestrained economic competition." Its ultimate effect would be that it "induces an unstable equilibrium by encouraging over-competition among its members. When the moment of over-competition is reached, a period of transition begins. I am inclined to believe that the United States is now entering upon such a period."

To the perceptive observer, there were signs that Adams's analysis was accurate. In his discussion of laissez faire, Bryce noted that, even in America, "New causes are at work . . . tending not only to lengthen the arms of government, but to make its touch quicker and firmer." Unlimited competition, he

The young men below were members of the Supreme Court of the Pow Wow Club at Harvard Law School in 1873. At that time almost every student at the Law School belonged to one or more clubs of this kind, whose purpose was to further the study of law through moot courts and the discussion of cases outside of regular classroom hours.

CHARLES WARREN, *History of the Harvard Law School,* NEW YORK, 1908

went on, pressed too hardly on the weak and, to restrain its abuses, the action of government was being carried into ever widening fields. This was true even though "the process of transition to this new habit [was] so gradual . . . that for a long time few but lawyers and economists became aware of it."

The law of the coming century was foreshadowed in state regulatory laws, the *Granger Cases*, the Interstate Commerce Act, and the Sherman Antitrust Act. As noted, the two federal statutes proved ineffective in curbing railroad abuses and monopolies. But indications early in the new century hinted that this situation would change. Theodore Roosevelt's "trust busting" policies and the 1904 *Northern Securities* decision presaged the beginnings of more effective enforcement of the antitrust law. Roosevelt also served as the catalyst for stronger railroad regulation. His 1905 annual message made adequate regulation a leading issue. It led directly to the Hepburn Act of 1906, which gave the Interstate Commerce Commission the powers needed for effective railroad regulation.

The theme of the next period of American development was anticipated by the repudiation of Spencerean philosophy by influential thinkers. By the late 1800's, William Graham Sumner was giving way to Lester Frank Ward and John Fiske to Richard T. Ely and Henry Carter Adams.

To the legal historian, Justice Holmes was to be the leading prophet of the new era. Holmes was part of the generation that had sat at the feet of Darwin and Spencer, and he could never shed his Darwinist outlook. Nevertheless, his Darwinism was tempered by an innate skepticism which made it impossible for him to accept the dogmatic approach of Spencer's legal

The Great Dissenter

Oliver Wendell Holmes, son of the American man of letters of the same name, was born in Boston in 1841. He was graduated from Harvard, served in the Union Army in the Civil War, was admitted to the Massachusetts Bar in 1867, practiced law in Boston, and was a professor at Harvard Law School in 1882. In the same year, he became an associate justice of the Massachusetts Supreme Court, rising in 1899 to become its chief justice. From 1902 until 1932, he was an associate justice of the U.S. Supreme Court. In 1929 *The Dissenting Opinions of Mr. Justice Holmes* was published. He died in 1935.

Without a doubt, he was the most famous dissenter in legal history, though he never thought of himself as such. In his very first dissenting opinion, in 1904, he stated that he was unable to agree with the U.S.

HARVARD LAW SCHOOL COLLECTION

Oliver Wendell Holmes, during his days as a young lecturer on law at Harvard

Supreme Court majority, but then went on to assert, "I think it useless and undesirable, as a rule, to express dissent." Why did he do so? His next sentence provided the answer: "Great cases like hard cases make bad law." Judicial dissent, he held, was justified when a particular decision disposed of a "great case" or a "hard case." If the case was an ordinary one, which did not have real importance in shaping the law, a separate statement of dissent was not justified merely because the judge happened to disagree with his colleagues.

While Holmes sat on its bench, the Supreme Court rendered decisions on just under six thousand cases. Holmes actually dissented only seventy times, leading his famous English correspondent, Sir Frederick Pollock, to ask, "Does he really dissent much

disciples. As early as 1873, Holmes wrote: "It has always seemed to us a singular anomaly that believers in the theory of evolution and in the natural development of institutions by successive adaptations to the environment, should be found laying down a theory of government intended to establish its limits once and for all by a logical deduction from axioms."

Above all, Holmes refused to confound intellectual dogma with the order of nature. "No concrete proposition," he stated in an 1897 speech, "is self-evident, no matter how ready we may be to accept it, not even Mr. Herbert Spencer's 'Every man has a right to do what he wills, provided he interferes not with a like right on the part of his neighbors.'" Though Holmes was eminently a legal historian, whose greatest work off the Bench was a historical analysis of common law doctrine, he rejected the negative attitude of Carter and the historical school. To him, there was no inevitability in either history or law, except as men made it.

When Holmes asserted in his *Common Law* that "The life of the law has not been logic: it has been experience," and that "The law finds its philosophy [in] the nature of human needs," he was sounding the clarion of twentieth-century jurisprudence. If the law reflected the "felt necessities of the time," then those needs rather than any theory, Spencerean or otherwise, should determine what the law should be. These were not the views of American judges and lawyers at the turn of the century—or even of the majority of the Court during Holmes's tenure on that tribunal. But the good that men do lives after them. If the nineteenth century was one of Legal Darwinism, the twentieth was, ultimately, to be that of Mr. Justice Holmes.

oftener than his learned brethren, or is the impression due to the weight rather than the number of the dissents?" The latter, indeed, was the truth. Moreover, "the fact that Holmes's most famous opinions were dissenting opinions by no means sets him down as a rebel or a no-sayer," observed his biographer, Catherine Drinker Bowen. "Holmes always regretted the necessity of dissenting, believing that too many dissents detract from the prestige of the Court."

Holmes's dissents emphasized two themes that have since become basic in the law. The first was expressed colorfully in one of his comments to Justice Harlan Fiske Stone: "About seventy-five years ago I learned that I was not God. And so, when the people . . . want to do something I can't find anything in the Constitution expressly forbidding them to do,

I say, whether I like it or not, 'Goddamit, let 'em do it!'" The responsibility for determining what measures were necessary to deal with economic and other problems lay with the people and their elected representatives, not the judges. The Constitution, Holmes declared, was not "intended to give us *carte blanche* to embody our economic or moral beliefs in its prohibitions."

But the theme of judicial self-restraint gave way to another Holmes theme in cases involving First Amendment rights. Here his overriding assumption was, as he put it in a 1919 dissent, "that the ultimate good desired is better reached by free trade in ideas—that the best test of truth is the power of the thought to get itself accepted in the competition of the market, and that truth is the

only ground upon which their wishes safely can be carried out. That at any rate is the theory of our Constitution."

Except in the area of free expression, Holmes's dominant approach was always that of tolerance toward legislative action. "I do not think," he asserted in 1913, "the United States would come to an end if we lost our power to declare an Act of Congress void." His dissents emphasized the limitations of judicial power and the danger of letting the Constitution become the embodiment of the justices' personal beliefs. "Judges," he said, "are apt to be naif, simple-minded men, and they need something of Mephistopheles." They "need education in the obvious—to learn to transcend our own convictions and to leave room for much that we hold dear to be done away with . . . by the orderly change of law."

VI

Welfare of the Community

Public Law: 1910–1950

In a 1913 address Theodore Roosevelt delivered a strong attack on "the function of the judge as an irresponsible lawmaker. . . . This is a function which American judges alone have arrogated to themselves, . . . the power to decide whether or not the people are to be permitted to have certain laws in the interest of social justice." The judges might be "well-meaning," but they had "no special fitness to decide non-judicial questions of social and economic reform. . . . They ought not to be entrusted with the power to determine, instead of the people, what the people have the right to do in furthering social justice under the Constitution."

The Roosevelt criticism was called forth by *Ives* v. *South Buffalo Ry. Co.*, in 1911, and similar court decisions that had stricken down legislative interventions in economic affairs. "Each decision told heavily against the interests of hardworking men, women and children unable to protect themselves, and each decision was in the interest of the wealthy and powerful. Each decision," Roosevelt charged, "was a decision against social justice."

The *Ives* decision in New York State, like its federal counterpart in *Lochner* v. *New York* in 1905, was a classic example of the impact of Legal Darwinism on American public law. At issue in *Ives* was the constitutionality of the 1909 New York Workmen's Compensation Act. "The statute, judged by our common-law standards, is plainly revolutionary," declared the state court. "Its central and controlling feature . . . is that the employer is responsible to the employee for every accident in the course of the employment, whether the employer is at fault or not, and whether the employee is at fault or not." The New York court ruled the statute invalid, holding that the liability sought to be imposed upon employers "is a taking of property without due process of law." That was true, according to the

Symbol of a new governmental responsibility: a welfare office in Franklin, Georgia.

Theodore Roosevelt stormed against the blocking of reforms by the courts.

Eight of the "nine old men" of the Supreme Court, flanked by the Attorney General and the Solicitor General, visit the White House during Herbert Hoover's administration. With a majority of its members still wedded to a philosophy of Legal Darwinism, the Court aborted many of the anti-Depression and social welfare laws instituted by Hoover's successor, Franklin D. Roosevelt.

judges, because, "When our Constitution was adopted it was the law of the land that no man who was without fault or negligence could be held liable in damages for injuries sustained by another." To change that principle by imposing "upon an employer, who has omitted no legal duty and has committed no wrong, a liability based solely upon a legislative fiat . . . is taking the property of A and giving it to B, and that cannot be done under our Constitution."

It was, indeed, amazing that American judges could "assert a constitutional right not to be held liable *in a civil action* without actual fault." Liability for fault alone was itself relatively new in the law. As shown in Chapter III, negligence did not develop as a separate tort before 1800; it was only during the nineteenth century that the principle of liability only for fault was fully developed. Despite this, a member of the *Ives* court could declare categorically, "I know of no principle on which one can be compelled to indemnify another for loss unless it is based upon contractual obligation or fault." Thus, the principle of immunity from fault, itself a product of recent legal development, was elevated into a right inherent in free government. "It seems to me," affirmed a member of the United States Supreme Court only a few years after the *Ives* v. *South Buffalo Ry. Co.* decision, "to be of the very foundation of right—of the essence of liberty as it is of morals—to be free from liability if one is free from fault."

As had been true in *Lochner*, a direct relationship existed between the *Ives* result and the economic philosophy of the judges in the early part of this century. To penalize even "the most thoughtful and careful employer," in the view of the same Supreme Court justice, was to proceed upon "a class distinction with its . . . invidious circumstances." Governmental intervention, said the jurist, could only be productive of ultimate harm. "Consider what the employer does: he invests his money . . . he takes all the risks of the adventure. Now there is put upon him an immeasurable element that may make disaster inevitable." Such governmental intervention could, as Spencer had asserted, only lead to weakening of the society itself. As Justice James C. McReynolds put it with regard to a law similar to that in *Ives*, "As a measure to stifle enterprise, produce discontent, strife, idleness, and pauperism, the outlook for the enactment seems much too good."

Nevertheless, *Ives* was an aberration even at the time it was decided. Certainly, by the turn of the century, workmen's compensation was an idea whose time had plainly come. The failure of the common law to provide for the injured worker had become intolerable, particularly since the worker had no means of protecting himself. The employer, on the other hand, said the Supreme Court in 1919, "takes the gross receipts . . . and by reason of his position of control can make such adjustments as ought to be . . . made, in the way of reducing wages and increasing the selling price." The pain and mutilation incident to production could legitimately be thrown upon the employer in the first instance and the public in the long run. In 1917 and 1919 the Supreme Court finally upheld state workmen's compensation laws, and the state courts, including those in New York, speedily followed suit.

Workmen's compensation laws, factory laws, and the like were, however, as far as the courts were willing to go in the first part of this century in permitting legislative regulation of the relations between employers and employees, as well as other aspects of the economic system. Due process was construed to authorize judges to hold laws unconstitutional that were contrary to their views of economic wisdom: "There was a time," noted a 1963 decision, "when the Due Process Clause was used by this Court to strike down laws which were thought unreasonable, that is, unwise or incompatible with some particular economic or social philosophy."

Decisions such as *Ives* and *Lochner* set the judicial pattern for a generation. Liberty, as contained in the Due Process Clause, was posited as permanent and absolute; impairment was not to be suffered, even in the form of experiments along new lines of social betterment: "The image," wrote Benjamin N. Cardozo in 1924, "was a perfect sphere. The least dent or abrasion was a subtraction from its essence. Given such premises, the conclusion is inevitable." Any legislative encroachment on the existing economic order became suspect as infected with unconstitutionality. The judges treated laws as unconstitutional because they offended what the judges strongly believed to be socially desirable. Despite a celebrated protest by Justice Holmes in the *Lochner* case of 1905, the Fourteenth

The cover of a 1922 issue of the Labor Herald expressed its sentiments over the Supreme Court's invalidation of a child labor law that year. The Court consistently found such legislation unconstitutional.

Amendment was increasingly measured by Spencer's *Social Statics*. The Supreme Court itself conceded in 1963 that, during the first part of the century, it had used "the 'vague contours' of the Due Process Clause to nullify laws which a majority of the Court believed to be economically unwise."

In no way did the due process approach have greater effect than in its impact upon governmental power to protect society against the abuses of industrialism. All too many legislative attempts at such protection could not successfully pass the due process test. In the first quarter of the century, the Supreme Court invalidated statutes regulating hours of labor, prohibiting child labor, guaranteeing minimum wages, barring so-called yellow dog contracts (making it a condition of employment that the worker will not join a union), or restraining the granting of injunctions in labor disputes.

During the first part of the century, in Justice Robert H. Jackson's characterization made in 1941, it was a fortunate and relatively innocuous piece of reform legislation that was able to run the gantlet of due process. Statistics document the impact of judicial control: in the period between 1890 and 1937, the Supreme Court held invalid 55 federal and 228 state statutes. Well might contemporary critics complain, as did Theodore Roosevelt, that "there has grown up the habit in our courts of using their great power with almost indiscriminate recklessness."

But the deficiencies of judicial review in operation lay even more in method than in result. It was not so much that the judges were interposing their veto "in a spirit of Toryism, of Bourbonism," as Roosevelt charged, as that they were arrogating for themselves a veto power never contemplated by the Constitution—"the political function which," said Justice Frankfurter in 1938, "American courts alone among the courts of the world possess." The frequency with which the courts interposed their power to negate social legislation led to charges, like that of Justice Brandeis in 1924, that they were exercising "the powers of a super-Legislature—not the performance of the constitutional function of judicial review." According to the English observer Harold J. Laski, "the inference is the unmistakable one that . . . the Supreme Court, by exercising this power of judicial review, is, in fact, a third chamber in the United States." In a similar vein, the leading French study of judicial review in the American system, published in 1921, was entitled *Government by Judiciary*.

The New Deal and the Court

"During the past half century," asserted President Franklin D. Roosevelt in 1937, "the balance of power between the three great branches of the Federal Government, has been tipped out of balance by the Courts in direct contradiction of the high purposes of the framers of the Constitution." Government by judiciary was dramatically illustrated by the judicial reception of the early New Deal program. Based on the need to resuscitate the depressed economy by extended governmental intervention, the New Deal program involved the negation of laissez faire; it meant a degree of economic regulation far greater than any previously attempted. If the country was to go forward, said President Roosevelt in his first inaugural address, "we must move as a trained and loyal army willing to sacrifice for the good of a common discipline, because without such discipline no progress is made, no leadership becomes effective."

The effort to move the nation forward came up against the restricted view of governmental power developed by the courts. The result was a series of decisions that invalidated most of the important New Deal legislation. In 1935 and 1936 cases, the Supreme Court struck down the two key New Deal antidepression measures—the National Industrial Recovery Act and the Agricultural Adjustment Act. Both measures were held beyond the reach of federal power. In another 1936 case, the same restricted approach was applied to rule against a federal law regulating the bituminous coal industry. Still another 1936 decision reaffirmed that a law fixing minimum wages was contrary to the freedom of contract guaranteed by due process.

The narrow interpretation of governmental power in these decisions was catastrophic. "We have . . . reached the point as a Nation," FDR declared, "where we must take action to save the Constitution from the Court." Elimination of manufacturing, mining, and agriculture from the reach of federal power had rendered Congress powerless to deal with problems in those fields, however pressing they might become.

In May, 1935, the Supreme Court unanimously struck down the National Industrial Recovery Act; one of the arguments against it was that it delegated unlimited legislative powers to the President. By 1937, however, reworked New Deal legislation was passing Court inspection.

Obviously the rejection of governmental power in the New Deal decisions fitted in perfectly with the restricted theory of governmental function that had dominated American thinking for the previous half century. The Constitution, stated Justice Holmes in a noted passage, "is not intended to embody a particular economic theory, whether of paternalism and the organic relation of the citizen to the State or of laissez faire." But it was most difficult for judges not to assume that the basic document was intended to embody the dominant economic beliefs on which they had been nurtured.

The grim economic background behind the New Deal measures, however, indicated how totally unrealistic was reliance on laissez faire. Giant industries prostrate, nationwide crises in production and consumption, the economy in a state of virtual collapse — if ever there was a need for exertion of federal power, it was after 1929. The market and the states had found the crisis beyond their competence. The choice was between federal action and chaos. A system of constitutional law that required the latter could hardly endure. The New Deal decisions, the Supreme Court itself was later to concede, "produced a series of consequences for the exercise of national power over industry conducted on a national scale which the evolving nature of our industrialism foredoomed to reversal."

The 1937 Reversal

President Roosevelt's answer to the judicial decisions was his "Court-packing" plan of February 5, 1937. (Under the plan, the President would have been given authority to appoint a new justice when an incumbent justice reached the age of seventy and failed to retire; this could have given Roosevelt as many as six new justices to appoint.) After lengthy hearings and public discussion, the Senate Judiciary Committee rejected it. Yet, if FDR lost the Court-packing battle, he was ultimately to win the constitutional war, for the Supreme Court itself was soon to abandon its restrictive approach to the proper scope of governmental power. Hence, in Justice Jackson's summary of the Court-packing fight, "Each side of the controversy has comforted itself with a claim of victory. The President's enemies defeated the court reform bill — the President achieved court reform."

A remarkable reversal in the Supreme Court's attitude toward the New Deal program took place early in 1937. From 1934 through 1936, the Court rendered twelve decisions declaring New Deal measures invalid; starting in April, 1937, that tribunal upheld every New Deal law presented to it, including some that were basically similar to earlier nullified statutes. It is, in truth, not too far-fetched to assert that in 1937 there was a veritable revolution in the Court's jurisprudence, which the author Edward S. Corwin characterized as "Constitutional Revolution, Ltd."

It is too facile to state that the 1937 change was merely a protective response to the Court-packing plan, to assert, as did so many contemporary wags, that "a switch in time saved Nine." The furor over the President's proposal obviously had repercussions within the Court's marble halls. As FDR himself expressed it, "It would be a little naive to refuse to recognize some connection between these decisions and the Supreme Court fight." At the same time, it misconceives the nature of the Supreme Court and its

In a cartoon in the Richmond Times-Dispatch, *President Roosevelt urges the Court to join the executive and legislative branches of the government in the effort to end the Depression.*

F.D.R. discusses his court-packing strategy with Senator Joseph T. Robinson (promised a Court seat if the scheme won).

manner of operation as a judicial tribunal to assume that the 1937 change in jurisprudence was solely the result of the Court-packing plan. The 1937 reversal reflected changes in legal ideology common to the entire legal profession. The extreme individualistic philosophy upon which the justices had been nurtured had been shaken to its foundations. If Spencerean laissez faire gave way to judicial pragmatism, it simply reflected a similar movement that had taken place in the country as a whole.

In any event, there *was* a real conversion in a majority of the Supreme Court, and its effects do justify the "constitutional revolution" characterization. And it is usually overlooked that the decisions first signaling the reversal in jurisprudence were reached before the President introduced his Court-packing plan. On March 29, 1937, Chief Justice Hughes announced a decision upholding a state minimum wage law, basically similar to one the Court had held to be beyond the power of both states and nation to enact only nine months previously. The Court's confession of error was announced over a month after the President's proposal, but the case itself was decided in conference among the justices about a month before the publication of the Court-packing plan on February 5. This circumstantial evidence strongly bears out the statement made some years later by Chief Justice Hughes to his authorized biographer: "The President's proposal had not the slightest effect on our decision."

In April, 1937, the Court decided *National Labor Relations Board* v. *Jones & Laughlin Steel Corp.* and upheld the constitutionality of the National Labor Relations Act. That 1935 law was the Magna Carta of the American labor movement; it guaranteed the right of employees to organize

The Consummate Legal Craftsman

The law," said Justice Oliver Wendell Holmes, "is not the place for the artist or poet. The law is the calling of thinkers." His successor on the Supreme Court, Benjamin N. Cardozo, was the rare exception to this statement. Cardozo was plainly one of the greatest American judges; except for Holmes himself, he has been the pre-eminent judge of the twentieth century. Yet he looms large not as a great decider of cases, but as the consummate legal craftsman—the master of the principles, ideals, and techniques of Anglo-American law. More than any other judge, as Roscoe Pound once pointed out, "he has known the tools of his craft and has known how to use them."

There was little drama in Cardozo's life. He was born in New York City in 1870, the son of a judge who was besmirched by his association with the Tweed Ring. During his youth, he had a number of tutors, including Horatio Alger. After study at Columbia and admission to the New York Bar in 1891, he became a lawyer's lawyer, to whom other attorneys referred difficult cases. He became a judge in 1914, serving eighteen years (five of them as chief judge) on the New York Court of Appeals and then six years (1932–1938) on the U.S. Supreme Court. During the Cardozo years, the New York court was recognized as the strongest in the country, and its judgments had a decisive influence on American law. When Holmes resigned from the Supreme Court, there was an unprecedented unanimity of opinion that Cardozo should succeed him. Though there were two New York justices and one Jew already on the Court, President Herbert Hoover yielded to public opinion and nominated Cardozo.

It is as a benefactor of what he called in an address to a Catholic audience "Our Lady of the Common Law" that Cardozo is remembered. Anglo-American case law stands as a structure fashioned by generations of judges, each professing to be a pupil, yet each a builder who added his few bricks. Cardozo was perhaps the greatest contributor to the common law's continuity during the twentieth century. He was a profound legal scholar who has been compared to Joseph Story. But his learning aided, and did not dictate, decision. According to Chief Justice Harlan Fiske Stone, Cardozo "believed . . . that the law must draw its

collectively and made it an unfair labor practice for employers to interfere with that right. The act was intended to apply to industries throughout the nation, to those engaged in production and manufacture as well as to those engaged in commerce, literally speaking. But this appeared to bring it directly in conflict with the Supreme Court decisions drastically limiting the scope of federal authority, including some of the 1934–1936 period on which the ink was scarcely dry. In *Jones & Laughlin*, these precedents were not followed. "These cases," laconically stated the Court, "are not controlling here." Instead, the opinion gave the federal power its maximum sweep. Mines, mills, and factories, which had formerly been ruled "local" and hence immune from federal regulation, were now held to affect interstate commerce directly enough to justify congressional control.

Starting with *Jones & Laughlin*, the decisions signaled a significant change in the Supreme Court's role in the constitutional structure. Where the Court had previously set itself up as virtual supreme censor of the wisdom of challenged legislation, it now adopted the view formerly expressed in dissent by Justice Oliver Wendell Holmes. Under the earlier approach, the desirability of a statute was determined as an objective fact on the Court's independent judgment. Now a more subjective test was applied: could rational legislators have regarded the statute as a reasonable method of reaching the desired result?

The change in the Court's approach had a tremendous impact on the doctrine of substantive due process. Few today doubt that the high tribunal went too far before 1937 in its application of the doctrine, or that the Court after that time was correct in deliberately discarding the extreme due process

vitality from life rather than the precedents and that 'the judge must be historian and prophet all in one.' He saw in the judicial function the opportunity to practice that creative art by which law is molded to fulfill the needs of a changing social order." To Cardozo, the job of the judge was to adapt the experience of the past so that it would best serve the needs of the present. "Logic and history," he wrote, "the countless analogies suggested by the recorded wisdom of the past, will in turn inspire new expedients for the attainment of equity and justice."

In a 1925 essay, Cardozo noted that people assert "that a judicial opinion has no business to be literature. The idol must be ugly, or he may be taken for a common man." Cardozo's own opinions were addi-

Justice Benjamin N. Cardozo
HARVARD LAW SCHOOL COLLECTION

tions to literature as well as law. He remains the acknowledged master of language as a legal instrument. The judge, he said, may be "expounding a science, or a body of truth which he seeks to assimilate to a science, but in the process of exposition he is practicing an art." By the lever of art, Cardozo, who died in 1938, lifted the most technical subjects to the heights. To read his opinions today is, in a sense, to string pearls. Typical of many was one he rendered in 1928: "A trustee," he wrote, "is held to something stricter than the morals of the market place. Not honesty alone but the punctilio of an honor the most sensitive, is then the standard of behavior. . . . Only thus has the level of conduct for fiduciaries been kept at a higher level than that trodden by the crowd."

This steelworker, voting for his choice of union at a Jones & Laughlin plant in 1937, was able to do so only after the Supreme Court upheld the Wagner Act of 1935 in a suit brought against the corporation by the government. In its 5-to-4 decision, the Court overrode its previous anti-union rulings.

philosophy. The Due Process Clause was not intended to prevent legislatures from choosing whether to regulate or leave their economies to the blind operation of uncontrolled economic forces, futile or even noxious though the choice might seem to the judges. Economic views of confined validity are not to be treated as though the framers had enshrined them in the Constitution.

In his dissent in the *Lochner* case in 1905, Justice Holmes had asserted, "This case is decided upon an economic theory which a large part of the country does not entertain." After 1937, both the economic and legal theories on which *Lochner* rested were repudiated by the Supreme Court. Early in 1937, the Court overruled its earlier holdings that a minimum wage law violated due process by impairing freedom of contract between employers and employees. "What is this freedom?" asked the opinion. "The Constitution does not speak of freedom of contract." The liberty safeguarded by the Constitution is liberty in a society that requires the protection of law against evils which menace the health, safety, morals, or welfare of the people. Regulation adopted in the interests of the community, the Court concluded, is due process.

Since 1937, the High Bench has had only two occasions directly to overrule due process decisions of its predecessors. The first occurred in 1941, when a 1928 decision voiding as inconsistent with due process a state statute regulating the fees charged by employment agencies had been relied on by a lower court to invalidate a similar Nebraska law; the Supreme Court speedily reversed, holding that the earlier case could no longer be deemed controlling authority. The second took place in 1973, when the Court overruled a 1928 case which required the stock of corporations controlling pharmacies to be owned by pharmacists operating and managing the pharmacies concerned. Here too, the earlier case was held a derelict in the law and overruled.

Although the Court has had no occasion directly to repudiate other specific due process decisions of the pre-1937 period, it would undoubtedly do so if the need arose, for recent decisions show how clearly the Court has rejected the earlier due process philosophy. From 1890 to 1937 the High Bench used the Due Process Clause as a device to enable it to review the desirability of regulatory legislation. In the middle of this century, the Court could declare, "The day is gone when this Court uses the Due Process Clause of the Fourteenth Amendment to strike down state laws, regulatory of business and industrial conditions, because they may be unwise, improvident, or out of harmony with a particular school of thought."

After 1936, no regulatory law was invalidated by the Supreme Court on due process grounds. The view that due process authorizes judges to hold laws unconstitutional because they believe the legislature has acted unwisely has definitely been discarded: "We have returned to the original constitutional proposition that courts do not substitute their social and economic beliefs for the judgment of legislative bodies who are elected to pass laws," said the Court in 1963. Above all, it is not for courts to judge the correctness of the economic theory behind a regulatory law. Not only has the Holmes view that the Constitution does not enact Spencer's *Social Statics* been emphatically adopted; in the Court's more recent words,

"Whether the legislature takes for its textbook Adam Smith, Herbert Spencer, Lord Keynes, or some other is no concern of ours."

The decline of substantive due process is now firmly ingrained in American public law. And the Court would say, such rejection is entirely consistent with the role of the judiciary in a representative democracy. To draw the pre-1937 due process line as a limit to regulatory action is to make the criterion of constitutionality what the judges believe correct as a matter of economic theory.

Law and the Welfare State

One of the most important public law developments during the second quarter of the twentieth century was the laying of the constitutional foundation for the emerging welfare state. If, by mid-century, the concept of the welfare state had come to dominate the polity, it cannot be denied that it came relatively late (by comparison with other countries) to the American scene. In large part, the reason for the American lag was a constitutional one. The restricted scope of governmental functions permitted by American public law during the first part of the century did not include most of the functions that have come to be associated with the welfare state.

Legally speaking, the trend toward the welfare state started with the

The Supreme Court in session, February 8, 1935. The photograph, by Dr. Erich Salomon, a noted pioneer in candid news photography, may be unique; it is believed to be the only one ever taken while the justices were actually hearing a case.

factory laws and workmen's compensation laws mentioned at the beginning of this chapter. More recently, such laws, designed to protect the worker against the hazards incident to industrial employment, have proved inadequate. The society has also sought to safeguard the individual against the uncertain nature of modern industrial employment. It has come to be recognized that the costs of maintaining superannuated workers and of unemployment, like the costs of industrial accidents, should be distributed as part of the costs of production, instead of being borne immediately by the individuals concerned. This has led to legislation establishing retirement and pension systems, as well as unemployment insurance systems.

These new laws were contrary to the restricted conception of governmental power which prevailed during the first part of the century. As late as 1935, the Supreme Court ruled an old age pension law to be an invalid interference with freedom of contract. Such a law, it declared, "is an attempt for social ends to impose by sheer fiat non-contractual incidents upon the relation of employer and employee . . . as a means of ensuring a particular class of employees against old age dependency."

This decision was one of the first casualties of the constitutional revolution of 1937. The *Social Security Act Cases* of that year definitely settled the constitutional authority to enact social legislation, such as that stricken down in 1935. The fundamental premise that has since governed judicial consideration of all such legislation is that society may take care of its human wastage, whether owing to accident, age, or some other cause.

The Social Security Act of 1935 brought the federal government extensively into the field of social insurance. It established a nationwide system of old age benefits to workers, as well as an extensive system of unemployment insurance. The systems were financed by taxes on both employers and employees. In the series of 1937 cases, the Supreme Court upheld the con-

People line up in 1936 to learn of the provisions of the new social security law. Though opponents called it socialistic, the measure was upheld by the Supreme Court.

stitutionality of both the old age and unemployment benefit provisions. In so ruling, the Court gave the broadest scope to the congressional power to tax and spend, holding that the Social Security Act provisions were valid exercises of that power. The 1937 decisions put an end to fears that unemployment insurance and old age benefit laws might prove beyond the power of either states or nation, as minimum wage regulation had been held to be under the pre-1937 decisions. Henceforth the United States was not to be the one great nation powerless to adopt such measures.

The significance of the *Social Security Act Cases*, however, extended far beyond the statute at issue. The opinions delivered furnished the doctrinal basis for the developing state. That state was characterized above all by the geometric growth of government largess. "Government," said Charles A. Reich in an article in the *Yale Law Journal* in 1964, "is a gigantic siphon. It draws in revenue and power, and pours forth wealth: money, benefits, services, contracts, franchises, and licenses." The field of benefactions came to occupy an ever-growing proportion of the efforts of government. The political order itself was compendiously called the welfare state.

The key instrument of the welfare state is the fisc, its motive force the power of the purse. The 1937 decisions construed that power most broadly. If Congress chose to tax and spend to operate schemes of old age benefits and unemployment insurance, that was a matter within its discretion. "For the past six years," the Court admitted finally in 1937, "the nation, unhappily, has been placed in a position to learn at first hand the nature and extent of the problem of unemployment, and to appreciate its profound influence upon the public welfare."

Under the *Social Security Act Cases*, the power of the purse could be utilized for whatever social purpose the legislature chose. The only restriction on that power in the Constitution was that it be exercised "to . . . provide for the common Defence and general Welfare." The *Social Security Act Cases* allowed the legislature to determine whether a given exercise of the power of the purse would promote the general welfare: "The line must still be drawn between one welfare and another, between particular and general. . . . There is a middle ground or certainly a penumbra in which discretion is at large. That discretion, however," said the Supreme Court, "is not confided to the courts. The discretion belongs to Congress."

The New Federalism

"The question of the relation of the States to the federal government is the cardinal question of our time," wrote Woodrow Wilson in 1908. If anything, the question became more pressing toward the middle of the century. The concept of federalism on which the Republic had been founded was by that time giving way to what was being termed "the New Federalism." This was part of a worldwide trend during the century toward consistent concentration of authority in the center of the political structure. But it was also fostered by the changing doctrines of public law already discussed.

The post-1937 decisions of the Supreme Court removed most of the limitations that had previously been placed on federal authority. The need for national regulation of the economy was met by judicial recognition of

Social security was a new concept to most Americans — as was the requirement (save for that of a temporary wartime draft) that each person be registered with a permanent government number. This poster was part of a nationwide public information campaign that launched the program.

In the New York City Post Office, typists process the first employees' social security forms in 1936.

the validity of such regulation. The basic theme was set in a 1940 opinion: "Congress under the commerce clause is not impotent to deal with what it may consider to be dire consequences of laissez faire." The decisions after 1937 recognized federal authority to regulate virtually every aspect of economic life. Nor was the Tenth Amendment ("The powers not delegated to the United States by the Constitution, nor prohibited by it to the States, are reserved to the States respectively, or to the people.") any longer a bar to federal regulation of local activities. "The amendment states but a truism," said the Court in 1941. Under it, no exclusive area of state authority served to limit the area in which federal action might be taken. Federal predominance had become the dominant legal theme in the American Union.

Equally important in making for a constitutional shift in the center of gravity in the federal system were the *Social Security Act Cases*. As noted, these decisions gave the broadest scope to the power of the purse, leaving to Congress all but unfettered discretion to tax and spend for any program deemed by it to provide for the general welfare. Under the decisions, Congress could plainly make financial grants to the states. Federal subsidies to the states were, of course, nothing new in the American system; they can be traced back to the preconstitutional Confederation. One must, however, note changes during the 1930's and 1940's that drastically altered the effect of the federal grant system.

During the 1930's depression, federal funds were first granted to the states on a really substantial scale. Many New Deal measures for social welfare, health, unemployment, agricultural, or other relief were carried out through federally aided state programs. In the following decade, the federal provision of grants-in-aid to the states grew by leaps and bounds. By mid-century, grants-in-aid were part of the warp and woof of the American governmental system. By then, about 15 percent of all funds spent by state governments derived from federal subventions, and the trend toward the use of federal aid was definitely on the increase.

In the second quarter of the century, the federal grant-in-aid changed, not only in degree, but also in kind. The grants made as part of the New Deal measures were no longer given without qualifications. Instead, substantial conditions were imposed by Washington on states that accepted its subventions, which made possible federal supervision of the programs of economic revival undertaken by the states. The practice of making grants conditional continued in the next decade; by mid-century the conditional grant-in-aid had become an established part of American federalism. "As used herein," stated a 1967 national study, "a 'Federal grant-in-aid' is a payment of funds by the National Government to a State or local government for a specified purpose . . . and in accordance with prescribed standards and requirements."

The constitutionality of the conditional grant-in-aid was sustained in the *Social Security Act Cases*. The act of 1935 provided for an unemployment compensation tax to be levied on employers. Employers in states that enacted satisfactory unemployment insurance laws were to receive credit up to 90 percent of the federal tax. Since the tax was to be collected whether or not any such state law existed, pressure was put on each state to enact unemployment compensation legislation meeting federal standards.

In one of the *Social Security Act Cases*, the Supreme Court rejected the claim that the 1935 act amounted to an unconstitutional attempt to control the states' efforts to deal with the unemployment problem. "Who then is coerced," asked the Court, "in the operation of this statute? . . . Not the state. . . . For all that appears she is satisfied with her choice, and would be sorely disappointed if it were now to be annulled. . . . To hold that motive or temptation is equivalent to coercion is to plunge the law in endless difficulties." In other words, no constitutional reason existed why the federal government might not supply motives for actions by the states. The power of Congress to make grants included the power to influence the action of the recipients so that the desired congressional ends would be attained.

According to Senator Edmund Muskie in 1967, "The grant-in-aid is likely to continue to be the most prominent and positive feature of contemporary federalism." Certainly, the grant-in-aid system made possible needed public services at a standard that many states by themselves would be unable to provide. At the same time, the growth of the grant-in-aid system was clearly helping to alter the balance between states and nation. Federal aid was extended only at the price of ever-increasing control by Washington over state legislation and administration: "all federal grants . . .," noted Jane Perry Clark in *The Rise of a New Federalism* in 1938, "drive stakes of important federal control into state administration. . . . The old adage that he who pays the piper calls the tune contains an element of truth in relation to grant-in-aid services." Further expansion of the system meant further aggrandizement of federal power. "Unquestionably it does," said the constitutional authority Edward S. Corwin, "for when two cooperate, even though they be a Hitler and a Mussolini, it is the stronger member of the combination who calls the tune. Resting as it does primarily on the superior fiscal resources of the National Government, Cooperative Federalism [as the grant-in-aid system is sometimes termed] has been, to date, a short expression for a constantly increasing concentration of power at Washington."

Hot and Cold War

In the first half of the twentieth century the United States was engaged in two world wars; American public law had to make an unprecedented accommodation to the demands of global conflict. Both wars saw the assumption by the nation of unparalleled authority, concentrated in the main in the executive branch.

Constitutional development during the two world wars emphasized (as it had in the Civil War) that presidential primacy is an inevitable concomi-

America's Gravest Miscarriage of Justice

The case of Toyosaburo Korematsu is unique in American law. As Justice Robert H. Jackson put it in 1944: "Korematsu was born on our soil, of parents born in Japan. The Constitution makes him a citizen of the United States by nativity and a citizen of California by residence. No claim is made that he is not loyal to this country. There is no suggestion that apart from the matter involved here he is not law-abiding and well disposed. Korematsu, however, has been convicted of an act not commonly a crime. It consists merely of being present in the state whereof he is a citizen, near the place where he was born, and where all his life he has lived." The difference between innocence and crime, so far as Korematsu was concerned, lay not in anything he did, said, or even thought, but only in his racial background. For Korematsu was a victim of what *Harper's* magazine was to term "America's Greatest Wartime Mistake," the forced evacuation of those of Japanese ancestry from the West Coast after the attack on Pearl Harbor.

Early in 1942, the Army issued Civilian Exclusion Orders, directing the moving of "all persons of Japanese ancestry, both alien and non-alien," from the West Coast (considered vulnerable to Japanese assault) to special inland Relocation Centers—which, in other countries, might have been termed more accurately concentration camps. Those who, like Korematsu, were forced into the Relocation Centers were deprived of their freedom because they were the children of parents concerning whom they had had no choice, and because they belonged to a race from which there was no way to resign. In the words of Justice Frank Murphy, "No less than 70,000 American citizens have been placed under a special ban and deprived of their liberty because of their particular racial inheritance. In this sense it bears a melancholy resemblance to the treatment accorded to members of the Jewish race in Germany and in other parts of Europe. The result is the creation in this country of two classes of citizens for the purpose of a critical and perilous hour—to sanction discrimination between groups

Japanese-Americans, taken from their homes,

tant of participation in a full-scale war. "This is a war of resources no less than of men, perhaps even more than of men," said President Wilson during World War I, and in accord with this viewpoint, the most drastic controls over the nation's resources were given him by Congress. Whereas Lincoln had often had to act without waiting for congressional authorization in order to avoid national disaster, Wilson was able to prosecute the war efficiently under the powers delegated to him.

Vast though the authority exercised by Wilson doubtless was, it remained for World War II to demonstrate the true extent of presidential primacy in wartime. The reality in this respect was shown even before Pearl Harbor. In the year and a half following the fall of France in 1940, the position of the nation was converted, on the initiative of the President, from that of a neutral to that of limited participant. From the transfer of fifty destroyers to Britain in September, 1940, to the October, 1941, order to American naval forces in the Atlantic to fire at sight on any Axis vessels or aircraft encountered, the President's acts were dominant. As Winston Churchill conceded, "The transfer to Great Britain of fifty American warships was a decidedly unneutral act. . . . It was the first in a long succession of unneutral acts

await transportation to Relocation Centers.

of United States citizens on the basis of ancestry."

Despite these sobering aspects, the Supreme Court upheld the Japanese evacuation in 1944 in the case of *Korematsu* v. *United States.* Korematsu had been convicted for remaining in California contrary to a Civilian Exclusion Order. Such an order, said the Court, could validly be issued after Pearl Harbor. In the face of a threatened Japanese attack on the mainland, citizens of Japanese ancestry could rationally be set apart from those who had no associations with Japan.

The *Korematsu* decision sustained the original relocation program. But the evacuated Japanese were detained for almost three years. That, ruled the Supreme Court in another case, *Ex parte Endo,* also in 1944, was going too far. Even the government conceded that the plaintiff, Miss Endo, was a loyal and law-abiding citizen. If that were true, said the Court, she was entitled to her unconditional release. The original evacuation program was justified as

a measure reasonably calculated to prevent espionage and sabotage by those affiliated ethnically with the enemy. But that justification could not apply to a concededly loyal citizen after sufficient time had gone by to enable the government to separate the loyal from the disloyal.

The *Endo* decision demonstrated both the strength and weakness of judicial review of exercises of the war power. The grant of habeas corpus to Miss Endo vindicated the rule of law, even in wartime. But the case also graphically revealed the limitations of judicial power as a practical check on military arbitrariness. Miss Endo had been evacuated from her home and placed in a Relocation Center early in 1942. In July, 1942, she had filed a petition for a writ of habeas corpus in a federal district court, yet it was not until December, 1944, that the Supreme Court ordered her released. She could take satisfaction in being immortalized in the *Supreme Court Reports,* but it was hardly an adequate recompense for her loss of liberty during the almost three years she had been confined.

which were of the utmost service to us. It marked the passage of the United States from being neutral to being nonbelligerent."

After Pearl Harbor, the basic question became one of the legal machinery needed to harness American resources for the demands of global conflict. Once again, the President was delegated the powers deemed needed to wage war successfully. He was given authority to mobilize both manpower and the economy to an unprecedented extent (at least for the American system). The powers granted included those of conscription of men, as well as so-called conscription of industry, requisition, priorities and allocation, price and rent control, wage stabilization, and control of labor disputes.

Under the war statutes delegating authority to him, President Roosevelt was vested with unexampled control over person and property. But such total power in the Executive was deemed essential. And the Supreme Court was in the forefront of those recognizing the necessity. The power to mobilize manpower had already been recognized during World War I. The World War II decisions upheld comparable power over property rights: "Mobilization of effort extended not only to the uniformed armed forces but to the entire population," the Court assented. The power to draft business organizations was ruled as great as that to draft fighting men.

During the war, the Supreme Court did little more than confirm the actions taken by the government, even such extreme actions as the evacuation of persons of Japanese ancestry from the West Coast and their detention in what were euphemistically termed relocation centers. Perhaps it is unfair to expect the justices to have done more than stamp their imprimatur on measures deemed necessary by those wielding the force of the nation. But the same was surely not true of the Cold War period that followed the cessation of hostilities. Doubtless some of the excesses committed during the postwar years are too close in time to be able to deal impartially with them. These excesses did, however, reveal that security, like the patriotism of which Dr. Johnson spoke, might also come to be the last refuge of a scoundrel: many of the things done in the postwar era in the name of national security would not have been tolerated in less tense times.

A basic problem for the American system of law is that of reconciling the antinomy between liberty and security. Both, to be sure, have always been essential elements in the polity, whose coexistence has had to be reconciled by the law. In the post-World War II period, nevertheless, security tended to dominate. The response to the tensions of the Cold War made American law security-conscious as it had never been before.

The governmental demand for security was articulated in laws and other measures restricting rights normally deemed fundamental. For the first time since the notorious Alien and Sedition Acts of 1798, a peacetime sedition law (making subversive speech criminal) put people in prison. The law in question—the Smith Act—was enacted in 1940; but the first significant prosecutions, those brought in 1948 against the leaders of the American Communist party, were a direct fruit of the postwar confrontation with the Soviet Union. The Communist prosecutions were upheld in *Dennis* v. *United States* in 1951, with the decision turning on the "clear and present danger" presented by Communist advocacy during the tense postwar period.

In addition, the Supreme Court upheld other significant Cold War restrictions, ranging from drastic restraints upon aliens to the loyalty-security programs instituted by governments in this country. The restrictions on Communist aliens were ruled within the plenary power of Congress over citizens of other lands, and the federal loyalty program was upheld under the settled principle that "The Constitution does not guarantee public employment." In addition, the Court refused to strike down restrictions on the procedural rights of notice and full hearing in cases where national security was involved.

These decisions occurred during the immediate postwar period, and may be understandable as a continued reaction from the excesses of pre-1937 judicial supremacy. Justices who had repudiated those excesses continued to display the same Holmesian approach of deference to the legislator. Nevertheless, one may wonder whether the Supreme Court did not go too far in standing aside in the face of the extreme restrictions imposed in security's name. A court overimbued with the dominant demand for security may tend to accede to that demand, even if the cost be distortion of accepted principles of constitutional law. Yet this can hardly be done without important effects on general jurisprudence. A supreme tribunal that molds its law only to fit immediate demands of public sentiment is hardly fulfilling its proper role. As Justice Frankfurter once put it, "The Court has no reason for existence if it merely reflects the pressures of the day." The doctrine of deference to the legislature may require abnegation on the part of the Court but hardly

The cold war concern for national security that followed World War II gave birth to another period of witch hunts against dissenters. This was the scene as the House Un-American Activities Committee held hearings in 1947 into alleged communists in the film industry. Among the committee members at the right was the then Representative, Richard M. Nixon.

abdication by it of the judicial function. Whatever may be said about the strains and stresses of the Cold War period, the enemy was not so near the gates that the nation had to abandon respect for the organic traditions that had theretofore prevailed in the American system.

From Property to Personal Rights

During the first half of this century, the courts began a shift in emphasis from property to personal rights that has been one of the major themes of twentieth-century American public law. For over a hundred years, the Bill of Rights had had little practical effect on governmental power. It was not until the second quarter of the present century that the first amendments began to be given practical meaning by the law.

To understand the course of development in this respect, one must first realize that the restrictions of the Bill of Rights were binding, as such, only on the federal government. During the early years of the Republic, there were few interferences from Washington with individual rights; hence there was little occasion for application of the Bill of Rights guaranties.

After the Civil War, significant limitations on state power were added to the federal Constitution. The postbellum amendments contained important guaranties of individual rights, particularly in the Fourteenth Amendment's Due Process and Equal Protection clauses. Yet, as noted in Chapter IV, the early impact of the new amendments was confined almost entirely to the economic sphere. When, toward the turn of the nineteenth century, the Supreme Court adopted the view that the Fourteenth Amendment (primarily in its Due Process Clause) was intended to work a fundamental change, its decisions were all but limited to property. For a generation thereafter, property rights, rather than personal rights, were the main concern of the courts. In 1922, a federal judge could still state, "it should be remembered that of the three fundamental principles which underlie government, and for which government exists, the protection of life, liberty and property, the chief of these is property."

During the second quarter of this century, the judicial emphasis began to change. The Supreme Court for the first time held the states bound by specific guaranties of the Bill of Rights. In so doing, it both provided protection for individual rights at the level of government where danger of abridgment has existed in practice and began to give substantive content to the guaranties contained in the Bill of Rights themselves. This development involved the selective incorporation, by a process of absorption, of guaranties of the Bill of Rights within the Fourteenth Amendment's Due Process Clause. As early as 1884, the Supreme Court had rejected the view that the Fourteenth Amendment automatically absorbed all the provisions of the Bill of Rights and thus placed on the states the exact limitations that had theretofore been placed on the federal government. The view the other way was urged in several cases and culminated in Justice Hugo L. Black's noted dissent in *Adamson v. California* in 1947, in which he urged that "one of the chief objects that the provisions of the Amendment's first section . . . were intended to accomplish was to make the Bill of Rights applicable to the states."

There was opposition to the nomination of Hugo L. Black (above) to the Supreme Court in 1937 when it was learned that he had briefly belonged to the Ku Klux Klan. But the Alabaman's record as a justice was progressive, and he became known as an ardent defender of the Bill of Rights.

Strikes like this one of Detroit auto workers in 1937 gained labor legal rights comparable to those of property.

Black's position on the matter has never been able to command a majority on the Supreme Court. What the Court did in the first half of the century was to develop the "fundamental right" test to determine whether a particular right guaranteed in the Bill of Rights is included in the Fourteenth Amendment: Is the right which the individual claims the state has violated so fundamental that it inheres in the concept of due process? According to a 1937 case, the line of division depends on whether the right at issue is one that is "of the very essence of a scheme of ordered liberty." If it is, the Fourteenth Amendment has absorbed it in the belief that neither liberty nor justice would exist if such a right were sacrificed.

In the second quarter of the century, the Supreme Court began to hold that specific guaranties of the Bill of Rights were so fundamental as to be included in due process. Two 1925 decisions held that the rights protected by the First Amendment "are among the fundamental personal rights and 'liberties' protected by the due process clause of the Fourteenth Amendment from impairment by the States." The domain of "liberty," withdrawn by the Fourteenth Amendment from encroachment by the states, was thus enlarged to include liberty of mind and belief as well as of action.

In 1923 the Supreme Court for the first time reversed a state criminal

The Clear and Present Danger Test

Early in the morning of August 23, 1918, the air above passersby at the corner of Houston and Crosby Streets in New York City was filled with leaflets thrown from a loft window. Written in lurid language, they contained a bitter attack against the sending of American soldiers to Siberia, urging a workers' general strike in support of the Russian Revolution and as a "reply to the barbaric intervention" by the U.S. troops. Six Russian factory workers who had printed and distributed the leaflets were arrested by the police and were convicted under the 1917 Espionage Act for the publishing of language which incited resistance to the American war effort by encouraging "curtailment to cripple or hinder the United States in the prosecution of the war."

The case, known as *Abrams v. United States*, went to the Supreme Court, which in 1919 affirmed the convictions, holding that, even though the defendants' primary intent had been to aid the Russian Revolution, their plan of action had necessarily involved obstruction of the American war effort against Germany. Justice Oliver Wendell Holmes, joined by Justice Louis D. Brandeis, dissented. The Holmes dissent, his famous one in which he set forth the foundation of the First Amendment as "free trade in ideas," which through competition for their acceptance by the people would provide the best test of truth, argued that the "silly" leaflets published by obscure individuals and thrown from a loft window presented no danger of resistance to the war effort. Not enough, he said, "can be squeezed from these poor and puny anonymities to turn the color of legal litmus paper."

According to Holmes, "Only the emergency that makes it immediately dangerous to leave the correction of evil counsels to time warrants making any exception to the sweeping command, 'Congress shall make no law abridging the freedom of speech.'"

Police cart off literature seized in a raid

conviction on the ground that the trial had departed from due process. In the next two and a half decades, the Court held an increasing number of the rights guaranteed by the Bill of Rights binding on the states. These included the Fourth Amendment's right against illegal searches and seizures, the Fifth Amendment's right against coerced confessions, the Sixth Amendment's right to a public trial, impartial jury, and counsel (at least in capital cases and where a "fair trial" could not be obtained), and the Eighth Amendment's right against cruel and unusual punishments.

True, the Court did not go as far as the dissenting justices urged. Left out of the due process catalogue, and consequently not yet binding on the states, were many rights that today are clearly considered fundamental: the rights against use of illegally seized evidence, double jeopardy, self-incrimination, that to a jury trial, and to counsel as a general proposition. But the Court by mid-century had only begun the process of absorption of the Bill of Rights. Most important, it had developed the tool by which an ever-increasing inventory of rights could be held binding on the states.

In holding governmental action violative of particular Bill of Rights guaranties, the judges were endowing those rights themselves with substantive content. This was especially true of that freedom which the Supreme

on communists during the red scare of 1919.

But when does such an "emergency" arise? Holmes himself had provided the answer a few months earlier in the case of Schenck v. United States: when "the words are used in such circumstances and are of such a nature as to create a clear and present danger that they will bring about the substantive evils that Congress has a right to prevent," he had said.

Under this Clear and Present Danger test, speech may be restricted only if there is a real threat—a danger, both clear and present, that the speech will lead to an evil that Congress has the power to prevent. In the Abrams case, Congress had the right to pass a law to prevent curtailment of war production; but, said Holmes, there was no danger, clear and present, or even remote, that the leaflets would have had any effect on production.

Holmes's Clear and Present Danger test was eventually adopted by the Supreme Court, providing a substantial guarantee in the protection of free speech. World War II did not see anything like the two thousand prosecutions under the Espionage Act, most of them involving anti-war speech, that had occurred during and just after World War I. Even the McCarthy Era of the 1950's did not witness anything as extreme as the reductio ad absurdum of the World War I Espionage Act cases—the conviction of the producer of a film titled The Spirit of '76 about the American Revolution, which included a scene showing British soldiers shooting and bayoneting women and children, a sequence charged with inciting hatred and enmity toward America's World War I ally! Adoption of the Clear and Present Danger test has, since the second quarter of the twentieth century, subjected such prosecutions to a "rule of reason," which makes it impossible for them to be brought successfully when the test is followed. As long as this occurs, cases like Abrams v. United States cannot be repeated.

The Supreme Court in 1944 declared "white primaries" in the South unconstitutional. Many blacks, like these voting in a 1946 primary in Marietta, Georgia, went to the polls and cast their ballots, despite threats of violence against them.

Court well termed "the matrix, the indispensable condition, of nearly every other form of freedom," namely, the freedom of expression protected by the First Amendment. Two developments with regard to that freedom were of particular significance.

First, the Supreme Court rejected the restrictive rule originally stated in 1897 by Justice Holmes (apostle of free speech though he was later to become) that government has the same unqualified power to bar speech in streets and other public places that "the owner of a private house [has] to forbid it in his house." In a series of cases during the 1930's and 1940's, many of which involved the Jehovah's Witnesses, the Court abandoned the rule. By mid-century the rule was definitively established that streets, parks, and other public places were held by government subject to the rights secured by the First Amendment. Under the new rule, public places could become vast forums for the presentation of unpopular views and opinions.

Second, the Supreme Court adopted the Clear and Present Danger Test enunciated in 1919 by Justice Holmes. Although that test has recently been criticized as too restrictive, it represented a real step forward in favor of free speech. "Correctly applied," said Justice Brandeis in 1920, "it will preserve the right of free speech both from suppression by tyrannous, well-meaning majorities and from abuse by irresponsible, fanatical minorities."

Mention should also be made of the movement in the law to give practical effect to the Fourteenth Amendment's Equal Protection Clause. That movement was not to become a leading one until the second half of the century; but it began before mid-century. As noted in Chapter IV, the purpose of the

Fourteenth Amendment to secure racial equality had largely been frustrated by the turn of the century. On the doctrine of "separate but equal" was built the whole system of Jim Crow that prevailed until after World War II.

During the war, the attitude of the Supreme Court to racial discrimination began to change. "Distinctions based on color . . . ," asserted a member of the Court in 1943, "are utterly inconsistent with our traditions and ideals. They are at variance with the principles for which we are now waging war." In 1944 the Court struck down as violative of equal protection the "white primary" that barred Negroes from effective participation in politics in most of the South. The next step was the invalidation of racial restrictions on property. In 1948 judicial enforcement of racial restrictive covenants was ruled contrary to equal protection. These decisions left untouched the Jim Crow system which, said the President's Committee on Civil Rights in 1947, "cuts across the daily lives of Southern citizens from the cradle to the grave."

The "separate but equal" doctrine had been laid down in 1896 in *Plessy v. Ferguson;* under it, segregation, as such, was not discriminatory and hence not violative of equal protection, provided substantially equal facilities were made available to both races. By mid-century, the Supreme Court had not overruled *Plessy.* But it began to interpret its doctrine in a manner which made its overruling only a matter of time.

The Court shifted the emphasis in the *Plessy* doctrine from "separate" to "equal"—to place increasing emphasis on judicial implementation of the requirement of equality in facilities. Starting in 1938, the Court ruled in a number of cases that given educational facilities provided for Negroes failed to meet the equality requirement. All of these cases involved education in colleges and universities, and by 1950 the Court had virtually adopted the doctrine that, where higher education was concerned, separate facilities for Negroes were inherently unequal. What the Court said of segregation in higher education was, however, also true of segregation as such. There can never be real equality in separated facilities, for the mere fact of segregation makes for discrimination. It was to be only a short next step to the holding that all segregation violated the Equal Protection Clause.

Administrative Agencies

At mid-century a leading judge stated that "administrative law [had] become the outstanding legal development of the twentieth century, reflecting in the law the hegemony of the executive arm of the government." Chapter v discussed how the archetype of the modern administrative agency, the Interstate Commerce Commission, was set up in 1887. But the ICC did not long stand alone; during the present century, a host of similar bodies was established. A system of administrative law was necessary to deal with the operation of these agencies—themselves the necessary implements for execution of the multifold functions assumed by the twentieth-century state. This development was acutely foreseen in 1916 by Elihu Root then president of the ABA: "There is one field of law development which has manifestly become inevitable. We are entering upon the creation of a body of administrative law."

The Plessy v. Ferguson *"separate but equal" doctrine of 1896 legalized segregated facilities all over the South. The part about them being "equal"* was usually ignored.

The Winds of Change

Even before the explosion of the blacks' civil rights struggle in the 1960's, changes in national attitudes were making it clear that the institution of Jim Crow and its legal base, the Plessy v. Ferguson decision, would not stand forever. To the blacks, it seemed that until the law changed, nothing changed. But by the 1930's public opinion had begun to shift and was laying the groundwork of support for the civil rights acts and judicial decisions that would eventually strike down Jim Crow. These photographs give some evidence of that change. At left, members of the Ku Klux Klan, a power in the 1924 Democratic convention and close to controlling several state governments, parade with impunity down Pennsylvania Avenue in the Nation's Capital in 1925. Fourteen years later, some 75,000 people, including government leaders, mass before the Lincoln Memorial, below, to honor black singer Marian Anderson after a controversy over her use of Constitution Hall, owned by the Daughters of the American Revolution.

Elihu Root, who warned of the need to limit the powers of administrative agencies, was Secretary of War and then Secretary of State under Theodore Roosevelt, a senator from New York, and an able representative of the United States at numerous international conferences.

Nevertheless, during much of the early twentieth century, American law was largely unaware of the developing system of administrative law. As late as 1927, Felix Frankfurter could complain that even scholars treated it as an exotic. Bench and Bar were still under the influence of A. V. Dicey's view, expressed in 1885, that administrative law was completely opposed to Anglo-American principles, and, therefore, "In England, and in the countries which, like the United States, derive their civilization from English sources, the system of administrative law and the very principles upon which it rests are in truth unknown." It was not until almost mid-century that administrative law received de jure status as a recognized rubric of American law, with its inclusion as a title in the *Fifth Decennial Digest* (1947) of the West Key Reporter System, which reports and digests the cases decided by American courts.

Yet if, before that time, "our Administrative Law has largely 'growed' like Topsy," as Frankfurter put it, grow it did and with a development that became inexorable after the Great Depression. The New Deal measures were carried out through the medium of administrative agencies: "As rapidly as — indeed, sometimes more rapidly than — causes could be isolated and problems defined," wrote James M. Landis in 1938, "administrative agencies were created to wrestle with them." It became imperative for these agencies of regulation themselves to be regulated by the law. "The limits of their power over the citizen must be fixed and determined. The rights of the citizen against them must be made plain," warned Elihu Root in 1916. The law could no longer continue to be distorted by Dicey's "misconceptions and myopia." Dialectic had to yield to reality; a system of administrative law was consciously developed.

The first task of the developing system was to legitimize the vast delegations of power made to administrative agencies, particularly during and after the New Deal period. In two 1935 cases, the Supreme Court had struck down the National Industrial Recovery Act, perhaps the most important early New Deal measure, on the ground that it contained excessive delegations of power because the authority granted under it was not restricted by any real standard. As the Court put it, with regard to the statute's grant of authority to prohibit, in the absolute discretion of the official concerned, the interstate transportation of so-called hot oil (oil produced in excess of state regulatory laws), "the Congress has declared no policy, has established no standard, has laid down no rule. There is no requirement, no definition of circumstances and conditions in which the transportation is to be allowed or prohibited."

In the next decade and a half, the Supreme Court all but abandoned the view exemplified in the 1935 decisions — that the courts must invalidate laws delegating power unless they contain limiting standards. The change in the judicial attitude was a reflection in the field of administrative law of the deference toward the legislator in economic affairs which marked American public law at mid-century. Judges who upheld legislative interventions in the economic area, even in fields previously ruled beyond the scope of governmental authority, were bound to take a more lenient attitude toward delegations of power in the same area.

At the same time, the changed judicial attitude encouraged Congress and the state legislatures to make broader delegations to administrative agencies than had formerly been their wont. Wholesale delegations became the rule rather than the exception; the broad grants made during the later New Deal, World War II, and the Cold War period were all sustained by the courts. Even a statute such as the Communications Act of 1934, which limited the authority conferred on the Federal Communications Commission only by the requirement that the commission act in the "public interest" — plainly no limitation at all — was sustained.

Thus if, as Justice Cardozo expressed it in one of the alluded-to 1935 cases, delegation without a standard is "delegation running riot," such delegation had by mid-century become normal. The touchstone of American government had, indeed, become the public interest criterion. As Charles A. Reich put it in his 1971 book, *The Greening of America*, "The basic theme was

The host of New Deal agencies, creating an "alphabet soup" of the various initials by which they were known, provided new subjects for the fun and satire of cartoonists. As the jibe below suggests, however, they did not amuse everyone, for their many new rules and powers posed serious threats to the nation and grave problems for the law.

Felix Frankfurter, at left, testifies before a Senate subcommittee considering his nomination to the Supreme Court in 1939. Though opposed by many as a radical, on the Court Frankfurter evinced respect for precedent in making his decisions.

simple: economic power . . . must be subjected to 'the public interest' " as defined by the administrator.

One consideration cut across the system of administrative law that the courts were constructing: deference to the administrative expert. As noted, the judges all but removed the restrictions on the powers that might be delegated to the administrator. In addition, they refused to intervene in the process of exercise of administrative power. In 1936 the Supreme Court had tilted a lance against the so-called institutional decision. But this attempt strictly to control the process of administrative decision was soon abandoned as an unwarranted judicial interference with agency autonomy. The dominant consideration was that articulated by Justice Frankfurter in 1941: "although the administrative process has had a different development and pursues somewhat different ways from those of courts, they are to be deemed collaborative instrumentalities of justice and the appropriate independence of each should be respected by the other."

The history of the developing system of administrative law was one of constant expansion of administrative authority accompanied by a correlative restriction of judicial power. If anything, there was an accentuation of this development as the law moved toward the middle of the century. The scope of judicial review of administrative decisions was consistently narrowed. The basic approach to the technical questions involved in most fields of regulation was that stated by the Court in 1942: "We certainly have neither technical competence nor legal authority to pronounce upon the wisdom of the course taken by the Commission."

The balance sheet at mid-century was, however, not all in favor of the administrator. Most notable on the other side of the ledger was the 1946 enactment of the Federal Administrative Procedure Act. That law was "a new, basic and comprehensive regulation of procedures in many agencies" and provided minimum standards of administrative procedure. Its enactment gave clear evidence of a congressional desire to call a halt to the process of administrative expansion. And the Supreme Court quickly indicated that the new law would be interpreted in such a way as to give full effect to its remedial intent. The friendliness of the Court toward administrative authority gave way to the doctrine of deference toward the legislator in the field of economic regulation.

Even more suggestive were indications of judicial doubts about the desirability of the trend toward expansion of administrative authority. "How to fit ancient liberties which have gained a new preciousness, into solution of those exigent and intricate economic problems that have been too long avoided rather than faced, is the special task of Administrative Law," wrote Justice Frankfurter in 1941. The judges began to realize that abdication of the field to the administrator was not a valid way of performing the task. "It will not do to say that it must all be left to the skill of experts," the Court declared in 1944. The judiciary, too, had a vital part to perform. "Courts no less than administrative bodies," the Supreme Court stated significantly, "are agencies of government. Both are instruments for realizing public purposes."

Farewell to Laissez Faire

Toward the end of his life, Herbert Spencer began to doubt his own optimistic philosophy of progress. His growing disillusionment culminated in an 1898 letter, prompted by his shock at American annexation of the Philippines: "the white savages . . . are over-running the dark savages everywhere. . . . There is a bad time coming; and civilized mankind will morally be uncivilized before civilization can again advance." During the next fifty years, history was to have its revenge on Spencer and his disciples. The present century has given the lie to the complacent Spencerean vision of the future.

In the law there was a generational lag until judges who were brought up when Spencerean philosophy was dominant were replaced by men ready to move the law into the twentieth century. After 1937, however, that movement took place, and its "first and foremost casualty . . . ," as Corwin pointed out in *Constitutional Revolution, Ltd.,* "was the *laissez faire* theory of governmental function." By mid-century, the courts were willing to recognize governmental interventions in the life of the community that would have been unthinkable a generation earlier. "The meaning of the Constitution," plaintively declared the dissenters in one of the 1937 cases upholding a regulatory law, "does not change with the ebb and flow of economic events." But the rigid constitutional construction of the pre-1937 period did give way before both the press of economic events and changing conceptions of governmental function.

As stated earlier, the main course of public law development during the first half of the century was one from Legal Darwinism to the Legal Realism of Justice Holmes. While the Supreme Court was increasingly equating the Constitution with laissez faire, men turned to Holmes's dissents as the precursors of a new era. The at-first-lonely voice soon became that of a new dispensation which wrote itself into American public law.

Yet, if Holmes furnished the principal jurisprudential foundation for the twentieth-century state, he did not necessarily concur in the assumptions upon which it was based. Holmes's attitude toward both law and life

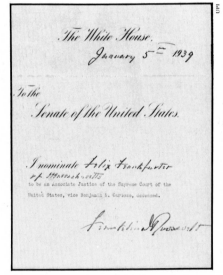

President Roosevelt's formal letter to the Senate nominated Felix Frankfurter of Massachusetts to fill the vacancy on the Bench created by the death of Justice Benjamin N. Cardozo.

The Great Monkey Trial

The law is a ass," observed Charles Dickens's character, Mr. Bumble, in *Oliver Twist*. In 1925 many Americans, watching with amazement the circus-like proceedings of the dramatic Scopes trial in Tennessee, found themselves echoing the same sentiments. "Isn't it difficult to realize that a trial of this kind is possible in the twentieth century in the United States of America?" demanded the lawyer for the defense, the famed Clarence Darrow. In truth, the case appeared a vestigial survival from an earlier day when people were

William Jennings Bryan at Dayton

prosecuted for witchcraft or for offenses like imagining the king's death. Headlined in the press as the Great Monkey Trial, it pitted the Biblical version of creation against the teachings of Charles Darwin, and did so in a courtroom atmosphere more closely resembling that of a revival meeting than a hall of justice.

The defendant, John T. Scopes, was a twenty-four-year-old high school teacher in Dayton, Tennessee, who was prosecuted for teaching evolution in violation of a state statute that prohibited the teaching in any public school of "any theory that denies the story of the divine creation of man as taught in the Bible, and to teach instead that man has descended from a lower order of animals." Conducted in the heat of July, the trial was a parody of all that a legal proceeding

should be. Dayton was ready for what it hoped would be the Waterloo of science. "One was hard put. . . ," an observer wrote, "to know whether Dayton was holding a camp meeting, a Chautauqua, a street fair, a carnival or a belated Fourth of July celebration. Literally, it was drunk on religious excitement."

The courtroom itself was decked with a large banner, exhorting everyone to "Read your Bible daily." Darrow finally got it removed by demanding equal space for a banner urging, "Read your Evolution." The stars of the trial were the lawyers: Clarence Darrow, perhaps the best known criminal lawyer in American history (Lincoln Steffens had called him "the attorney for the damned"), representing Scopes and, indirectly, Darwin and evolution, and, against him, William Jennings Bryan, the Great Commoner, orator of the famed "Cross of Gold" speech in 1896, three-time candidate for President, and Secretary of State under Woodrow Wilson, who had volunteered to direct the prosecution. Aging and sanctimonious, Bryan was the leading Fundamentalist of the day. "I am more interested in the Rock of Ages than in the age of rocks," he proclaimed.

At the trial's beginning, Darrow said later, "the judge . . . with great solemnity and all the dignity possible announced that Brother Twitchell would invoke the Divine blessing. This was new to me. I had practiced law for more than forty years, and had never before heard God called in to referee a court trial." Darrow's objection to the blessing was overruled, and each day's session began with prayer by a different preacher. The high point of the trial saw Darrow put Bryan himself on the stand as an expert on "religion." The *New York Times* described this as the most amazing court scene in history, and out-of-state reporters and observers like the iconoclast H. L. Mencken had a field day conveying the in-

congruous proceedings to the nation. Bryan stuck doggedly to his insistence on the literal truth of the Bible, refusing, in Darrow's phrase, "to choose between his crude beliefs and the common intelligence of modern times."

In the end, the local population felt it won a righteous victory when the jury found Scopes guilty. But the judge imposed only a $100 fine, and, on appeal, the Tennessee Supreme Court reversed the decision on a technicality: the court, rather than the jury, had set the fine. The case

Bryan's opponent, Clarence Darrow

itself was more dramatic than significant—unless it deserved remembrance as an example of the law at its worst. "I think," said Darrow during the trial, "this case will be remembered because it is the first case of this sort since we stopped trying people in America for witchcraft." On another plane, Darrow's withering examination during the trial went far to discredit Fundamentalist dogma. Though anti-evolution laws remained on the books in what H. L. Mencken referred to as "the Bible Belt" of the South, they were never again enforced. And in 1968, the U.S. Supreme Court finally struck down an Arkansas anti-evolution law, though admitting that by then "the statute is presently more of a curiosity than a vital fact of life."

was grounded on an innate skepticism which made him doubt the economic nostrums that were acquiring increased currency as the century progressed. His personal views often ran counter to regulatory legislation based upon the new theories. To Sir Frederick Pollock, Holmes admitted that he shared to a great extent a "contempt for government interference with rates etc.," as well as a belief that the Sherman Act was "a humbug based on economic ignorance and incompetence" and a "disbelief that the Interstate Commerce Commission is a fit body to be entrusted with rate-making."

Above all, Holmes's skepticism led him to be dubious of dogma and decision based upon dogmatic cliché: "no general proposition is worth a damn," he said. Delusive exactness he saw as a source of fallacy, particularly in the application of the purposed vagueness of constitutional provisions. His philosopher's stone was "the conviction that our constitutional system rests upon tolerance and that its greatest enemy is the Absolute." It was not at all the judicial function to strike down laws with which the judge disagreed. "There is nothing I more deprecate than the use of the Fourteenth Amendment . . . to prevent the making of social experiments that an important part of the community desires . . . even though the experiments may seem futile or even noxious to me," he declared in one of his dissents. Not the judge but the legislator was to have the primary say on the policy considerations behind a regulatory measure. The judge's business was to enforce even "laws that I believe to embody economic mistakes."

By mid-century, the Holmes approach of judicial self-restraint had become established doctrine. Nevertheless, an important difference existed in this respect between Holmes and his disciples who had virtually taken over the post-1937 Bench. The latter did not share Holmes's doubts about the wisdom of much regulatory legislation. On the contrary, they tended to be vigorous adherents of the changed conception of the state and the need for its intervention in economic affairs. Many of them had been active in the New Deal and shared its philosophy of assuming economic leadership in the public interest.

At mid-century, the judge who was best known as a conscious disciple of Justice Holmes was Felix Frankfurter, who—after the death of Justice Cardozo—had succeeded to the Holmes seat on the High Bench. Describing the man whom he always considered his mentor on the Bench, Frankfurter wrote that Holmes "privately distrusted attempts at improving society by what he deemed futile if not mischievous economic tinkering. But that was not his business." Yet it was emphatically Frankfurter's business throughout his career. As early as 1930, Professor Frankfurter published a book, *The Public and Its Government*, advocating effective regulation; during the next decade, he was the Academic Eminence behind the New Deal. For Justice Frankfurter to follow the doctrine of self-restraint in the economic area was to uphold laws that coincided with his own views on the proper scope of governmental functions. "The helplessness of the individual employee to achieve human dignity in a society so largely affected by technological advances" made him willingly reject "the shibboleths of a pre-machine age" which equated "the constitutional conception of 'liberty' . . . with theories of *laissez faire*."

The Holmesians on the post-1937 Bench firmly believed, in the words of Justice Brandeis, that "Regulation . . . is necessary to the preservation and best development of liberty." Feeling that way, they enthusiastically ensured that the law mirrored the society in the transition from laissez faire to the welfare state.

"Of course," as Holmes said, "a general proposition is simply a string for the facts." The law at mid-century differed sharply from that of a generation earlier, not only in general doctrines but also in its approach to the facts. The decisions in cases such as *Ives* and *Lochner* early in the century were based upon the constitutional system as a perfect, but closed, sphere; the least dent was an invalid subtraction from its essence. In determining public law issues, the black-letter approach—exact adherence to the letter of cases and statutes—was the only one permitted. Said the *Ives* court in reply to an appeal based upon "the economic and sociological arguments" urged in support of the challenged law: "We have already admitted the strength of this appeal to a recognized and widely prevalent sentiment, but we think it is an appeal which must be made to the people and not to the courts."

During the first part of the twentieth century, the judges reached their restrictive conclusions deductively from preconceived notions and precedents; by mid-century, the judicial method had become inductive, reasoning more and more from facts. The constitutional system came to resemble a rubber ball: the dent pushed out of one side promptly reappeared on the other. Economic liberty became fluid and inconstant, dependent upon the particular circumstances of time and place. The Brandeis Brief replaced the black-letter judge with the man of statistics and the master of economics and other disciplines. Compare the opinion in the *Jones & Laughlin* case of 1937, with its emphasis throughout on the economic and social conditions that called forth the challenged statute, with that in the *Ives* case of 1911, where those factors were expressly ignored. The difference is as marked as that between the poetry of T. S. Eliot and Alfred Austin.

Still, as Holmes emphasized, theory is the most important part of the law, as the architect is the most important man in the building of a house. When one sums up the change in twentieth-century public law, the altered approach to doctrine stands out most clearly. Lecturing at Harvard at the turn of the century, A. V. Dicey summarized a comparable earlier change in England: "The current of opinion," he said, "had . . . been gradually running with more and more force in the direction of collectivism, with the natural consequence that by 1900 the doctrine of laissez faire . . . had more or less lost its hold."

Over the next fifty years a similar development took place in the United States. By mid-century the welfare state had conquered American law as it had taken the rest of the society. The invisible hand of Adam Smith was replaced by the "public interest," as increasingly determined by government and its agencies. In the changed social context, the elaborate system constructed by Herbert Spencer became ever more irrelevant; the philosophy of Spencer and his legal disciples had been not so much repudiated as bypassed.

The powerful dissents delivered by Oliver Wendell Holmes from 1902 to 1932 set the theme for twentieth-century law.

VII

Gone with the Frontier

Private Law and Institutions
1910–1950

August 29, 1906, was a pleasant summer evening in St. Paul, Minnesota. The twenty-ninth annual meeting of the American Bar Association had convened in the Capitol building that morning. Now the members (some 370 out of a total of 5,400) were seated in the auditorium to hear an address by "Mr. Roscoe Pound, of Lincoln, Nebraska." The title was "The Causes of Popular Dissatisfaction with the Administration of Justice." The typical ABA address of the day would have been delivered by a lawyer of national eminence, who would cheer his professional brethren by a eulogium on the law as the most refined system of justice yet devised by man. The present speaker was far different; he was a lawyer in his middle thirties, unknown outside his own state. And he did not intimate, but devoted his whole paper to the proposition that American law was something less than perfect.

Pound began his talk with the theme that "Dissatisfaction with the administration of justice is as old as law." But then he jolted his audience by asserting that that did not justify overlooking the fact "that there is more than the normal amount of dissatisfaction with the present-day administration of justice in America," and he proposed to point out the causes of current popular dissatisfaction. As his dry voice read out a bill of particulars, his conservative hearers sat in dismay: "Our system of courts is archaic." "Our procedure is behind the times." "Our courts have seemed to obstruct public efforts to get relief." They "have been put in a false position of doing nothing and obstructing everything." They "are made agents or abettors of lawlessness . . . and their time is frittered away on mere points of legal etiquette." "Putting courts into politics . . . has almost destroyed the traditional respect for the Bench."

The State Capitol in St. Paul

Roscoe Pound, about 1909, when he was teaching law at Northwestern University

As a leading judge put it half a century later, "Pound's famous address . . . elicited hostile, almost virulent, criticism, although the address was merely a factual and analytical presentation." Today Pound's speech can be viewed as the catalyst for the reform efforts made during this century in the administration of justice—"the spark that kindled the white flame of progress," in a flamboyant characterization by American legal scholar John H. Wigmore.

The Pound catalogue of causes of dissatisfaction may serve as the starting point for an inventory of American law during the first half of the twentieth century. From it can be seen how the nation's law and legal institutions had developed by mid-century. In Pound's list of defects in the law, the following stand out most sharply:

(1) the mechanical operation of legal rules;
(2) the difference in rate of progress between law and public opinion;
(3) the individualist spirit of the common law;
(4) the doctrine of contentious procedure;
(5) the deficiencies of judicial organization and administration.

The discussion that follows of the different branches of private law and legal institutions during the first half of the century will benefit from the perspective of Pound's list. The causes of dissatisfaction that Pound noted at the turn of the century appear to have had a valid basis at the time. If there was progress during the next fifty years, it consisted in large part of efforts to ensure that the Pound catalogue would no longer reflect reality.

Chapter VI dealt with fundamental changes that occurred in American public law. As we have seen, three of the items in the Pound list definitely applied to public law in the first part of the century: (1) the mechanical application of constitutional law, particularly in the delusive exactness with which the judges applied the Due Process Clause; (2) the individualist

Schoolmaster of the American Bar

Roscoe Pound was to the twentieth century what Joseph Story had been to the nineteenth—America's greatest legal scholar. Dean of the Harvard Law School from 1916 to 1936, the period usually considered the Golden Age of that institution, he was a brilliant writer and teacher whose impact on the law and lawyers gained him the title of Schoolmaster of the American Bar. Yet he came to law himself after starting life as a botanist. Born in Lincoln, Nebraska, in 1870, he attended the University of Nebraska, studying botany, acquiring an M.A. and a Ph.D., and directing the Nebraska Botanical Survey, during which he discovered a lichen which was named *Roscoepoundia* for him. In 1889 Pound decided to study law

and entered Harvard Law School.

The following year, without having yet received his law degree, he passed the Nebraska Bar and started in practice in Lincoln. Eleven years later, in 1901, he was appointed a judge of the Nebraska Supreme Court and served until 1903, when he became dean of the Nebraska Law School. An address he made in St. Paul in 1906—the first speech to the American Bar Association by a law teacher—boldly criticized the deficiencies of the American legal system and brought him national attention. He was invited to teach at Northwestern and Chicago, and in 1910 he was appointed Professor of Law at Harvard. He stayed there until 1947, achieving an international reputation as a legal

thinker. Pound is one of the "two best men that I know of in this country," Oliver Wendell Holmes wrote about him as early as 1911.

Pound, perhaps, is best remembered for the years he served as dean at Harvard. Under his leadership, the faculty included outstanding men in most fields of the law, and the school attracted the cream of the country's law students. But Pound continued active in legal scholarship long after his retirement. His five-volume *Jurisprudence*, containing a compendium of a lifetime of thought on the subject, was published in 1959 when he was almost ninety years old, five years before his death in 1964.

His greatest contribution was to

spirit carried to its extreme; and (3) the lag between the law as applied by judges molded by Legal Darwinism and public opinion, which, as in England, was becoming more and more collectivist in outlook. The last chapter also demonstrated how, by the mid-1900's, the situation had altered completely. Judges had rejected extreme individualism and had become among the firmest adherents of the welfare state. Attempts at mechanical application of legal rules had given way to a balancing approach that weighed the claims of different interests in the organic scale. As the century went on, the balance tipped increasingly in favor of the social interests that might be furthered under expanding conceptions of governmental power.

This chapter notes a comparable development in the different areas of private law. The individualistic spirit of the common law, which had dominated contracts, torts, property, and other private law branches at the turn of the century, was being replaced fifty years later, we will see, by an entirely different spirit, which emphasized the welfare of the community even at the cost of individual rights of property, contract, and the like. In addition, a movement to revitalize legal institutions, particularly the courts, had begun to gather momentum.

What then had become of the Pound catalogue of complaints at mid-century? It would be erroneous to assume that it had been rendered academic by changes and reforms. Yet it would distort reality even more to assume that no progress had been made in removing the causes of popular dissatisfaction that Pound had noted.

Protection of the Individual

The law at the turn of the century aroused popular dissatisfaction most by its extreme adherence to the doctrine of freedom of contract. As applied

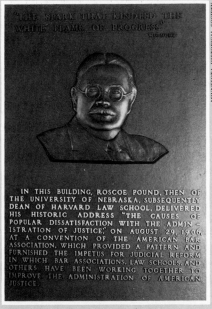

IN THIS BUILDING, ROSCOE POUND, THEN OF THE UNIVERSITY OF NEBRASKA, SUBSEQUENTLY DEAN OF HARVARD LAW SCHOOL, DELIVERED HIS HISTORIC ADDRESS "THE CAUSES OF POPULAR DISSATISFACTION WITH THE ADMINISTRATION OF JUSTICE," ON AUGUST 29, 1906, AT A CONVENTION OF THE AMERICAN BAR ASSOCIATION, WHICH PROVIDED A PATTERN AND FURNISHED THE IMPETUS FOR JUDICIAL REFORM IN WHICH BAR ASSOCIATIONS, LAW SCHOOLS, AND OTHERS HAVE BEEN WORKING TOGETHER TO IMPROVE THE ADMINISTRATION OF AMERICAN JUSTICE.

Roscoe Pound plaque, Minnesota Capitol

bring to American legal thought a broader approach than analytical concentration upon legal rules alone. He synthesized the work of the great European jurists and made their thinking available to American lawyers and law teachers. Above all, he brought into the law and the teaching of law a sociological approach in which the actual claims made upon the law and the impact of recognizing them upon society were considered as the bases for applying rules, principles, and standards.

Justice Holmes once termed him a uniquity. The range of his learning and his ability to call upon it at will were prodigious, if not awesome. The number of things Pound knew, said Holmes, "drives me silly." A Harvard colleague declared that "Pound knows three times more about every subject we teach than the man who teaches it." His knowledge was legendary, but was used without pretension; Pound assumed that his encyclopedic mind was not unusual. In his famous Jurisprudence Seminar, he would discuss the books students should read, listing German, French, and Italian, as well as English and American, volumes. Finally he would refer to a work in Portuguese, then add, "For those of you who may not read Portuguese, there is an excellent summary in Italian."

"Now how," demanded his Harvard colleague, "can you get on with a man like that?"

by the judges of the day, that doctrine exemplified the main deficiencies to which Pound called attention in his 1906 address: the extreme individualism of the common law applied with mechanical rigor, even while popular opinion was moving away from freedom of the individual will as the dominant factor in social progress.

In 1909 the Supreme Court dealt with problems of contract in the industrial society as if the parties were two neighbors bargaining in the rural community of an earlier day. The autonomy of the individual will was still a pillar of the common law. In Walter Bagehot's characterization, "men's choice determines nearly all they do"; the free wills of those concerned made the law for them. The law of contracts was the archetypical branch of "legal science"; Langdell, who began the case method of teaching law, awarded it the honor of the first casebook. By the first part of the twentieth century, the treatise writers had woven contract law into a rational and harmonious system grounded on freedom of contract.

As the century went on, judges continued to talk in terms of freedom of contract and autonomy of the individual will. But the notion of contractual equality on which they were based was relegated to the realm of abstract theory by the reality of the modern industrial society. "There is grim irony in speaking of the freedom of contract of those who, because of their economic necessities, give their services for less than is needful to keep body and soul together," said Justice Harlan Fiske Stone in a 1936 dissent. The same was true of most private individuals who entered into contractual relations with the corporate and governmental entities with which they increasingly had to deal — whether as consumers, purchasers of utility and similar services, tenants, insured or would-be insured persons, or in other relationships. The standardized mass contract, or contract of adhesion, began to replace the kind whose detailed terms were freely negotiated; more and more mass contracts presented take-it-or-leave-it terms.

The courts themselves started to undermine the concept of freedom of contract by imposing terms upon parties who consented to a particular kind of transaction, relation, or status, and by refusing to enforce contracts, though freely entered into, which they considered unduly unequal and unfair. By 1942, Justice Frankfurter could ask, "Does any principle in our law have more universal application than the doctrine that courts will not enforce transactions in which the relative positions of the parties are such that one has unconscionably taken advantage of the necessities of the other?" The courts began to read a virtual requirement of reasonableness into the obligation of contracts — to equitable-ize the terms fixed by the parties. At mid-century, Pound could state that though, fifty years earlier, "The free wills of the parties made the law for them . . . this idea has been disappearing all over the world."

To the law at the beginning of the century, free contract was the sine qua non of the free society. The very notion of social progress was deemed intimately connected with the extension of contractual liberty. Sir Henry Maine's celebrated dictum on the progress from status to contract was seized upon as a fundamental axiom which the society could violate only at the peril of social retrogression.

Samuel Gompers, president of the American Federation of Labor until his death in 1924, symbolized a new force in American industrial life. The old concept that each worker was free to make his own contract with management was dying, and the idea of a collective voice for labor was being gradually accepted by the law.

S. J. Atwood's Employment Agency

12 STATE STREET, NEW YORK

STATEMENT of LABOR CONTRACT

in accordance with Chapter 700 of the Laws of 1910.

Name of Employer / Name des Stellungsgebenden / Imię pracvdającego / Alkalmazást ado neve / Pracu dajucebo meno / Namn af arbetsgifvaren / Nome del padrone	Cohoes Company
Address of Employer / Adresse des Stellungsgebenden / Adres pracydającego / Alkalmazást ado címe / Pracu dajuceho adressa / Adress af arbetsgifvaren / Direzione del padrone	Cohoes N.Y.
Name of Employee / Name des Angestellten / Imię robotnika / Alkalmazott neve / Robotnikow meno / Namn af arbetstagaren / Nome del Lavorante	Uno Palmer
Address of Employee / Adresse des Angestellten / Adres robotnika / Alkalmazott címe / Robotnikow adressa / Adress af arbetstagaren / Direzione del Lavorante	4219 - 7th Ave Bklyn
Nature of work to be performed / Art der auszuführenden Arbeit / Jaka praca / A munka minősége / Jaka robota / Det arbete som skall utföras / Specie di Lavoro	Carpenter on Concrete forms..
Hours of Labor / Anzahl der Arbeitstunden / Ilość godzin roboczych / Munka órák száma / Kelo hodini robit / Arbets-timmarne / Ore di Lavoro	9 hours per day
Wages offered / Angebotener Lohn / Jaka płaca / Felajánlott munkabér / Kelo placu / Den lön som erbjudes / Paga offerta	35 to 40 cent per hour
Destination of the persons employed / Bestimmungsort der Angestellten / Miejsce przynaczone do roboty / Az alkalmazottak küldetési helye / Dza je poselanim / Destinationen af de anstälda personerna / Destinazione delle persone impiegate	Cohoes N.Y.
Terms of Transportation / Transport-Bedingungen / Warunki jazdy / Szállítási feltételek / Jak budu poslane / Villkoren för deras transportering / Condizione di viaggio	Paid own fare........
Remarks / Anmerkungen / Uwaga / Megjegyzések / Poznamka / Anmärkning / Osservazioni	

If more than one person is engaged, list of names and addresses will be found attached.

New York, ...June 29th...................... 1914

Workers, and particularly newly arrived immigrants, were usually in no position to protect themselves under the freedom of contract concept—as evidenced by this 1914 labor contract form, printed in seven languages, and in this case binding a carpenter to wages of thirty-five to forty cents an hour for a nine-hour day.

"There was to be a swing, later in the 20th century, away from this excessive emphasis on liberty of contract," observed Jerome Frank, a circuit court judge, in 1941. The preferred place that the autonomy of the individual will should have in the society was still recognized, as well as the ameliorating role that extension of the sphere of contract had actually played in legal history. But men began to reject the notion that the movement from status to contract represented the one and only path of social progress. Freedom of contract gave way to social welfare and the maintenance of a

Chicago garment workers hail a union victory in 1915. Such celebrations by strikers were subject to police harassment, and most strikes were broken by employers' injunctions and the use of professional strikebreakers.

CHICAGO HISTORICAL SOCIETY

In 1927 anarchists Sacco and Van-
zetti, *above, were executed for murder after a controversial prosecution.
Many believed that they were innocent and died only because of their
unpopular beliefs. Below, their fu-
neral procession in Boston.*

fairer standard of work and living. The coming of the welfare state severely
reduced the descriptive validity of Maine's maxim.

This was true even of so rudimentary a welfare measure as workmen's
compensation. As long ago as the turn of the century, A. V. Dicey acutely
noted that the Workmen's Compensation Act, which had just taken its place
in the English statute book, had severely cut down the contractual capacity
of both workmen and master: "The rights of workmen in regard to compensation for accidents have become a matter not of contract, but of status." A
quarter-century later, the U.S. Supreme Court followed a similar approach.
In ruling that workmen's compensation laws were not open to objection
because they abrogated common law defenses or imposed liability without
fault, the Court stated that "Workmen's Compensation legislation rests
upon the idea of status, not upon that of implied contract. . . . The liability
is based, not upon any act or omission of the employer, but upon the existence of the relationship which the employee bears to the employment."

In the field of industrial accidents, then, the legal consequences flowed,
not from the will of the parties or any fault which might be said to result
from their volition, but from the mere existence of the employment relationship to which the law now attached defined incidents of risk and
liability.

What was true of workmen's compensation extended to many other laws

enacted in the second quarter of the century. By mid-century, the society had surrounded the freedom of the individual with new status conditions. The earlier ideal of the abstract free individual will had given way to a tendency to think of man in society in every sort of relation with his fellow man, and man's legal activities as having to do with those relations.

Wherever one looked in the law, there was a growing importance of status as opposed to contract — if we mean by status the attachment of legal consequences to the position of the individual concerned, irrespective of his volition in the matter. Legal consequences resulted more and more from a given calling or situation — as employer, worker, landowner, tenant, insurer, consumer — rather than from the exercise of free will by an independent individual.

This was particularly apparent in the field in which freedom of contract had enjoyed its widest sway, that of employment. The position of employer, under the law, had become very much akin to status, as we have been using that term. Duties and liabilities were imposed upon him not because he had so willed, or because he was at fault, but because the nature of the employer-employee relationship was deemed to call for them. In all too many cases, the employer could no longer terminate the relationship by exercise of his will, or even control the choice of employees. He was compelled to enter into relation with an organization of workers, regardless of his choice in the matter. He was required to comply with laws providing for wages, hours, and other conditions of employment. When the employment relation existed, there was no longer complete freedom of contract, any more than there had previously been full freedom of contract between a trustee and beneficiary.

The community began to be organized about relationships rather than wills. The law itself increasingly tended to rest on relationships and duties, not on isolated individuals and rights. In this respect, the position of the individual in society was somewhat comparable to that before the industrial revolution. In the twentieth-century economic order, business, industry, and government had become the dominant activities. They stood in the society where landholding stood in the Middle Ages. The typical man found his greatness not in himself and in what he did, but in the business, labor, or governmental organization he served. It was his relationship to the organization that gave rise to the most significant legal consequences that attached to his existence and activities. The sphere of contract, in yielding to relational regulation, might even be said to signal a reversion to the medieval ideal of relationally organized society.

Restraint of the Antisocial

Twentieth-century developments in the law of property were essentially similar to those noted with regard to contracts. In the first part of the century, the emphasis remained on the rights of the property owner. Merely to repeat the 1922 statement of a federal judge "that of the three fundamental principles which underlie government, and for which government exists, the protection of life, liberty, and property, the chief of these is property" is to show how far out of line such a statement is with the present-day legal scale of values. If, at the turn of the century, unrestricted acquisition and use of property was at its broadest, it was progressively narrowed as the century went on. Some years ago, one of the greatest of modern jurists, the German Rudolf von Jhering, formulated the matter thus: "Formerly high valuing of property, lower valuing of the person. Now lower valuing of property, higher valuing of the person."

In the first part of this century, the law of property was still that described in Chapter v. The rights of property had reached their climax. In property, as in contract, the will theory was dominant; the law dealt with property almost entirely in terms of the will of the owner. During the first half of the century, the courts continued to use the broad language of unlimited ownership and use. As late as 1952, a court could assert that "Property is more than the physical object which a person owns. It includes the right to acquire, possess, use and dispose of it without control or diminution." By mid-century, however, "that sole and despotic dominion" of which Blackstone spoke was giving way to what one writer, Harry M. Cross, termed "the diminishing fee." The rights of the property owner became increasingly subject to regulation in the public interest. Fee simple ownership, in the Blackstone sense of absolute dominion, was being replaced by an ownership having fee simple duration, but only in limited or specified uses. The owner of property no longer had the unrestricted right to use his property completely as he chose. Whatever might have previously been the case, the law increasingly recognized that the owner might be barred from using his property in a wasteful or antisocial manner.

Chapter v also mentioned the doctrine of so-called abuse of rights, using the building of a "spite fence" as the typical case. The law at the beginning of the century allowed no redress for the aggrieved neighbor; by mid-century, the courts had shifted their view and tended to apply the doctrine of abuse of rights, holding that the right of property ended where abuse began. By the middle of the century, however, the limitations imposed by law on the *jus utendi* (the right to use) had gone much further than the prohibition of the spite-fence type of abuse. The change in this respect was characterized by Pound as one which "strikes at the foundation of the will theory . . . by giving up full free individual self-assertion as the purpose of the legal order."

The law was working toward a basic limitation on property rights which restrained their "antisocial" exercise. Wasteful use of property was increasingly restrained by laws providing for proper utilization of the soil and conservation of natural resources. In urban areas, too, serious limitations were imposed on the owner's right to use his property as he wished. The doctrine of reasonable use was furthered by zoning and town planning legislation and the regulation of billboards. Said the Supreme Court in the leading case upholding the zoning power, "Until recent years, urban life was comparatively simple; but, with the great increase and concentration of population, problems have developed, and constantly are developing, which require and will continue to require, additional restrictions in respect of the use and occupation of private lands in urban communities." The freedom of owners to use their land without control by others had given way with industrialization and population pressures.

This cartoon appeared at a time of many antilabor injunctions. The Supreme Court, as well as numerous U.S. courts, followed the lead of Chief Justice William Howard Taft (1921–1930), who was outspoken about "the irresponsibilities of labor unions."

CHARLES HARBUTT, MAGNUM

The changing law could be seen in the increasingly hospitable attitude of the judges toward limitations on property rights imposed to accomplish aesthetic objectives. Chapter v noted that the law at the beginning of the century refused to recognize aesthetic ends as legitimate concerns of public power. As the century went on, this refusal gave way to grudging acceptance and then to unqualified approval. The courts first ruled that if zoning, billboard regulations, and the like could be justified by traditional health and safety factors, the fact that aesthetic considerations might have played a part in their adoption did not affect their validity. As a judge somewhat lyrically put it in 1932, "Beauty may not be queen but she is not an outcast beyond the pale of protection or respect. She may at least shelter herself under the wing of safety, morality or decency."

Two decades later, the courts were ready openly to acknowledge aesthetic ends as proper. The Supreme Court (in a case concerned with urban redevelopment in Washington, D.C.) could now state that governmental power to restrict property rights included values "that are spiritual as well as physical, aesthetic as well as monetary. . . . If those who govern the District of Columbia decide that the Nation's Capital should be beautiful as well as sanitary, there is nothing . . . that stands in the way."

By the middle of the century, then, a principle of reasonable use, as de-

The construction of mass real estate developments like the one above accelerated limitations on property rights, subjecting builders to planning and zoning regulations that protected the common good.

fined by the relevant authorities, was coming to supersede the idea that the owner of property might do with it as he pleased. The law of property had undergone a veritable transformation in fifty years. In the early part of the century, property had, as much as any branch of the law, exemplified the causes for popular dissatisfaction that Pound noted in 1906. By mid-century, a completely altered law now increasingly emphasized the social, rather than the individual, aspect of property. The absolute bundle of rights which, to our fathers, could scarcely be impaired without subverting the very conception of property was no longer beyond the reach of public power.

Transformation of Tort Law

Writing in 1914, Jeremiah Smith, a prominent law professor of the day, foresaw with trepidation the extension of the principle of strict liability into many new fields. At mid-century, a leading text could state, "The extension is taking place, and undoubtedly will continue, as new social viewpoints impose greater responsibilities upon the defendant. Thus far, at least, the dire consequences once anticipated have not occurred."

To Smith and his contemporaries, "the fundamental principle of the modern common law of torts" was "that fault is requisite to liability." That principle had come to dominate American tort law. Not only was it supported by the economic considerations discussed in Chapter III, but it was also seen to have a definite moral base, founded as it was upon a moral appraisal of the individual actors in each case and the belief that the blameworthy should compensate the blameless. When the requirement of fault finally replaced the "unmoral standard of acting at one's peril," it was hailed as the crowning triumph of reason and morality toward which the common law had been groping for centuries.

When Jeremiah Smith wrote, workmen's compensation laws had already been enacted in almost half the states (and the states involved had well over half the nation's population). Under workmen's compensation, as a critic put it early in the century, "The time-honored principles of the law of torts have been cast aside, a wider rule of responsibility has been framed, and no man can now say what will be the ultimate effects of the new doctrine." Workmen's compensation involved a rejection of fault as the basis for liability; instead, liability was based on the concept of protection of individuals from the consequences of industrial accidents, regardless of culpability on their part. The presence or absence of negligence played no part; the fundamental principle was that of liability without fault, with recovery provided for all injuries arising out of and in the course of employment. Loss from industrial accidents was a cost of the enterprises that entailed them, and one which should be borne by them. In such circumstances, the element of moral fault became irrelevant.

What most concerned Jeremiah Smith was the possibility that the workmen's compensation principle would become the governing principle throughout the law, with the consequence that tort law based upon fault, as it existed in 1900, would virtually disappear. By the middle of the century, the Smith forebodings had not yet been realized; but the principle of liability without fault had made substantial inroads into tort law.

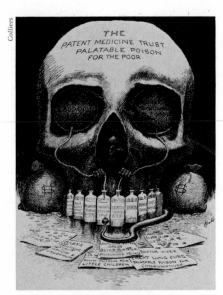

Not until 1906 did the Pure Food and Drug Act place the first restrictions on the sale of fraudulent, and even harmful, patent medicines. Prior to then, the public had little or no protection against such products, as reflected by the angry cartoon above.

First, there was an extension of the compensation principle of strict liability into other fields. Legislation provided for responsibility without negligence for deficiencies in railroad equipment required by law, as well as for injuries to child labor. Pure food laws made the manufacturer or seller of defective food liable to the injured consumer, even though he had used reasonable care. In addition, an increasing number of courts adopted, and even extended, the doctrine of the case of *Rylands* v. *Fletcher* in 1868, which laid down the rule of absolute liability upon a landowner who brought on his land anything likely to do mischief if it escaped. The *Restatement of Torts* could generalize that doctrine in terms of "ultra-hazardous activities," thus extending it from dangerous substances collected or brought onto land to all activities that posed an undue risk to the community.

Second, the concept of negligence itself was being transformed. By mid-century, it had been so widened by the courts that commentators could speak of "negligence without fault" or "negligence in name only." This development was most striking in the cases holding sellers of goods liable for defects that caused harm to the purchaser under a theory of an "implied warranty" which courts read into the contract, and which permitted recovery without any proof of negligence. A trend had started to hold the manufacturer liable to the ultimate consumer upon the theory of a warranty "running with the goods." The manufacturer, by placing a product (for example, an automobile) on the market, was considered to assume a responsibility to the consumer, resting not upon contract or tort in the

Food products were also affected by the Pure Food and Drug Act. Here, an inspector checks the produce being sold from a pushcart in the 1930's.

traditional sense, but upon the relation arising from the purchase and the fact that harm was foreseeable in a large proportion of cases.

What the law was doing was to substitute the idea of social responsibility for that of individual fault. Fault itself was transformed by the objectivization of fault liability, which involved the elimination of moral factors from an expanding area of tort law. Liability still nominally based on traditional concepts of negligence more and more involved no "real" fault in defendants themselves. In particular, railroad and motor vehicle operators became liable not for a particular "fault" occurring in their operations but for the inevitable consequences of their inherently dangerous activities; "negligence" for them was reduced to a "quasi-strict" liability for dangerous enterprise.

The law of torts was also being transformed by public opinion exercised through the medium of the jury verdict. Early in the century, tort law may have lagged substantially behind public opinion in its extreme individualist philosophy. The gap was reduced as jury verdicts reflected the popular view that people ought to be protected financially against the hazards of life in the industrial community. The consequence was a growing tendency by juries to award judgments regardless of whether fault was adequately proved, a tendency reinforced by the knowledge that most defendants carried insurance. The growth of insurance, indeed, bid fair to render much of tort law obsolete. The spreading of risks through insurance was increasingly seen as the common-sense substitute for a system that awarded reparation only when negligence could be proved. In practice, the vast majority of accident claims were settled by insurance carriers without litigation; insurance had brought about a closer approach to absolute liability in practice than in tort theory.

At the turn of the century, the nation's tort law reflected most of the defects described by Pound in his 1906 address. A half-century later, Pound himself noted the changes. What is it, he asked, that has been driving us in the present century thus to transform tort law? "It is the annual total of nine million victims of personal injury to which total of injured, maimed, and slain must be added the widows, orphans, and dependents deprived of maintenance." The toll taken by accidents had become a major problem for social justice; during World War II, there were more casualties in this country from accidents than on all our battlefields. The mere numerical dimensions of the problem in the industrial, mechanized, motorized, plane-traveling society necessitated revision of the common law system of providing for fault by law and no-fault by charity.

In the present century, the main function of the law of torts has been seen as the reasonable adjustment of economic risks, not the expression of moral principles. The goal stressed by the fault concept in the last century was deterrence; compensation itself was a secondary factor. The emphasis has changed. The stress has been transferred to compensation. The society has come to demand a system in which the loss from those tort harms loosely termed accidental injuries will not fall on the unfortunate individuals who suffer them; in one way or another the burden must be shifted. The law of torts has steadily moved from a fault to a social insurance basis.

The transformation was accompanied by a narrowing of the immunities

A Sears, Roebuck advertisement early in the century guarantees its product, acknowledging the "implied warranty" which the law was coming to recognize as part of every sale.

previously recognized by the law. Most important was the enactment of legislation abandoning the doctrine of sovereign immunity, which had completely barred tort suits against government. The older view had been expressed by Justice Holmes, when he asserted that there could be no legal right as against the state which makes the law and the courts on which the right depends: "It seems to me like shaking one's fist at the sky, when the sky furnishes the energy that enables one to raise the fist." But the state, like the description of the common law in a famous Holmes dissent, is neither a brooding omnipresence in the sky, nor the sky itself. The state may consent to be sued and such consent was given in the Federal Tort Claims Act of 1946, under which Congress, according to the Supreme Court in 1949, showed "that it was ready to lay aside a great portion of the sovereign's ancient and unquestioned immunity from suit." The states began to enact similar statutes. In addition, the courts were starting to do away with the other immunities that existed in tort law, notably that of charitable institutions, especially hospitals.

The changing conception of tort law also made the courts receptive to new doctrines which altered the rigid emphasis of the common law. The strict rule of contributory negligence began to give way to the idea of

Women welders are seen at work on an aircraft carrier in 1943. Some wear no protective headgear, a practice that helped make World War II accident rates high. Yet under modern law such negligence did not leave the workers without legal remedy.

243

apportionment of damages under a doctrine of so-called comparative negligence. The courts were also abandoning the narrow notion that equitable relief (often the only effective relief in tort cases) would be given only to protect *property* rights. Interests of personality were increasingly brought within the pale of injunctive protection. In particular, the right of privacy received increasing recognition. Soon after the *Roberson* v. *Rochester Folding Box Co.* decision of 1902, which refused to accept that right, the supreme court of Georgia rejected its holding and affirmed the right to privacy. The Georgia decision was widely followed; by mid-century, invasion of the right of privacy as an actionable tort was recognized nationwide.

The historical development of tort law has been marked by a general broadening of the interests the law would protect. In its common law origins, tort law started with protection against torts (civil wrongs) to realty. Even when the law expanded to include protection of other interests, the property limitation continued. It has only been during the present century that this restriction has been giving way. Protection of property in the older sense has become an ever smaller part of the subject. The vast majority of tort cases involve accidents and injuries to economic relations. The latter has, in fact, become so important as to outgrow the original tort classification. Unfair competition, copyright, labor law, and the like (originally treated as minor parts of tort law) have so developed that they have become separate

CULVER PICTURES

J. Pierpont Morgan brandishes his cane at an aggressive news photographer. The year was 1910, when the courts were just beginning to recognize the right to privacy.

A Model T Ford slumps after an accident in 1917. The rapid increase of motor vehicles, and of accidents caused by them, has had a continuing effect on liability and insurance law.

branches of the law, each an arcane specialty, with its own corps of specialists.

The Growth of Corporate Power

Chapter IV discussed the Supreme Court ruling in 1886 that corporations were "persons" within the protection of the Due Process and Equal Protection clauses of the Constitution. Until 1938, innumerable cases were decided on the unquestioned assumption that corporations were entitled to the constitutional protection. Soon after his appointment to the Supreme Court in 1937, Justice Hugo L. Black challenged the assumption: "I do not believe the word 'person' in the Fourteenth Amendment includes corporations." Though Black was later joined in his position by Justice William O. Douglas, legal history has gone the other way. No other judge, before or since, has questioned the rule that corporations are "persons" within the meaning of the Fifth and Fourteenth amendments.

The Black-Douglas dissents are, nevertheless, of great significance, since they point up the changed position of the corporation in the second quarter of this century. From the post-Civil War period to the 1930's, no responsible legal authority would have thought of questioning the established status of the corporation in American law. By the turn of the century, the legitimacy of the business corporation had been fully established. For a generation thereafter, the law was concerned solely with ensuring that the corporate device would be permitted to serve the needs of the business community. The emphasis was on utility rather than responsibility insofar as corporate power was concerned.

The predominant theme in the first third of this century was that of ensuring the fullest utilization of the corporate device, unhindered by governmental restrictions which interfered with such utilization. The corporate instrument was made available on terms most responsive to the

Puck, May 8, 1912

CORPORATION LAWYER

CORPORATION PRESIDENT

CORPORATION LAWYER

POOR MAN'S LAWYER

A POOR MAN TRYING TO WIN A CASE AGAINST A CORPORATION

A Puck *cartoon of 1912 asked, "What stands less chance than a snowball in hell?" and answered, "A poor man trying to win a case against a corporation lawyer." Even the judge was depicted as insignificant compared to the powerful corporation forces.*

wishes of businessmen. The law was used to enlarge the maneuverability of private power, with the correlative that government regulation of such power must be strictly limited. The end of the law in this area was to facilitate businessmen's use of the corporation.

During the last century, general incorporation laws were passed that enabled corporate status to be acquired for almost any economic venture, without a need for the legislature to pass a special act of incorporation. By 1930, stimulated by competitive chartering in states such as Delaware and New Jersey, a new type of law had become common, which offered incorporation on terms of increasing liberality. The key element was the permissive attitude displayed: a standard corporate structure was provided, but the statute allowed it to be varied by such departures as draftsmen might insert into the corporate articles and bylaws. In effect, businessmen could legally create whatever arrangements they found most serviceable.

In sanctioning such corporate arrangements as businessmen chose to create, the law placed its imprimatur on control by insiders—promoters, entrepreneurs, management. Promoters were given freedom to mold the corporate contract as they desired, and management to modify almost without limit the business to be done and rights in earnings and assets.

The results were mixed. Certainly, under the encouragement given by the law, the corporation became the dominant factor in business and industry; as such, it played a principal part in transforming the economic life of the nation. But the liberality of corporation law was far from an unmixed blessing. The freedom of promoters and management meant subjecting investors, workers, and the community itself to new dangers. The removal of limitations on size brought corporate giants into existence. Granting limited liability to enterprises with only nominal capital led to increasing financial irresponsibility. The holding company device mushroomed and posed increasing problems for investors and the public.

In the first part of the present century, the law was shaped to fit the real or supposed needs of economic expansion. When the Great Depression indicated that uncontrolled expansion was itself a will-o'-the-wisp, the law, like the society, began to reconsider the place of corporate power. Such reconsideration was based, first of all, on realization of the gap that had developed between the corporation in legal theory and the corporation in economic practice.

The law had adopted a hands-off policy in the face of corporate power, assuming that abuses would be prevented both by the competitive market and the self-interested care of those who put their capital at risk. By the 1930's, confidence in these controls had all but disappeared. The now-classic study, *The Modern Corporation and Private Property* by Adolf A. Berle and Gardiner C. Means, provided the factual basis for an understanding of the transformations that had occurred during the century. As summarized by Means in a later volume, what he calls the "Corporate Revolution" involved: (1) the increasing extent to which economic activity is conducted under the corporate form; (2) the increasing role played by corporations of tremendous size; (3) the increasing dispersion of stock ownership; and (4) the increasing separation of ownership and control in the modern corporation. These developments negated the effectiveness of the controls on which the law had relied to prevent corporate abuses. By 1930, two hundred nonfinancial corporations controlled a major part of the economy; the trend toward concentration continued (though at a decreasing rate) in the next two decades. Neither market discipline nor shareholder control could adequately restrain the economic giants.

The inability of the market and their theoretical owners to discipline the new corporate concentrations placed an increasing burden on the law to deal with the problem of corporate responsibility. By mid-century, the law had only begun to cope with the problem. The legal answer during the second quarter of the century proceeded along two main lines. First, there was a renewed emphasis on government efforts to restrain corporate abuses. Earlier attempts, notably in the Sherman Act's ban on monopolistic combinations and restraints and the prohibitions against unfair competition contained in the Clayton Act and Federal Trade Commission Act, were mere negative stabs at reinforcing the free market and proved largely ineffective (though they were becoming more than the empty form they had been when they were first enacted).

Corporate abuses and the Great Depression led to more positive government efforts at regulation, first through blue-sky laws enforced by state commissions, then through the New Deal regulatory laws. These provided both for positive regulation of crucial industries (notably transportation, power, and communications) and general regulation of the securities markets and investment practices.

In addition, there was an effort to make stockholder control more effective. Legislatures and courts sought to foster a flow of corporate information to shareholders. Statutes extended the common law right to inspect books and records, and the Securities and Exchange Commission exercised its powers in favor of full disclosure. Attempts to protect stockholder voting rights were made as well. The courts also tried to enforce the duties of loyalty and care owed by management to shareholders; so far as possible, they tried to tighten the standards of behavior of those exercising corporate power, holding them not to the morals of the marketplace, but to the trustee's punctilio of honor.

By mid-century, nevertheless, it was apparent that the legal efforts were scarcely adequate. It cannot be denied that public regulation in particular profoundly influenced the course of economic development. "But," as Abram Chayes pointed out in *The Corporation in Modern Society*, "the general problem that was addressed—the domestication of the private social and economic power derived from the new technology organized in corporate form—this continued unabated." Grown to tremendous proportions, a "corporate system" had evolved—as once there had been a feudal system—that had attracted to itself a combination of attributes and powers comparable to those enjoyed by government. The giant corporation, wrote the economist Peter F. Drucker, had become "the institution which sets the standard for the way of life and the mode of living of our citizens; which leads, molds and directs; which determines our perspective on our own society." It had become a focus of power whose only competitor was the state. It virtually enjoyed the status of a private government, sharing sovereign power with government itself.

The stage was thus set for a conflict between public sovereignty and private power reminiscent of that between Church and State a thousand years earlier. If the ultimate outcome was to be a corporate Canossa, it was not yet clear at mid-century who was to play the role of Pope and who that of Emperor.

Increased Government

The prior portions of this chapter have shown a substantial modernization in American substantive law during the first half of the twentieth century. If, at the turn of the century, contracts, property, torts, corporations, and the other private law branches all suffered from the deficiencies Pound noted in 1906, the situation had completely changed by the middle of the

Mediocre legislators and the machine control of politics were the butts of this 1910 cartoon by William A. Clark. Its title was "They are not in politics for their health."

century. The extreme individualist basis on which the different branches of the law had been grounded had either disappeared or was giving way as the century progressed. If the modernization did not proceed as rapidly as some desired, still, considerable progress was made. Whether we talk of the law of the welfare state or the "socialization of law," the developing law did mirror the evolution of the society itself.

A different picture is presented by the institutions that make and administer the law. As pointed out in the first chapter, the basic institutions of American law were already in existence at the founding of the Republic. Moreover, they had attained the form and structure that was to characterize them throughout the nation's history. The main legal agencies—legislatures, Executives, and courts—have changed very slowly during the two centuries since independence. The jobs these institutions perform have, of course, altered tremendously over the years; their important work in the middle of the twentieth century dealt with issues that scarcely existed before 1870. But the institutions in operation in the twentieth century would not have been unfamiliar to the lawyer of a hundred years ago. He would have found little that was strange on Capitol Hill or in a typical state courthouse in 1950.

The element of familiarity would have been particularly evident in a visit to Congress or a state legislature. Few institutions have changed so little in two centuries as the American legislature. By 1950, there had been, to be sure, a substantial broadening of the franchise as well as provision for

Men wait in a breadline for their Christmas dinner in New York, 1931. The free-wheeling economy had led to a collapse and depression that would bring about a much stricter regulation of corporations.

direct election of senators. That did not, however, change legislative operation and procedure or bring about the modernization that was so sorely needed.

The caliber of American legislators was still a source of both learned and lay criticism. There was some improvement over the situation that prevailed during the period of Reconstruction and the Gilded Age. Yet, considering the needs of the new century, the level of legislative ability continued depressingly low. According to an English observer in 1948, "most members of the House are mediocre men and women who do not differ greatly from one another." The Senate contained some outstanding men, he added, but, even there, "every Congress contains a number of senators whose election is hard to explain, and still more difficult to justify." Both Houses were "open to profound criticism" both with regard to their personnel and the manner in which they functioned. The situation in the state legislatures was, if anything, worse. The "machine" was still the primary factor in choosing state legislators, though its influence was lessening as the century went on.

American legislatures operated by and large as they had a century earlier. The dominant feature was a concentration of control in the leadership, which was itself increasingly determined by longevity of service. The seniority principle hung like an albatross on the effective functioning of legislative bodies. As a critic put it, "Congress is probably alone among all private or governmental bodies charged with any kind of responsibility which lets leadership depend exclusively upon the accident of tenure." One who worked in or with Congress soon found that that institution was not so much a coherent governmental organ as a series of fragmented individual power bases. The senior members of the two Houses could be compared to a group of feudal chieftains. The chairmen of major committees each had their own baronial fiefs—tied together by often vague alliance to party but dominated most of all by the desire to conserve the power and perquisites pertaining to each particular barony.

What compounded the problem was the expanded role of the twentieth-century legislature. It was in this century that legislation began to play a positive role in ordering the society. As in Benthamite Britain, statute law became the great instrument of advance. More and more, legislatures asserted control over matters formerly deemed outside the range of governmental concern.

As legislative business expanded, there was a correlative loss in initiative in molding the law. The twentieth-century legislature had neither the interest nor the talent to revive the codification movement that had played so important a part in an earlier day. Leadership passed to other bodies, notably the American Law Institute; the legislative function was exhausted in the confirmation of unifying laws recommended by the National Conference of Commissioners on Uniform State Laws.

Even more important was the emergence of the Executive as a key force in the initiation and formulation of legislation. In lawmaking, as in other fields, knowledge is power. This century has seen a growing tendency for legislation to originate in executive expertise. As administrative problems became increasingly technical, the legislature turned more and more to the

A cartoon of 1928 recognized the vast expansion of the role of the U.S. Presidency. It has grown immeasurably more since that day.

Franklin D. Roosevelt campaigns in a West Virginia mining area in 1932. Elected four times as President, he was a strong Chief Executive who left an enduring impact on the laws and institutions of the nation.

Executive for guidance in drafting laws. A leading judge, Arthur T. Vanderbilt, wrote in 1953: "Fully 80 per cent of the important legislation of the first three years of the administration of President Franklin D. Roosevelt originated in the White House or in the executive departments. The habit then formed has not disappeared, especially in fiscal and economic matters. . . . In effect the President has acquired the powers of the English prime minister over the introduction of legislation without the correlative duties to the legislative branch imposed on the prime minister under the English practice." It was a far cry from the attitude of the Senate in 1908 when a furor was created because a Cabinet member sent to that body the complete draft of a proposed bill. By the middle of the century, the drafting of legislation by the executive departments had become common practice.

The problem of the legislature in the twentieth-century world was well put by the director of the Bureau of the Budget in 1945: "We are up against the fact that legislative bodies have not changed very much but the kinds of problems with which they must cope have changed radically." Despite passage of the Legislative Reorganization Act of 1946, neither Congress nor the state legislatures had really come to grips with this situation. The legislature in operation at mid-century scarcely gave confidence to those who believed in representative government and sought to preserve it as a flourishing institution even in an atomic age.

251

"If not good law," said Justice Robert H. Jackson in 1952, "there was worldly wisdom in the maxim attributed to Napoleon that 'The tools belong to the man who can use them.' " The vacuum created by legislative ineffectiveness was increasingly filled by executive ascendancy. The twentieth century was becoming the century of the White House. Wherever one looked, he was met by the reality of executive authority. During this century the Chief Executive had come so far to overshadow all others that almost alone he filled the public eye and ear. Men such as Woodrow Wilson and the two Roosevelts had shown that the Bryce dictum — "Great men are not chosen Presidents" — was no longer accurate.

The century was also turning out to be the century of the administrator; the movement toward the welfare state was a movement toward the administrative state. Conscious use of the law to regulate the society, particularly in its economic and social affairs, required the creation of a growing bureaucracy at all levels of government. The administrative agency came into its

The Problem of the Fourth Branch of Government

As modern U.S. business life has grown more complex, Congress has delegated the power to regulate essential industries to specially created administrative agencies, modeled upon the first of them, the Interstate Commerce Commission (established in 1887). These agencies are unique in the American governmental structure in that they act independently of each of the three traditional branches of the federal government, but combine the functions of all of them.

There are seven major agencies, sometimes called the "big seven":

Two regulate carriers — the Interstate Commerce Commission (rail, motor, and water carriers, and pipelines) and the Civil Aeronautics Board (air carriers).

Two regulate other utilities — the Federal Power Commission (electric and gas utilities) and the Federal Communications Commission (radio, television, telephone, and telegraph).

One regulates the investment business — the Securities and Exchange Commission.

Two regulate special fields that affect industry generally — the Federal Trade Commission (unfair trade practices) and the National Labor Relations Board (unfair labor practices).

Few tasks performed by the government are more vital than those assigned to this "headless fourth branch of government." Land and air transportation, energy from gas and electricity, communications, the investment markets, labor relations, and competitive trade practices are among the key areas regulated by the decrees of these groups. Every time a person turns on a television set, buys an airplane or railroad ticket, switches on an electric light or a gas stove, or succumbs to the lure of a radio or TV commercial, he or she is influenced by the power of the "big seven." The values involved in their decisions exceed many times the annual dollar value of all money judgments rendered by federal courts.

But there is another side of the coin. The powers given to the administrative agencies are so broad that they are vested with virtual life-and-death authority over the businesses affected. This has made the businesses unwilling to run the risk of hostile agencies. Thus, for example, those engaged in commercial broadcasting have felt that they must at all costs avoid an unfriendly Federal Communications Commission. This has

own as a primary governmental institution. The Interstate Commerce Commission had spawned a progeny that threatened to exhaust the alphabet in the use of initials to characterize the new bodies.

The administrative agency was the governmental instrument par excellence of the New Deal. Through it, Washington hoped to work a progressive modification of the economy and the society, comparable, at the very least, to the great English Reform Movement of the last century. Many went even further and saw in the administrative process the ultimate supplanter of private industry, which would take over the role of economic leadership in the "public interest." This was the ultimate view that enthralled the extreme New Dealer; this was the specter that terrified private industry.

By mid-century, neither the thrill nor the chill adequately reflected reality. After noting the rise of the administrative process, Felix Frankfurter could state that, "Concerning its efficacy, however, pessimism has supplanted the earlier feeling of hope." What was clear was that the rise of the administra-

A few of the agencies that do so much of the government's work today. Opposite page, from top: corporation lawyers before the National Labor Relations Board; the Federal Trade Commission; the Federal Power Commission during a pipeline hearing. This page, from top: members of the Civil Aeronautics Board take their oath of office; a hearing before the Federal Communications Commission.

stimulated determined efforts on the part of the broadcasters to influence the commission and try to ensure that it will favor their interests.

Such attempts by the regulated to control the regulators have created problems in all the agencies. At times, the attempts have been so successful that it has appeared that the "public interest" has become a mere fiction, masking the reality of regulation for the benefit of the regulated. In 1966 Chief Justice Warren E. Burger, then on the Court of Appeals for the District of Columbia, characterized the notion that the FCC can effectively represent the interests of the public as "one of those assumptions we collectively try to work with so long as they are reasonably adequate. When it becomes clear, as it does to us now, that it is no longer a valid assumption which stands up under the realities of actual experience, neither we nor the Commision can continue to rely on it."

The influence of regulated upon regulators has tended to increase progressively as the administrative agencies have gone through what has been seen to be their typical "life cycle." The federal commissions have all experienced periods of youth, maturity, and old age, with their development dominated by what has been termed the progressive law of ossification. It is only during its youthful stage that a commission is vigorous in fighting for the public interest. As time goes on, it loses its early enthusiasm, and apathy increasingly replaces administrative aggressiveness. During the phase of maturity, the regulated direct their efforts toward taking over the regulators, and the commission tends more and more to equate the "public interest" with the interests of the regulated groups. This development is carried further in the commission's old age, when it has more or less come to terms with those whom it is ostensibly regulating. Over the years, there is created a relationship which is best described as regulatory symbiosis: regulators and regulated have learned to live with each other and have, in fact, grown intimately dependent on each other. For the system of regulation in the "public interest" that was intended by Congress, the nation has had substituted, in each of the "big seven," a system that has become essentially one of self-regulation.

Richard Frankensteen, CIO organizer (left), appears before the National Labor Relations Board in 1937 to tell about antilabor violence committed during a Ford plant strike. The NLRB was one of the most powerful agencies established during the New Deal.

tive agency meant a drastic shift in the legal center of gravity, so far as lawmaking was concerned. The legislature did, it is true, continue to enact an increasing number of laws and the courts applied them in an increasing number of decisions. Legislative and judicial lawmaking were, however, being dwarfed by the administrative lawmaking function.

The distinguishing feature of the modern administrative agency was its possession of the power to determine, either by rule or by decision, private rights and obligations. The typical agency had vested in it both legislative and adjudicatory authority: the legislative power to promulgate rules and regulations having the force of law and the judicial power to decide individual cases. In impact on those subject to administrative power, agency rulemaking and adjudication were at least comparable in importance to the powers exercised by legislatures and courts themselves. In volume, administrative lawmaking was far greater. From its beginning in 1935, the *Federal Register* (in which rules and regulations are published) vastly exceeded in size the *Statutes at Large* (in which laws enacted by Congress are published). The quantitative picture was the same with regard to adjudications. "The values affected by [administrative] decisions," wrote Justice Jackson in his 1955 book *The Supreme Court in the American System of Government*, "probably exceed every year many times the dollar value of all money judgments rendered by the federal courts. They also affect vital rights of the citizen." A host of controversies as to private rights was no longer decided in courts. By mid-century, Justice Jackson could state that administrative agencies "have become a veritable fourth branch of the Government, which has deranged our three-branch legal theories as much as the concept of a fourth dimension unsettles our three-dimensional thinking."

The Unwieldy Mass of Law

What was lacking was an effective attempt to reduce the products of the lawmaking process to manageable scope. Legislatures continued to grind out laws; the sheer bulk of legislation was discouraging. In 1952–1953 alone Congress and the state legislatures enacted 29,938 statutes, and these merely supplemented the existing statutory compilations that filled 931 thick volumes. The mass of administrative regulations was even more appalling. The *Federal Register* for 1947 contained 8,902 large pages. But, to check all the federal regulations, one had to search the *Code of Federal Regulations*, with its fifteen volumes of 17,193 pages, and the cumulative supplements for 1943–1946, containing a total of 57,242 pages. It was estimated that the new edition of the *Code of Federal Regulations* then being prepared would contain approximately 11,000,000 words—fourteen times as many as in the Bible and twelve times as many as in a complete Shakespeare.

Even greater was the mass of reported American judicial decisions. By 1950, their number stood at 2,100,000, as compared to about 60,000 a century earlier. What is more, the number was increasing at the rate of 22,000 a month. Well might Oliver Wendell Holmes suggest that the law could get along with the reports of its own day alone: "We could reconstruct the corpus from them if all that went before were burned." And Holmes had said this in 1897, when the number of reported decisions was less than a quarter of the number half a century later and before the rise of administrative law. No one could even hazard a guess as to the volume of administrative decisions, but at mid-century the reported decisions of four federal agencies alone approximated in volume the reports of all the federal district courts and courts of appeals.

The historical answer to such an unmanageable mass of law has been codification. That answer was not, however, given by twentieth-century legislatures, even though the need was much greater than when the codification movement had almost succeeded in the previous century under the leadership of David Dudley Field. Instead, there was given the peculiarly American answer of what Pound termed "private codification."

Private codification in American law has been primarily the work of the American Law Institute, an organization founded in 1923 by a group of leading lawyers, law teachers, and judges. At its inception, the main task of the ALI was "to promote the clarification and simplification of the law and its better adaptation to social needs." The objective of adaptation of the law to social needs was soon subordinated to promoting its clarification and simplification. "The eminent in the law have been gathering here," wrote Holmes of the first ALI meeting, "yearning for the upward and onward—specifically the restatement of the law . . . by members of their body." The *Restatement of the Law* was the ALI answer to the need to mitigate the uncertainty and complexity of American law.

The *Restatement* intended to present "an orderly statement of the general common law of the United States, including in that term not only the law developed solely by judicial decision, but also the law that has grown from the application by the courts of statutes that have been generally enacted and have been in force for many years." From 1923 to 1944, nine legal subjects were restated: Agency, Conflict of Laws, Contracts, Judgments, Prop-

A cartoon titled "The Majesty of the Law" ridicules a judge peering at a pinhead and searching for technicalities. Even today the law is often charged with looking for loopholes.

erty, Restitution, Security, Torts, and Trusts. These summaries of the law took up 24 volumes totaling over 17,000 pages.

The *Restatements* were instruments of private codification: they were not prepared under public authority; they have no legally binding force, but only such influence as Bench and Bar accord them. Despite Brandeis's cynical remark, "Why I am restating the law every day," the *Restatements* had substantial impact. At a minimum they provided clearer statements of the common law than had theretofore been available. As a picture of contemporary law by the foremost members of the profession, they became a guide which, though not authoritative in the strict sense, was accepted by Bench and Bar "as prima facie a correct statement of the general law of the United States."

The *Restatements*, according to a leading torts writer, were "in no sense intended to be a code in the scientific meaning of that word"; nor did they cover more than a small part of the corpus of American law. It is erroneous to assume that they filled the need for codification that the unwieldy mass of American law presented. At the same time, however, much of the work of the National Conference of Commissioners on Uniform State Laws was carried on in cooperation with the American Law Institute. Its work in drafting proposed uniform laws to serve as legislative restatements of particular subjects continued during the first half of the century and culminated in 1952 in the Uniform Commercial Code, the most ambitious project yet undertaken by both the Commissioners and the ALI.

Bench and Bar

"You say . . . ," wrote Justice Holmes to Sir Frederick Pollock in 1919, "that we are an illiterate profession. My dear boy, if you can say that in England, what could I say that was adequate about us here! I see and hear things daily that would make me shudder if I had not grown hardened." It must be remembered that Holmes sat at the apex of the legal system. If he could direct his strictures at the Supreme Court Bar, what could be said about the lower ranks of the profession throughout the country?

The candid observer must concede that the Holmes comment was not too much overdrawn. It was true that there were leaders at the Bar who would have been outstanding in any day — men such as Arthur T. Vanderbilt, Charles Evans Hughes, John W. Davis, and Clarence Darrow. But even these great advocates lacked the broad perspective of their counterparts of a century earlier. Gone were the days when the practitioner might emulate the example of James Kent who, as a lawyer, "steadily divided the day into five portions and alloted them to Greek, Latin, law and business, French & English." The twentieth-century practitioner had neither the inclination nor the time to devote to intellectual activities not directly connected with his professional pursuits.

Two trends dominated the legal profession in the first part of the twentieth century — that toward specialization and that toward service as a business adjunct. Both trends had begun before the turn of the century, but they gathered momentum in the years that followed. In 1910 Woodrow Wilson noted that "Lawyers are specialists. . . . The general, broad, universal field

After a long deadlock among candidates at the 1924 Democratic convention, John W. Davis, the outstanding legal advocate of the day, was chosen as that party's nominee for President.

As chief justice of the Supreme Court from 1930 to 1941, Charles Evans Hughes took a middle course during the New Deal years, gradually reshaping the law to fit changing times.

of law grows dim and yet more dim to their apprehension as they spend year after year in a minute examination and analysis of a particular part of it." The lawyer was becoming a mere technician, concerned with the minutiae of his own craftsman's skill. "He has less time for reflection upon other than immediate professional undertakings." Increasingly rare were the great practitioner-statesmen. In their place was a professional mass that looked upon their narrow specialties in tax law, commercial law, accident law, and the like as all there was to know about the law.

Specialization was compelled by the growing commercialism of the profession. A study published in 1916 was entitled "The Law: Business or Profession?" As the century went on, the answer was more and more in favor of business. The whole tendency of the present century in the profession has been toward commercialism. The descent from honor to affluence has been as characteristic of the profession as of the society itself.

In 1934 Justice Harlan Fiske Stone asserted that commercialism "had made the learned profession of an earlier day the obsequious servant of business, and tainted it with the morals and manners of the marketplace in

"We'd love to have you associated with us, but you see how it is."

In this 1936 New Yorker magazine comment on the size of legal firms, a young lawyer is turned away because there is no room left for another name on the firm's door.

its most anti-social manifestations." No longer did the list of lawyers' clients represent a cross section of the society. The trend toward the legal profession as an adjunct of the business community reached its climax in the first third of the century. "Has not the lawyer," asked Woodrow Wilson, "allowed himself to become part of the industrial development, has he not been sucked into the channels of business, has he not changed his connections and become part of the mercantile structure . . . ?"

The result was a vast change in the nature of law practice itself, with the law firm tending to resemble the corporate entities it served. "The successful lawyer of our day more often than not is the proprietor or general manager of a new type of factory, whose legal product is increasingly the result of mass production methods," said Justice Stone. The growth of the urban "law factory" was a striking development in the twentieth-century legal system. Speaking in 1914, Joseph H. Choate could already note a difference between practice then and in the mid-nineteenth century: "The conduct of law business in those primitive days," he said, "was very different in every particular from the strikingly commercial methods into which the profession has fallen, or risen, in recent years." About this time there were 3 partners and 16 associates in the Cravath firm in New York. By 1940, this had risen to 22 partners and 72 associates; the clerical staff alone was close to 150. The firm resembled nothing so much as the executive offices of a large business corporation. Departmentalized into as many branches of the law as were practiced by the firm, with a long list of seniors and associates, each with his own particular specialty, with scores of assistants, typists, telephone operators, secretaries, bookkeepers, cashiers, a compre-

The "Green Goods" Lawyers

The practice of law has not yet developed a General Motors or even a Merrill Lynch, Pierce, Fenner and Smith, but during the second half of the twentieth century there was no doubt that Justice Louis D. Brandeis's "curse of bigness" had come to the legal profession. In 1963 New York City's twenty-three largest law firms ranged in size from 55 to 134 lawyers; ten years later the same firms contained 77 to 189 lawyers. The trend to bigness was not confined to New York. In the 1970's, Chicago, Cleveland, Houston, Los Angeles, Philadelphia, San Francisco, and Washington, D.C., each had firms with over 135 lawyers.

These "urban law factories," the new power elite of the legal profession, have served a significant interest, creating the legal framework for a new economic system built around the giant corporation. In the public mind, their members are "the Wall Street lawyers," the leading spokesmen for, and adjuncts of, big business. More than a century ago, Tocqueville saw the legal profession as the American aristocracy. Today, many Americans would agree that Wall Street lawyers fill that role. According to sociologist C. Wright Mills, "The inner core of the power elite also includes men of the higher legal . . . type from the great law factories."

The large law firms, wrote Erwin O. Smigel in *The Wall Street Lawyer*, "seem to have combined the atmospheres of a university, offices for a group of physicians or a 'Mayo type clinic,' a country law firm and a big business." The typical ones house their lawyers on three or four floors in the Wall Street district, preferably on Wall or Broad Streets or in the new Chase Manhattan Bank Building. In recent years, there has been some movement uptown to the Pan American Building on Park Avenue or other prestigious addresses nearby.

The urban lawyer in apotheosis is a partner in one of these firms, with an office high up in the mecca of the blue-chip Bar—1 Chase Manhattan Plaza. On his wall are photographs of himself with presidents, Cabinet members, governors, senators, and the like. His desk is elegant, its neatness far removed from the typical clutter of a lawyer's office of not so long ago. His telephone has several push buttons, and there may be as many as twenty channels on his intercom. Many of the old-timers, and even

hensive library—the lawyer's office had become another modern business.

In 1920 New York City had a score of law firms with staffs of at least 20 lawyers each; by mid-century, the number had grown to 73, and there were 284 such firms in cities throughout the country. These great law offices symbolized the new role of the Bar; they reflected the demands of big-business clients. They set the professional tone, even though numerically they contained a minority of the country's lawyers. The trend toward this service of business reached its peak in the 1920's. It was then that the profession's role was summed up in the blunt statement that a good lawyer was one who would tell his client not what he could not do, but how to do what he wanted to do.

This situation changed drastically during the Great Depression and the New Deal. The New Deal programs were largely devised and operated by lawyers. Expanding government regulation required an unprecedented number of attorneys. The new administrative agencies were lawyer-dominated agencies. For the first time in the century, the cream of the nation's law school graduates thought of Washington, D.C., rather than Wall Street, as their goal. Traditions of public service started to re-enter the profession. Law-trained men were once again in the seats of public power, working a transformation in the economic and governmental systems.

Toward mid-century, the lawyer had become a government lawyer as well as a lawyer for business. In 1949, almost one-eighth of the 180,000 lawyers in the country were employed by government. At the policy-making level their influence was far greater than mere numbers indicate. In the words of Fred Rodell, a leading critic, in 1939: "It is the lawyers who run

some of the newer men, try to think of themselves as members of a law firm of an earlier day and attempt to create in their offices the atmosphere of a country law firm, with pictures of Lincoln, old-fashioned furniture, and "folksy" decorations and memorabilia. But their practice has little to do with that of a Lincoln or even with the dramatic kind of law popularized on television in such programs as *Perry Mason*. Resembling the environment of a big corporation rather than that of a law office of a century ago, their business is marked by a constant paging of lawyers, long corridors of maze-like offices, and enormous file systems whose cabinets consume an ever-larger portion of available space.

The work of these law firms occurs mostly outside of courtrooms; the partners almost never appear before a judge and jury—a testament to Elihu Root's dictum that "a lawyer's business is to keep his clients out of litigation." Most of the time is spent in the giving of advice and the preparing of legal papers. Big money is made in the drawing up of contracts, particularly those dealing with corporations and involving large transfers of property, huge bank loans, mergers, and so forth. As Martin Mayer observed in *The Lawyers:* "God can make a tree; only lawyers can make a corporation." Doing so has been especially profitable; Wall Street lawyers affectionately refer to the shepherding of new stock issues as the handling of "green goods."

The existence of such firms reflects the increasing complexity of modern society—the problems of big corporations, big unions, and big government, the last with its high taxes and bewildering mass of regulations. The lawyers fill a growing need to ensure that contracts are foolproof in law and that daily transactions will pass muster with the Justice Department, the Treasury, and the myriad of regulatory agencies. If the requirements of the corporations created the large law firms, however, they themselves have developed in the corporate image. The difference between the lawyer and the client has become a matter of degree. The law firms, too, are big businesses; increasingly, the question has become only, how much money can be made? Despite a passion for anonymity, the Wall Street lawyer has gained a controversial image as an instrument of big business.

our civilization for us. . . . Most legislators are lawyers; they make our laws. Most presidents, governors, commissioners, along with their advisers and brain-trusters are lawyers; they administer our laws. All the judges are lawyers; they interpret and enforce our laws. There is no separation of powers where the lawyers are concerned. . . . As the schoolboy put it, ours is 'a government of lawyers, not of men.' "

One of the major consequences of lawyer domination of governmental institutions was the legalization of the developing administrative process. The trend that had started with the Interstate Commerce Commission continued in the growing number of agencies set up during this century. These agencies, too, were cast in the lawyer's mold. Most agency heads were lawyers; their staffs were dominated by lawyers; their procedures were patterned on those followed in the courtroom. Adversary judicial procedure became their outstanding characteristic, increasingly disabling them from operating efficiently in the public interest. When the welfare state established its own agencies to administer its burgeoning benefactory programs, there was a natural tendency to burden them with the panoply of full judicial procedure developed in the earlier regulatory agencies. This tendency

In 1935 artist William Gropper looked over the United States Senate and found it a place where one man could orate on the perils facing the Republic while his fellow senators dozed or read their newspapers.

was to pose one of the most difficult problems for the nation's public law in the second half of the century.

A primary test of whether a profession is worthy of the title is whether it has made the effort necessary to adjust its field to the needs of the time. The legal profession has inevitably been a conservative influence in society. This truism continued to be valid during the first half of the century. Far too few lawyers were willing to incur the trouble and unpopularity attendant on crusades for reform. Despite the apathy of the vast bulk of the Bar, however, the century did see progress both in reform of the law and the standards of the legal profession. Above all, the judges, themselves the pinnacle of the profession, transformed American public and private law to serve the needs of the emerging twentieth-century state and society.

In the profession itself, the first half of the century saw an intensification of the movement to raise professional standards that had begun before the turn of the century. Before 1890, only four states had had boards of Bar examiners; in no more than half a dozen had there been written Bar examinations. This situation changed completely. Bar examiners and written examinations became standard after 1900. By mid-century, the written Bar examination was required in thirty-nine states; the other nine permitted graduates of certain schools to be admitted to the Bar without examination. The Lincoln-type attorney, who prepared for the profession by self-directed reading, had become a thing of the past.

The effort to improve the caliber of the profession also had its effect on the courts and the judges who manned them. The leveling influence on judicial caliber had been the political selection of judges, particularly through the elective process. As seen in Chapter v, the trend toward judicial election had reached its climax by 1905. The years that followed saw the beginnings of a reversal of that trend. For the first time since the movement toward election of judges had begun a century earlier, a number of states shifted to other methods of judicial selection. Notable in inaugurating the new trend was the adoption by the organized Bar of the American Bar Association plan, also called the Missouri plan, because it was used in the selection of appellate judges in that state after 1940. In Missouri, judges are appointed from three persons nominated by a judicial commission; after a year in office, they run unopposed at the next election. Also significant was the provision for appointment of judges in the modernized court system set up under the 1947 New Jersey Constitution. The extent of the new trend should not be exaggerated, however. At mid-century, thirty-five states still provided for the popular election of judges. Nevertheless, the bar associations in a majority of those states were in favor of a change to the Missouri plan, and the second half of the century would see election increasingly give way as a method of judicial selection.

Methods of selection have always had a direct bearing upon the caliber of judges. Professional and scholarly opinion has always held that appointment produces a much higher quality on the Bench than election. This has been characterized as a mere verdict of opinion, resting on no substantial evidence of historical inquiry. Yet it cannot be denied that the decline in judicial capacity in the last century coincided with the spread of popular election. During the first half of this century, the level of judicial competence gradually improved. Significantly, among the best judges toward mid-century were Arthur T. Vanderbilt of New Jersey, Laurence M. Hyde of Missouri, and Roger Traynor of California — all appointed judges.

Federal judges have, of course, always been chosen by appointment, and every qualified observer has noted their superior caliber. During the first half of this century, there were judges who ranked with any who ever sat on the federal Bench. Chief Justices Hughes and Taft were leaders of the Supreme Court who must be placed just below Marshall and Taney themselves. Justices Holmes, Brandeis, Cardozo, Stone, Black, and Frankfurter deserve, by any standards, to be listed among the greats of American judicial history. It was during this period, too, that the lower federal courts were staffed by outstanding judges such as Learned and Augustus Hand, Charles E. Clark, John J. Parker, and Jerome Frank — men who would have graced any court.

When Pound spoke in 1906 of the deficiencies in the courts, he referred not to judicial personnel, but to judicial organization and procedure. "I venture to say," he emphasized, "that our system of courts is archaic and our procedure behind the times." The multiplicity of courts and the lack of effective organization kept American law where English law had been before the Judicature Act of 1873 in that country. Procedures that were technical and contentious made the courtroom atmosphere congenial only to American counterparts of Dodson and Fogg and Serjeant Buzfuz.

Substantial improvements were made in the first half of this century in both judicial organization and procedure. At mid-century, Judge Vanderbilt, in his book *The Challenge of Law Reform*, was able "to show how the law

Learned Hand and the Spirit of Liberty

Among all of America's great judges who were never appointed to the Supreme Court, the best known, perhaps, was Learned Hand of New York. After Justice Benjamin N. Cardozo's death in 1938, Hand was considered by many to be the nation's greatest living judge. His judicial career was spent on what he delighted to call an "inferior court," although for years he was the virtually unanimous choice of the legal profession for the next Supreme Court vacancy — a choice that went unrecognized by any President.

Born in 1872, Hand was appointed to the federal district court at the age of thirty-seven in 1909, one of the youngest men ever named to be a federal judge. In 1924 he was elevated to the United States Court of Appeals for the Second Circuit, where he made his greatest legal contributions. When he died in 1961, he had served for fifty-two years on the federal Bench, longer than any other jurist. His stature stemmed not from the few great cases that came to him, but from the notable way in which he dealt with a multitude of small cases that covered every subject in the legal lexicon. "Repeatedly," said Chief Judge Henry J. Friendly of the Court of Appeals, "he would make the tiniest glow-worm illumine a whole field." Over the years, his eminence grew by the cumulative weight of opinion after opinion — painstaking, eloquent, and illuminating. No judge, not even those on the Supreme Court, was more frequently cited by name. He was, indeed, often called the tenth

Judge Learned Hand in 1959

has in certain jurisdictions at least thrown off the shackles of complicated court systems, of technicalities and fictions in procedure and pleadings, and how it has substituted instead a simple court structure, flexible rules of procedure aiming at the elimination of technicalities and surprise, and finally the shortening and improvement of trials by pretrial conferences and modernized rules of evidence."

In most parts of the country, the multiplicity of courts and judges remained an outstanding feature of the legal system. Nebraska, early in the century, had more judges than all of England; New Jersey had seventeen courts or parts of courts as late as 1947. The situation in these states was far from atypical. Special pleading, with its confused agglomeration of technicalities, was still in vogue in some states in the first part of the 1900's.

Procedural reform in this century dates from the Federal Rules of Civil Procedure, adopted in 1937. Their goal was admirably stated in Rule 1: "They shall be construed to secure the just, speedy, and inexpensive determination of every action." The Federal Rules served as the catalyst for adoption of similar simplified state rules, notably in California and New Jersey. Closely connected with procedural reform was the movement to vest the judges with power to promulgate rules of procedure. The Federal Rules themselves were put into effect only after the Supreme Court was given rule-making power. By mid-century, almost half the states had followed the federal lead and vested rule-making authority in their courts.

Even more important was the provision of a simplified modern court structure—with a trial court of general jurisdiction over all matters (civil, criminal, equitable, and probate) and a court to hear appeals (with an intermediate appellate court if the size of the state and the volume of its

Supreme Court justice, so often did his judgments guide theirs.

Hand, however, was more than a judicial master of the law. His character was summed up in one sentence by Judge Friendly: "He was Ariel, and Prometheus, and Jove, with a goodly touch of Mephistopheles, too." Like Justice Oliver Wendell Holmes, he was an unabashed epicure, with a liking for pretty women, scabrous stories, and good food and drink. A colleague once told of "the pangs he suffered . . . when a velvet Burgundy had to go unquaffed one night in Paris, on his physician's advice and, more important, Mrs. Hand's orders." Like Holmes and Cardozo, also, Hand was an artist on the Bench, who employed language as a tool to adapt the law to contemporary needs and, in so doing,

also enriched America's literature.

To the general public, Hand was best known for his occasional papers and addresses—in particular for the moving remarks he made to newly naturalized citizens at ceremonies in New York's Central Park in 1944. The speech was widely published and is held by many to be the finest statement on the spirit of liberty written in this century. In it, Hand wondered whether we place too much hope in constitutions, laws, and courts:

"These are false hopes; believe me, these are false hopes," said the jurist. "Liberty lies in the hearts of men and women; when it dies there, no constitution, no law, no court can save it; no constitution, no law, no court can even do much to help it. While it lies there it needs no consti-

tution, no law, no court to save it."

Then came his stirring peroration: "What then is the spirit of liberty? I cannot define it; I can only tell you my own faith. The spirit of liberty is the spirit which is not too sure that it is right; the spirit of liberty is the spirit which seeks to understand the minds of other men and women; the spirit of liberty is the spirit which weighs their interests alongside its own without bias; the spirit of liberty remembers that not even a sparrow falls to earth unheeded; the spirit of liberty is the spirit of Him who, nearly two thousand years ago, taught mankind that lesson it has never learned, but has never quite forgotten; that there may be a kingdom where the least shall be heard and considered side by side with the greatest."

Courthouse Square, the town center of Llano, Texas, in the early 1900's

Rural folks exchange news and opinions outside

Shirtsleeve law in the courthouse of historic Fairfax County, Virginia

The County Courthouse

A familiar hub of hometown life, it is a seat of the law, a center of politics and gossip, and occasionally the scene of an epic like the murder trial of labor leader Bill Haywood, defended by Clarence Darrow, in Boise, Ada County, Idaho, 1907 (right).

the courthouse in Versailles, Kentucky, in 1940.

An election-year (1938) façade of the courthouse in Waco, Texas

judicial business required it). Once again, the federal courts led the way. By mid-century, however, only California, Delaware, and New Jersey had followed the federal lead. Judicial administration had become a recognized discipline; but establishment of modern court systems still remained high on the agenda of legal progress. Action in the second half of the century remained essential if the courts were not to be increasingly bypassed by arbitration and administrative tribunals.

Crucial to whatever reforms were accomplished in both substantive law and legal institutions during the first half of the century were the growth of professional organizations and legal education. The membership of the American Bar Association grew from 1,718 in 1902 to 42,121 in 1950. There was a comparable growth in state and local bar associations. By 1923, there was an active bar association in every state or territory. In 1921 the movement for a racially integrated Bar began with the State Bar of North Dakota. By mid-century, over twenty states had integrated Bars. The most important work of the bar associations was in improving educational and professional standards. They were also active, though to a lesser extent, in the movements to reform substantive and procedural law, as well as that which led to the Federal Administrative Procedure Act in 1946. From a broader point of view, their influence was not entirely beneficial. They all too often reflected the interests of their larger clients and served, through most of this period, as a damper on much of the effort to bring the society and its institutions into the twentieth century.

During this century, the American law school came into its own. At the turn of the century, a majority of lawyers still received no formal training in law before admission. By 1950, the apprentice-trained or self-read lawyer had become a disappearing anomaly. According to a 1951 survey, over 94 percent of the country's lawyers had attended some law school prior to admission. Within the law schools themselves, the American Bar Association and the Association of American Law Schools had been largely successful in elevating standards. Both associations adopted minimum standards for approved law schools. The effort to raise standards inevitably moved slowly. In 1928 only a third of American law students were in ABA-approved schools; in 1936 the figure had risen to 55 percent. By 1951, of a total of 164 law schools in the country, 124 had received ABA approval. In addition, there was a gradual elevation of law school admission requirements. In 1921 the ABA and AALS amended their standards so that two years of prelegal college work were required. In 1950 three years became the standard. In practice, the better law schools required a college degree. And almost all the law schools demanded three years of study (or four years of part-time attendance) before the law degree could be received. The schools themselves were nearly all professional schools of a college or university; the proprietary law schools tended to disappear in most parts of the country.

In the law schools, the case method not only reached full bloom, but even began to wilt. Early in the century, Langdell's innovation had become standard practice. It had a most salutary effect in rescuing American legal education from the theoretical incursions into dogma that still characterized

law teaching in other countries. It furnished precisely the kind of training the potential lawyer needed and the older textbook method had neglected: training in intellectual independence, in individual thinking, in digging out principles through penetrating analysis, and reasoning from them in a legal manner. Concepts, principles, and rules of law were studied, not as dry abstractions, but as realities arising out of actual cases decided in the community. As a general proposition, one had to agree strongly with Harold J. Laski's conclusion that the case method "makes for a far higher standard of legal education."

Nevertheless, the middle of the century also saw indications of rising dissatisfaction with the case method as the only method of legal education. Langdell's successors were inevitably concerned primarily with precedents and technique. There was assiduous analysis of what courts had done and their manner of doing it, but little reflection on the relationship of law to the social, economic, and political forces that produced it or its function as a means of social control. The case method treated law from only one per-

Efforts during the past half century to raise and standardize law school requirements have been largely successful. Above: law student exams.

Legal Aid for the Poor

The year 1876, the centennial year of the nation, saw the establishment of the first legal aid office in the United States. Opened by the German Society in New York City, its original purpose was to provide legal assistance to German immigrants. "Our Society," announced its president, Edward Salomon, "provides not alms, which these applicants do not ask and would not accept, but justice." In time, needy persons of other backgrounds appealed to the organization for help, and the little agency, intended only to assist newly arrived Germans, be-

accounting for the inflation of the twentieth century, now appear ridiculously small. The early work of the society focused on the protection of seamen (against shanghaiing, which was still prevalent on the waterfront) and in behalf of claims for payments for services. In 1910 an aggressive campaign was instituted against the unjust practices of personal loan companies and installment sellers of furniture. Great effort went into the raising of even the modest sums required by the society for its expanding work. Its annual opera benefits

and hearing a glazier describe his inability to recover $6.60 for work that he had performed. The expenses of a suit would exceed the amount involved. No wonder, said Roosevelt, the poor thought of American justice as containing only laws to punish, never to help. This, he wrote in a 1917 article, led directly to contempt for law, disloyalty to government, and the planting of the seeds of anarchy.

Gradually, the Legal Aid Society became a major organization, with offices throughout New York City and an annual budget of over $4,000,000. In 1972 it received 231,078 requests for assistance, three quarters of them involving criminal cases. Its idea, meanwhile, had spread to other cities, starting with Chicago in 1886. By 1916 thirty-seven cities had some form of legal aid in operation; at mid-century there were ninety-two legal aid offices in the country (seventy-three in cities of over 100,000 population). In 1949 a National Legal Aid Association was set up to serve the various groups on a country-wide basis, and today virtually every large city has its own legal aid organization (there were some 250 of them throughout the nation in 1973).

During the century, it became recognized, also, that legal aid of this type was not enough to secure legal justice for the growing numbers of the country's poor and needy. Starting with Los Angeles, many cities established public defender offices as defense counterparts to district attorneys. The defenders were public officials whose job it was to handle cases for those who were accused of crimes and were too poor to engage lawyers of their own. In the 1960's, as part of its "war on poverty," the federal government also entered the scene, providing substantial funding, through the Office of Economic Opportunity, for legal services for the urban and rural poor and such economically deprived groups as the American Indians and other minorities.

Waiting one's turn at a New York Legal Aid Society branch office about 1912

came a busy law office for all poor persons in New York City. In 1896 it adopted the name by which it is still known in New York, "The Legal Aid Society."

Its first period of growth occurred in the last decade of the nineteenth century when it acquired a full-time staff and opened branches in different parts of the city. The number of applicants, two hundred in 1876, rose to over fourteen thousand in 1900, yet in 1901 the society's total expenses were $17,980 and the approximate cost per applicant was only one dollar—amounts that, even

once drew a letter from Mark Twain, saying that there was no need to urge attendance on those who had come to previous years' performances: "There are enough of those to fill the house," he said. "I know this, for when I was there, there was but one vacant seat, and I was in it."

One of the society's most important functions was the publicizing of the need for legal services for the poor. Recounting how he was once taken to the society's office to observe its activities, Theodore Roosevelt told of sitting at the interviewing desk

spective: that of appellate court decisions. It isolated law study from other threads in the pattern of the society.

Critics of the case method were becoming increasingly articulate. The newer casebooks were more than mere compendiums. The cases used were the products of careful editing, with unessentials compressed or eliminated. More and more, textual commentary and legislative and administrative materials were included. Seminars were added to the curriculum. Still, by and large, the curriculum and method of instruction remained what they had been a generation earlier. The newer fields of law were coming in, but at a pace that did not mirror the century's law explosion. If one could not yet trace a trend for the reorganization of law study, there were signs that such a trend might emerge in the second half of the century.

The Ends of Law: 1950

The expansive confidence of American law began to give way to the increasing skepticism and pessimism of the twentieth century. The law of an earlier day had been molded by the seemingly limitless reaches and economic opportunities of the frontier. The spirit of American law had been the spirit of the pioneer. Now the memory of the frontier was fading. The frontiersman's jealousy of law and administration changed to a growing demand for supervision and restraint. The call to protect men from themselves and the failures of the market replaced the feeling that man was ruled best when he was ruled least. Government paternalism increasingly removed the stamp of the pioneer from the legal order.

The complacent arrogance of the law of 1900 could scarcely survive the realities of twentieth-century life. With all its callousness, Legal Darwinism had been based on an essentially optimistic view of society and its institutions. Progress, if not perfectibility, was the lodestar that guided Herbert Spencer and his legal disciples. Even a cynic such as Justice Holmes could believe that high-mindedness was natural to man.

But the confidence engendered by optimism seemed increasingly out of place to the twentieth-century jurist. "Now days are dragon-ridden, the nightmare/Rides upon sleep. . . ," the poet Yeats had written in *Nineteen Hundred and Nineteen*. The assurance that we were living, also, in the best of all possible legal systems was supplanted by doubt that the nation's legal institutions were adequate to meet the needs of the day. Conviction became ever more difficult during the transition to a valueless world.

The comparative certainty of the last century could withstand neither the facts nor the intellectual currents of twentieth-century history. Einsteinian relativist physics, with its challenge of what had been supposed the fixed order of the universe, and Freudian psychology, with its challenge of the fixed order of the mind, combined with Marxian determinism to undermine the assumptions on which the legal order had been based. Time, distance, and mind had lost their absolute values; reality was more complex and less stable than man had imagined.

The problem was that the legal universe, like the physical one, had no center. Everything was seen to be relative: "Nothing is more certain in modern society," declared the Supreme Court at mid-century, "than the principle that there are no absolutes." The world of law, like that of physics, was perceived only as the relativity of one value compared with another.

For the first time, a new conception of law itself, unrelated to traditional theories, developed. A new school of jurisprudence, self-styled realist, gave voice to this conception. It took for its starting point the Holmes dictum that "The prophecies of what the courts will do in fact, and nothing more pretentious, are what I mean by the law." From this, it was a short step to Jerome Frank's assertion that law was "only a guess as to what a court will decide. Law then . . . is either (a) actual law, *i.e.*, a specific past decision . . . or (b) probable law, *i.e.*, a guess as to a specific future decision." The law was not to be found in the authoritative guides to which jurists had always looked. Instead, the realists urged, "Don't get your law from rules, but get your rules from the law that is."

The realists performed a valuable service in emphasizing the difference between law in the books and law in action—between what legal institutions said and what they did. Awareness of this was essential if the law was to attain the ends deemed appropriate by the middle of the century.

Realism in jurisprudence was, however, used in the sense in which artists employ it rather than in the philosophical sense. Because the ugly existed in nature, it was true; and the realist in art insisted on portraying the ugly as truth, even in exaggerated ugliness. Similarly, the juristic realists insisted on the alogical and irrational features of the legal process, stressing them to the exclusion of all else. The notion that "The Law is, in the main, an exact science," they characterized as a hoax. "No pretense was ever more absurd." The search for legal certainty they termed a myth, a childish longing to recapture the world of "the Father-as-Infallible Judge."

It may be, as Holmes skeptically put it with regard to the influence of jurisprudence, "I don't believe most judges knew or cared a sixpence for any school." But the impact of the legal realists has been all-pervasive during the present century, changing the very way in which men have been accustomed to consider law. By mid-century, the law had succumbed to the century's preoccupation with relativism and behaviorism. It appeared psychologically impossible to do what men had believed they were doing by law. The law was not the master but the slave of societal behavior; the concept of law as self-sufficient and independent had been based on false premises. The law was not an impartial agency of social control, holding down the prejudices and individual inclinations of those in public power. It was merely what judges and officials did, motivated by their prejudices and personal propensities. The result was similar to that reached by Marxian determinists, though with less emphasis upon economic factors.

What was clear was that the certainty with which the law had been regarded at the turn of the century was now a thing of the past. Gone too was the general consensus on the ends to be served by twentieth-century law. The ends men had agreed upon in 1900 were increasingly called into question. In the early part of the century, economists, sociologists, and political scientists had become aware of the need for change, when jurists were still repeating nineteenth-century formulas. New theories of the ends of law were articulated in terms of a contrast between social justice and legal justice, emphasizing the need for a shift in emphasis from individual claims in property and promised advantages to concern for the individual life. "The old justice in the economic field," affirmed John Dewey, "consisted chiefly in securing to each individual his rights in property or contracts. The new justice must consider how it can secure for each individual a standard of living, and such a share in the values of civilization as shall make possible a full moral life."

The pressure of unsecured or inadequately recognized interests pushed the law toward a new approach to legal problems. The change began with the recognition of interests as the ultimate idea behind rights. Individual interests were placed on a lower plane than social interests and obtained their juristic significance from the social advantage in giving effect to them. This resulted in a shift in stress from individual interests to social interests. The changing conception saw justice in terms of wants rather than wills. Juristically, the emphasis was transferred from the social interest in the general security (in the security of acquisitions and transactions) to the social interest in the individual life.

The law now took for granted the fact that it must look at life in the concrete rather than man in the abstract. Its watchword became the satisfaction

A busy early-century scene at the New York Legal Aid Society. Not all applicants for help were poor; some were immigrants whose legal troubles were compounded by their unfamiliarity with American ways.

of human wants. The law, like government, was a social siphon, its essential function that of ensuring an equitable apportionment of the community's resources. The great change was from the abstract equality of the nineteenth century to an adjustment of burdens and redistribution of resources.

By the middle of the century, Pound could state two emerging postulates on which the law was based:

"(1) Everyone is entitled to assume that the burdens incident to life will be borne by society.

"(2) Everyone is entitled to assume that at least a standard human life will be assured him."

In the first half of the century, the law had gone far toward accepting these postulates. This meant an inevitable expansion in the role of the legal order in the society. But here the new conception of law played a crucial part in undermining its effectiveness. As the role of law expanded, confidence in its ability to accomplish its ends started to decline. Legal skepticism led to skepticism about the law as an effective instrument of social change. Holmes had said that the Golden Rule was that there was no Golden Rule; the realists took this to mean that there was no Rule at all. If only the nonrational element in the law was real, how could the expanded ends of law themselves be rationally achieved? In the second half of the century, the skepticism inherent in the new conception of law would become a growing doubt about the very legitimacy of the legal order and its institutions.

And what of the inventory of legal deficiencies with which Pound began the century? At mid-century, Arthur T. Vanderbilt updated the Pound catalogue. Looking at substantive law, he saw the primary need as that to simplify and make knowable the law. The volume of legal sources and materials had become completely unmanageable. Yet, even though substantive rules and doctrines still needed modernizing, the situation was not nearly as critical as it had been when Pound delivered his address. The complaints of the people were no longer directed at the substantive law; the first half of the century had seen the individualist spirit of the common law substantially modified, with a consequent lessening of the gap between law and public opinion. The law still suffered from mechanical operation of rules, but this too was giving way before the realist conception of law.

Public dissatisfaction was now focused "primarily . . . at the men who administer the law in the courts and the way in which they administer it," said Vanderbilt. With all the efforts at reform in procedure and judicial administration that had been made, the problems in those areas noted by Pound still persisted. In most jurisdictions, contentious procedure still made trial too often a battle between the parties rather than a rational search for truth on the merits. More serious, calendar pressures, ineffective administration, and archaic procedures made the law's delays worse than ever. The courts themselves were approaching a crisis in organization and administration. Popular sentiment mirrored the growing judicial inability to dispense justice efficiently. Distrust went beyond the lack of effective judicial administration. According to a 1939 national survey, 28 percent of the people did not even consider the judges of their local courts honest. Lack of trust was greatest in states where judges were selected through election; in many of them, belief was widespread that judgeships were the subjects of bargain and sale.

What made the situation at mid-century different from what it had been half a century earlier was the existence of proven remedies for the law's defects. Judicial caliber could be raised by the spread of the Missouri plan. The Federal Rules furnished a model for the supplanting of antiquated procedures. Minimum standards of judicial administration had been formulated by the American Bar Association. Judicial administration itself was becoming a science; it had already produced modernized court systems, such as those in California and New Jersey. Those systems could easily be adapted for use in any state. With all of this, Vanderbilt could complain in 1949 of "the general indifference of the legal profession to the technicalities, the anachronisms, and the delays in our procedural law." The leaders of reform were but the tip of the professional iceberg. The great mass of lawyers kept aloof from the reforming effort; their inertia was still the strongest factor in favor of the status quo.

By mid-century, however, the contrast between the efficiency of the assembly-line age and the cumbersome methods of the law could no longer be ignored. The scientific methods of modern management and the patchwork caricature that passed for administration in most courts appeared (as they indeed *were*) products that were centuries apart. The second half of the century would tell whether this situation would continue. If effective steps to ameliorate deficiencies were not soon taken, growing popular dissatisfaction might well extend to the legitimacy of the legal process itself.

The federal government's response to the economic plight of the American people during the depression of the 1930's established its acceptance of responsibility for the public's welfare. Programs of the WPA provided employment for millions, including artists like Moses Soyer, who did this canvas in 1936 of fellow WPA painters at work on mural panels in New York.

VIII

Search for New Values

Public Law Since 1950

W
e may well wonder in view of the precedents now established,"
declared Charles Evans Hughes not long after World War I,
"whether constitutional government as heretofore maintained
in this Republic could survive another great war even victoriously waged."
During the second half of the twentieth century the problem became, if anything, more pressing, though not in the specific terms posed by Hughes.

When World War II ended, it was apparent that Hughes's dire prediction
had not materialized. The basic constitutional structure had emerged from
a second global conflict essentially unimpaired. Hughes's query has since
been given renewed pertinence by the presidential power to wage war even
without a congressional declaration. So far-reaching has that power become
that it has threatened to alter the very organic balance of the American governmental system. The dominant constitutional fact during the second half
of this century has been the commitment of the nation to two major wars on
the authority of the President alone.

True, American intervention in Korea was a direct response to the June
25, 1950, resolution of the United Nations Security Council. That resolution
determined that the North Korean invasion was a breach of international
peace, called for withdrawal of the invading troops, and requested member
nations to "give every assistance to the United Nations" in coping with the
situation. When President Truman ordered American forces to help repel
the invasion, he stated that he did so in order to support the Security Council resolution.

The nation's obligation under the Charter of the United Nations was assumed under the treaty that provided for American membership in the world
organization. But it was the President alone who decided whether to use

Protesting for civil rights: the
Reverend Martin Luther King at
the Lincoln Memorial in 1963

Symbol of the turbulent 1960's: marchers oppose the war in Vietnam.

force to protect the interests of the nation abroad and carry out its treaty obligation. And he did so on his own authority, both as Chief Executive and commander in chief. "Prompt action was imperative," said Mr. Truman, in explaining his action to Congress a month after he had moved. In such a case the President has the power to act immediately, without any obligation to seek legislative approval. The reality of the twentieth-century world—if not the strict letter of the Constitution—makes presidential primacy a compelling necessity, even to the extent of taking belligerent action without congressional consent.

This has been true under all the Presidents since World War II. The Truman action in Korea had its counterparts in the 1958 intervention in Lebanon by Eisenhower, the 1962 confrontation over Cuba under Kennedy, the 1965 landing in the Dominican Republic under Johnson, and in Nixon's 1970 deployment of the fleet to deter an invasion of Jordan. In those cases, also, the President directed the use of the armed forces—though, in them, such use was not met by any opposing force.

But it was the Vietnam war that proved to be the constitutional crucible of the period. It increasingly exerted a distorting pressure that made what was previously plain appear uncertain, and before which even established doctrines had to bend. For the President to commit over half a million men to an obscure part of the world, where the interests of the nation were not

"The Most Oppressive of All Kingly Oppressions"

Article I of the Constitution empowers Congress "to declare war." But the effective power to "make" war inheres in the President, whom the Constitution expressly makes commander in chief of the armed forces. This is more than a ceremonial title; the President, under the Commander in Chief Clause, is the actual head of the armed forces. Constitutionally, he may assume personal command of forces in the field, as Washington did in 1794 when he accompanied the troops dispatched to suppress the Whiskey Rebellion. He may, as Lincoln did in 1862, order a military advance or interfere directly in command decisions. He may, as Franklin D. Roosevelt did in World War II, map the strategy of global conflict from the White House. He may even, as Woodrow Wilson did in 1917, place American forces under foreign command. Moreover, President Truman himself made the final decision in 1945 to employ the atomic bomb.

Can a President, however, "make war" when the Congress has not "declared" the war? Throughout the nation's history, Presidents have assumed that their power as commander in chief includes that authority. Even in the case of wars waged with formal congressional declarations—save for the War of 1812 and the Spanish-American War—the declarations merely confirmed states of war already entered into, largely upon the initiative of the President. In addition, there have been countless cases in which Presidents, without a declaration of war, have employed American forces within the territory of, or against the forces of, another country. These actions did not lead to formally declared wars because the countries involved were not able to retaliate. As Felix Frankfurter said in 1914, when he was asked whether the seizure of Vera Cruz in Mexico by American troops should be treated as an act of war, "It would be an act of war against a great nation; it isn't against a small nation."

Even weak Presidents have not hesitated to use American forces in such actions abroad on their own authority. William Howard Taft sent Marines to put an end to an insurrection in Nicaragua while he was President. Years earlier, Franklin Pierce had ordered the naval bombardment of a town in the same country. When a property owner sued the naval commander for damages, a federal court in 1860 ruled that the President could direct the use of force to protect American interests abroad even without congressional authorization.

The dangers involved in such a power were noted by Abraham Lincoln in 1848. "Allow the President to invade a neighboring nation whenever he shall deem it necessary . . .," he said, "and you allow him to do so, whenever he may choose to say he deems it necessary for such purpose and you allow him to make war at pleasure." During the twentieth century, the President has been able vir-

clearly threatened, appeared to do violence to the constitutional division of powers. If the Constitution gave Congress alone the power to declare war, how could the President carry on such a long and costly conflict without any congressional declaration?

The constitutional issue cannot be avoided by saying, as a federal judge once did, that the President is powerless to declare war, go to war, or put the nation into war without the formal action of Congress. According to the Supreme Court, war is "That state in which a nation prosecutes its right by force." If the nation prosecutes its interests by force which is resisted, a state of war exists as a fact, regardless of congressional inaction. In such a situation, it is the fact that makes "enemies," and not any legislative declaration. Although there was never a formal declaration, by every other criterion the Korean action did, in fact, constitute war; a holding that "the Korean War is not War — in the face of 128,000 American casualties — is," as one state court put it, "so unrealistic and legalistic as to be utterly unjustifiable." Similarly, it would be difficult to convince those who served in the Vietnam conflict that it was not war in every sense of the word. "Lack of a formal declaration of war did not mitigate the suffering of the wounded nor the sorrow of the families of the dead," declared another state court.

Nor should the reality of presidential power be blurred by the fact of congressional participation in both the Korean and Vietnam conflicts. In

President Johnson exhorts troops in Vietnam.

tually "to make war at pleasure," free of legal and political controls. Attempts at congressional control have proved ineffective. When Congress refused in 1917 to authorize President Wilson to arm American merchantmen, the President proceeded to take the action on his own authority, assigning the necessary men and equipment from the Navy. After Congress in 1941 provided that the Lend-Lease Act did not authorize the convoying of merchant ships to belligerents, President Roosevelt ordered the Navy, anyway, to convoy supplies to Britain as far as Iceland. Although the Neutrality Act of 1939 remained technically in force until Pearl Harbor, Roosevelt acted directly to support Great Britain in its war effort with both supplies and air and naval forces in what Edward S. Corwin called "the War before the War."

The only time the Supreme Court has considered the legality of presidential exercises of the power to "make war" was in 1863. Though the case came up at a critical time, during the Civil War, the Court was willing to rule on the issue. By only a bare majority it upheld Lincoln's blockade of the South on his own authority. Since then, notably during the Korean and Vietnam wars in the twentieth century, the Court has refused to consider the validity of presidential uses of the armed forces. The result has been for the constitutional case against presidential warmaking without a congressional declaration of war to go by default. The power to involve the people in war, Lincoln wrote in 1848, was "the most oppressive of all Kingly oppressions," and the framers of the Constitution, he observed, had resolved "that *no one man* should hold the power of bringing this oppression upon us." During the twentieth century, however, practice, if not the letter of the Constitution, has, again in Lincoln's words, all but placed "our Presidents where Kings have always stood."

the one case that dealt with the legality of the Vietnam war, a federal court ruled that Congress and the President had taken mutual and joint action in the prosecution and support of military operations in Southeast Asia from the beginning of those operations. Congressional action, including the Tonkin Gulf Resolution of 1964 and the furnishing of manpower and materials of war for protracted military operations in Vietnam, was held sufficient to authorize or ratify the nation's actions in Vietnam. The intent of the Constitution's framers in authorizing Congress alone to declare war was judged not defeated by permitting such an inference of legislative authorization.

In the strict letter of the law, the court may have been correct. The first draft of the Constitution vested in Congress the power "to make war." This was changed on the floor of the Convention to the present provision empowering Congress "To declare War." Clearly implied was a difference between the power to *declare* and that to *make* war, with only the former vested exclusively in Congress. The implication has been borne out by the war power throughout American history. From Thomas Jefferson's dispatch of a naval squadron to the Barbary Coast in 1804–1805 to the Vietnam war, the nation's Presidents have acted on the assumption that they have authority to make war, whether or not there has been a congressional declaration. In actual fact, the nation has been at war more often without, than with, a formal declaration by Congress.

On this point we may recall Engel's law on the passage of quantity into quality. The undeclared wars of the second half of the twentieth century have been so much greater than anything comparable in previous American history that the change of quantity *was* simultaneously a change of quality. It is one thing to talk about the power of the President to order belligerent acts such as the Pershing punitive raid into Mexico in 1916, the Boxer expedition into China in 1900, or even the sending of troops into the territory in dispute with Mexico in 1846. All of those involved acts of war, but they were, quantitatively speaking, not of great consequence for the nation and its constitutional system. That was not the case with the Korean and Vietnam wars, full-scale conflicts, as intensive as any wars in which the nation has been engaged. Nor were their effects limited to the areas in which they were waged. Vietnam in particular turned out to be the most disruptive conflict internally since the Civil War.

The framers of the Constitution may, as Lincoln once said, have vested Congress with the power to declare war to ensure that no one man might hold the power to involve the nation in war. Vietnam showed how different constitutional reality can become. In this respect, practice, if not the organic text, has all but placed "our Presidents where Kings have always stood."

Most significant perhaps was the failure of the law to play a part in deciding the legality of the presidential power to wage war. In 1863, just before Gettysburg, the Supreme Court ruled on the legality of Lincoln's exercise of the war power. The same was not true during the Korean and Vietnam wars. A number of cases were brought challenging the authority of the Executive to wage war in Vietnam. Over vigorous dissents, the Su-

U.S. soldiers in Korea move toward the front in 1951, passing refugees who are streaming away from danger.

Many American Presidents have stretched the dimensions of their constitutional powers. This is a Chicago Tribune cartoon comment on President Truman's request for more White House authority in 1951.

preme Court refused to consider the matter, presumably on the ground that the use of the armed forces abroad constitutes a political question over which the courts do not have jurisdiction. Judicial abstention was consistent with the precedents on the matter, but it prevented a legal resolution of the most important public law issue of the century.

King for Four Years?

The power to wage war was only one aspect of an unprecedented growth of presidential authority that marked the second half of the twentieth century. Paralleling that phase were White House assertions of power over domestic affairs that increasingly shifted the constitutional center of gravity from the Capitol to the other end of Pennsylvania Avenue. This trend of executive aggrandizement reached a climax in the claims of presidential power by Richard M. Nixon during the late 1960's and early 1970's.

Nixon's boldest assertions sought to short circuit the position of Congress as a check upon executive power. The President is, of course, the head of the executive branch; he appoints all the key officials in the federal departments and agencies. His power here, however, is subject to the requirement of senatorial confirmation. This legislative check was increasingly bypassed by the vesting of control over the executive branch in special assistants to the President, who were appointed without any confirmation. During Nixon's first Administration, it was well known that the conduct of foreign policy was in the hands of the President's foreign affairs adviser, Henry A. Kissinger, rather than the Secretary of State, who had formal control. The functions of other Cabinet departments were similarly (albeit less spectacularly) shifted to the White House. The White House staff grew to the size of a major agency (over two thousand persons in 1973); it originated and supervised most of the important policies followed by operating departments and agencies. Yet none of its personnel was confirmed by the Senate or was subject to congressional scrutiny, through committee testimony or otherwise.

This was particularly true of the Office of Management and Budget (set up in 1970, with a staff of hundreds), which exercised virtually complete fiscal control over the executive branch, as well as over supposedly independent agencies such as the Federal Trade Commission. The OMB did not limit itself to fiscal control. It asserted the power to require federal agencies to obtain its approval for requests for information from private individuals and companies. This enabled the OMB, for example, to frustrate efforts by the FTC to investigate companies the commission suspected of improper business practices. Though the Constitution requires senatorial confirmation for all federal officers, none of the OMB officials, from the director down, was ever voted on by the Senate. In 1973, Congress passed a bill to

The 1973 Senate Watergate hearings, below, helped illuminate for the country the abuse resulting from the vast authority, much of it unaccountable to the people, that had become entrenched in the White House. Such investigatory hearings, common throughout U.S. history, reflect the congressional role as "grand inquest of the nation."

DENNIS BRACK, BLACK STAR

require Senate confirmation of the OMB director, but it was vetoed by the President and the veto was not overridden.

Central to congressional control of the Executive is legislative investigatory power. Without information, congressional oversight becomes more form than substance. Here the old saw that knowledge is power has its widest scope; as President Harry S. Truman once said, "An informed Congress is a wise Congress; an uninformed Congress surely will forfeit a large portion of the respect and confidence of the people." The White House staff, however, was insulated from congressional inquiry by the doctrine of executive privilege. After mid-century, that doctrine was pushed to new limits. President Nixon asserted it not only to cover the expanded White House staff, but also any federal official whom the President directed not to testify before a congressional committee. Nixon went so far as to claim the power to withhold from both Congress and the courts any evidence that he chose, even though it might be crucial to a pending criminal case.

Even the power of the purse, the constitutional birthright of the Anglo-American legislature, was not immune from presidential intrusion. Nixon's assertions in the area of appropriations added the word "impoundment" to the federal lexicon and threatened a major constitutional confrontation. The overriding issue was that of who controlled the purse strings. The Constitution gives Congress the power to pass appropriation laws and imposes on the President the duty to "take Care that the Laws be faithfully executed." Nixon refused to execute appropriation statutes, impounding funds voted by Congress for housing, water pollution, highways, education, and other areas. During his first five years in office, he impounded over fifty billion dollars on the ground that the programs involved were "inflationary" and incompatible with his own set of budget priorities. In effect, he was asserting the power which the Constitution gives to Congress — the determination of what moneys should be spent by the federal government.

None of the powers claimed by Nixon were original with him. Appointment of unconfirmed White House officials, as well as claims of executive privilege and impounding power, were made by earlier Presidents. Nixon's assertions, however, were quantitatively so much greater than those of his predecessors that once again there was a difference in the *quality* of the claims. It was Nixon who expanded the White House staff to its greatest extent and sought to give it effective control over the details of executive operations. Nixon claimed executive privilege more than any prior President, capping a recent trend toward secrecy in government. Over two-thirds of executive refusals to give information to Congress came in the period 1953–1973, with more than half of these falling in Nixon's first four and a half years in office. Presidents had, though rarely, asserted power to impound funds voted for a specific purpose. Nixon, for the first time, exercised a wholesale impoundment power, refusing to spend funds for a wide range of programs voted by Congress.

The movement toward an "imperial Presidency" did not proceed unchecked. In political, as in natural, science, Newton's third law operates. Action which moves too far in one direction ultimately provokes an equivalent reaction in the opposite direction. Awesome though the Presidency may

White House Rug

This 1972 cartoon by Herblock depicts executive privilege as a rug of secrecy under which the murky transactions of an administration can be swept from public sight.

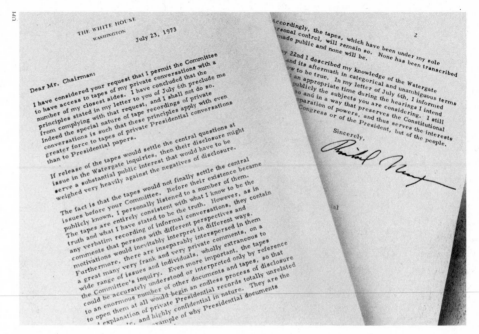

The letter at right was sent by President Nixon to the Senate Watergate Committee in 1973, arguing that the constitutional separation of powers supported his refusal to turn over to the Committee tape recordings of White House conversations it had requested from him.

have become, it is not, any more than any other institution, wholly exempt from the law of the pendulum.

The self-inflicted wound of Watergate resulted in the first contemporary attempts to check inflated presidential pretensions. The broadside claims of executive privilege were met by vigorous congressional investigations and court decisions which rejected the heresy that the President alone was above the law and immune from judicial process. Cast aside was a rhetoric of defiance of the courts that had not been heard from the White House since pre-Civil War days. Executive privilege is not recognized in the Constitution or statutes; thenceforth, at the least, the precedent that it was subject to judicial control would govern.

During 1973 a number of federal courts ruled that the impounding power asserted by the President was illegal. In addition, both Houses passed bills giving Congress the power to review and override impoundment decisions, though it was not clear at the end of 1973 that they could resist an expected veto. Another law eliminated the power of the Office of Management and Budget over Federal Trade Commission demands for reports and other information. Most important in the attempt to curb presidential power was the passage, over presidential veto, at the end of 1973 of a law limiting the President's power to commit American forces to hostilities abroad. It has been said that, if the Constitution were rewritten to reflect modern realities, Article II on presidential powers could be reduced to one sentence: The President is commander in chief. Now, for the first time, the power of the commander in chief was limited by law. Under the 1973 enactment, combat action abroad ordered by the President would have to end in sixty days (subject to another thirty-day extension if the President certified it was necessary for the safe withdrawal of forces) unless Congress authorized the action. At any time during the sixty- or ninety-day periods, Congress could order an immediate removal of forces by concurrent resolution.

One may, all the same, express a doubt that the post-Watergate waning of presidential power would be more than temporary. If the presidential troubles provided an opportunity to restore the constitutional balance, one would have to be oversanguine to expect a congressional resurgence as a result. There were all too many indications that even a wounded Presidency remained the predominant force in the polity. At the end of 1973, even after a series of adverse court decisions, the President impounded money voted earlier in the year for development of water and sewage systems, despite an express directive in the appropriation law that the money be spent. In addition, Congress indicated its own sense of powerlessness by increasing delegations of power. When an energy crisis arose, the solution was to confer vast new chunks of authority on the President, with little attention given to the need to limit the power delegated.

Even the war powers law could turn out to be a two-edged sword. It confirmed the presidential power to wage war for at least a limited period and might well prove useless as a practical check. It is hard to see Congress refusing to vote support for an armed action involving American forces, however it was originally begun. Lincoln, in an 1848 letter, told why he voted for the bill declaring war against Mexico, although he opposed the war. The Administration, he said, "brought in a bill with a preamble, saying — Whereas war exists by the act of Mexico, therefore we send Gen: Taylor men and money. . . . They could not vote *against* sending help to Gen: Taylor, and therefore they voted *for* both together." The same would doubtless happen whenever American troops were again engaged in action.

In recent years, the nation heard arguments on behalf of the Presidency such as were not presented in the English-speaking world since the time of Charles I. As Senator Jacob Javits of New York put it in a 1973 book,

Demonstrators in the fall of 1973 bring their demand to the front of the White House. A federal court had just legalized such protests outside the White House on weekends, after four years in which large demonstrations there had been banned.

"Watergate came about, at least in part, because the Presidency had become an office of such awesome authority that those close to an incumbent Chief Executive seemingly could be led to believe that they were above the law, especially when they felt able to cite 'higher' grounds of loyalty to the President . . . as justification for their actions." The overriding constitutional need became that of somehow reducing the Presidency to "life-size." The alternative was the view attributed to William H. Seward over a century ago: "We elect a king for four years and give him absolute power."

The Warren Court

The tenure of Earl Warren as chief justice of the Supreme Court from 1953 to 1969 accelerated another trend—that toward emphasis on personal rights which was noted in Chapter VI. "When the generation of 1980 receives from us the Bill of Rights," Warren declared in 1955, "the document will not have exactly the same meaning it had when we received it from our fathers." The Bill of Rights as interpreted by the Warren Court had a meaning much different from that handed down by its predecessors.

Not too long ago, legal observers expected the post-1937 "constitutional

The Warren of the Warren Court

From 1953 to 1969, the Supreme Court bore the image of its chief justice, Earl Warren of California, as unmistakably as the earlier courts of John Marshall and Roger B. Taney had reflected the unique leadership of those two men. Although the chief justice (apart from his title and a slightly higher salary) is not legally superior to his colleagues, there is an extralegal potential inherent in his position. As director of the Court's business, he presides over the body of nine jurists, both in open court and in the even more important work of deciding cases in the conference chamber. In conference, he has the right to call and discuss the individual cases before the other justices speak, and he can exercise guidance, and even control, over the deliberations. His role in the conference, in effect, is like that of striking the pitch for an orchestra, for his example, most often, sets the tone of the entire session.

Warren brought more authority to the chief-justiceship than it had had since the Court of Charles Evans Hughes (1930–1941). In the intervening years, the dominant theme had been discord; all too often, the Court had presented a spectacle of internal atomization. To be sure, judicial dissension did not end with Warren's appointment to the central chair. Sharp divisions still existed. But they were no longer reflections of personal antagonisms, as they had all too often been before. Under Warren's leadership, intellectual issues once again came to be dealt with purely as such, and dissonance ceased to be a major Court characteristic. It may be, as John Winthrop said in 1644, that "Judges are Gods upon earth." But a pantheon of gods who speak with nine inconsistent voices can hardly project a feeling of divine certainty. In this respect, the restoration of an institutional ethos to the Court was Warren's primary contribution, even outranking the great contributions he made to substantive law.

Warren (1891–1974) was born in Los Angeles. Admitted to the California Bar in 1914, he practiced law in San Francisco and Oakland until World War I. From 1917 to 1918, he served in the U.S. Army. He became deputy city attorney in Oakland in 1919 and eventually rose through politics to become district attorney in Alameda County and, from 1939 to 1943, attorney general of California. In 1943 he was elected governor of California, serving in that office for ten years. During that period, his warm, human personality and increasingly liberal approaches to public issues gained him the support not only of members of his own Republican Party, but of large numbers of Democrats and independents. His national reputation increased quickly, and in 1948 he was the Republican nominee for Vice President. Five years later, President Dwight D. Eisenhower appointed him to the chief-justiceship of the Supreme Court.

It is a mistake to conceive of the chief-justiceship solely in terms of learning in the law. Of course, the Supreme Court is a law court, but it is—and has been, since John Marshall—unique among courts. Elevation to it requires an adjustment from preoccupation with the restricted problems of private litigation to the more exacting demands of public law. On

revolution" to signal a permanent decline in the Supreme Court's position. The subdued role played by the Court in the later New Deal period, during World War II, and in the early postwar years led many to expect the Court to wither away, much as the state was supposed to do in Marxist theory. Yet, one thing is clear: neither the Soviet State nor America's high tribunal has withered away in the second half of the century.

Still, the work of the Supreme Court differed from earlier periods. As seen in Chapter VI, the emphasis in the Court had started to shift before mid-century from the safeguarding of property rights to the protection of personal rights. In enforcing the liberties guaranteed by the Bill of Rights, the Supreme Court forged a new and vital place for itself in the constitutional structure. More and more the Court came to display its solicitude for individual rights. Freedom of speech, press, religion, the rights of minorities and those accused of crime, those of individuals subjected to legislative and administrative inquisitions—all came under the Court's fostering guardianship.

There were three principal developments in the Warren Court regarding the protection of personal rights: (1) acceptance of the preferred position

© KARSH. FROM RAPHO GUILLUMETTE

Chief Justice Earl Warren

the High Court, a justice must be even more a statesman than a lawyer. This is particularly true of the man who sits at the center of the Court.

In Warren's political career—especially during his three terms as governor of California—he had displayed a high type of statesmanship that was soon reflected, as well, in his new position on the Bench. Not interested in technicalities, he was usually moved by the question, "Is this fair and just?" The main monument of his judicial statesmanship was, without a doubt, the 1954 decision in the *School Segregation Case.* Under his leadership, the Court seized the vital constitutional issue by the bit (the same issue meticulously avoided under Warren's predecessor, Chief Justice Fred M. Vinson) and unanimously outlawed school segregation. Warren's accomplishment of achieving unanimity in this decision cannot be overemphasized. It was not a slight feat for the Court's neophyte (as he then was), vested only with the moral prestige of the chief-justiceship, to induce eight individualists, accustomed to arriving at decisions in their own ways and never hesitant at articulating their separate views, to join in the unanimous decision—without even a single concurring voice to detract from the majesty and forth-

rightness of the opinion which Warren wrote.

Aside from Warren's gift of leadership was his profound influence on the substantive law which the high tribunal dispensed during his years as chief justice. His legal approach, in this regard, differed drastically from that of his predecessor. In cases involving conflicts between government and the individual, Chief Justice Vinson had usually been on the side of officialdom. Warren, on the other hand, started with a strong feeling for the individual and his rights. Under Warren's leadership, the Court, which almost invariably had been on the side of governmental authority, changed into a tribunal inclined to look with a far more friendly eye on claims of violation of individual rights. In the Warren Court, indeed, individual rights received greater protection than in any previous court. When Warren resigned in 1969, it could be said that, in all of American history, only John Marshall's Court had played so large a role in reshaping the law to meet the needs of the day.

theory; (2) extension of the trend toward holding Bill of Rights guaranties binding on the states; and (3) broadening of the substantive content of the rights themselves.

The preferred position theory was first stated by Justice Harlan Fiske Stone in 1938. Under Chief Justice Warren it became accepted doctrine. The theory is based on the view that the Constitution gives a preferred status to personal, as opposed to property, rights. The result is a double standard in the exercise by the courts of their review function. The tenet of judicial self-restraint does not rigidly bind the judge in cases involving civil liberties and other personal rights. The presumption of validity gives way far more readily in cases where life and liberty are restrained. In those cases, the legislative judgment must be scrutinized with much greater care.

Critics say that the preferred position approach, with its elevation of personal rights, creates a hierarchy of rights not provided for in the Constitution. It should, however, be recognized that each generation must necessarily have its own scale of values. In nineteenth-century America, concerned as it was with the economic conquest of a continent, property rights occupied the dominant place. A century later, in a world in which individuality was dwarfed by concentrations of power, concern with the maintenance of personal rights had become more important. With the focus of concern on the need to preserve an area for the development of individuality, judges were naturally more ready to find legislative invasion when personal rights were involved than in the sphere of economics.

Chapter VI noted how Justice Black had revived the constitutional issue originally set to rest in *Barron* v. *Mayor of Baltimore* in 1833. The Court had ruled at that time that the Bill of Rights was not binding on the states; but Black urged that the adoption of the Fourteenth Amendment had changed that result. The Supreme Court majority never accepted the Black thesis that the entire Bill of Rights was incorporated in the Fourteenth Amendment's Due Process Clause, adopting instead a selective approach, under which only those rights deemed "fundamental" were included in due process. Yet if Justice Black seemingly lost the Bill of Rights incorporation battle, he was to come close, after mid-century, to winning the due process war. For the Court, without formally abandoning its selective incorporation approach, held virtually all of the Bill of Rights guaranties to be fundamental and hence absorbed by due process.

The key decisions were those in *Mapp* v. *Ohio* in 1961 and *Gideon* v. *Wainwright* in 1963, which reversed earlier refusals to hold the right against the use of illegally secured evidence, and that to counsel, to be so fundamental as to be included in due process. Both the *Mapp* and *Gideon* rulings spoke in broad terms of the need to protect individual rights; they signaled a trend to include ever more of the Bill of Rights guaranties in the Fourteenth Amendment. In the following decade the courts held these rights fundamental and hence binding upon the states: rights against double jeopardy and self-incrimination; that to jury trial in criminal cases; to a speedy trial; to confrontation; and to bail.

Add to these rights those which had been held binding on the states before mid-century, and they include all the rights guaranteed by the Bill

WIDE WORLD

In its landmark decision against illegal search and seizure, the Supreme Court in 1961 dismissed charges against Dollree Mapp because police had forcibly searched her home without a warrant. Above, Mrs. Mapp is arrested nine years later after police (with a search warrant) found drugs in her apartment.

of Rights except for the right to a grand jury indictment and that to a jury in civil cases involving over twenty dollars. The two exclusions hardly alter the overriding tendency to make the Due Process Clause ever more inclusive. As a result, the Fourteenth Amendment now includes well-nigh all the rights safeguarded by the Bill of Rights. The controversy between those who urge that due process incorporates the entire Bill of Rights and those who take a contrary view is rendered all but academic.

But the Warren Court did more than hold the important rights of the Bill of Rights binding on the states. It also broadened the substantive content of the rights, giving virtually all personal rights a wider meaning than they had theretofore had in American law. This was particularly true in two crucial areas: freedom of expression and criminal justice.

Although the Supreme Court did not adopt the absolutist view of free speech urged by Justices Black and Douglas, it placed increasing emphasis on freedom of expression as a preferred right. The "firstness" of the First Amendment was firmly established. The right to use the streets and other public places as public forums was extended to those using them for civil rights protests and demonstrations. Most criticisms of the conduct of public

"Integration, Supreme Court" is the title of Ben Shahn's 1963 painting of the justices who in 1954 had ruled that segregation in public schools was a denial of equal protection.

287

officials and public figures were exempted from the law of libel. Freedom of the press was broadened; censorship laws were stricken down, and the power to restrain publication on grounds of obscenity drastically limited. Even claims of national security were not strong enough to make the prohibition against prior restraints give way.

Protection of the rights of criminal defendants also became a primary concern of the Supreme Court. So zealous did the judges become in ensuring fairness for defendants that many critics supported President Nixon when he contended in 1971 that they "have gone too far in weakening the peace forces as against the criminal forces in our society." Criticisms were directed particularly at the restrictions imposed upon police interrogation and the use of confessions. Under the 1966 decision of *Miranda* v. *Arizona*, for the police to be able to use any confession, they must show that they had given full warning to the defendant that he had a right to remain silent and to the presence of an attorney, either retained or appointed. Decisions such as *Miranda* worked a drastic change in the criminal law and its application by policemen, prosecutors, and judges.

Protection of personal rights and liberties thus became the very focus of the contemporary Constitution. With property rights constitutionally curtailed, compensatory scope had to be given to personal rights if the ultimate social interest — that in the individual life — was not to be lost sight of. The need to broaden the constitutional protection of personal rights received added emphasis from the growth and misuse of governmental power in the twentieth-century world. Totalitarian systems showed dramatically what it meant for the individual to live in a society in which Leviathan had become a reality. The "Blessings of Liberty," which the framers of the Constitution took such pains to safeguard, were placed in even sharper re-

"But Gideon Did Write That Letter"

If an obscure Florida convict named Clarence Earl Gideon had not sat down in his prison cell with a pencil and paper to write a letter to the Supreme Court," said Attorney General Robert F. Kennedy, "and if the Court had not taken the trouble to look for merit in that one crude petition among all the bundles of mail it must receive every day, the vast machinery of American law would have gone on undisturbed. But Gideon *did* write that letter, the Court *did* look into his case . . . and the whole course of American legal history has been changed."

Gideon was an unfortunate American, but typical of many others. Poor, without influence or standing, a social reject with a prison record

Clarence Gideon

for four felonies, he seemed scarcely destined to serve as the catalyst for crucial legal change in the United States. "Judging from the externals," wrote Anthony Lewis in his book, *Gideon's Trumpet,* about the case, "it would be hard to imagine a figure less likely to be the subject of a great case in the Supreme Court."

But Gideon was in jail again, and this time he had composed a handwritten petition and mailed it directly to the Supreme Court in Washington. He referred to "my limited education and also the utter folly and hopelessness [of] parts of my life." But he noted: "The question is very simple. I requested the [Florida] court to appoint me attorney and the court refused." As an indigent, he had

lief in a world that had seen so clearly the consequences of their denial.

When the Constitution and the Bill of Rights were written, government was only an arbiter, allowing the individual to go unrestrained except at extreme limits of conduct. In the century and a half that followed, the system gradually shifted to one in which government had a positive duty to promote the welfare of the community, even at the cost of individual property rights. From a constitutional, as from a political, point of view, the welfare state was by mid-century an established fact.

But the problem had ceased to be one of the exertion of governmental authority over property rights to further the public welfare. In the words of Justice Douglas, "the welfare state is a side issue. The central problem of the age is the scientific revolution and all the wonders and the damage it brings." The machine, which George Orwell called "the genie that man has thoughtlessly let out of its bottle and cannot put back again," had created new concentrations of power, particularly in government, which utterly dwarfed the individual and threatened individuality as never before. "Where in this tightly knit regime," asked Justice Douglas, "is man to find liberty?"

"Legal Equality"

During the second half of the twentieth century, American law, in W. H. Auden's phrase, "found the notion of equality." The constitutional right of equality was a century old in 1968, but it was not until the latter half of this century that it was vigorously enforced by the courts. The period of vigorous enforcement began with the appointment of Earl Warren to the Supreme Court's central chair. The first important decision of the Warren Court was *Brown* v. *Board of Education* in 1954.

A policeman in Knoxville, Tennessee, carries a box of seized literature, allegedly pornographic. The year was 1973, after the Supreme Court had ruled that local standards should prevail in determining obscenity.

been unable to afford a lawyer in his trial for burglary, and the court had declined to appoint one for him. Under the governing decisions, the refusal of a state to provide a lawyer for an indigent defendant did not violate the Constitution, and Gideon, without the aid of a lawyer had been found guilty and sent again to jail.

Gideon's letter bore fruit, and his case, *Gideon* v. *Wainwright* (the director of the Florida Division of Corrections), was accepted by the Supreme Court. The Court appointed Abe Fortas, himself soon to be named a justice of the Court, to represent him, and in 1963 the decision came—categorically proclaiming the right of indigents to court-appointed counsel.

"Reason and reflection," declared the opinion, "require us to recognize that in our adversary system of criminal justice, any person haled into court, who is too poor to hire a lawyer, cannot be assured a fair trial unless counsel is provided for him. This seems to us to be an obvious truth."

The Supreme Court's decision not only reversed Gideon's conviction (at his new trial, with the help of a lawyer, he was acquitted); it also signaled an increasing concern of the justices for the rights of criminal defendants. In the years following the *Gideon* ruling, decisions in case after case extended the Bill of Rights protections for those accused of crimes in state, as well as federal, prosecutions. Ultimately, however, as Anthony

Lewis wrote, the 1963 case of *Gideon* v. *Wainwright* was "a testament to a single human being." Against all odds, Gideon had insisted upon, and won, the right to a lawyer. The poorest and least powerful of men could now take his cause to the highest court and triumph. "Maybe this will be one of those small steps forward," Gideon had written to Fortas after his victory. Vindicating his claim had meant a fundamental change in the law that would benefit untold future defendants. "Like the Gideon of old, who was summoned by an angel of the Lord to lead Israel and overcome the Midianites," said the *Washington Post*, "Clarence Earl Gideon . . . championed the cause of justice for all indigent defendants."

For the title of his drawing above, artist Andrew Rush quoted former Supreme Court Justice Robert H. Jackson: "No mob has ever protected any liberty, even its own." Depicted is a crowd of whites shouting epithets at a black child who is being escorted into a public school.

The decision overruled the "separate but equal" doctrine and declared racial segregation violative of the equal protection guaranty. The *Brown* ruling was subjected to criticism as severe as any directed against a judicial decision since the *Dred Scott* case in 1857, ranging from extreme vituperation to more reasoned censure based upon an alleged lack of legal craftsmanship in the Court's opinion. Two decades later, such criticisms had lost their relevancy. Perhaps the Court did not articulate as clearly as it should have the juristic bases of its decision. But the *Brown* opinion was so clearly right in its conclusion that segregation denied equality, that one wonders whether additional labor in spelling out the obvious was really necessary.

What is clear is that the case has taken its place in the forefront of historic High Bench decisions. Its impact on a whole society's way of life can be compared only with that caused by political revolution or military conflict. Its ruling signaled an expansive attitude of the courts toward the Equal Protection Clause which marked the nation's public law during the third quarter of the century. For one thing, enforcement of *Brown* demanded a new activist role for the judges, far removed from the traditional limitations of the judicial function. When the *Brown* Court declared that the lower courts were to ensure that Negroes be admitted to schools on a nondiscriminatory basis "with all deliberate speed," it led to learned controversy on the origins of that phrase. In actuality, as Oliver Wendell Holmes had pointed out years before, it had been a common practice in Chancery to use the "delightful phrase, with all deliberate speed." More important was a remedial role which the *Brown* statement required federal judges to assume. They had to supervise actively the operation of school systems to ensure compliance, thus becoming superboards of education in many parts of the country.

From the field of racial equality involved in *Brown*, the Supreme Court spread the equal protection mantle over an increasingly broad area, notably in the field of political rights and the rights of criminal defendants. The key political rights decision was *Baker* v. *Carr* in 1962, in which the federal courts were ruled competent to entertain an action challenging legislative apportionments as contrary to equal protection. It has become constitutional cliché that *Baker* v. *Carr* has worked a drastic change in legislative representation throughout the land. That is true because, in 1964, the Court held that the Equal Protection Clause lays down an "equal population" principle for legislative apportionment. The Constitution, under this principle, demands substantially equal representation for all citizens. The result has already been a substantial shift in the political structure, with a reduction of the disproportionate influence of rural areas and a transfer of the legislative balance to those urban and suburban concentrations in which the bulk of Americans now live.

Reapportionment involved the judges in a veritable "political thicket," which compelled them once again to go beyond traditional notions of judicial power. In historical perspective, the *Reapportionment Cases* of 1964 stand as the culmination of the development of the right of suffrage. The judges worked a reform comparable to that achieved by Parliament in translating the program of the English Reform Movement into the statute book. To do so, they had to act as virtual censors of the electoral process, even exercising the legislative function of redistricting when necessary.

In addition to racial and political equality, the Supreme Court moved to ensure equality in criminal justice. The basic theme there was that "all people charged with crime must, so far as the law is concerned, 'stand on an equality before the bar of justice in every American court.'" To achieve this goal, the Constitution was used both to ensure equality between rich and poor defendants and to eliminate the inherent inequality that exists between the prosecution and the defendant—the latter dwarfed by the State as he inevitably is when he finds himself in the dock.

If one great theme has recurred in recent public law, it has been that of equality: equality as between races, between citizens, between citizens and aliens, between rich and poor, between prosecutor and defendant. The result has been what Justice Abe Fortas called "the most profound and pervasive revolution ever achieved by substantially peaceful means." More, it has been that rarest of all political animals: a judicially inspired and led revolution. Without the Supreme Court decisions giving ever-wider effect to the right to equality, most of the movements for equality that permeated the society would never have gotten started.

Nor may it be assumed that egalitarian development has reached its terminal point. On the contrary, as Tocqueville acutely noted, "the desire of equality always becomes more insatiable in proportion as equality is more complete." Equality before the law as it is now understood will scarcely be the ultimate stage of egalitarian evolution.

In the second half of the century, doubts arose whether the problem of

The Supreme Court's "one man, one vote" decision in 1964 made reapportionment necessary in much of the country, and the two political parties did not always see eye-to-eye on where new district boundaries should be drawn. Above, a New York Republican state senator examines his party's proposal for the redistricting of Manhattan.

equality could be resolved by "legal equality." The law in this century has come to recognize the claim that each individual have assured to him the conditions of a minimum human life. That recognition is, however, now questioned as inadequate. Instead, the claim is coming to be one for conditions comparable to those enjoyed by others. A claim for equal conditions of life is now pressing, and one cannot even put the matter as to what is recognized with assurance, as one could have done only a generation ago.

In public law, the dominant theme is starting to go beyond the formal equality before the law established by the Equal Protection Clause. Legal equality, presented in traditional negative terms, is being seen as inadequate to deal with the problems presented by factual inequalities. Ensuring that equal justice be afforded to rich and poor alike may require more than adherence to formal equality in the application of legal precepts and doctrine. The existence of true equality in an actual case may depend, not only on the absence of disabilities, but also on the presence of abilities.

Even legal equality can exist only insofar as each member of the community possesses in fact, not only in form, equal chances of using his natural endowments. In proportion as the capacities of some are sterilized or stunted by their social environment, while those of others are favored or even pampered by theirs, the right of equality becomes an elegant but anemic euphemism. Hence results the claim with which society and the legal order are being presented, that there is a social duty to make "compensation" for the inequalities under which less-favored members of the community have had to live—a claim that the law is urged to support.

The dynamic, even explosive, nature of the contemporary thrust for equality is evident. The law itself is plainly in a state of flux and transition. Concepts and principles that, not too long ago, appeared unduly radical have become accepted rules of law. All that can be stated with confidence is that society, in the latter part of the twentieth century, is in the midst of a tremendous evolutionary development, destined still to produce changes in the law fully as profound as those it would bring about in the society at large.

Upholding Civil Rights Laws

In an address concluding the centennial celebration of the Fourteenth Amendment, Chief Justice Warren noted the limitations in judicial enforcement of the amendment's pledge of equality. The "courts cannot seize the initiative and devise innovative solutions to pressing social problems," he said. They are restricted to cases brought by outside litigants and are "far more limited than a legislature in devising effective remedies, a shortcoming which is particularly apparent when broad social problems are at issue." Judicial enforcement of the Equal Protection Clause must be complemented by the greater institutional flexibility of the legislature. Increased participation by Congress was necessary in the task of translating the Fourteenth Amendment's promise of equality into meaningful action.

During the 1950's and 1960's, Congress, for the first time since 1875, assumed an active role in enforcement of the Fourteenth Amendment. In this respect, the years after 1957 resembled the Reconstruction period,

The High Court's Brown v. Board of Education *decision in 1954, ordering an end to segregation in public schools, resulted from the protest of Linda Brown, above, a pupil in a segregated school in Topeka, Kansas.*

CARL IWASKI. COURTESY *Life*

when Congress enacted a whole series of civil rights laws designed to give effect to the Fourteenth Amendment's guaranty of equality.

The end of Reconstruction had seen the end also of congressional attempts to enforce the Fourteenth Amendment. In 1894 Congress repealed the most important of the civil rights statutes that had not already been stricken down by the Supreme Court. For over half a century thereafter, the federal legislators kept hands-off in the field of civil rights. But, if the Congress was a legislator who slumbered from Reconstruction to the post-World War II period, it made considerable amends by its spate of activity in the civil rights field after the middle of the twentieth century. The Supreme Court decisions and the resistance to them, "The Negro's peaceful demonstrations . . . and the violent reactions to those demonstrations awakened the nation's conscience to the realities of racial injustice," said Chief Justice Warren. "Demands for effective legislative action grew, and Congress responded. . . ."

Starting in 1957, five civil rights laws (those of 1957, 1960, 1964, 1965, and 1968) were added to the federal statute book—and three of them (those of 1964, 1965, and 1968) were as far-reaching as any Reconstruction enactment. The legislation started innocuously enough with the Civil Rights Acts of 1957 and 1960. Those laws had little substantive impact; their weakness made their effect largely symbolic, primarily as indicating a renewed congressional concern with civil rights. But the same was not true of the Civil Rights Acts of 1964 and 1968 and the Voting Rights Act of 1965. Those measures marked the reassumption by Congress of a leadership role in enforcing the constitutional command of equality.

Three principal factors led to the enactment in 1964 of the most significant civil rights legislation since the post-bellum period. First was a dramatic change in the national climate that had occurred in the racial field. That change had been brought about by Supreme Court decisions (starting with *Brown* v. *Board of Education* in 1954) and a "new Negro evangelism," which had replaced a century's passivity with increasingly militant attempts to secure full equality. The Negro recourse to direct action as a means of protest had culminated in 1963 (in full view of the television camera) in the use of fire hoses and police dogs against demonstrators in Birmingham, Alabama. The events in Birmingham both roused the national conscience and stimulated a previously lukewarm administration into becoming a firm supporter of strong civil rights legislation.

Then came the second factor—the assassination of President Kennedy. It would be out of place here to assess how much is real and how much artificial in the legend of the martyred President. History may ultimately rate Kennedy as a latter-day Garfield rather than a twentieth-century Lincoln. Yet it can scarcely be denied that his death had a devastating effect on the national conscience. The civil rights program that Capitol Hill had kept dangling was now seen as a legislative legacy which Congress owed to the Kennedy memory.

The third factor that led to enactment of the 1964 Civil Rights Act may be termed the civil rights conversion of Lyndon B. Johnson. It does not really matter whether the public contrast between Senator Johnson and President

WIDE WORLD

Civil rights protests, inspired by Martin Luther King, took place in many cities, North and South, in 1963, and often led to violence. In the photograph above, police dogs are being used against black demonstrators in Birmingham, Alabama.

OVERLEAF: *More violence in Birmingham in 1963: firemen use high-pressure hoses against blacks. The employment of force against people whose only reply was passive resistance shocked the nation and created sympathy for the civil rights cause.*
CHARLES MOORE. BLACK STAR

Johnson was a consequence of conviction or convenience. With the master legislative strategist of the day in the Oval Office, enactment of the strongest civil rights measure since Reconstruction soon became a reality.

On June 18, 1964, the day before the Senate voted passage of the 1964 statute, Senator Richard Russell of Georgia, the leader of the southern bloc in the upper House, declared, "the moving finger is writing the final act of the longest debate and the greatest tragedy ever played out in the Senate." Those who had been so long deprived of their rights could scarcely agree with this assessment. The 1964 statute sought to protect three basic rights: the right to equality in public accommodations, the right to have federal funds spent in a nondiscriminatory manner, and the right to racial and sexual equality in employment.

Title II of the 1964 act was, in many ways, the most important provision for racial equality since the Fourteenth Amendment. It barred racial discrimination in all public accommodations, if their operations affected commerce (including hotels and other places of lodging, restaurants, gasoline stations, theaters and motion picture houses, stadiums, and other places of exhibition or entertainment). As such, it was the modern counterpart of the 1875 Civil Rights Act and was intended to secure equal access to public facilities in a manner comparable to that intended by the earlier statute. Title II of the 1964 act was, however, drafted to avoid the limitation of the *Civil Rights Cases* of 1883. Unlike the 1875 statute, it relied not on the power

In a demonstration for equal rights, James Meredith, second from left, marches with supporters from Memphis to Jackson, Mississippi, in 1966. Meredith, whose enrollment four years before at the University of Mississippi had caused bloodshed, was shot during the march, but was able to complete the long walk.

VERNON MERRITT, BLACK STAR

to enforce the Fourteenth Amendment, but on the commerce power. Although, as Chief Justice Warren put it, "It is a rather sad commentary on the development of Fourteenth Amendment doctrine that Congress felt compelled to equate Negro rights with the movement of goods to enact civil rights legislation," this did enable Title II to be upheld despite the *Civil Rights Cases* decision of the nineteenth century.

Crucial in the civil rights movement has been the attempt to vindicate the right of suffrage guaranteed by the Fifteenth Amendment. In its impact on that right, the Voting Rights Act of 1965 (as extended by the Voting Rights Act Amendments of 1970) was the most far-reaching statute ever enacted by Congress, going beyond even the drastic provisions of the Force Act of 1871, on which it was in certain respects modeled. The 1965 act provided for the supplanting of state election machinery by federal law and ad hoc federal officials, where that was necessary to eliminate a pattern of Fifteenth Amendment violation. Where the 1965 statute applied, it worked a virtual displacement of state authority over elections. To southern senators this might make the measure one which could be characterized as "tearing the Constitution . . . asunder" and one worthy of Hitler or Genghis Khan. To the rest of Congress and to the country it represented, the time was long overdue for a measure that had more than hortatory effect in enforcing the Fifteenth Amendment.

The congressional enforcement picture was completed with the Civil Rights Act of 1968, which prohibited racial discrimination in housing. In passing it, Congress assumed that it was enacting the first federal fair housing law in this country. Two months later, it learned from the Supreme Court that the nation already had an even broader open housing law on the statute book in the Civil Rights Act of 1866. We have already discussed the merits of the Court's elevation of the 1866 act from legislative limbo to an enforceable ban against any housing discrimination (see page 125). Here we need note the decision only as an indication of the new judicial attitude toward congressional enforcement of the post-bellum amendments.

According to Chief Justice Warren, "Perhaps the most significant development in recent years has been the changed attitude of the Supreme Court toward congressional enforcement powers." The history of judicial frustration of civil rights legislation toward the end of the last century has emphatically not been repeated in our day. The Supreme Court unanimously upheld the Civil Rights Act of 1964 and the Voting Rights Act of 1965. Equally significant were decisions in 1966 which went far toward removing the restriction that the *Civil Rights Cases* had imposed on congressional enforcement power. That power is no longer restricted by the reach of the Fourteenth Amendment itself. Though the amendment alone speaks only to "state action," legislation protecting rights secured by the amendment may reach private action in which states do not participate. Purely private discrimination is no longer beyond the reach of public power.

Human Rights Agencies

"Law's weakness," said Arnold Toynbee, "is that its range is not coextensive with social life. There are many kinds of social relations that cannot be

The U.S. Supreme Court in session: judgments handed down in this room become the ultimate law of the land.

How the Supreme Court Works

Unlike most other courts, the U.S. Supreme Court can decide which cases it will hear and which it will not. Cases come to it on appeal, for review and final settlement, from 103 lower federal courts—ninety U.S. District Courts, eleven U.S. Courts of Appeals (which receive cases after they have first been heard in the District Courts), the U.S. Court of Customs and Patent Appeals, and the U.S. Court of Claims—as well as from state courts in cases involving federal questions. In recent years, the number of such cases reaching the Supreme Court has mounted spectacularly, increasing 300 percent between 1953 and 1973. In the face of this growing workload, the number of appeals turned down by the High Court has also increased. During the 1972 term (from October, 1972, to June, 1973), the Court was asked to rule on 3,824 cases. It accepted and rendered decisions on only 177.

The rising caseload and growing number of issues left unsettled have distressed litigants, as well as the Court itself, and Chief Justice Warren E. Burger, among others, has advanced proposals to reduce the High Court's workload. In the meantime, it must not be lost sight of that the Supreme Court is—and has been—essentially a tribunal to settle only those questions which the justices believe involve a sufficient public concern to warrant a decision by the highest bench in the land. From that point of view, how does it dispose of the mass of appeals that come to it from the lower courts?

Almost all cases reach the Court through petitions for certiorari (petitions, in effect, for the Court to ask a lower court for the records so that it can review a case and decide it on its merits). Some cases, by their specialized nature, have a "right" to be heard by the Supreme Court, but since 1925, such "appeals as of right" have been sharply limited. The justices, as noted, have discretionary power to grant or deny the petitions for certiorari, and actually do dispose of the vast majority of cases by the simple denial of the petition—thus refusing to hear the case. No petition is even considered by the justices, in fact, unless at least one of them believes it important enough, and no case will be accepted unless at least four justices decide in favor of granting certiorari.

Many lawyers, from time to time, have suspected that the justices' law clerks (each justice is entitled to three—recent graduates of law schools) constitute a kind of junior court which decides the fate of the petitions. "This idea of the law clerk's influence," Justice Robert H. Jackson once said, "gave rise to a lawyer's waggish statement that the Senate no longer need bother about confirmation of Justices but ought to confirm the appointment of law clerks." So far as one can tell, however, it is the justices themselves who do make the decisions, though their clerks help in screening the large volume of petitions. The principal criterion for acceptance is whether a case raises an issue worth considering, a standard most cases would seem not to meet.

In the Supreme Court Building's courtroom, the attorneys' arguments (as well as the eventual reading of the opinions) are conducted publicly. The crucial work on an accepted case, however, occurs in the private research and reflection of each justice, and in the conferences that are held by the Court as a whole. Such group discussions take place about once a week during a term in an oak-paneled conference chamber, and it is there that the decisions are actually made. Upon entering the conference room, each justice shakes hands with all those present, a custom that has been followed for generations. Only the justices are present during the conference; there are no clerks, stenographers, or secretaries in the room. The practice is followed to maintain secrecy until the decisions are announced. Years ago, the Court was convinced that an informational leak existed. At that time, two pages waited on the justices in conference. The Court decided that the leak must have come from one of the pages and adopted the rule, followed ever since, of barring all non-justices from the room when cases were being discussed. As it turned out, a lawyer, making an educated guess, had been the source of the alleged leak.

During their conference, the justices sit in order of seniority around a large rectangular table. The cases are discussed by the justices in the same order, starting with the chief justice, who can control the order in which the cases are called and generally guides the discussion and sets the tone in which a case is considered. His right word at the right time may lead to a compromise needed for decision. After discussion, a vote is taken, this time beginning with the newest justice and moving up through the ranks of seniority, with the chief justice last—a procedure followed since John Marshall's day. At the end of the conference, the cases are assigned for the writing of opinions. This is done by the chief justice, save when he is with the minority. In that instance, the assigning is done by the senior justice for the majority opinion.

Hallowed by many years of writing and making history, the Court is awesome in its traditions. But it is also much that is the United States. "A proper degree of dignity is required and observed in the Supreme Court," wrote a French visitor to Washington in 1833. "Business is there conducted as it ought to be in every court of justice." Despite the problems of the Court's growing caseload, those words are still true.

regulated by legislation." When we talk of laws that curb racial discrimination, we are dealing with legal regulation of conduct normally thought beyond the reach of the legal order. The traditional approach has been that we cannot legislate morals. According to an early English judge, "The devil himself knoweth not the mind of man," and the law is no better equipped when it seeks to control man's moral processes.

Yet the attainment of moral ends motivated the enactment by Congress of the civil rights laws of the 1960's. Nor was the passage of such laws limited to the national legislature. Laws prohibiting racial discrimination in different aspects of life were passed at all levels of government after the middle of the century. In 1964 the Supreme Court could say, "There is nothing novel about such legislation. Thirty-two States now have it on their books . . . and many cities provide such regulation." In the next decade many other states and localities added to their statute books laws prohibiting racial discrimination in public accommodations, housing, employment, and other fields.

The social and moral objectives of these laws did not affect their validity. "That Congress was legislating against moral wrongs . . . rendered its enactments no less valid," said the Supreme Court. The same was true of state laws on the matter: "a State may choose to put its authority behind one of the cherished aims of American feeling by forbidding indulgence in racial prejudice," Justice Frankfurter had said in 1945. In 1964 the Supreme Court affirmed that "the constitutionality of such laws stands unquestioned."

Nevertheless, these laws would scarcely prove effective if their enforcement were left to actions instituted by those private persons affected, or even to sanctions imposed by the ordinary criminal law. To ensure effective enforcement, states and municipalities established special administrative agencies charged with the duty of enforcing the different antidiscrimination laws. These agencies were generally of the commission type and were given such titles as Commission Against Discrimination, Commission on Human Rights (or Relations), and Fair Employment Practices Commission. They were vested with various powers, ranging from attempts at persuasion and conciliation to the power to issue binding cease and desist orders directing the termination of particular discriminatory practices and even to decree affirmative relief, such as orders to hire or to rent premises, and to order the payment of damages.

The growing use of the administrative process to enforce the public policy against racial and other discrimination has been one of the most significant public law developments in the second half of this century. An expanding field was found for the administrative process at the very time when it was increasingly censured as inadequate in its traditional area of regulation. The new legislation aimed at a range of human and social problems very different from the economic conflicts and abuses that the Interstate Commerce Commission-type agency was designed to combat. The administrative device was to become the legal instrument for attaining the goal of racial equality—the ultimate moral commitment of American government.

The roots of racial discrimination, of course, go far deeper than legislatures, commissions, and courts can penetrate. Yet, while there are practical limits to the effectiveness of legal action that seeks to go too far and too fast in improving morals, this does not mean that the law must adopt a do-nothing attitude. Most criminal prohibitions can be traced to some moral principle or inspiration. Hopefully, the attempt to elevate moral standards in the race relations field will ultimately be as accepted as criminal prohibitions against murder and theft, which originally reinforced specific commands of the Decalogue.

Yet the implications of success were almost as disturbing as those of failure. Was the human rights agency to be but the forerunner of similar organs through which a Brave New World would seek increasingly to control conduct, albeit for the lofty purpose of elevating moral standards and eradicating antisocial behavior?

The Rights Explosion

"There seems to be," said a federal judge, "a kind of spontaneous generation about the federal constitution; the more questions about it are answered, the more there are to be answered." During the second half of the twentieth century, this has been particularly true of the Bill of Rights. There has been a spontaneous generation in the field of individual rights all but unprecedented in legal history. The egalitarian revolution, already discussed, has been but one phase of an era of expanding rights.

The task of the legal order is to reconcile the interests that press for recognition in any society and to choose which among them shall be recognized as rights to be enforced by the law. Until this century that task was thought of in negative terms, in accordance with Justinian's celebrated definition—"Justice is the set and constant purpose which gives to everyone his own"—at the beginning of his *Institutes*. "The great end of government," said Dr. Samuel Johnson when the American Republic was founded, "is to give every man his own." The framers of the Constitution, like Dr. Johnson, thought of such "own" essentially in terms of private property. The primary function of government was conceived in terms of protecting that system of external "meum and tuum" of which Kant wrote.

In twentieth-century society, the "own" that government must secure has become broader than the physical possessions to which the individual has a title of right. Americans have come to think of the government role in the positive sense of securing for each individual the conditions necessary to proper human existence. The goal of the society is becoming that of ensuring that each individual be able to live an adequate human life therein—if all human wants cannot be satisfied, they be satisfied so far as is possible and at least to the extent of a decent human minimum.

A society in which the exercise of governmental power must find its ultimate justification in the realization of this goal is bound to be characterized by a continuing rights explosion. In the second half of the twentieth century new interests pressed upon the law as almost never before, seeking recognition in the form of legal rights. The law came increasingly to acknowledge their existence, raising ever more rights to the legally protected plane. These new rights fell into two broad categories: those asserted by particular groups and those applicable to all in the community.

The civil rights demonstrations of 1963 were climaxed by a "March on Washington" in August by 250,000 black and white Americans. Above is the scene as Martin Luther King delivered his "I Have A Dream" speech at the Lincoln Memorial.

301

Perhaps the most important of the rights in the first category were those of women and those dependent on public largess. In the field of women's rights, the present century has seen a virtual transformation of the law. According to the famous epigram of Frederick W. Maitland, "A woman can never be outlawed, for a woman is never in law." Until the present day, American law displayed a similar attitude. The first case under the Fourteenth Amendment, in 1873, denied the right of women to practice law: "The paramount destiny and mission of woman are to fulfill the noble and benign offices of wife and mother. This is the law of the Creator," declared the Court at that time.

A century later, the law of the Creator was being construed differently. The common law jeremiad against women had been abandoned; virtually all disabilities based upon sex were being eliminated, either by statute or judicial decision. Political rights, economic rights, the right to share in public services and benefactions—these were almost all placed beyond governmental power to make sexual classifications.

The removal of sexual disabilities was the culmination of a century's development. But the recognition of legal rights in the field of government largess was entirely a product of the latter part of the twentieth century. Until the late 1960's, indeed, it was hornbook law that no one had any "right" to the largess dispensed by government. On the contrary, such largess was considered, in the law, a mere gratuity, which might be withheld, granted, or revoked at the pleasure of the governmental donor. This was true regardless of the nature of the given largess—whether it was a job, a pension, welfare aid, veterans' disability benefits, a government contract, or any other benefit to which the individual had no pre-existing "right." The result was to place those dependent on public largess in a legal status subordinate to that of others in the community. If the governmental benefaction was a mere "gratuity" or "privilege," it could be withheld or revoked without adherence to the procedural safeguards that would otherwise be required by the Due Process Clause.

Such a legal approach was rendered obsolete by the reality of twentieth-century society. The welfare state was distinguished by its distribution of economic benefactions to persons and classes in the community; for more and more persons, in fact, the government represented the primary source of income and other economic benefits. But there were signs that the mid-century welfare state itself was rudimentary in comparison with the augmented role of government that was emerging. Norbert Wiener, the author of *Cybernetics,* wrote that "the first industrial revolution . . . was the devaluation of the human arm by the competition of machinery." The second industrial revolution, that of this century, was devaluing the human brain itself; when it was accomplished, the vast bulk of the population would have practically nothing to sell that would be worth anyone's money to buy. The community would then have to supply the economic needs that the individual could no longer meet fully by his own efforts. In such a society, a legal system based upon the principle that government largess is a mere "privilege" would place in the hands of those possessing public power an effective means of controlling most individual rights. Though even the recipient of a

Student protesters at UCLA conduct a 1970 demonstration against U.S. intervention in Cambodia. Women were among the leaders in both the antiwar and civil rights movements.

The 1969–70 term of the Supreme Court marked the hundredth anniversary of the admission of the first woman to practice before the Court. In 1969, on the first day of the new term, 37 of the 90 lawyers admitted that day were women. Here, they pose behind officers of the National Association of Women Lawyers.

"privilege" remained theoretically free to exercise his constitutional rights, he would know that the price of free exercise would be the risk of loss of the largess upon which he had come to depend.

The law has now started to make the welfare state itself a source of new "rights" and to surround the "rights" in public benefactions with legal safeguards comparable to those enjoyed by the traditional rights of property. The landmark case was *Goldberg* v. *Kelly* in 1970, in which due process was held to require "a full 'evidentiary hearing'" before welfare benefits might be terminated. It was ruled no answer to the due process claim to argue that welfare benefits are a "privilege" and not a "right": "It may be more realistic today to regard welfare entitlements as more like 'property' than a 'gratuity.' . . . Such benefits are a matter of statutory entitlement for persons qualified to receive them."

Goldberg v. *Kelly* was soon applied to other cases involving government largess: unemployment compensation, public housing, public employment, and government contracts. In all these cases, the "privileges" of not too long ago were transformed into virtual "rights" entitled to the full procedural protection afforded to traditional property rights. The law was thus beginning to resolve the basic issue of fair dealing by government with those dependent on it.

In addition to the rights asserted by particular groups such as women and welfare clients, the law began to recognize a broad range of new rights that protected all individuals in the community. Foremost among these was the right of privacy. In Chapter v we saw how, in an 1890 article, Louis D. Brandeis and Samuel D. Warren had urged the existence of a legally protected right of privacy. What Brandeis and Warren were advocating was the individual's right of privacy as one the law should protect as against infringement by other individuals—a right that would be vindicated by the traditional tort action for damages and an injuction. In a 1928 dissent, Jus-

Connecticut's law forbidding the use of contraceptives was challenged by Mrs. Estelle Griswold, above, and struck down by the U.S. Supreme Court in a 1965 decision that viewed it as a denial of a constitutionally protected personal right.

tice Brandeis emphasized another aspect of the right of privacy: "The makers of our Constitution . . . conferred, as against the Government, the right to be let alone—the most comprehensive of rights and the right most valued by civilized men. To protect that right, every unjustifiable intrusion by the Government upon the privacy of the individual, whatever the means employed, must be deemed a violation of the [Constitution]."

In this dissent Brandeis was speaking, not of an asserted common law right against other private individuals, but of a constitutional right valid against government itself. "This notion of privacy is not drawn from the blue," Justice William O. Douglas asserted in 1961. "It emanates from the totality of the constitutional scheme under which we live." In the 1960's the law began to accept the notion of a general right to privacy as against government as part of the area of personal right protected by the Constitution. *Griswold* v. *Connecticut* in 1965 expressly recognized the existence of such a constitutionally protected right of privacy—a right said to be within the protected penumbra of specific Bill of Rights guarantees ("specific guarantees of the Bill of Rights have penumbras, formed by emanations from those guarantees that help give them life and substance. . . . Various guarantees create zones of privacy," the Court held). The right of privacy was a "penumbral right" protected by the Constitution.

Most cases enforcing the right of privacy against government involved the particular zone of privacy protected by the Fourth Amendment ("The right of the people to be secure in their persons, houses, papers, and effects, against unreasonable searches and seizures, shall not be violated, and no warrants shall issue, but upon probable cause, supported by oath or affirmation, and particularly describing the place to be searched, and the persons or things to be seized"). That protected area was expanded by decisions holding the amendment's restrictions fully applicable to the states, as well as to electronic eavesdropping, and administrative inspections. Perhaps Canute-like, the Supreme Court increasingly interposed the Fourth Amendment in the face of a proliferation of electronic and other devices to violate privacy that were the dubious gift of modern science. The right of privacy was also extended beyond the search and seizure situation to what the Supreme Court once called the "private realm of family life which the state cannot enter." Marital privacy was ruled beyond the reach of public power, and a law prohibiting the use by married couples of contraceptive devices was held an unconstitutional intrusion upon "a right of privacy older than the Bill of Rights."

Even broader in its impact than the right of privacy was the right to a habitable environment which the law started to vindicate in the third quarter of the century. In the 1960's both the judge and the legislator began to place increasing stress on environmental issues. Decisions recognized the duty of federal agencies to give weight to ecological as well as economic factors in reaching decisions affecting the environment. In the *Scenic Hudson* case in 1965, the Federal Power Commission's grant of a license to construct a power plant in the Hudson Valley was set aside because the FPC had not adequately developed the environmental case against the license. The commission might not "act as an umpire blandly calling balls and strikes"; the rights of the public in environmental protection "must receive active and affirmative protection," said the decision.

In 1969 Congress elevated the public interest in the environment to the status of a legal right. The Environmental Policy Act expressly recognized "that each person should enjoy a healthful environment." The statute made the obligation imposed by *Scenic Hudson* on the FPC one generally applicable to all agencies. Those whose activities affected the environment must show that the ecological impact was compatible with the developing environmental right.

In addition, a trend developed to broaden public participation in governmental decisions that would have environmental effects. Statutes began to require public hearings in the affected localities before highways, public housing, urban development schemes, and the like could be built. Members of the public had a right to be heard in such cases, as well as in other administrative proceedings that directly affected the public interest. The courts were also recognizing the standing of members of the public and organizations representing their interest in the environment to challenge decisions that had ecological impact. Standing itself was being rapidly expanded beyond its restricted sense of pocketbook interest. Citizens and organizations with environmental complaints were now permitted to sue:

The Scenic Hudson decision in 1965 recognized the public's right to environmental protection. Projects like this atomic power plant, seen being constructed on the Hudson River in 1966, must now be subjected to increasingly stiff state and federal environmental regulations.

WIDE WORLD

"the public interest in environmental resources . . . ," said a 1970 decision, "is a legally protected interest affording these plaintiffs, as responsible representatives of the public, standing."

Toward the Brink of Absurdity

Legal rules, unlike those in the physical sciences, do not have fixed areas of strains and stresses. There is a tendency to stretch legal rules to the breaking point. "You cannot blame the Minister for trying it on," said an English official over a generation ago about his superior's willingness to stretch the law. Today, you cannot blame those whose rights are first coming to be legally recognized for similarly seeking to "try it on."

In the rights explosion of the second half of this century, the law has recognized rights that had previously scarcely even pressed for recognition. They cut across the entire legal spectrum, ranging from extensions of traditional rights (such as those to freedom of expression and equal protection) to the emerging rights discussed in the last section. The difficulty has been one of drawing lines beyond which the "new" rights might not be pushed. The law has always had to draw lines; all of law depends upon differences of degree, at least as soon as it is civilized. The most delicate and shifting of the balances which the law is expected to maintain is that between competing rights, especially between those of the individual and those of the society. The protection of individual freedom inevitably means a limitation of the power of the majority: "the power of the Court to protect individual or minority rights has on the other side of the coin the power to restrain the majority," wrote Justice Robert H. Jackson.

Beneficiaries of the newly emerging rights have not unnaturally sought to vindicate those rights as far as the law will permit. It is after all not their job, but that of the courts, to work out the defining limits. When the courts fail to work out such limits, the law runs into difficulties. For the first time in American history, the free speech guaranty was used to restrict governmental power to deal with obscenity—a use that had its basis in the 1957 *Roth* decision. In the next decade and a half, the Grapes of *Roth* were harvested. The Supreme Court's failure meaningfully to define obscenity resulted in a virtual abdication of public power; proliferation of pornography was a direct consequence of the law's failure to draw workable lines.

On all sides, the law was subject to the pressure of rights pushed to their logical extremes. Advocates of women's rights urged that sexual equality be extended to prohibit even the protective classifications in laws that limit the employment of women in occupations deemed particularly arduous or hazardous. The right to a habitable environment was relied on to insist that ecological factors prevail in all governmental decisions—that environmental values might never be subordinated to economic factors, regardless of the economic needs of the community.

The right to privacy was being expanded into a right to personal autonomy, with emphasis on the right to control the use of one's body. The Supreme Court upheld the right of married couples to use contraceptives free from governmental restrictions. Some saw this decision as a mandate to the judges to work out a broad area of bodily autonomy, similarly immune from

This vivid display in the newsroom of the Houston Chronicle in 1970 dramatized the women employees' demand for equal treatment in pay and job opportunities on the paper.

public control. Society's continuing effort to regulate sexual conduct was being questioned. The courts were starting to strike down laws prohibiting sexual acts performed in private between consenting adults. The right of control over one's body was also used to question statutes restricting abortions. Such restrictions were held by the Supreme Court to be impermissible invasions of each woman's constitutional rights. The courts were also starting to strike down governmental attempts to draw adverse consequences from private homosexual conduct. In addition, cases were questioning laws punishing alcoholism and making narcotic addiction a criminal offense.

One commentator remarked that the emerging law was based on the proposition that "society may properly regulate the behavior of competent adults only if that behavior demonstrably threatens the rights, safety, or interest of others." It was rightly pointed out that this was but another version of the maxim stated by John Stuart Mill: "that the individual is not accountable to society for his actions, insofar as these concern the interests of no person but himself." A Michigan court used this Mill maxim as

the basis of decision in invalidating a statute requiring motorcyclists to wear crash helmets. The law was found to be related solely to the safety of the motorcyclist and hence invalid under the Mill maxim.

It is, as Learned Hand once said, most irksome to be ruled by a bevy of Platonic Guardians. That is particularly true when their decisions are based on outdated philosophical premises. However valid the Mill conception may once have been, it has been overtaken by the march of governmental power. In a society characterized by interdependence and concern for the welfare of all, there are few, if any, areas in which, in Mill's words, "a man's conduct affects himself alone." Even where harm would come only to the individual, he is not permitted to contract out of a scheme of social legislation, such as that set up by the Social Security Act. Similarly, if a man lives in society, it is not simply his own concern whether he can operate a motorcycle safely. The safety of the motorcyclist is directly related to the safety of others using the highway. The society that pays the bills may require precautions that cut down the number of highway accidents.

The difficulties involved in the undue extension of rights were compounded by the revival, after a century, of the problem of civil disobedience. The second half of the century saw a broad extension of the First Amendment to new forms of expression. The Supreme Court refused to limit the

A nostalgic image of the flag-conscious past is provided by the nineteenth-century picture above and by the view below of Washington, D.C., schoolchildren pledging allegiance in 1899. Today, the Supreme Court has ruled that no one may be forced to salute the flag.

right of free speech to mere expression of words. Even before mid-century, it held that the display of a red flag and a refusal to salute the American flag were protected by the First Amendment. A similar result was reached in 1969 with regard to the wearing of black armbands in protest against the Vietnam war.

The notion of nonverbal speech was also extended to include civil rights demonstrations and comparable conduct. Whether involving picketing, massing in the streets, or sit-ins, such a demonstration, as Justice Harlan put it in 1961, "is as much a part of the 'free trade in ideas' . . . as is verbal expression, more commonly thought of as 'speech.' " But here the law had to draw lines. Though verbal speech is subject to relatively little governmental interference, the same is not true when speech is combined with conduct. The First Amendment does not immunize street demonstrations, however laudable their motives, from public control. Significantly, it was the leading free speech advocate on the Supreme Court, Justice Hugo L. Black, who led the law in distinguishing between "speech pure" and "speech plus."

That distinction was the basis of the law's attempt to deal with the civil disobedience problem. One of the most difficult issues for any system of philosophy is that presented by the unjust law. From a purely legal point of view, there can be no such issue. A valid law must be treated by the courts as laying down a binding legal norm; its enforcement may not be defeated by its supposed injustice. The rule of law itself becomes meaningless if the law recognizes in the individual a right, derived from a higher "moral law of the universe," not to comply with any law he considers unjust.

In the 1960's the claim was increasingly put forward that civil disobedience was a right protected by the First Amendment. In its extreme form, it was asserted that the violation of a statute restraining nonverbal conduct was, as a protest against that statute, itself a form of expression protected by the Constitution. Here was the right of expression pushed to the brink of absurdity. Under it, every violation of law could be elevated into a protest against the law concerned, vested as a form of expression with immunity against governmental action.

The claim that nonverbal violation of the law was a form of constitutionally protected protest was made most frequently in connection with the destruction of Selective Service registration certificates and records, on the theory that such destruction was intended as a public protest against particular uses of the armed forces. The claim of constitutional protection for the alleged protest could not, however, serve to defeat a prosecution for violation of the congressional prohibition against destroying draft cards and records. The statute was a reasonable provision implementing the Selective Service Act, and its violation might be punished even though intended as a symbolic act of protest.

The legal answer to the asserted right to disobey the law as a form of protest was the only one that could be given. "Civil disobedience," Martin Luther King conceded," can never be legal. These would certainly be contradictory terms. In fact, civil disobedience means that it is not legal." Regardless of individual claims of conscience, the law must treat the violator of an allegedly unjust law upon the same basis as any other law violator.

When the Supreme Court upheld a conviction for destroying draft cards, it was a libertarian judge, Chief Justice Warren, who declared, "We cannot accept the view that an apparently limitless variety of conduct can be labeled 'speech' whenever the person engaging in the conduct intends thereby to express an idea." In this respect, at least, the law refused to permit the First Amendment to be stretched to the point of absurdity.

Social Welfare and the Courts

In his 1969 Cardozo lecture, Edward H. Levi referred to the temptation to modify the primarily negative role of law in a world that admires positive action. "This in itself creates temptations and tensions — ," he said, "a desire to involve law in programs which have little to do [with] or are perhaps contrary to its discipline. This contributes to the laxity of lawyer-legislators toward enactments which are deceptive in their incompleteness and require restrictions or meaning to be worked out elsewhere. . . . It is an added factor in encouraging courts, which have unusual power within our system, to assume a more affirmative role, dwarfing legislative consideration of policy matters and skewing their consideration as constitutional issues."

The enlarged judicial role, to which Levi referred, has been one of the outstanding features of American law since the middle of the twentieth century. Traditional restrictions on the scope of judicial power have been abandoned, with the courts assuming an activist role in the polity in more and more areas. In the public mind at least, the distinction between law and policy has become increasingly blurred. The penumbra between constitu-

Civil Disobedience and the Rule of Law

Throughout American history, civil disobedience has posed a problem for the law. From the time of the Boston Tea Party to the era of Prohibition and the decade of the Vietnam War, Americans have felt free to disobey laws which they considered unjust. Perhaps the period of the most widespread confrontation between the adherents of civil disobedience and the law were the years before the Civil War when persons opposed to slavery condemned the Mexican War (as an immoral plot to extend slavery), participated in the "underground railway," and defied laws passed for the slave-owning interests. It was then, in 1849, that Henry David Thoreau wrote his notable essay *On the Duty of Civil Disobedience*. Advocating obstruction of government as a means of protest, Thoreau declared, "When a sixth of the popula-

© 1968 BENEDICT FERNANDEZ. *In Opposition*

Young men defying the law by burning their draft cards in New York City in 1965

tionality and desirability has progressively widened as the courts have come to assume a virtual Ombudsman function in the society.

The change in this respect can be illustrated through developments in one particular field—social welfare. Here the courts (and especially the Supreme Court) have acted in a manner far removed from the customary limited role of the judge. One may wonder, in fact, whether a British observer of recent American welfare decisions would not be tempted to repeat Harold J. Laski's stricture against the Supreme Court as "a third chamber in the United States."

As noted earlier in this chapter, welfare assistance was, until recently, considered a mere "privilege" in the law—to be granted or denied at the will of the government and on the conditions laid down by it. Before the Social Security Act of 1935, the provision of welfare assistance was entirely a state and local function. Local welfare agencies dispensed largess free from control by the federal government or the courts. Neither public opinion nor the law contemplated any recourse for a rejected applicant.

Both public attitude and the law were markedly changed by the Great Depression and the federal government's response to it, culminating in the Social Security Act. The result was a broad extension of welfare assistance programs and the assumption by the society of an obligation to provide for broad segments of the community who did not come within the conception of the traditional "poor." The depression led to a virtual democratization of poverty that in turn was reflected in increased concern with the objectivity and fairness of the welfare system.

One of the draft card burners, pictured below on the opposite page, is taken to jail in 1968 from the New York courthouse where he lost his final appeal of his conviction three years before. Shown passively resisting imprisonment, he had received a sentence of six years, which was later reduced to six months.

tion . . . are slaves, and a whole country [Mexico] is unjustly overrun and conquered by a foreign army, and subjected to military law, I think that it is not too soon for honest men to rebel and revolutionize." Thoreau was too much the theorist to put civil disobedience to more than a token test. A prison, he wrote, may be "the only house in a slave State in which a free man can abide with honor." But earlier, in 1845, when he had refused to pay his poll tax in protest against slavery, he had been satisfied to spend a single symbolic night in the Concord, Massachusetts, jail, leaving in the morning after his aunt had paid the tax for him.

His doctrine, however, has served to justify Americans more activist than he, from the abolitionists of his day to civil rights protestors of more recent times. They have as-

serted their duty to a "higher law," which made it necessary for them to flout unjust man-made laws such as the Fugitive Slave Law of 1850 or late-nineteenth-century statutes requiring racial segregation. That those laws were voted by the people's representatives did not deter them. Believing with Thoreau that "any man more right than his neighbors constitutes a majority of one," they claimed the right to judge the justness of laws, even those accepted by the vast majority of the people.

Martin Luther King (1929–1968) was one of the foremost exponents of Thoreau's civil disobedience theory. But it was relatively easy for the law to deal with the challenge raised by King and his followers in civil rights demonstrations in the 1960's. The discriminatory laws which they disobeyed were themselves contrary

to the constitutional command of equal protection. King's refusal to obey those acts was ultimately justified by the courts. If the courts had decided otherwise, King and his followers could have been sent to jail for each violation. Despite the demonstrators' deep moral conviction, the law could not have accepted their flouting of constitutional statutes. "Civil disobedience," Supreme Court Justice Abe Fortas affirmed, "is violation of law." The rule of law requires law violators to be punished regardless of moral purpose. The theory of civil disobedience observed by men like Martin Luther King and Mohandas K. Ghandi in India recognizes this. King urged that civil disobedience must be done openly and peacefully, and with willingness to accept the penalties imposed by the law.

A line of unemployed, persons with qualifying low incomes, and others not working because of strikes wait in St. Louis in 1970 for the distribution of federal food stamps through a relief program administered by various state and local agencies.

Until the 1960's, changes in American social welfare law were brought about entirely by legislators and administrators (particularly by imposition of federal standards to which state administrations had to conform to secure grants under the Social Security Act). The courts had adopted a complete hands-off policy, asserting the absence of judicial jurisdiction in the field of public largess. As recently as 1966 the federal district court in the District of Columbia could dismiss a suit by a welfare recipient for injunctive relief against warrantless night searches by welfare workers on the ground that there was no "right" to welfare and the court should not, therefore, determine the propriety of the practice. At the beginning of 1967, a commentator noted that the federal courts had seen only one finally adjudicated action on welfare grants.

This situation has changed completely. In the past few years the courts have decided a plethora of welfare cases. So numerous have they become that Commerce Clearing House now publishes the *Poverty Law Reporter* to inform practicing attorneys of litigation and court decisions in this field. But it is not so much the quantity, as the quality, of such decisions that is so noteworthy. The judges have completely abandoned their attitude of abnegation and have instead assumed an affirmative role in welfare cases that (paraphrasing Edward Levi) dwarfs both legislative and administrative consideration of policy matters and presents their consideration as constitutional issues upon which the courts have the last word. As a result, the judge has become a virtual rulemaker in the field of welfare administration and one superior to the traditional legislative and administrative rulemakers because his is ultimately the final rule laid down in the matter. Justice Jackson's famous animadversion, "We are not final because we are infallible, but we are infallible only because we are final," applies with peculiar appropriateness to the courts' decisions in welfare cases.

What is most striking is that some of the most important welfare decisions turn on the Supreme Court's disagreement with the policies followed by welfare administrators (although the Court has been astute to articulate the the disagreement in constitutional terms). This has been seen in a consideration of the judicial reception of the so-called man in the house rule (denying assistance to a mother and her children when she lived with a man not the children's father) which had been basic to the policy of American welfare administrators for many years.

The "man in the house" rule had been based upon two considerations. The first was the long tradition that aid should be given only to the "worthy" poor. The second was the fact that the mother was cohabiting with a man who might be considered a source of income as a "substitute parent" for the children concerned. After all, the eligibility of most children for aid depended on the "absence" of the father from the home. If the mother had a de facto husband, did not her children necessarily have a de facto father?

Whether one approves or disapproves of the "man in the house" rule, he must recognize it as a matter of policy that, in other countries, would be for the legislator and administrator to resolve. In the United States, on the other hand, it is difficult not to conclude that it was the judges' strong disapproval of the policies behind the "man in the house" rule that led them to strike it down in *King* v. *Smith* in 1968. The Supreme Court decision there was based upon its reading of the Social Security Act, but it is fair to say that its voiding of the rule on federal statutory grounds could hardly have been anticipated by anyone familiar with the structure and history of the Social Security Act. According to the Court, the federal statute required a state to provide assistance to all children deprived of parental support because of the "absence" of a parent, regardless of whether a "substitute parent" lived in the house. But the relevant federal agency had always interpreted the act to allow the states to adopt a "substitute parent" rule and the statute itself is really silent on the matter. What the Supreme Court was actually doing was to substitute the judicial for the administrative judgment on the desirability of the "man in the house" policy.

What is clear, at any rate, is the consequence of *King* v. *Smith*: no welfare

Protesting inadequate welfare payments with which to support her children, this New York woman threatened to give birth to her ninth child in the office of the Borough President of Manhattan (left). She was taken to a hospital in time for the event.

A "Poor People's March," organized principally by followers of Martin Luther King to focus attention on the plight of the nation's poor, arrives in Washington, D.C., in 1968.

administrator may follow anything like a "man in the house" rule, no matter how firmly he may be convinced of its desirability as a matter of administrative policy. The Department of Health, Education, and Welfare immediately issued new regulations to implement the Supreme Court decision (expressly adopting the prohibition of the "man in the house" rule in all its aspects as administrative policy), and these regulations (laying down the new administrative policy in conformity to the Supreme Court decision) became binding on all welfare administrators in the United States.

In the area of welfare policy covered by the "man in the house" rule, the judge has led and the administrator has followed. The same has been true in the field of welfare procedure. There also the development has been one of administrative response to litigation in the courts. Before 1967, none of the states administering welfare programs provided for a hearing prior to termination of welfare assistance. In June, 1967, the lack of such a hearing was challenged in a suit in a federal court in Mississippi. Rather than go to trial, the state agreed to give pretermination hearings, and an amendment was made to the Mississippi welfare manual, continuing assistance in all termination cases pending a fair hearing.

Other lawsuits followed in other states, challenging those states' failure to provide pretermination hearings. Of particular importance was the action filed in New York, which ultimately became the already discussed case of *Goldberg* v. *Kelly* (1970). While that case was pending in the lower court, the Department of Health, Education, and Welfare was considering a new regulation requiring continuation of welfare payments pending a hearing in termination cases. The new regulation was issued the day the lower court decided that due process required a pretermination hearing, and the public announcement stated that the new policy was "in line with" the court decision. Before the Supreme Court rendered its decision affirming the lower court and laying down the broadside right to a hearing in welfare cases, the agency had already amended its regulation to provide for such a hearing. The administrative action was doubtless taken in response to the lower court decision and in anticipation of the expected Supreme Court decision.

These welfare cases have seen a virtual reversal between the roles of legislator and administrator, on the one hand, and that of judge, on the other. Policy has been set, not by Congress (which had remained largely passive on the questions) or the administrator (who has followed court decisions—either handed down or anticipated), but by the courts (whose intervention has brought the administrative rule-making process to life). Nor should we be deceived by the fact that the policy decisions have been framed in legal terms in the judicial opinions. "I would have little, if any, objection," caustically declared Justice Black's dissent in *Goldberg* v. *Kelly*, "to the majority's decision in this case if it were written as the report of the House Committee on Education and Labor."

Most suggestive is the ultimate potential of the judicial assumption of a supervisory role over welfare policies. The traditional trial-type procedures of American administrative law, however fair they may be in theory, may not be wholly appropriate in a field such as welfare. In that field, as Chief Justice Warren E. Burger pointed out, "the history of the complexity of the administrative process followed by judicial review as we have seen it for the past thirty years should suggest the possibility that new layers of procedural protection may become an intolerable drain on the very funds earmarked for food, clothing, and other living essentials."

Decisions such as *Goldberg* v. *Kelly* may well make the administration of the welfare system so inefficient, in terms of diverting administrative emphasis from the end of aiding the poor to the means of complex procedural protection, that the system itself may prove unworkable. Before that extreme is reached, the legislature may decide to replace the costly welfare system with a simpler system of direct grants to the poor. The decisions of the judges in the welfare field may thus lead directly to a substantive revamping of systems of aid to the poor—which points up as much as anything the role played by judicial review in the legal system.

The Changing Constitution

Not long ago, the attitude of Americans to their constitutional system was that described by Edmund Burke: "We ought to understand it according to our measure; and to venerate where we are not able presently to comprehend." With the approach of the nation's bicentennial, Burke's attitude appears as quaint as the costume of his time. During the present century, veneration has too often given way to vituperation, as men have begun to doubt so much that had always been taken for granted in the polity. At a minimum, we no longer assume that, with the contemporary constitutional

Soon after this Goldsboro, North Carolina, welfare recipient was photographed with her television set, her county welfare board ordered all persons on relief to give up either their TV sets or their right to welfare. Such administrative rulings have been challenged in suits, making the courts become supervisors over welfare policies and procedures.

system, the ultimate stage of organic evolution has been reached. We know that the system is continuing to evolve beyond the "perfection" that Americans at the turn of the century (who looked upon all of constitutional history as only a dress rehearsal for the stage reached in their day) assumed it had attained.

The historian who looks at American public law after two centuries is struck by the way in which it has illustrated the antinomy inherent in every system of law: the law must be stable and yet it cannot stand still. The essential outlines of the constitutional system are still those laid down at the beginning; there is here a continuity in governmental structure that is all but unique in an ever-changing world. But the system still proves workable only because it has been continually reshaped to meet two centuries' changing needs.

American public law in operation has directly reflected the history of the nation: the main thrust has been to meet the felt needs of each period in the nation's history. There have been aberrations, but by and large the law has remained true to Marshall's polestar—that we must never forget "it is a *constitution* we are expounding," a living instrument that must be construed to meet the practical necessities of contemporary government.

At the outset, the primary needs of establishing national power on a firm basis and vindicating property rights against excesses of state power were met in the now classic decisions of the Marshall Court. A generation later, the needs of the society had changed. If the Taney Court was to translate the doctrines of Jacksonian Democracy, and particularly its emphasis on society's rights, into constitutional law, that was true because such doctrines were deemed necessary to the proper development of the polity. In addition, they furthered the growth of corporate enterprise and prevented its restriction by the deadening hand of established monopoly. If in the latter part of the nineteenth century the law was to elevate the rights of property to the plane of constitutional immunity, its due process decisions were the necessary legal accompaniment of the industrial conquest of a continent. The excesses of laissez-faire-stimulated industrialism should not lead us to overlook the vital part it played in American development. Nor should it be forgotten that the decisions exalting property rights were a necessary accompaniment of the post-Civil War economic expansion.

The present-day picture has completely altered. We have come to recognize that property rights must be restricted to an extent never before permitted in American law. At the same time, unless the rights of the person are correlatively expanded, the individual will virtually be shorn of constitutional protection—hence the recent shift in emphasis to the protection of personal rights. The judges, like the rest of the population, have been disturbed by the growth of governmental authority and have sought to preserve a sphere for individuality even in a society in which the individual stands dwarfed by the power concentrations that confront him.

Despite the law's efforts, the concentration of governmental power has continued unabated. The second half of the century has seen an acceleration of the public law trends noted in Chapter VI: the growth of federal power at the expense of the states and the increase of presidential power.

Ralph Nader, who began his career as a crusader for safer car designs by the auto industry, became the nation's best-known ombudsman for the consumer, bringing together public-interest lawyers and specialists in consumer affairs to press for reforms in numerous industries and within agencies of the federal government.

Right: ITT draws the anger of New York antiwar protesters in 1972.

Shadowed

Foreshadowing the Watergate revelations, this Herblock cartoon of 1971 aimed at the government's increasing invasion of personal privacy.

FROM HERBLOCK'S *State of the Union*, SIMON & SCHUSTER, 1972

Regarding the first of these, federal predominance has remained the outstanding aspect of our federalism. This has involved a continuing increase both in the federal authority (in areas as diverse as the electoral process, education, and welfare administration) and in state dependence on federal funds. Political efforts to redress the balance, such as the Nixon program for revenue sharing, appear unlikely to alter the inevitable. Discerning observers may even question the ultimate fate of the states themselves. They may still have something of the magic of Athens and Rome, of Venice and Florence. But they may also suffer the fate of those entities, so far as the reality of governmental power is concerned.

Within the federal government, the augmentation in the power of the President has proceeded without letup. The dominant feature of the contemporary Constitution has been the paramount position of the President. The fulcrum of the polity has moved ever more steadily from Capitol Hill to the other end of Pennsylvania Avenue. In drama, magnitude, and prestige, the President now so far overshadows all others that, almost alone, he is the focus of public attention.

During the second half of the century, the vital issues of war and peace have rested primarily with the Chief Executive. He has committed the nation to two major undeclared wars, and also made the decisions whether and when to terminate those conflicts. If the Vietnam war led to increasing congressional efforts to restrain presidential power, it is still too soon to say whether those efforts will prove successful. And when, in the 1970's, price and wage stabilization were imposed on a national scale, Congress authorized the President to set up the stabilization program. The delegation was unprecedented, except for that in the National Industrial Recovery Act which the Supreme Court had stricken down in 1935. This time, however, the wholesale delegation was upheld without difficulty. Could it be doubted that, even when Congress was able to act, it would deal with future emergencies by comparable examples of "delegation running riot"?

W. B. Yeats wrote that "All States depend for their health upon a right balance between the One, the Few and the Many." The maintenance of that balance is peculiarly the task of American public law. More particularly, it is the job of the judges since, following the famous Hughes aphorism, the Constitution is essentially what the judges say it is. It is their unique function to serve as the guardians of the organic ark. To enable them to do so effectively, they are armed with the awesome authority to nullify any governmental act deemed by them to be in conflict with any provision of the basic document.

Not too long ago, the golden age of judicial innovation appeared to have come to an end. The work of the Warren Court proved how erroneous that appearance was. As a federal judge put it in 1970, the 1960's turned out to be "the most innovative and explosive era in American constitutional law" since the days of John Marshall.

The Warren Court, however, gave way to the Burger Court. This by itself says much, for the retirement of Chief Justice Warren marked a legal watershed. As prior portions of this chapter show, the Supreme Court under Warren rewrote much of the corpus of the nation's public law. The Burger

Court could be considered primarily a Court of consolidation. Transforming innovation, in the law as elsewhere, can take place for only so long; the new legal principles must then be digested, their details worked out, and the principles themselves run the gantlet of practical operation.

In an address in 1971 announcing two Supreme Court appointments, President Nixon referred to the common tendency to label justices as "liberals" or "conservatives." One may wonder whether the liberal-conservative dichotomy accurately describes either judges or courts. To those who engage in the pastime of labeling judges, Felix Frankfurter used to pose something of a problem. From Academic Eminence behind the New Deal to leader of the conservative Court cabal—that was the way critics tagged Justice Frankfurter. Yet, to one familiar with the justice's personal libertarian views, the characterization was a one-dimensional distortion of reality.

In the 1970's Warren Burger suffered from the same type of distortion. That it was a distortion is clear to anyone familiar with Burger's opinions in the field of administrative law over the years. That field is particularly pertinent, since it is the one area of public law in which the Warren Bench did not make any fundamental contributions. It is becoming increasingly apparent that a concern with individual rights that does not focus upon the rights of the individual vis-à-vis the administrative process is bound to be only partially effective. In our evolving society, the relationship between administrative power and individual rights is becoming of ever-greater importance, particularly in the area of social welfare law.

Before his appointment as chief justice, Burger made some of the most important judicial contributions to American administrative law. Two of his opinions rank as landmarks in the movement to broaden the due process rights of individuals in their dealings with administration. To one familiar with *these* Burger opinions, the labeling of the chief justice as "conservative" has an ironic ring. Although Burger has a more restricted view of the judicial role than some, a propensity for tilting at windmills is not necessarily an attribute of judicial liberalism. The Burger opinions in the field of administrative law are as solicitious in their protection of individual rights as any rendered since mid-century.

The inappropriateness of categorizing judges within the liberal-conservative dichotomy may be illustrated by a 1970 decision restricting a constitutional right recognized by the Warren Court. In question was the right not to be subjected to an administrative inspection without a search warrant. *Camara* v. *Municipal Court* in 1967 had ruled that the right was guaranteed by the Fourth Amendment and was so fundamental as to be incorporated within the Fourteenth Amendment's Due Process Clause. A companion case, *See* v. *Seattle,* also in 1967, had held that the right existed for business, as well as residential, premises. A 1970 decision—*Colonnade Catering Corp.* v. *United States*—held that the *See* requirement of a warrant for inspection of business premises was not applicable to a closely regulated business, such as the liquor business. In such a business, the legislature could validly provide for warrantless inspections by the relevant regulatory agencies. If the legislature is not restricted in the area of liquor regulation, it is presumably likewise unrestricted in other fields of economic activity

When he was convicted for refusing to permit a fire inspector to enter his warehouse without a warrant, Seattle businessman Norman See, above, went all the way to the Supreme Court. As a result, the conviction was overturned, and the Court ruled that commercial property merited the same protection under the Due Process Clause as residential property.

subjected to pervasive regulatory power, such as those under the laws vesting regulatory authority in the Interstate Commerce Commission and similar agencies.

Which is the truly "liberal" decision—that which vindicates only the right of the businessman and frustrates the regulatory authority to uncover violations, or that which recognizes that in a closely regulated business the public interest in ferreting out violators may justify a different rule to protect the consumer and the community? Where the public is so dependent on the product or service furnished by the business concerned as to justify pervasive regulation, should not the legislature be permitted to design broad powers of inspection to uncover any evils that may exist? In the case of an agency like the ICC, the *See* limitation might well make effective regulation virtually impossible.

One cognizant of the values involved in the Bill of Rights cannot but feel sympathetic toward the protective zeal shown by the Supreme Court during the Warren years. All the same, it is not mere caviling to point out that judicial predisposition toward the libertarian result may be a two-edged sword. Properly employed, it can maintain the essential balance between liberty and authority. Carried to its extreme, however, judicial libertarianism can lead the judges to assume undue authority over the other branches.

What was it that the Supreme Court had done in the years before 1937 to which much of the country objected so strongly? It was the erection by the justices of their personal predilections into due process dogmas that could not be touched by the legislature. True, the old Court's action in that respect was almost entirely limited to the economic field; yet that was so because it was in that field that legislative action was upsetting the justices' precon-

The Fifteenth Chief Justice

In 1969 Warren Earl Burger succeeded Earl Warren as chief justice of the Supreme Court. American chief justices, said President Richard M. Nixon, in announcing Burger's appointment, "have probably had more profound and lasting influence on their times and on the direction of the Nation than most Presidents have had." At the time, there had been thirty-seven Presidents and ninety-one Congresses, but only fourteen chief justices. Their longer tenure had enabled them to make the enduring impressions on American history that Nixon had pointed out.

Burger, born in St. Paul, Minnesota, in 1907, was the epitome of the self-made lawyer. Unable to accept a Princeton scholarship which his academic record had earned him (it was not large enough to pay his living expenses), he spent two years at the University of Minnesota and four in an evening law school, working during the day as a life insurance salesman. Although he graduated in the Depression year of 1931, his record secured him a job with a leading St. Paul law firm. Within five years, he had become a partner. In 1953 he became an assistant attorney general, and, in 1956, a judge of the Court of Appeals for the District of Columbia. He served on that court, often ranked only second in importance to the Supreme Court, until his elevation to the High Court as fifteenth chief justice.

Burger's appointment drew some criticisms, among them complaints that the President had not chosen another Cardozo. But where, it might have been asked, was another Cardozo to be found in an age of mediocrity in which the courts were the characteristic institution of the period? In addition, it may have been doubted that the talents of a Cardozo were called for in the holder of the highest judicial office. What was needed, rather, was the ability to lead the Court in molding the law to meet the needs of the day. That a new chief justice, moreover, perceived those needs differently than his predecessor—another argument made against him—was not necessarily cause for denigration. In terms of legal change, the Warren Court had moved farther and faster than any Bench in history. Burger was to lead a Court at ebb tide because of the need to consolidate. Neither the Court nor the nation could

ceptions. Today, none of the justices has difficulty in accepting governmental regulation that would have seemed all but revolutionary to the Court majority before 1937. In the economic area, then, deference to the other branches accords with the personal convictions of the present Court. The same is not true in the area of personal rights. Here legislative restrictions run counter to the libertarian predispositions of many of the justices. But are these justices necessarily more justified in writing their private predilections into the Constitution than were their pre-1937 predecessors?

Of course, any jurist who writes of the changing law in his own day runs risks, particularly when he seeks to indicate future trends. Few authors are as rash as those who venture into print with attempts to forecast coming constitutional developments. As a newspaper once put it, with regard to the present writer's effort to predict future Supreme Court tendencies, "He would be on much safer ground trying to forecast the winner of the . . . Derby, for which nominations have not even been made as yet." Perhaps all we can say with assurance is to repeat, with Camus, that "the wheel turns, history changes." American public law will continue to evolve, as it has until the present, to meet the changing needs of the society it serves. The law, like other institutions, has its epochs of ebbs and flow. The outlook now is for a period of consolidation and restraint. As compared with the Warren flood tide, American public law may be moving into a receding period. Yet, as Yeats wrote,

> Though the great song return no more
> There's keen delight in what we have:
> The rattle of pebbles on the shore,
> Under the receding wave.

Chief Justice Warren E. Burger flanked by British judges during a visit to London

live in a permanent state of constitutional revolution.

Will Rogers once said, characterizing Chief Justice William Howard Taft: "It is great to be great. It is greater to be human." That comment is also applicable to Chief Justice Burger. Like Taft, Burger has proved to be a quietly effective leader of the highest court. His impact on history may not be as great as that of some other chief justices, but in the future he may loom as just what the Court required after the turbulence of the Warren years. Like Taft, also, his greatest contribution may be to improve the Court's administrative effectiveness and prevent it from becoming unequal to its task in the face of its ever-exploding caseload.

IX

Era of Transition

Private Law and Institutions Since 1950

I do not think I overstate the matter," declared Brooks Adams in a lecture early in the twentieth century, "when I say that this community lives very largely in defiance or in disregard of the law. Wherever you look you mark the same phenomenon. Last spring Secretary Taft gave an address at Yale upon the failure of the criminal law. . . . You have only to read in the newspapers . . . of crimes of violence, of undetected murders . . . and of those numberless criminal frauds which go unpunished . . . to find abundant confirmation. The family is disintegrating. Marriage has ceased to be a permanent state and has become an ephemeral contract."

The remarks of the Brahmin cynic confirm that the crisis confronting law in the second half of this century is not unprecedented. From the law's beginnings, harsh words have been directed at the declining moral climate and its adverse effect on law enforcement. This has been particularly true in the United States. Concern about the interplay between law and morals has been a constant feature in American legal history, with the moral graph of the nation, according to contemporary critics, always showing decline.

Of course, men tend to place exaggerated emphasis on developments in their own day. As Teilhard de Chardin wrote in 1959, "In every epoch man has thought himself at a 'turning-point' of history." Still, he continued, there are moments in history when such an impression is justified. "We are, at this very moment, passing through an age of *transition*. The age of industry, the age of oil, electricity and the atom; the age of the machine, of huge collectivities and of science — the future will decide what is the best name to describe the era we are entering. The word matters little. What does matter is that we should be told that . . . life is taking a step, and a decisive step, in us and in our environment."

Technological growth and progress affect the quality of life and raise new problems that challenge laws and traditional institutions.

A California storefront legal clinic, with low costs to clients

Whitney North Seymour, center, presides at the 1970 "Is Law Dead?" symposium of the Association of the Bar of the City of New York. Flanking him are, left, the symposium's director, Dean Eugene V. Rostow of the Yale Law School, and one of the speakers, Robert P. Wolff.

Yet, aware though we may be that we are living through an era of decisive transformation, our awareness is accompanied by increasing apprehension. "The men of today are particularly uneasy, more so than at any other moment of history," Chardin noted. This uneasiness is linked directly to recurring doubts about the position of the individual in a world so unlike that in which his forebears lived. Can the individual exist as an end in himself — with all the scope for individuality that that concept implies — in an age in which the machine tends more and more to despoil human personality?

In addition, men are troubled, as almost never before, about the legitimacy of governing institutions. A crisis in confidence leads increasing numbers to question the continuing capacity of our system to respond to today's demands. On all sides, men repeat the Brooks Adams-type clichés about law enforcement breakdown. Underneath it all is a growing malaise about the relevancy of law in the traditional sense to the problems of an atraditional age. That "law indifferent to blame or praise," which the poet Yeats sang early in the century, now seems but a will o' the wisp — and, what is more, one that, even if attainable, may be inadequate to serve the needs of the contemporary community.

To celebrate its centennial in 1970, the Association of the Bar of the City of New York convened a symposium to "ask itself whether its premise, faith in law and in the value of trying to mold it and its institutions to fit the needs of a changing society, was still valid." The papers delivered were published under the title "Is Law Dead?" The symposium's answer was, as one critic pointed out, as predictable as a conclusion from a Vatican conference on whether God was dead. But the mere fact that the question was asked by the most prestigious bar association in the country was significant.

The title "Is Law Dead?" was intended to suggest a parallel between law and theology, where the so-called Death of God theologians have had such great impact in recent years. An age that personifies Laplace's famous denial of the need for God does not find it untoward to make similar denials of the need for law. Like the God of organized religion, the law is said to be less relevant to more people now than at any other time in history.

Can there be a legal order without law? A society that has seen the construction of theological systems modeled upon the *Mécanique Céleste* does not find such a question ridiculous. To the present century, indeed, the problem of the death of law has become very real. Both the extreme right and the extreme left of twentieth-century juristic thought have posited the disappearance of law as we know it from society. Their legal theories, which reached their culmination in the writings of Nazi and Soviet jurists, are reversions to justice without law. Under them, cases are decided, not according to strictly defined authoritative precepts, but according to "healthy public sentiment" or "socialist conceptions of justice." "Not the *corpus juris Romani*," said Lenin, "but our revolutionary consciousness of justice ought to be applied to 'Civil Law relations.'"

Soviet jurists, working from the Marxist starting point of the withering away of the state, assumed that law would also disappear with the attainment of true communism. In the socialist state, there would be no more law, but merely technical regulation; legal rules would be replaced by "social-technical" rules. As Professor E. Paschukanis, the leading exponent of this theory, explained, "The more consistently the principle of authoritative regulation, excluding all references to an independent autonomous will, is carried through, the less room remains for an application of the category of law." This was but another form of Friedrich Engels's famous thesis that the government of persons would be replaced by the administration of things. Law, in the sense of the rule of law, was to be wholly replaced by administration.

Perhaps the best commentary on Paschukanis's theory can be found in a 1942 lecture by Roscoe Pound: "The professor is not with us now. With the setting up of a plan by the present government in Russia, a change in doctrine was called for and he did not move fast enough in his teaching to conform to the doctrinal exigencies of the new order. If there had been law instead of only administrative orders it might have been possible for him to lose his job without losing his life."

It is, to be sure, possible to have a legal order without law. Those who urge the irrelevancy of law in the traditional sense are really urging the replacement of law by administration in the Paschukanis sense. In fact, as we shall see, one important aspect of contemporary legal development has been a movement to expand the sphere of administrative justice. But that movement has been caused less by the failings of the law than by the in-

In 1972 a Supreme Court decision directed that no person could be sentenced to jail, even for a misdemeanor, unless he or she had been offered free legal counsel. In a New York house of detention, above, inmates in private booths receive legal help in preparing their cases.

adequacy of the institutions that administer it. The current crisis in the law is primarily a crisis of confidence in our legal institutions.

The basic theme in American legal history in the second half of this century has been essentially a continuation of that noted in Chapter VII. The substantive law has continued its efforts to modernize itself; substantial changes continue to be made in substantive rules and doctrines in the law's effort to remold itself in the image of the evolving society. Where a legal lag has existed, it has been in the movement to reform the institutions that make and administer the law. Not that the reforming movement noted in Chapter VII petered out after mid-century; if anything, its efforts increased in intensity in recent years. The need for reform also intensified as the century's societal problems gathered momentum. Despite the continuing effort to modernize the courts and other legal institutions, the gap between need and performance widened. Law was not dead, but its institutions were becoming increasingly ineffective.

Or, to put it more accurately, the community was becoming more aware of the inadequacies of its legal institutions. This was but one aspect of the growing hostility toward social institutions that characterized the contemporary society. During most of the nation's history, Americans took for granted the superiority of their political, legal, economic, social, and other institutions. Now, at all levels of society, men rage at all their institutions. In every area the rise in human expectations leads men to demand more and more of institutions and to want their demands met "Now!" The institutions alter, but never fast enough to meet the demands.

Of course, as already indicated, the complaints about the law's decay are not new. What is new is the institutional crisis of our time. Legal institutions, like all others, are caught in a crossfire between the need for drastic alteration and their inability to keep up with the leaping aspirations of the day. Intransigent frustration is the increasing response of the community.

This frustration is leading Americans, for perhaps the first time in their history, to question the legitimacy of their legal institutions. The twentieth century, already witness to the collapse of traditional religion, may also see a collapse of traditional law. Whether this will happen depends in large part upon the ability of our legal institutions to transform themselves now — not a century from now. Effective institutional reform has become the categorical imperative for survival of the law as Americans know it.

New Trends in Contract Law

That the law's problems are primarily institutional, rather than substantive, may be seen from developments in contract law after mid-century. The substantive law of contracts has been substantially modified to meet the needs of the twentieth century. The abstract autonomy of the individual will, previously the pillar of contract law, has ceased to be the all-dominant factor in contract cases. As indicated in Chapter VII, the courts have begun to refuse to enforce contracts, though freely entered into by the parties, which they consider unduly unequal and unfair. In addition, they are starting to equitable-ize the terms of agreements as fixed by the parties, starting to read a virtual requirement of reasonableness into contracts. These develop-

Long court delays — in some instances stretching out five years and more — were deplored by this 1955 cartoon.

ments toward fairness have gained force in the second half of the century.

The law also began to question various contractual devices that tipped the balance unfairly against one party to a contract. These devices had been widely used in contracts of credit and sale, and operated in practice to give creditors and sellers an undue advantage. Perhaps the most burdensome of these was the wage garnishment which was widely incorporated into installment sales and loan contracts. The Supreme Court has shown "the grave injustices made possible by . . . garnishment"—"garnishment . . . may as a practical matter drive a wage-earning family to the wall." In 1969 the Court held prejudgment wage garnishment illegal on the ground that it deprived the wage earner of his property without prior notice and hearing. At least one state went further and abolished garnishment completely.

Other abusive practices were also curbed, both by courts and by legislatures. These included deficiency judgments, rules of confession of judgment, and the holder in due course doctrine. Most important in this respect were the enactment by Congress of the Consumer Credit Protection Act and the promulgation by the National Conference of Commissioners on Uniform State Laws of the Uniform Consumer Credit Code. The latter statute was termed "a revolutionary restructuring of credit laws." It restricted the power of creditors, particularly in the use of the contractual devices just mentioned. It also extended the judicial authority to invalidate consumer credit contracts on grounds of unconscionability. The courts, too, applied the theory of unconscionability on their own motion. A leading case held unconscionable an installment contract for the sale of an expensive stereo set to a woman on welfare with eight children. The gross inequality of bargaining power was said to make for an absence of meaningful choice. "Did each party to the contract, considering his obvious education or lack of it, have a reasonable opportunity to understand the terms of the contract, or were the

A woman with her baby checks the crowded schedule of the New York City Night Court. The row of notices on the board reflects the huge number of cases handled by this overworked court and, also, the antiquated manner in which information on cases is conveyed to concerned parties.

While most courts still cling to out-moded ways of functioning, modern business institutions utilize the latest technological aids for numerous operations, including those dealing with legal matters. Above, checks are electronically scanned and sorted in a New York bank.

important terms hidden in a maze of fine print and minimized by deceptive sales practices?" asked the federal court.

One familiar with the developing law of contracts in areas such as those described must be impressed with the extent to which the law was being re-molded in the 1960's and 1970's by both courts and legislatures. Changing conceptions of social justice were definitely having an impact on the substantive law of contracts. The emerging law was placing on American legal institutions an ever increasing responsibility for ensuring fairness in contractual dealings, regardless of the terms agreed upon by the abstract free wills of the parties.

Yet, paradoxically, as the substantive law of contracts was being remade to fit the demands of the contemporary society, it was playing a diminishing practical role in the life of the community. As far as ordinary business dealings were concerned, it may be doubted that more than a small minority of contract cases were decided by the law of the land as made and administered by the courts. The present century has seen a trend to arbitration, which has become more pronounced as time goes on. Today it can be doubted that as many as 10 percent of contested contract cases are litigated in courts. The growth of arbitration is directly related to the inadequacies of the courts as institutions for dispensing justice. Businessmen have developed their own arbitration tribunals to enable them to avoid the delay, cost, inconvenience, and publicity associated with courtroom proceedings. True, not all agreements to arbitrate are voluntary. Arbitration clauses are put in most contracts of adhesion, particularly in insurance policies and contracts entered into with large corporations. Standard form contracts of this type leave the citizen with no real freedom of choice. They also remove an increasing number of commercial transactions from the sphere of the courts.

Realistically speaking, as far as the businessman and those who dealt with him were concerned, the courts had become primarily glorified debt collection agencies. The main work of the lowest tier of civil courts was the collection of debts; they provided a mechanism by which merchants and tradesmen, finance companies, banks, and other businesses could collect from those who allegedly owed them money. In the field of debt collection, the inadequacies of the courts led to their being used as instruments of harassment and oppression. To the courts in these cases, the debtor was usually a cipher who did not even appear in his own defense. In New York's Manhattan Civil Court alone, there were over 100,000 default judgments per year. "Sewer service" (where the summons is not served on the defendant, but instead "thrown down a sewer," or its equivalent), inconvenient local venue, and the cost of litigation ensured that the judicial process in this area was as impersonal and inexorable as an IBM computer. To that part of the public who had dealings with them, the civil courts had served as expensive adjuncts of their local finance companies.

In the second half of the century, therefore, the substantive law of contracts flourished as almost never before, with the basic trend that of what might be called an equitable-ization of an entire branch of the common law. But all this was becoming less relevant to both business and the judicial process. The creative cases were increasingly decided by arbitrators, not judges. At a lower level, mechanical debt collection cases left little room for application of principles of contract law, however much the judges were refashioning them to accord with changing conceptions of social justice.

Changes in Tort Law

Almost a century ago, Holmes pointed out that "The state might conceivably make itself a mutual insurance company against accidents, and distribute the burden of its citizens' mishaps among all its members." The law has not yet gone this far. But the evolving law of torts during this century indicates that the Holmes forecast is not as far-fetched as it may once have seemed. Certainly the whole approach of the law to the subject of torts has altered drastically in recent years. Most important has been the changing conception of the very purpose of tort law.

In traditional terms, the function of the law of torts is to fix the dividing line between those cases in which a man is liable for harm done by him, and those in which he is not, its primary purpose to adjust the conflicting claims of the litigating parties. The present century has brought an increasing realization that more than the interests of the litigants may be involved in tort cases; the interests of the society may also be concerned, though the parties are purely private litigants. The administration of the law has become more than a process of weighing the interests of plaintiff against those of defendant. The interests of the community are thrown into the scale and, more often than not, tip the balance. The interests of individual litigants are balanced against one another, but only in the light of what will best serve the public interest. From this point of view, the century has seen increasing publicization of tort law, as, indeed, it has of most branches of private law.

The law has been moving toward virtual socialization of compensation for injuries. It increasingly accepts as the overriding social interest the protection of individuals from the consequences of pecuniary loss through such vicissitudes of life as accident, old age, sickness, and unemployment. That interest has been furthered through the century's social legislation, starting with workmen's compensation laws and culminating in the Social Security Act of 1935 and more recent laws. In the second half of the century, it has begun to influence the whole development of tort law.

In this respect, workmen's compensation may be taken as the model for much of the coming law of torts. At the turn of the century the law of torts proved inadequate to deal with the enormous burden of industrial accidents. As noted in Chapter VII, the burden was shifted from tort law and the courts to workmen's compensation tribunals; by mid-century, all of the states had enacted workmen's compensation statutes. The basic principle governing the law of industrial accidents became that of reparation: the requirement of fault and other restrictions worked out by tort law became irrelevant.

During the remainder of this century, the principle of reparation for harm done could be expected to make substantial inroads into what was left of the traditional law of torts. This was already apparent in the third quarter of the century, which saw an intensification of the trends noted in Chapter VII. Thus, the narrowing of the immunities from liability recognized by tort law continued. The immunity of charitable institutions, particularly hos-

Legal Services for Everyone

In the 1970's, attention was given to the question of how available legal services were to all Americans. The large corporations and the wealthy could command the resources of the blue-chip law firms. Those below the poverty line were increasingly able to obtain free legal services under court decisions that had expanded the right to counsel, and through federally funded programs of legal services for the poor. But, as an American Bar Association report stated, the middle 70 percent of the population, living generally on tight budgets and rarely able to afford a lawyer, was "not being reached or served adequately by the legal profession." The failure of law and lawyers to reach the bulk of those who were neither rich nor indigent be-

lied the concept of equal justice to all.

Various efforts have been initiated within the legal profession to remedy the situation. In a number of areas, pilot programs have been set up to test the feasibility of prepaid legal services for subscribers. The best known is the Shreveport Plan, instituted in Shreveport, Louisiana. The program provides its members with different legal services much as the Blue Cross and Blue Shield plans give medical services to their members, paying the lawyers with funds previously withheld from the subscribers' paychecks. The idea has been endorsed by the ABA, and similar prepaid group plans are in operation or being planned in states throughout the country. Moreover, a 1973 congressional amendment to

the Taft-Hartley Act permitted employer contributions to defray the cost of legal services for union members. This will undoubtedly become a standard part of many labor contracts, accelerating the spread of prepaid legal service programs.

Another innovation has been the legal clinic, one of which was opened in 1972 in a storefront office in Los Angeles. According to the head of the consumer organization which established it, the purpose of the clinic was to provide "an effective legal delivery system to handle the day-to-day problems of the consumer." Its concept was simple: through efficient operation and large volume, legal services could be delivered cheaply and effectively for the middle-income

pitals, was virtually overthrown; by 1971 it persisted fully in only three states. More important has been the judicial overruling of the sovereign immunity doctrine (the immunity of state and local governments from tort liability). Before mid-century, no court had been willing to repudiate that doctrine, though an increasing number of judges conceded its inconsistency with modern conceptions of justice. The picture has since changed. Starting with a 1957 Florida decision, an increasing number of state courts abolished immunity from tort liability of state or local governments, or both. By 1974, sovereign immunity had been overruled in about half the states.

In addition, the movement toward comparative negligence continued, though not as rapidly as some had hoped. Statutes providing for general apportionment of fault were enacted in a number of states; the anachronistic doctrine of contributory negligence was expected to give way still further as the principle of reparation gained ground.

Most important was the continuing diminution of the role of fault in tort law. In part, this was true because of the continued spread of insurance. Cases covered by insurance rarely came to court; most of them were settled with little regard to the question of fault. Compensation was coming to be based, not on fault, but on the existence of insurance. In litigated cases, the inarticulated major premise was the jury's willingness to return verdicts that would be paid by insurance companies. Plaintiffs' attorneys were increasingly adroit in insinuating the existence of insurance coverage and even that was being rendered unnecessary by the extension of laws making insurance compulsory.

The inadequacies of tort law were most apparent in the field of automo-

individual. The fees were fixed and published in a brochure, ranging from $15 for an initial consultation to $100 for default divorces and $200 for bankruptcies and most misdemeanor offenses. The clinic's storefront office was designed to be as accessible as a drugstore or any other neighborhood shop. Overhead was cut by the use of paralegal counselors and a systems approach to legal problems, most of which fell into standard patterns.

The problem of providing legal services for the middle class will undoubtedly become more urgent as people find it increasingly difficult to cope with the legal complexities of modern life. It is one which the legal profession must resolve, not alone because of the public need, but also in terms of enlightened self-

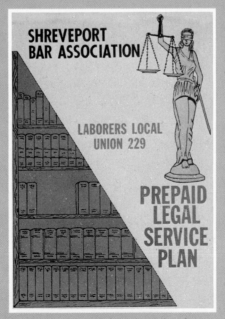

Cover of a booklet describing the Shreveport Plan's provision of legal services.

interest. A glut of lawyers threatening to result from the geometric growth of law school enrollments may be avoided by meeting the unsatisfied needs of those who are normally unable to obtain legal services. But the reaction of the Bar has not yet been hospitable. A long campaign was required to induce the ABA to approve the principle of prepaid legal services, and legal clinics like the one in Los Angeles have met with considerable hostility. Yet, as many lawyers agree, the Bar more than any other group has an interest in making legal services less costly and more available. The alternative, in the long run, could be a socialization of law practice that would ultimately mean the end of the American legal profession as it has been known.

bile accidents. The automobile accident case was the greatest incubus of the system of civil justice. It was both ineffective as a means of securing fair compensation for those who most deserved and needed it and destructive of the proper functioning of the civil courts. By the 1970's, the automobile accident calendar had mired the courts in a miasma of inefficiency and injustice. *Jarndyce* v. *Jarndyce*, the outrageous case described by Charles Dickens in *Bleak House*, was becoming the norm; the pity was that there was no Dickens to describe its effects as he had done in his novel—it "so exhausts finances, patience, courage, hope, so overthrows the brain and breaks the heart, that there is not an honourable man among its practitioners who would not give . . . the warning, 'Suffer any wrong that can be done you rather than come here!' "

As the slaughter on the highways continued its geometric climb and the problem of the uncompensated victim became ever more acute, it became increasingly apparent that the precedent of workmen's compensation furnished the feasible remedy. Even before the middle of the century, writers had advocated the extension of the workmen's compensation principle to automobile accidents. Notable among these was the so-called Columbia Plan recommended by a prestigious committee in 1932. After mid-century, there was increasing interest in the matter. No state has yet adopted an auto-

Highway carnage like this clogs the courts with suits to fix blame and direct the payment of damages.

WIDE WORLD

mobile accident compensation scheme, though one was set up in Puerto Rico under a 1968 law. Since then, steps in the direction of compensation systems have been taken in states that enacted no-fault automobile insurance laws. By 1974, such laws were enacted in a dozen states. Despite the obvious need for action, further expansion of no-fault was met by strong opposition in the legal profession. The obstructive role of many lawyers belied the public concern of the contemporary bar association with law reform.

The overriding fact was the aggravation of the problem and the inability of tort law to deal with it. The accident rate continued to mount, most victims remained uncompensated, and the social cost of caring for them became ever greater. Sooner or later, the law would have to give. Whatever the cost of automobile accident compensation, it would ultimately have to be borne, because the cost of the existing system in ruined human lives far exceeded it.

Property and the Social Interest

Not too long ago, property meant power. So far-reaching had the rights of the property owner become in American law that Morris Raphael Cohen could write an article in 1927 on "Property and Sovereignty." That article could scarcely be written today. The whole course of development in twentieth-century law has been away from emphasis upon property rights. If, at the turn of the century, property meant power, three quarters of a century later, insofar as the law was concerned, it had come to mean responsibility.

On all sides, the property owner in the latter part of the present century was met by legal restrictions affecting his rights of ownership. His virtually absolute right to use his land as he chose was giving way to an overriding principle of reasonable use, as defined by the relevant authorities. That principle was further developed during the third quarter of the century. Zoning and comparable regulations became ever more pervasive, increasingly limiting the use that could be made of property. In addition, the law was starting to develop ecological limitations. The power of the property owner to befoul the environment, pollute adjoining air and water, dispose at will of sewage and sludge, was limited by legislators, administrators, and courts. T. S. Eliot's "Clear the air! clean the sky! wash the wind!" had become the rallying cry for an environmental policy that imposed more and more restrictions on the property owner.

Property law, like tort law, was increasingly infused with public law elements. The rights and obligations of property owners were determined not only by the common law developed by the judges, but even more by the statutes, regulations, and decisions made by legislators and administrators. As the society moved toward a controlled economy, the details of the *jus utendi* were dependent as much on government as on the will of the individual property owner.

One who looks at the developing law must conclude that the century has seen a complete change in the relationship between the law and individual rights of substance. True, property has always rested on the law; property unprotected by law remains only an academic conception. Until almost the present day, however, the role of American law vis-à-vis private property was largely to secure it from encroachment by others. Within the limita-

The concept of property in the past, which allowed owners to misuse what they possessed, permitted the degrading of the quality of air and water, even if it affected others. Today pollution like that shown above often leads to legal actions.

George Tooker's painting, "Government Bureau," conveys the depersonalization of the individual attempting to cope with modern-day bureaucracy. In recent years, the courts have tried to protect the rights of the individual; the law's present problem is to strike a balance between public and private rights.

tions of the *sic utere* maxim ("use your property so as not to injure that of another"), the owner was left with the widest dominion over the use and disposition of property. This has all been drastically altered. The law has brought about a social transformation of property that can be compared, both in its importance and its effect upon the society, only with the institution of the feudal and then the free enterprise systems, and the notions of property upon which they were based.

It should not, however, be forgotten that the legal transformation of property has been not an end, but a means—the means of vindicating the different social interests furthered by the law. Nor should it be overlooked that the fundamental social interest in our system is in the individual life. The basic goal of contemporary society may be taken as that of ensuring that each individual be able to live a human life therein—that, if all individual wants cannot be satisfied, they be satisfied at least insofar as is reasonably possible and to the extent of a human minimum. The interests the law vindicates must find their ultimate justification in the realization of this goal.

Difficulty arises because, in the law, society and individual are too often conceived in competing terms. In weighing the claims of different interests, the courts have increasingly balanced the property right of the individual against the competing social interest. Yet, if these are the weights put in the scales, it is scarcely surprising that the balance is usually struck against the individual. When the judges pose one claim as an individual interest and the other as a social interest, they virtually decide the question in advance.

The present century's shift away from property rights contrasts sharply with the original emphasis of American law. "An accurate view of the matter," it was declared in 1787 during the Philadelphia Convention, "would . . . prove that property was the main object of Society." Without property rights, the Constitution's framers knew, all other rights would be without practical value. "Property must be secured," affirmed John Adams, "or liberty cannot exist."

Such an emphasis on property now seems misplaced. In today's hierarchy of legal values, property rights have been relegated to a lesser level. Yet, as already stressed, it should not be lost sight of that the ultimate social interest is that in the individual life, nor that the fulfillment of that interest is impossible without the protection of private property. If the individual is deprived of hope to acquire property, asked Pope Pius XII, what other natural stimulus can be offered him? The very maintenance of individuality is closely entwined with the property rights of the individual: "You take my life, When you do take the means whereby I live," runs the line in *The Merchant of Venice.*

The emphasis in the recent law of property on the conflict between individual and social interests may be unduly simplistic. If balance we must, should we not place on the individual's side the importance of the institution of property in the free society? The vindication of property rights themselves may be stated in terms of social interests. "Both human rights and property rights are foundations of our society," said President John F. Kennedy. Individual property rights should be secured because, and to the extent that, they coincide with social interests.

Harnessing the Giant Corporation

It is still not settled whether the giant corporation in America is to be placed in "its proper place as the servant, not the master, of society." The second half of the century had not seen any abatement in the growth of corporate power. If anything, the trend was the other way. "In the second half of the twentieth century," observed James Willard Hurst in 1970 in *The Legitimacy of the Business Corporation in the United States*, "the business corporation — especially the very large corporation — plays leading roles of bewildering diversity on a world stage, and not only in the United States." The corporate device, fashioned as the prime legal instrument of economic expansion, had now come to dominate the economy and the society. We had become a nation of wage earners who worked, in the main, for corporations. The average American found his greatness not in himself and in what he did, but in the corporate entity he served. Whether men spoke of the corporate revolution, the new industrial state, or the military-industrial complex, their terminology assumed that the contemporary age continued to be characterized by corporate predominance.

Despite, or perhaps because of this, the second half of the century might still see a renewed subordination of the corporation to law. There were signs that the law of corporations would repeat the law of property's shift from power to responsibility. As pointed out in Chapter VII, this was a new

Appointed to the Supreme Court in 1939 after having served as chairman of the Securities and Exchange Commission, Justice William O. Douglas quickly made a mark as a staunch defender of human rights.

posture for American law. Until well into this century, the law, like the society, was concerned almost entirely with the utility of the corporation as an instrument of economic expansion. The prime functional need for the law was to serve the utility function. Corporation law was to provide a ready instrument to muster capital, put it under central direction, and endow that direction with the authority to serve both the general economy and more specific interests. Even before mid-century, the legal emphasis in this area started to alter. Since then the law has seen a continuing reconsideration of the place of corporate power.

In broad terms, a movement was beginning to subject corporate power to the rule of law. Both legislatures and courts were starting to look at industrial corporations as quasi-public institutions—virtually as arms of the state subject to some of the legal principles that control the acts of government agencies themselves. There was a growing willingness of government and law to intervene in the workings of large corporations. Though the law continued to speak in terms of "private" policy and "private" decisions, decision making by the great industrial complexes was coming to be regarded as private only in the strictest technical sense. Phrases such as "private government," which had been a previous generation's metaphor, had become legitimate tools for analysis of the new reality.

The development of corporation law gave indication of following that of the nation's public law itself. The latter has been a history of successive attempts to make power responsible—to subject governmental conduct to the rule of law. The emerging law of corporations was starting to repeat this history. Corporate conduct was not yet clearly governed by rules that would assure equity to the various interests involved. But one could expect successive attempts to clarify rights and to make corporate power, like governmental power, "responsible." The time had come to explore the dimensions of corporate power in terms of values more generally associated with the allocation of political power. Corporation law was confronted, as a leading corporation lawyer conceded, with a constitutional problem: that of imposing some form of constitutionalism upon the corporate economy.

Most suggestive in this respect was Justice William O. Douglas's concurring opinion in *Bell* v. *Maryland* in 1964. That case involved the invocation of police protection against Negroes participating in a sit-in in a restaurant owned by a corporation. The state urged that the corporate owner was a "person" having the right to choose those with whom it would deal. Justice Douglas seized the occasion for attacking the whole concept of analogizing corporate personality and individual personality. Giving corporations the status of individuals and guaranteeing them the same rights of privacy in the use of their property would in effect "give corporate management vast dimensions for social planning," he said. It would vest them with power through intracorporate regulation to determine practices in race relations; it "would make corporate management the arbiter of one of the deepest conflicts in our society."

The implication was that the corporate owner should be subject to the requirements of fair play imposed by the Fourteenth Amendment. Such a result was advocated by an increasing number of writers on corporation law, notably by A. A. Berle who had helped awaken both the law and the society to the realities of corporate power. Constitutional limitations such as due process and equal protection were designed to shelter citizens from the rapacities, cruelties, and compulsion of arbitrary governmental power. Did we not now need similar protection from these neo-statist organizations of economic power? "Governing power, wherever located," said one writer, "should be subject to the fundamental constitutional limitation of due process." The alternative would be (to use the Douglas approach) to make corporate management the uncontrolled arbiters of vital aspects of American life.

It would be premature to assert that the law has already adopted the Douglas-Berle approach to the control of corporate power. Yet indications suggest it may have started to move in that direction. Legislation designed to protect automobile dealers' franchises is an outstanding example. A 1956 statute enacted by Congress was a direct attempt to impose a virtual "due process" prescription for corporate accountability. Arming the dealer with a legal complaint if his franchise was terminated flew directly in the face of the accustomed reliance on freedom of customer selection and rejection. But, where free bargain had given way to ultimatum, and existing laws proved inadequate to deal with the impotence of corporate satellites, the constitutional-type avenue of redress was tried.

From this perspective, much of traditional antitrust law had been intended to curb what Senator John Sherman had called the "kingly prerogative" of giant corporations back in 1890. So far as the law sought to protect competitors or suppliers or buyers who were satellites of corporate concen-

To entitle his painting of an American jury, artist Andrew Rush drew on a quotation by the great jurist, Justice Joseph Story.

"Where is to be found a nobler institution than the trial by jury, that impregnable bulwark of civil liberty." —STORY

STEVE SHAPIRO. BLACK STAR

Campus unrest over the Vietnam war and civil rights in the 1960's was typified by this student demonstration at Columbia University in 1968. Calls to revolution had little substance, following, or staying power and scarcely made a dent on the solidity and strength of traditional American institutions.

trations, it was motivated more by an "equal protection" spirit than by the rationale of competitive economics. Similar "equal protection" considerations might one day become the explicit basis of more rigorous insistence that the vertically integrated corporation could not favor itself against those who competed with it at one stage and dealt with it at another.

When all was said and done, however, it was by no means clear that the law was doing enough to subject corporate power to the requirement of social responsibility. The conception of corporate constitutionalism itself was still at the rudimentary stage. Perhaps we are in the process of a "revolution" in corporation law, as some contend, which will result in a redirection of business goals and conscious assumption of broad social responsibility. To whatever extent such a revolution may be taking place, does it meet the need for the legal canalization of responsibility which the burgeoning of corporate power demands?

The "curse of bigness" is not only still with us; it has grown to an extent that Justice Brandeis would have thought impossible. Today's giant corporations, observed A. A. Berle, "are units which can be thought of only in somewhat the way we have heretofore thought of nations." That was in 1957. In 1971 a study showed that of the world's one hundred leading "money powers," measured in terms of gross national product or net sales, more were corporations (51) than countries (49). The remedy of "corporate democracy" for the feudalism of the large corporation has already proved unattainable. The hopes for corporate constitutionalism or some comparable limiting conception may also prove incapable of realization. Perhaps the legal answer will be to impose upon corporations a "public interest" requirement such as that imposed by law upon governmental agencies. "Today it is generally recognized that all corporations possess an element of public interest," said Justice Douglas as early as 1940. Tomorrow the law may demand that their actions run the gantlet of a legally enforceable public interest standard. Yet, can we really expect the law to succeed here when it has failed so signally in making administrative agencies themselves live up to the public interest standard?

One may go further and doubt whether the problems posed by the corporate society can be resolved by the law. A leading authority, Bayless Manning, asserted in 1962 that "corporation law, as a field of intellectual effort, is dead in the United States. . . . We have nothing left but our great empty corporation statutes—towering skyscrapers of rusted girders, internally welded together and containing nothing but wind." Corporation law by that time had become of little effect because it provided scant controls over those who wielded practical power within most corporations. But it would be erroneous to think of corporation law as more than an instrument of wants and energies derived from sources outside the law; it has never been the prime mover. If the law is to impose needed controls on corporate power, it will be because society itself is ready for such controls. The giant corporation has become so thoroughly integrated into the American business culture that to suggest a drastic change in the scope or character of corporate activity is to suggest a drastic alteration in the structure of society. If this comes about, it will take place not because of changes in the law but because of much more radical changes.

Mediocrity in Government

As far as the institutions that made and administered the law were concerned, two things were apparent as the nation approached its bicentennial: (1) the existence of a crisis in popular confidence and (2) the likelihood that our legal institutions would remain essentially unaltered during the remainder of the century.

The first of these facts was underscored by a 1971 survey which found that only a small minority of Americans retained confidence in "the Government." According to the survey director, recent years had seen "a massive erosion of the trust the American people have in their Government." Cynicism had become the order of the day; the manner in which our institutions were functioning provided justification for the prevailing mood.

"What if there's nothing up there at the top?" asked the poet Yeats. All too many Americans had concluded that it would make little difference in the actual life of the community.

With this recognized, it would still require a rash observer to predict anything like an institutional upheaval during the remainder of the century. The situation in this respect was acutely noted by a British commentator, C. P. Snow, in 1970: "The worry I have met . . . among Americans is a fear of revolution. This is totally unrealistic. . . . The underlying structures—as the young call them—of American society are immensely strong. By structures I mean the institutions that the radicals get cross about. . . . I would be prepared to make a bet, though I shan't be there to collect, that by the year 2000, the essential framework of [the United States] . . . will be remarkably similar to what it is today."

American law was confronted with an institutional dilemma: its institutions were in a confidence crisis of such proportions that people had begun to doubt their very legitimacy, but those same institutions were the ones that would make and administer the law during the remainder of the century. The basic question was whether those institutions could be reformed sufficiently to enable them to overcome popular disillusionment.

One would have to be singularly sanguine to assume that an affirmative answer must be given to that question. Observation of American legal institutions in the second half of the twentieth century reveals all the deficiencies noted in Chapter VII. This is particularly true of the legislature, which, at both the federal and state levels, has seemed more than ever a parody of what a legislature should be. It would take an act of faith to assume that there has been an improvement in legislative caliber since mid-century. If anything, the contrary has been the case. The Congress has been the very epitome of governmental mediocrity and, at the state level, the situation has been worse. Leaving aside the grosser manifestations of congressional

Watergate and the Lawyers

The many scandals of the Nixon Administration, known collectively as Watergate, placed the U.S. legal profession under a cloud. Most of those who were implicated, including the President himself, were highly placed lawyers, sworn guardians of the law. Yet the Vice President of the United States, members of the Cabinet, top presidential aides and counsels, and other policy-making officials of the government, many of them lawyers, were charged as participants in crimes or in attempts to obstruct justice. Even the top law enforcement officers of the country, including two attorney generals and the acting director of the FBI, were caught up in the skein of illegalities.

The hypocrisy and lack of ethics reflected by the justifications and explanations for the crimes and cover-ups were no less shocking to the nation. After Vice President Spiro Agnew, a lawyer, admitted to a federal crime, he told newsmen and a TV audience that he had done nothing wrong. John Ehrlichman,

one of the President's top aides and also a lawyer, testified to the Senate Watergate Committee that he could not answer the question of whether the President of the United States had the right to commit murder. And on the theory that two wrongs make a right, various illegal actions, including political use of the IRS and other federal agencies to reward friends and punish enemies, were justified because previous administrations were alleged to have done the same thing.

The underlying problem, revealed so explosively by Watergate, had long been felt. The Code of Professional Responsibility holds lawyers to the highest standards. But economic pressures had increasingly made the lawyer an adjunct of businessmen. Most lawyers had paid far more attention to the interests of their clients than to ethical issues. Clients expect lawyers to do anything to win their cases, and, too often, the end of winning had led to neglect of the moral content of the means. "I have had many lawyers

who have told me what I cannot do," J. P. Morgan is said to have complained at one time. "Mr. [Elihu] Root is the only lawyer who tells me how to do what I want to do." In recent years, all too few lawyers have been willing to tell their clients, "You cannot do that."

The identity of interests between business and its lawyers was sharply illustrated also by Watergate-associated scandals that involved the raising of campaign funds by illegal methods. Using the "carrot-and-stick" of a governmental intention to reward or punish, administration officials induced corporation leaders and their attorneys to commit wrongdoing. The chairman of American Airlines, for instance, who was himself a lawyer, contributed illegally to a campaign fund for the President, believing that this would help the interests of his company. Nor was he alone. Officials of major oil, insurance, manufacturing, and other firms did the same, undoubtedly with the concurrence of their companies' attorneys.

decay—the diminution in prestige, the venality and conflicts of interest that permeate Capitol Hill, the common attitude reflected in the congressman as a staple butt of popular humor—one has only to look at the manner in which Congress functions to realize its manifest inadequacy for today's needs. About the only thing American legislatures have done efficiently in recent years has been to vote themselves hefty increases in pay and unvouchered expense allowances, and to do so in indirect ways so that the public has been unaware of their action.

Of course, to paraphrase the celebrated statement attributed to Mark Twain, everyone talks about the legislature, but no one does anything about it. Though many people have ideas on what to do, there is little real consensus, except on the need to eliminate the seniority system. And on that there is certainly no agreement on any workable alternative. One can apply to the American legislature Churchill's comment about democracy—it is the worst possible form of government until we consider the alternatives. One may, nonetheless, wonder whether that really justifies the ineptitude of the nation's primary lawmaking organ.

There may be reason for hope in the effects starting to be felt from the Supreme Court decisions in the *Reapportionment Cases* of 1964. As noted in Chapter VIII, they have already begun to shift the legislative balance from

Watergate figure John Mitchell, right

It is unrealistic, perhaps, not to expect the legal profession to play a major part in any Watergate-type scandal. In a lawyer-dominated society, lawyers are bound to have a vital role in any large undertaking, including a corrupt one. This was true in all past episodes of significant corruption; lawyers and judges were infamous characters in the activities of the Tweed Ring, the affair of the Crédit Mobilier, and in the Teapot Dome scandal.

Some urge that the problem can be dealt with by the teaching of ethics in law school, with specific examples of what may and may not be done. Legal education, until now, has never stressed ethics; law professors have answered calls for such courses with the bromide that morality cannot be taught, any more than it can be legislated. While a greater emphasis on ethics in legal education can do no harm, the difficulty is that such a course might tend to become one in platitudes. Moreover, it is doubtful whether ignorance of ethical rules contributed to the lawyers' involvement in the Watergate scandals. Those who were concerned knew that what they were doing was illegal; one does not have to be a Benjamin Cardozo to know that breaking and entering, perjury, and the like are criminal acts.

But lawyers, in one view, may be considered only a reflection of the society in which they operate. The legal profession is guardian of the law and its standards; but only the rare lawyer actively practices the role of acolyte. To the average lawyer, the law is a means of livelihood. For all the talk about public service, he treats his practice as his business, and his ethics inevitably fuse with those of the businessman. By an ethical Gresham's Law, the morals of the marketplace take over in the law as they do in the rest of society. And this, in truth, may illuminate the real problem. "Watergate," declared the American Bar Association president in 1973, "with all its related events— and . . . the spirit of the times in which such things can happen and result for some in so little sense of outrage—seems to me to be at least a threat to our liberties and to our very sense of decency."

rural areas to the urban and suburban centers in which most Americans now live. The provocative possibility is that this may lead to the needed revitalization of the legislature. Not so long ago, during the "Court-packing" struggle of the mid-1930's, Congress preserved the Supreme Court as an effective judicial institution. Is it too fanciful to hope that, when all the ramifications of the *Reapportionment Cases* have been revealed, it will this time be the Court that comes to the rescue of the legislative department and furnishes the catalyst for sorely needed legislative rejuvenation?

During the second half of the century, the vital center of the governmental structure remained 1600 Pennsylvania Avenue. This was true despite a decline in presidential caliber which revived (hopefully only temporarily) the descriptive validity of the Bryce dictum—"Great men are not chosen Presidents." To be sure, the lowered presidential level has been obscured by the magnitude of White House power and by public relations techniques. All too frequently, euphoria overshadows lack of program, platitude outweighs mediocrity, and rhetoric seems to impart substance to shallowness. Perhaps these words are overcensorious. Our leaders are not unique in their mediocrity. "So universally is that shared," wrote Dean Acheson in 1971, just before his death, "that our age might be called the apotheosis of mediocrity."

The executive manner may have been ordinary, but that has scarcely affected the concentration of executive power that has characterized our era. A notable feature of contemporary law has been the continuing growth of administrative authority. This is all the more striking because the period saw a climax in the disillusionment with the administrative agency that had begun even before mid-century. All that has been said about other legal institutions applies with special force to the administrative agency. In everything except power, it has been in steady decline since the New Deal days. In 1964 Eugene ("Bull") Connor, of Birmingham police-dog notoriety,

The stacks of folders at right contained bills awaiting action by the New York State Assembly in 1973. Some of them were important, some frivolous, and some almost duplicates of others. Similar situations in other state legislatures, the national Congress, and in the courts slow the people's business to a snail's pace.

was elevated to the chairmanship of the Public Service Commission of Alabama, the most important administrative agency of his state. That simple fact tells more about the current state of the administrative agency than any lengthy dissertation. Yet these were the bodies on which men of the caliber of William O. Douglas, James M. Landis, and Jerome Frank once sat.

The goal of cheap and inexpensive justice by experts, one of the chief reasons for setting up administrative tribunals, proved illusory. The administrative process proved even more expensive and time-consuming than the judicial process. Virtually every study emphasized this dreary reality. Even more important was the increasing failure of administrative agencies to protect that very public interest they were created to serve. The administrative process, which had been vigorous in fighting for the public interest in the 1930's, had gone through successive stages of apathy and ossification. The regulatory agency had become part of the economic status

"Because of Our Computer's Mistake"

The facts as set forth by plaintiff," said judge Harold R. Tyler of the federal District Court in Manhattan in a 1972 case, "suggest an Orwellian nightmare of computer control which breaks down through mechanical and programmers' failures and errors." It had, indeed, been a nightmare for the plaintiff, but it was to become one, also, for the defendant and possibly for many giant corporate enterprises in the future.

The case had been brought by a Mrs. Eloise Bronson, an elderly widow living on welfare in Brooklyn, against the Consolidated Edison Company after the New York public utility had shut off her electricity for allegedly being behind in the payment of her bill. The company had acted even though Mrs. Bronson had personally delivered a check in payment, after a dispute concerning the amount she owed. Through a computer's error, the check had not been credited to her account, and her service had been halted. With the help of the Legal Aid Society, Mrs. Bronson sued, claiming that the company's electricity cut-off procedures violated the Due Process Clause of the Fourteenth Amendment. Due process, she argued, required a hearing in which a consumer could have an opportunity to rebut the company's claims before it cut off service.

This was something new. As interpreted by the courts, due process clearly required a hearing before a *governmental agency* acted in a manner which injured a particular individual. But a *privately owned company* like Consolidated Edison had not been held subject to the Constitution's due process requirements. Nevertheless, Judge Tyler ruled in Mrs. Bronson's favor. In the case of a government unit, once it provides a service to the public, said the judge, it must comply with due process before it can terminate access to that service. The same should rule for electric service, which is as vital to the existence and livelihood of an individual as any state-provided service. Here, as in government, Judge Tyler declared, the individual "is confronted by an impersonal bureaucracy held together by computers, wherein inefficiency and a resultant high level of error are the norm, and unresponsiveness or 'run-arounds' the only answer to his inquiries." Hence, due process required notice and hearing prior to termination of service.

"It was just our luck," said a Consolidated Edison official, "to be faced with this poor old woman living in the dark because of our computer's mistake." The implications of the case, however, went beyond the

court's sympathy for Mrs. Bronson. The 1972 decision was the most striking example of a recent legal tendency to hold corporate power to the demands of due process. The Due Process Clause has served as the principal judicial instrument for curbing abuses of governmental authority. Now, with the power of huge corporations so unrestrained, either by the market or by public regulation, there is a search for other controlling devices. The answer supplied by the Bronson case may be applied as well to all other corporations which furnish products and services on which the modern community depends. The result could subject major corporations to the same requirements of notice and hearing prior to decision now imposed on government agencies.

The developing law in this area underscores the recent tendency of constitutional rights to expand into domains traditionally regarded as those of private law. But it also raises serious questions regarding the suitability of hearings and other adjudicatory procedures in nongovernmental operations. Are procedures which have proved so burdensome and ineffective in regulatory administrative agencies the proper model for decision making in the area of corporate activity? The answer must still be provided.

quo. It had come to terms with those it was ostensibly regulating; the "public interest" was equated more and more with the interest of those being regulated. For the age-old central question of political science, *Quis custodiet ipsos custodes?* ("Who will regulate the regulators?"), American law had given a new answer: Those who are regulated themselves.

To speak of public institutions as endowed with life is more than metaphor. The governmental body, like the animal, has periods of vigor and decline. The vital spark had gone out of the administrative agency. Even undue influence and corruption — cancers of the governmental organ — had begun to appear. Yet there was no effective movement to reduce administrative power; if anything, the trend continued the other way.

Just when the administrative process had proved that it was, indeed, a lost hope, the law found new worlds for it to conquer. The trend toward extension of administrative power into areas of social legislation, which had begun with the Social Security Act of 1935, was intensified after mid-century. Disability, welfare, aid to dependent children, health care, and a growing list of other services came under the guardianship of the administrative process. The traditional area of regulation was now completely dwarfed by the growing field of social welfare. The law pressed these newer areas into the judicialized mold of the regulatory process. Procedures that had become a travesty on the courtroom and were proving ever less effective in the regulatory area were now imposed on the expanding administrative apparatus of the welfare state.

More important in its implications was the expansion of the administrative process into areas traditionally occupied by the courts. We have seen that the future of much of tort law lies in the extension of the principle of compensation, particularly in the field of automobile accidents. Puerto Rico has already established an Automobile Accident Compensation Administration. By the end of the century we may expect similar agencies in many of the states. Even the criminal law has not proved exempt from administrative intrusion. New York has transferred jurisdiction over traffic offenses from the courts to administrative tribunals. Not too long ago, administrative criminal jurisdiction would have been deemed violative of basic conceptions. Constitutional niceties have had to give way in the face of the growing inadequacies of the courts in areas such as traffic violations. We may expect increasing efforts to transfer other lesser offenses, notably those involving violations of sumptuary laws, from the courts to administrative agencies.

Bench and Bar

"To see what is in front of one's nose," said George Orwell, "needs a constant struggle." This is particularly true when one seeks to examine the contemporary situation in one's own profession, a profession so crucial in a lawyer-dominated system. In terms of impact upon the society, the lawyer's role in the second half of the twentieth century has been as vital as ever. If anything, it has been magnified by the evolving nature of the society. Regulation and benefaction from cradle to grave have meant an inevitable expansion in the lawyer's place in the community.

Artist Hank Virgona's impression of a courtroom: affairs move along so tediously that even the judge grows weary.

It has also meant a constant increase in the ranks of the legal profession. In 1971 there were 355,242 lawyers in the United States. The American legal profession is about fourteen times the size of England's, counting both barristers and solicitors in that country. On a per capita basis, it is still more than three times the size of England's.

Since mid-century, the profession in this country has prospered as never before. Applications to law schools have grown at a geometric rate; while many may have been motivated by the lawyer's ability to play an important social role, the majority were attracted by the rising material rewards of the profession.

Despite this, the legal profession has been afflicted with singular un-easiness during the third quarter of the century. According to a 1967 address by Chief Justice Warren, "In a century which has been characterized by growth and modernization in science, technology and economics, the legal fraternity is still living in the past. We have allowed the mainstream of progress to pass us by."

The prosperity of the profession cannot belie the truth of the Warren comment. "On the whole, it is fair to say that neither the law schools, the practicing profession, nor the Bench has eagerly reached out to inquire whether new tools and new techniques can be put to good use in the law," wrote Bayless Manning in 1968. The computer has become an indispensable adjunct of business, government, the military, the university, and most other institutions of the society. "But our law schools and the general institutions of the law (except, significantly, the Internal Revenue Service) remain largely innocent of the computer's existence," Manning noted. This has been the century of the managerial revolution. Yet the legal profession has not really changed its organizational and operational methods. It has, indeed, been said that the only significant innovations in the technology of law practice since the turn of the century have been the Xerox copier and the looseleaf service. The endless delays, burdensome expense, and blizzards of papers

involved in law practice contributed significantly to growing disesteem of the profession. "Can the way of doing business in the law remain indefinitely in a nineteenth-century mold when all around us is changing?" asked Manning.

Still, the Bar of the late twentieth century differs greatly from the Bar of the late nineteenth. As noted, the number of lawyers has substantially increased—a proportioned increase far larger than that of the American population as a whole. In 1951 one lawyer served 696 of the population; in 1971 the ratio was one to 572. The methods of practice also continued to change, as the trends noted in Chapter VII intensified. The day of the single practitioner was starting to pass. The number, size, and proportion of lawyers practicing in firms continued to grow; the "law factories" became bigger than ever. Law firms with over a hundred lawyers and two or three hundred supporting personnel appeared on the scene. Over fifty New York law firms had more than fifty lawyers; fifteen had one hundred or more lawyers. These large law firms were increasingly considered as spokesmen for big business.

Nevertheless, the Wall Street lawyer represented the popular image of the profession less than he had before mid-century. The percentage of lawyers in private practice was sharply decreasing, dropping from 89.2 to 72.7 percent from 1948 to 1971. More lawyers were working for government, either as government lawyers in the traditional sense or in the newer programs providing legal services for different sections of the community. The public service lawyer was now a prominent part of the profession. For an increasing minority of law students, he was the professional model they hoped to emulate.

The profile of law practice was also changing. Some staples of legal work a century ago had been, or were in the process of being, lost to others outside of the legal profession. Land title work, still a mainstay of the profession in England, had moved from the American Bar into the hands of more

This small army of lawyers—112 of them—was employed to defend twenty-nine oil companies in a single antitrust suit in 1957. Corporations often use such massed legal talent.

efficient institutions. This process was repeated in the trust field, and the lawyer also lost most of the tax field to the accountant. Similar developments may be expected in the remainder of the century. The tort case will doubtless give way to compensation or no-fault insurance. Other areas will increasingly surrender to government officials and lay experts; that may well be the outcome of the unsatisfactory state of domestic relations and probate law. Arbitration will replace judicial decision in more and more business cases. In addition, government and groups will take over more of the practice provided by the independent attorney. Programs furnishing legal services for the poor will be expanded, ultimately seeking to meet the legal needs of an ever larger part of the community. Group legal services, received with growing favor by the Supreme Court, may also assume an increasing role in the legal services provided by independent practitioners.

The resulting decline in practice should be more than balanced by the increase in professional opportunities provided by the expanding law of the contemporary society. A whole set of new legal rights is emerging in the second part of the century. These rights will be further developed and vindicated by lawyers. In addition, opportunities for the lawyer will increase with the continuing growth of government. If the welfare state is necessarily an administrative state, that means more law and more scope for lawyers.

The basic trend in the twentieth-century Bar has been from a profession to a business; the law firm has more and more resembled a business corpora-

These lines outside the Supreme Court Building in 1961 were composed of more than four hundred lawyers from New York City who were about to be admitted to practice before the High Court. The dramatic gathering was organized by the New York County Lawyers' Association.

On its seventy-fifth anniversary, in 1953, the American Bar Association was addressed by Attorney General Herbert Brownell (left). The ABA has tried to be the conscience of the legal profession, but Watergate disclosures in the early 1970's reminded that lawyers sometimes ignore its ethical standards.

tion. Projections anticipate ever larger and more businesslike firms. Lawyers who are not partners in them will increasingly become salaried employees, working for other lawyers, government, or corporations. Can the professional ethos and status be maintained or will the law evolve from the first part of the century's adjunct of business to only a business itself? Hopefully that will be avoided, notably by a growing social consciousness of the Bar. Yet such an answer is by no means foreordained by developments thus far in this century.

The growth of the Bar after mid-century was paralleled by the growth of the bar associations. By June, 1972, the American Bar Association had expanded its membership to 157,182, almost half of the lawyers in the country. Comparable figures for state and local bar associations are not available, but no doubt their memberships also continued to increase, particularly in view of the fact that over half the states now had integrated Bars.

The legal profession continued to play a leading part in the movement for law reform. The American Law Institute went forward in its work of restating the law. New editions of the *Restatements* were being prepared and *Restatements* in other fields were issued as well. In addition, the ALI and the National Conference of Commissioners on Uniform State Laws continued to promulgate model statutes and codes. The *Restatements* and codifications were of great value, but they scarcely filled the need for legal codification. As the proliferation of statutes, regulations, decisions, and other legal materials accelerated, the law became ever more unmanageable. Yet no discernible codification movement appeared comparable to that led by David Dudley Field over a century ago. Perhaps the one thing that would save the law in this respect was technology. To survive in the wilderness of legal materials may now be beyond the human ken; the same will not necessarily be true when the law is reduced to computer form.

The bar associations were taking a more active part in the movement for the reform of legal institutions, particularly the courts. Much was accomplished, but, in terms of the needs of the day, the progress was agonizingly slow. The law reformer in the second half of the century felt stranded on a treadmill: the harder he went in the direction of reform, the less ground it seemed he had covered. This was true even of the giants of reform such as Arthur T. Vanderbilt, who had been the leader in the movement for court reform and reorganization in New Jersey. "Without doubt," said John P. Frank, "he was the country's most effective man in one state in this century." But, for all his valiant efforts, by 1971 there was an average waiting time in New Jersey of over two years for personal injury cases, with the time in the two largest counties closer to three years. In other states, the situation was worse. In Philadelphia and Chicago in 1973, the average such case took 53 and 49.8 months respectively from the date of answer to the date of trial; in New York City, the time lag in the different boroughs varied from 31.1 to 50.2 months.

To be sure, *Jarndyce* v. *Jarndyce*, the fictional case in *Bleak House*, had taken far longer. But nobody outside Bedlam would consider that case a model for a working legal system. And it had taken place in the England of the 1820's, well before the great reforming efforts of the past century. It is ludicrous in the age of automation and efficiency for the victim of an automobile accident to have to wait an average of three to five years for the trial of his case.

The congested calendar is a symptom — not, as apologists would have us believe, a cause — of the present state of judicial justice. Dickens told of the Chancery judge who admitted that there had been "a trivial blemish or so" in the Court of Chancery's operation, "but this . . . had been entirely owing to the 'parsimony of the public'; which guilty public, it appeared, had been . . . bent in the most determined manner on by no means enlarging the number of Chancery Judges appointed." The same has been the common plaint of American judges. Yet it should be clear that the increases that have occurred in the number of judges during the past generation have done comparatively little to solve judicial deficiencies.

Parkinson's Law operates in the courts as well as in the executive department: the more judges, observed a federal judge testifying before the Senate Judiciary Committee in 1967, "the more inefficiency creeps into the whole system." New York City has more judges than all of England, with new judgeships constantly being added. Does anyone doubt which has the better judicial system? "We have learned by sad experience," said Chief Justice Warren, "that merely adding judgeships will not solve the problem of judicial administration. Indeed, adding more judges to courts using outmoded methods of administration is more likely to retard production than it is to stimulate it."

The key to what almost all commentators term the "crisis in the courts" is to be found in the outmoded methods the chief justice mentioned. The first essential in their elimination is a proper judicial selection process. In terms of reform this means moving away from popular election to the Missouri-plan type of selection process. According to the American Judica-

In the modern computer age, artist Hank Virgona depicts a familiar scene —a judge still the prisoner of rubber stamps, ledger books, and other archaic devices. Many distinguished members of the Bench and Bar, including Chief Justices Warren and Burger, have warned that the rule of law in the United States might collapse completely unless the court system undergoes modernization.

ture Society, "Since 1951, the pace at which states have returned to appointive-elective selection of judges has quickened." Perhaps so, but one may doubt that it has quickened enough to bring about the needed elevation in judicial caliber. Since mid-century, several more states have adopted versions of the Missouri plan. But over thirty states still provide for the popular election of the judges of major courts.

Just as important as selection is court organization and procedure. As pointed out in Chapter VII, the essentials of a modern unified court structure have been recognized for years. Movements to reorganize the nation's court systems have been gaining momentum. But they have succeeded in establishing unified judicial systems in less than a quarter of the states, and effecting lesser reforms—notably the replacement of justices of the peace with courts staffed by full-time, salaried, professional judges—in a few others. In the majority of states, the courts remain "Wrapt in the old miasmal mist," to use T. S. Eliot's phrase; diversity of courts, multiplicity of jurisdictions, and lack of effective administrative responsibility continue as characteristic features.

Although many of the states have provided career administrators for at least their major courts, this alone has done little to resolve the deficiencies of judicial administration. Modern management techniques have passed the courts by even more than the rest of the legal profession. Except for the Xerox copier, the office machine has had scarcely any effect on judicial operation. According to Chief Justice Burger, "the ancient ledger type of record books, sixteen or eighteen inches wide, twenty-four or twenty-six inches high, and four inches thick are still used in a very large number of courts. These cumbersome books, hazardous to handle, still call for longhand entries concerning cases." For judges who have clung thus tenaciously to old ways, the computer is still an unattainable dream in the mind of its originator,

Embodying legal wisdom and judicial efficiency, Chief Justice Vanderbilt was architect of the reform of New Jersey's courts.

Arthur T. Vanderbilt of New Jersey

There were gentlemen and there were seamen in the navy of Charles II," wrote Thomas Babington Macaulay in his *History of England*. "But the seamen were not gentlemen, and the gentlemen were not seamen." In American courts, it has somewhat similarly been said, there are judges and there are administrators. But the judges are not administrators, and the administrators are not judges. Except, that is, for Arthur T. Vanderbilt, who, from 1948 to 1957, was chief justice of the New Jersey Supreme Court. Emphatically a judge who was also an administrator, Vanderbilt was the most effective judicial administrator in American history. His administrative accomplishments as his state's chief justice so overshadowed his juristic ability that even lawyers have tended to forget that he was one of the nation's outstanding judges of this century.

Before his appointment to the Bench, Vanderbilt was one of the leaders of the American Bar, a president of the American Bar Association who had acquired a reputation as perhaps the most effective advocate of the day. Born in 1888, he was not, despite his name, a member of the moneyed branch of the Vanderbilts, but was a self-made man. He often said that his name, if anything, had been a handicap, since it led people to assume that he was a dilettante who did not have to pursue the law seriously as a means of livelihood.

Financial success at the Bar enabled him to take public interest cases without fee long before that became fashionable. The first one was a 1928 civil liberties case involving striking workers and the American Civil Liberties Union. Vanderbilt secured the reversal of a conviction for participating in a procession without a permit. Describing the facts in court, he stated that the procession had been led by "two beautiful girls carrying American flags." One of the judges interposed, "Mr. Vanderbilt,

I have read the record, and I see no evidence to support your statement that these girls were beautiful." "Surely your Honor will take judicial notice of the fact that any girl carrying the American flag is *ipso facto* beautiful," came back Vanderbilt's unruffled answer.

As a lawyer, Vanderbilt was a reincarnation of the Bar's earlier-day giants, who regarded their practice as only a part of their career. He was active in politics, organizing a good government movement that overthrew a corrupt political machine in his home county in New Jersey. But his two overriding interests were legal education and law reform. In 1914, a year after his admission to the Bar, he became a professor at New York University Law School, continuing to teach classes there long after his practice had become a booming one. Former students recall his vigorous manner, which did not end with the classroom bell; animated discussions continued as members of the class walked with him to his transportation back to New Jersey. As dean of the school from 1943 to 1948, he transformed the institution into one of the country's top law schools, and the New York City building in which it is now housed is named for him.

The challenge of law reform (which in 1955 was the title of one of his books) became his great passion. He was the rare example of a reformer, who not only designed, but was given the opportunity to implement his ideas. Years of effort culminated in the setting up of a modern integrated court system in New Jersey in 1947, a reform of which he was the principal architect. He was then appointed chief justice of the state's supreme court, which made him the administrative head of the new court system. Under his leadership, the New Jersey courts, long a byword for judicial inefficiency, speedily became the model judiciary in the country. Calendar

lag was virtually eliminated, as the new chief used his powers to bring court management into the twentieth century.

Vanderbilt's guiding principle was expressed in the title of a lecture he gave in the year of his death, 1957 — *The Application of Sound Business Principles to Judicial Administration*. How he adhered to what he preached was described after his death in a memorial address by Supreme Court Justice William J. Brennan, Jr., who had been Vanderbilt's colleague on the New Jersey court: "Never one to indulge notions he was convinced were misguided, he grasped the nettle on his first day as Chief Justice. He announced rules of administration controlling the day-to-day work of the judges which, it is an understatement to say, produced initial consternation in judicial ranks. The rules prescribed fixed court hours and court days throughout the state to be observed by all judges by their actual presence on the Bench throughout the hours prescribed. Conduct of judicial business in chambers was expressly forbidden. Judges were required to file weekly a report detailing the matters attended to during the prescribed court hours and noting any matters wherein decision was reserved. The noting of reserved matters was required so that the Chief Justice might keep a watchful eye on the time taken by the judges to dispose of such matters."

Vanderbilt's whole career gave substance to the assertion that great men do make a difference, even in the law. He was, said former Yale law professor John P. Frank, the most effective law reformer in any state in this century. Yet even the Vanderbilt model of judicial efficiency could not long survive the man. Within a decade after his death, the New Jersey courts were as far behind in their work as those in other parts of the country.

An advance in the service of justice: a computer, providing a printout of jury selection lists, speeds up a formerly time-consuming step in jury trials in New York City's busy Criminal Courts Building.

Charles Babbage. Judicial business has gone on unaware that the Age of Gutenberg has been supplanted by the Age of McLuhan.

Joined to all this has been the declining level of judicial ability. The courts have become the characteristic institution of an age of mediocrity. Gone are the giants of an earlier day and even the great judges who still added luster to the Bench at mid-century. The general level in recent years has been depressingly undistinguished. To be sure, this is a value judgment not shared by all others. It is, however, the felt impression of one for whom the law reports constitute staple reading. Increase in the number of judges has meant a noticeable dilution in quality.

One must, of course, avoid the example of Dickens's Lord Boodle who "really does not see to what the present age is tending. A debate is not what a debate used to be; the House is not what the House used to be; even a Cabinet is not what it formerly was." Yet, there are times when the tendency to view with alarm is justified. In 1921 Learned Hand made his oft-quoted assertion that, "As a litigant I should dread a lawsuit beyond almost anything short of sickness and death." Half a century later, the groping and floundering condition of the courts makes the Hand assertion more valid than ever.

When an institution consistently fails to perform the job that the community reasonably expects of it, its legitimacy ultimately comes into question. This is what has happened to the courts in the second half of the century. Their inadequacies, said Chief Justice Earl Warren in 1958, are "corroding the very foundations of government." Since mid-century the public has come to realize what the lawyers already knew: the administration of justice in the United States is in a state of disaster. And nothing that is being done will really cure the situation. The law itself is at a low point in creativity in dealing with it. "Unless something new and effective is done promptly . . . ," declared Warren in 1967, "the rule of law in this nation cannot endure."

Legal Education

For the first time since Christopher Columbus Langdell discovered his new world in the case method, substantial changes were taking place in the methods of legal education. During the first half of the twentieth century, the case method had taken over the country's law schools. After mid-century it continued as the basic method in legal education, but it was more and more supplemented by other methods. The case method was attacked as both too narrow and too uneconomical a way of learning law. In particular, it was considered ill adapted for teaching the newer subjects in the curriculum.

The expansion of law during the century has been directly reflected in the changing law school curriculum. The traditional rubrics of the law still found their place, especially in first-year law. But they were supplemented by an ever-growing list of subjects that were virtually unknown a short time ago. All the new areas of the law—administrative law, urban law, environmental law, poverty law, consumer law, and a host of others—were now in the law school catalogue. Most of the newer courses used materials of instruction that were increasingly far removed from traditional casebooks. The proliferation of courses also made it impossible for all of them to be covered in the three years of law school study. The solution was to allow students to choose their subjects. The traditional required curriculum gave

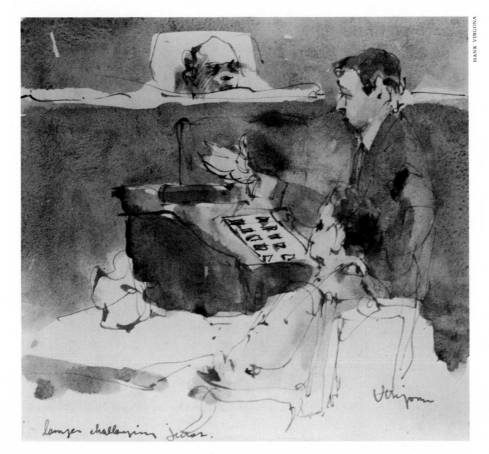

HANK VIRGONA

lawyer challenging juror.

A jury selection scene by Hank Virgona pictures a lawyer at a lectern with a board bearing slips of paper carrying the names, addresses, and occupations of the prospective jurors. The slips have been taken from a drum, one at a time. As some of the jurors are rejected by the lawyers, new names are drawn from the drum and placed on the board.

At the Antioch Law School in Washington, D.C. — a new type of law school that concentrates on clinical work — students assist real-life clients in need of legal aid. At right, a student confers with a client in a combination law office/classroom.

way to a growing number of elective courses, with the required courses occupying an ever smaller portion of the law student's time.

After mid-century, there was a renewed attempt to give a more practical cast to legal education. This took two directions. First, "skill" courses were added, which taught such things as the drafting of conveyances and wills and the mechanics of handling particular types of litigation. These courses were not really new; drafting-type courses had entered the curriculum years before. But the range of these offerings was greater, as the law schools made a conscious effort to impart more of the basic skills of the lawyer.

More important was the development in the 1960's of "clinical" legal education. Patterned on medical education, the new clinical training focused on direct involvement by law students (under faculty supervision) in actual litigation in selected fields, including direct client representation in courts and administrative agencies. Clinical programs appeared in most law schools — with the range running from a semester of off-campus work with a public interest law firm in Washington, D.C., to programs in the criminal courts, prison counseling, police work at precinct level, and the like.

The attempts to change legal education have been part of the law's efforts to meet the needs of the lawyer in the changing society. Nevertheless, one may wonder whether they do not constitute at least a partial step back to the apprentice system of an earlier day. Development of the modern law school was based upon recognition of the difference between "academic" and "practical" training in the law. The law school provided academic instruction in the classroom; practical training came after graduation, usually by working in a law office at the beginning of legal practice.

One must, to be sure, recognize the disquiet with legal education in the second half of the century. The case method of teaching has taken on a growing hit-or-miss quality; more and more it seems a method in search of a purpose, particularly after completion of the basic courses of the first year. But, is the solution a smorgasbord of courses, of increasingly esoteric character, into which the student is free to dip as fad or fancy moves him? Law students should be thoroughly drilled in all subjects basic to legal thinking. Even in a relativist age, all subjects are not created free and equal.

A "modest doubt" also surrounds the shift of emphasis to "practical" training. The law school as a strictly "how-to" school is not necessarily an improvement. The law school has until now not been successful in providing effective "practical" training outside the school. The simplistic analogy of the medical school does not justify converting the law classroom into the law clinic. Clinical work may have a place, but that does not warrant substituting it for the classroom, at the cost of complete grounding in the basic subjects. The law school remains the only place where most lawyers have an opportunity to think about law in anything like the grand manner. To substitute a proliferation of bread and butter or topically relevant courses and apprenticeship will hardly impart a wider perspective.

The second half of the century has seen a tendency to look critically at legal education. Too many have failed to do justice to the truly remarkable contribution law schools have made to American law. They did this as professional schools offering professional training all but unique in its intensity and discipline. However law schools evolve in the remainder of this century, they cannot retain their excellence by continued dilution of their academic content.

The Ends of Law Since 1950

"The pace of change in human affairs . . . ," said Arnold Toynbee, "has been accelerating constantly since the earliest date from which any record

Another aspect of the clinic system: students at the New York University School of Law participate in a simulation of a case to be tried by those in the clinical program in a real court.

of human affairs has survived." During the present century, the rate of acceleration took a quantum leap forward. Perhaps never before has there been a period of such fundamental change in society. This has been true not only with regard to the quantity, but also the quality, of change. At the turn of the century, far-reaching proposals were met with the comment that they were as impossible as flying. Yet the changes go deeper than the awesome gifts of applied science. Like Alice through her looking glass, we may still see the old safe world behind it—that *other* room in which everything was as solid as it seemed, where chairs were actually chairs and tables, tables. But the century of stability and order has become a lost world.

In his novel *Slaughter-House Five*, Kurt Vonnegut tells of education at an American university after World War II: "At that time they were teaching that there was absolutely no difference between anybody. . . . Another thing they taught was that nobody was ridiculous or bad or disgusting." Relativism has become the basic philosophy of a much-divided civilization. "It keeps drumming into our hearts," said Alexander Solzhenitsyn in his Nobel Lecture, "that there are no stable and universal concepts of justice . . . that all of them are fluid." The absolutes of an earlier day appear increasingly out of place in the century of Einstein and Freud.

In a relativist world, it may no longer be meaningful to talk about the ends of law. The law, according to Brooks Adams, "is the envelope with which any society surrounds itself for its protection." When the society expands or contracts regularly and slowly, the envelope tends to conform without difficulty; when the society breaks suddenly with its past, the law itself may be rent. The present civilization differs so from the civilization of our fathers that our fathers' law has, in many respects, become a sorry guide—

A Day with the Highest Court

On December 17, 1973, reflecting as usual the diversity of interests that make appeals to it, the Supreme Court took the following actions as summarized by The New York Times:

Advertising: Declined to review a decision prohibiting the Firestone Tire and Rubber Company from contending that its super sports wide oval tire "stops 25 per cent quicker" without conducting adequate scientific tests under typical road and weather conditions (No. 73-543, Firestone Tire and Rubber Company v. Federal Trade Commission).

Airlines: Let stand a decision upholding a $500 limit on airlines' liability for lost baggage against a claim by a scientist that three years of research work had been lost when his bags disappeared (No. 73-680, Sechler v. Trans World Airlines Inc.).

Civil Service: Declined to review a decision upholding the right of a Florida fire department to refuse to employ a telephone operator because she was 53 pounds heavier than the civil service weight limit on grounds that the rules were reasonably related to overall health (No. 73-548, Wolfe v. Metropolitan Dade County). Dissenting: Douglas.

Court Martial: Agreed to review a decision that an army captain could not be court-martialed for the possession and sale of marijuana when the offense involved activity off the base during off-duty hours when the officer was not in uniform (No. 72-662, Schlesinger v. Councilman).

Education: Let stand a decision reinstating a California high school English teacher who was discharged for reading to a class an essay of his own composition containing obscene language that local school officials found offensive (No. 73-620, Governing Board of Torrance v. Linduros).

Equal Rights: Agreed to review a decision that authorized disability benefits for pregnant women who had previously been denied them on the grounds that only illness and injury were covered (No. 73-640, Geduldig v. Aiello).

Agreed to review two decisions holding that the Corning Glass Works had illegally paid higher wages to male inspectors on the night shift than to female inspectors performing the same work during the day (No.

and in none more than in the values it sought to maintain. A law without values has become the secular reflection of contemporary society.

The traditional ends of law have been giving way during the present century. At the century's beginning, law's watchwords were opportunity and security. Although equality had been raised to the constitutional plane, it was construed narrowly to mean equality of opportunity in the marketplace. The security of acquired interests was emphasized, even, if need be, at the expense of the interests of the community. These ends were increasingly called into question as the century progressed.

The second half of the century appears to be a period of transition insofar as the ends of law are concerned. We seem to be moving from an ideal of individual self-assertion to one of cooperation; in the law, as in the society, competition has changed to interdependence. How many individuals are freely competing today and how many more are doing their part cooperatively, in however modest a way, as employees in some corporate or public enterprise, finding reflected glory in its greatness and giving it service in a relation suggestively like the old one of lord and man?

As indicated in Chapter VII, the evolving law is taking as its watchword the satisfaction of human wants. A maximum of abstract free self-assertion, as the measure of values, has been replaced by the maximum of human control over nature, both external nature and human nature, toward the satisfaction of human wants. The task of the law is seen as that of adjusting or harmonizing conflicting human wants or expectations so as to achieve the values of civilization with a minimum of friction and waste.

From this point of view, we may be moving toward a legal order whose primary function is distributive rather than regulatory. The law has been

73-29, Corning Glass Works v. Brennan, and No. 73-695, Brennan v. Corning Glass Works).

Labor: Held that a labor union attempting to organize a plant cannot offer to waive initiation fees for employes who agreed to join the union before the issue went to a vote and that an employer in such a situation is not required to bargain with the union if it wins the election (No. 72-1231, National Labor Relations Board v. Savair Manufacturing Company). Dissenting: White, Brennan and Blackmun.

Negligence: Dismissed an appeal involving a challenge to the legality of New Jersey's rule that 6 per cent interest must be paid on negligence judgments from the time the lawsuit was instituted until the date of the award (No. 73-685, Levine v. Busick).

Pollution: Ruled that lakeshore property owners suing an industrial polluter for damages cannot bring a class action unless they establish that each member of the class suffered the minimum $10,000 damage needed to qualify for Federal court consideration (No. 72-888, Zahn v. International Paper Company). Dissenting: Brennan, Douglas and Marshall.

Postal Service: Agreed to review a decision denying a postal union local the right to seek a court injunction against a private postal system that is reducing job opportunities for its members (No. 73-532, American Postal Workers Union v. Independent Postal System of America).

Probation: Agreed to review a decision that convicted criminals can be required to pay court charges and attorney fees before they are freed on probation (No. 73-5280, Fuller v. Oregon).

Property: Held that title to land that was submerged by riverbank erosion and then resurfaced when the river was rechanneled belonged to the original private owner and not to the state, which ordinarily has title to riverbed property (No. 72-397, Bonelli Cattle Company v. Arizona). Dissenting: Stewart. Not participating: Rehnquist.

Taxation: Agreed to review a decision denying the State of Ohio the right to levy personal property taxes against business machines built to order to foreign specifications but not yet exported (No. 73-629, National Cash Register Company v. Kosydar).

moving toward acceptance of postulates that indicate the assumption by it of such an essentially distributive role. The postulates in question permit us to assume that the financial burdens incident to life will increasingly be borne by the society and that the individual will be assured at least the minimum requirements of a standard human life.

The ends sought by these postulates are essentially economic in nature. Indeed, throughout its history American law has been primarily economics-oriented. Its overriding thrust has been to provide the economy with the legal tools and incentives needed for the economic conquest of the continent. The law, like the society, was geared toward constant increases in material quantity—the need to make everything more, the danger of making anything less.

After mid-century Americans began to realize that, in Yeats's words, "a State founded on economics alone, would be a prison house. A State must be made like a Chartres Cathedral." In the law, as in the society, men became concerned with the quality, as well as the quantity, of life. A new jural postulate started to emerge: everyone is entitled to assume that a habitable environment will be provided for those who live in the society. Such a proposition makes for a reversal in emphasis in the traditional trilogy of life, liberty, and property. For the first time, the law is assuming a positive obligation to protect the *quality* of life.

In other respects, too, the fundamental postulates of the legal order appear to be changing. A conception of equality is emerging that goes far beyond any previous notion of equality before the law. The classical distinction used to be between *égalité de droit* and *égalité de fait*—between formal or legal equality and practical or factual equality. Until the present day, the primary aim of reformers was the achievement of the first, since once that was established, the second (insofar as was desirable) would, it was thought, establish itself. Now the law recognizes this approach as too narrow. The end of law is seen to be, not only vindication of legal equality, but also provision of equality in fact with regard to more and more of the elements that make life meaningful in the contemporary community. The law is beginning to recognize a claim for conditions comparable to those enjoyed by others. The postulate that men might assume that a standard human life would be assured them may give way to a broader assumption that they are entitled to equal conditions of life as compared with their fellows.

It is still too soon, as Pound pointed out in 1959, to attempt to lay out these lines with assurance. The legal system is still too much in transition. The immediate direction, however, seems to be that of seeking to satisfy the maximum of the range of human wants or demands insofar as this may be done through the legal order.

Accomplishment of the ends deemed appropriate in the latter part of the twentieth century requires the law and its institutions to expand their role in the society at an accelerating rate. As President Nixon put it, "The nation has turned increasingly to the courts to cure deep-seated ills of our society, and the courts have responded. As a result, they have burdens unknown to the legal system a generation ago." This tendency shows no signs of decreasing. "And now," Nixon added, "we see the courts being turned to, as they

The ABA meets, 1957, in Westminster Hall, where the common law developed.

PAULUS LEESER

The architecture of the old and the new Hudson County courthouses in Jersey City, right, suggests the old and the new in law; the imposing old structure of yesterday is succeeded by one that could be an office building housing a business—which, in many ways, the practice of law has become.

should be, to enter still more fields—from offenses against the environment to new facets of consumer protection and a fresh concern for small claimants."

Expansion of the law's role brings into sharp focus the inadequacies of American legal institutions. The law cannot long continue trying to do more and more with less and less. The expanding role of law has been accompanied by increasing skepticism about its ability to keep up with society's needs. Hannah Arendt informs us that erosion of governmental authority is caused by government's inability to function properly. The inability of our legal institutions to function properly has led to widening doubts about their legitimacy, doubts that are not being resolved by the current reform measures.

The ends of law are starting to come full circle. Popular dissatisfaction has led to increasing emphasis upon the public interest in the general security and the need to make the law an effective instrument for maintaining "law and order." This is going back to the end of law in the origins of the legal order. In its beginnings law has for its end, and its sole end, to keep the peace. As it grows mature, the law acquires broader purposes, leading in our own day to ends far beyond the scope of those traditionally associated with the legal order. These more-inclusive ends will be rendered meaningless by the failure to further the public interest in the general security. A major part of the current dissatisfaction with the law is based on the ineptitude of American legal institutions in fulfilling the elementary end of any legal order: to keep the peace.

We are told by a leading judge that "The judicial process is at its core a fundamentally inefficient process." It does not follow, however, that an institution so appallingly inefficient must retain its central place in the society. Toward the end of the twentieth century, the danger is not that the rule of law will formally end, but that it will become increasingly irrelevant. Unless American legal institutions are remade to meet the needs of the community, they will be, not eliminated, but bypassed by growing segments of the society.

History confirms that courts which become bywords of incompetence may continue formally in full dress and ceremony — but the society finds means of carrying on its business without them. Maitland pointed out that, at the end of Queen Mary's reign, "the judges had nothing to do but 'to look about them.'" The inadequacies of the common law and the expense and delay involved in lawsuits had led the bulk of the community to avoid the courts at all costs. The jurisdiction of the judges was superseded by other tribunals, notably the Star Chamber and Chancery.

The law in Tudor and Stuart days met the challenge. "Then, as now," wrote Arthur T. Vanderbilt, "the administration of the common law left much to be desired. Then, as now, what was needed was more administration in the courts of justice and more of the fundamental principles of justice in the . . . tribunals." The courts reformed through infusion of then-modern concepts of law and administration and elimination of undesirable elements in the newer justice. The rest was judicialized and fitted into its proper place in the legal order. Asked Vanderbilt: "The common lawyers of the sixteenth century met their problems and mastered them. The challenge of today is so clear that it does not need to be stated. The only question is can we meet it?"

The mural "The Power of the Law," hanging in the Appellate Division of the New York State Supreme Court, was painted by Edwin Howland Blashfield in 1899, when the law in America was more sure of itself. Caught by the demands and restlessness of a changing society, the law now gropes for a relevancy to modern needs, while at the same time remaining true to the foundation of the American system and the fundamental law of the land, the United States Constitution.

"This…Constitution [is] intended to endure for ages to come and, consequently, to be adapted to the various crises of human affairs."

CHIEF JUSTICE JOHN MARSHALL,
McCulloch v. Maryland (1819)

THE CONSTITUTION OF THE UNITED STATES

We the People of the United States, in Order to form a more perfect Union, establish Justice, insure domestic Tranquility, provide for the common defence, promote the general Welfare, and secure the Blessings of Liberty to ourselves and our Posterity, do ordain and establish this CONSTITUTION for the United States of America.

ARTICLE I

SECTION 1. All legislative Powers herein granted shall be vested in a Congress of the United States, which shall consist of a Senate and House of Representatives.

SECTION 2. The House of Representatives shall be composed of Members chosen every second Year by the People of the several States, and the Electors in each State shall have the Qualifications requisite for Electors of the most numerous Branch of the State Legislature.

No Person shall be a Representative who shall not have attained to the Age of twenty-five Years, and been seven Years a Citizen of the United States, and who shall not, when elected, be an Inhabitant of that State in which he shall be chosen.

[Representatives and direct Taxes shall be apportioned among the several States which may be included within this Union, according to their respective Numbers, which shall be determined by adding to the whole Number of free Persons, including those bound to Service for a Term of Years, and excluding Indians not taxed, three fifths of all other Persons.].[1] The actual Enumeration shall be made within three Years after the first Meeting of the Congress of the United States, and within every subsequent Term of ten Years, in such Manner as they shall by Law direct. The Number of Representatives shall not exceed one for every thirty Thousand, but each State shall have at Least one Representative; and until such enumeration shall be made, the State of New Hampshire shall be entitled to chuse three, Massachusetts eight, Rhode-Island and Providence Plantations one, Connecticut five, New-York six, New Jersey four, Pennsylvania eight, Delaware one, Maryland six, Virginia ten, North Carolina five, South Carolina five, and Georgia three.

When vacancies happen in the Representation from any State, the Executive Authority thereof shall issue Writs of Election to fill such vacancies.

The House of Representatives shall chuse their Speaker and other Officers; and shall have the sole Power of Impeachment.

SECTION 3. The Senate of the United States shall be composed of two Senators from each State, [chosen by the Legislature] thereof, for six Years; and each Senator shall have one Vote.[2]

Immediately after they shall be assembled in Consequence of the first Election, they shall be divided as equally as may be into three Classes. The Seats of the Senators of the first Class shall be vacated at the Expiration of the Second Year, of the second Class at the Expiration of the fourth Year, and of the third Class at the Expiration of the sixth Year, so that one-third may be chosen every second Year; [and if Vacancies happen by Resignation, or otherwise, during the Recess of the Legislature of any State, the Executive thereof may make temporary Appointments until the next Meeting of the Legislature, which shall then fill such Vacancies].[3]

No Person shall be a Senator who shall not have attained to the Age of thirty Years, and been nine Years a Citizen of the United States, and who shall not, when elected, be an inhabitant of that State for which he shall be chosen.

The Vice President of the United States shall be President of the Senate, but shall have no Vote, unless they be equally divided.

The Senate shall chuse their other Officers, and also a President pro tempore, in the absence of the Vice President, or when he shall exercise the Office of President of the United States.

The Senate shall have the sole Power to try all Impeachments. When sitting for that Purpose, they shall be on Oath or Affirmation. When the President of the United States is tried, the Chief Justice shall preside: And no Person shall be convicted without the Concurrence of two-thirds of the Members present.

Judgment in Cases of Impeachment shall not extend further than to removal from Office, and disqualification to hold and enjoy any Office of honor, Trust, or Profit under the United States: but the Party convicted shall nevertheless be liable and subject to Indictment, Trial, Judgment, and Punishment, according to Law.

SECTION 4. The Times, Places and Manner of holding Elections for Senators and Representatives, shall be prescribed in each State by the Legislature thereof; but the Congress may at any time by Law make or alter such Regulations, except as to the Places of chusing Senators.

The Congress shall assembly at least once in every Year, and such Meeting shall [be on the first Monday in December,] unless they shall be Law appoint a different Day.[4]

SECTION 5. Each House shall be the Judge of the Elections, Returns, and Qualifications of its own Members, and a Majority of each shall constitute a Quorum to do Business; but a smaller Number may adjourn from day to day, and may be authorized to compel the Attendance of absent Members, in such Manner, and under such Penalties as each House may provide.

Each House may determine the Rules of its Proceedings, punish its Members for disorderly Behavior, and, with the Concurrence of two thirds, expel a Member.

Each House shall keep a Journal of its Proceedings, and from time to time publish the same, excepting such Parts as may in their Judgment require Secrecy; and the Yeas and Nays of the Members of either House on any question shall, at the Desire of one fifth of those Present, be entered on the Journal.

Neither House, during the Session of Congress, shall, without the Consent of the other, adjourn for more than three days, nor to any other Place than that in which the two Houses shall be sitting.

SECTION 6. The Senators and Representatives shall receive a Compensation for their Services, to be ascertained by Law,

---

[1] *The part in brackets was repealed by section 2 of amendment XIV.*
[2] *The part in brackets was repealed by section 1 of amendment XVII.*
[3] *The part in brackets was changed by clause 2 of amendment XVII.*

[4] *The part in brackets was changed by section 2 of amendment XX.*

and paid out of the Treasury of the United States. They shall in all Cases, except Treason, Felony and Breach of the Peace, be privileged from Arrest during their Attendance at the Session of their respective Houses, and in going to and returning from the same; and for any Speech or Debate in either House, they shall not be questioned in any other Place.

No Senator or Representative shall, during the Time for which he was elected, be appointed to any civil Office under the Authority of the United States, which shall have been created, or the Emoluments whereof shall have been encreased during such time; and no Person holding any Office under the United States, shall be a Member of either House during his Continuance in Office.

SECTION 7. All Bills for raising Revenue shall originate in the House of Representatives; but the Senate may propose or concur with Amendments as on other Bills.

Every Bill which shall have passed the House of Representatives and the Senate, shall, before it become a Law, be presented to the President of the United States; if he approve he shall sign it, but if not he shall return it, with his Objections to that House in which it shall have originated, who shall enter the Objections at large on their Journal, and proceed to reconsider it. If after such Reconsideration two thirds of that House shall agree to pass the Bill, it shall be sent, together with the Objections, to the other House, by which it shall likewise be reconsidered, and if approved by two thirds of that House, it shall become a Law. But in all such Cases the Votes of both Houses shall be determined by Yeas and Nays, and the Names of the Persons voting for and against the Bill shall be entered on the Journal of each House respectively. If any Bill shall not be returned by the President within ten Days (Sundays excepted) after it shall have been presented to him, the Same shall be a Law, in like Manner as if he had signed it, unless the Congress by their Adjournment prevent its Return, in which Case it shall not be a Law.

Every Order, Resolution, or Vote to which the Concurrence of the Senate and House of Representatives may be necessary (except on a question of Adjournment) shall be presented to the President of the United States; and before the Same shall take Effect, shall be approved by him, or being disapproved by him, shall be repassed by two thirds of the Senate and House of Representatives, according to the Rules and Limitations prescribed in the Case of a Bill.

SECTION 8. The Congress shall have Power To lay and collect Taxes, Duties, Imposts and Excises, to pay the Debts and provide for the common Defence and general Welfare of the United States; but all Duties, Imposts and Excises shall be uniform throughout the United States;

To borrow money on the credit of the United States;

To regulate Commerce with foreign Nations, and among the several States, and with the Indian Tribes;

To establish an uniform Rule of Naturalization, and uniform Laws on the subject of Bankruptcies throughout the United States;

To coin Money, regulate the Value thereof, and of foreign Coin, and fix the Standard of Weights and Measures;

To provide for the Punishment of counterfeiting the Securities and current Coin of the United States;

To Establish Post Offices and post Roads;

To promote the Progress of Science and useful Arts, by securing for limited Times to Authors and Inventors the exclusive Right to their respective Writings and Discoveries;

To constitute Tribunals inferior to the supreme Court;

To define and punish Piracies and Felonies committed on the high Seas, and Offenses against the Law of Nations;

To declare War, grant Letters of Marque and Reprisal, and make Rules concerning Captures on Land and Water;

To raise and support Armies, but no Appropriation of Money to that Use shall be for a longer Term than two Years;

To provide and maintain a Navy;

To make Rules for the Government and Regulation of the land and naval Forces;

To provide for calling forth the Militia to execute the Laws of the Union, suppress insurrections and repel Invasions;

To provide for organizing, arming, and disciplining the Militia, and for governing such Part of them as may be employed in the Service of the United States, reserving to the States respectively, the Appointment of the Officers, and the Authority of training the Militia according to the discipline prescribed by Congress;

To exercise exclusive Legislation in all Cases whatsoever, over such District (not exceeding ten Miles square) as may, by Cession of particular States, and the acceptance of Congress, become the Seat of the Government of the United States, and to exercise like Authority over all Places purchased by the Consent of the Legislature of the State in which the Same shall be, for the Erection of Forts, Magazines, Arsenals, dock-Yards, and other needful Buildings;—And

To make all Laws which shall be necessary and proper for carrying into Execution the foregoing Powers, and all other Powers vested by this Constitution in the Government of the United States, or in any Department or Officer thereof.

SECTION 9. The Migration or Importation of Such Persons as any of the States now existing shall think proper to admit, shall not be prohibited by the Congress prior to the Year one thousand eight hundred and eight, but a tax or duty may be imposed on such Importation, not exceeding ten dollars for each Person.

The privilege of the Writ of Habeas Corpus shall not be suspended, unless when in Cases of Rebellion or Invasion the public Safety may require it.

No Bill of Attainder or ex post facto Law shall be passed.

No capitation, or other direct, Tax shall be laid, unless in Proportion to the Census or Enumeration herein before directed to be taken.[5]

No Tax or Duty shall be laid on Articles exported from any State.

No preference shall be given by any Regulation of Commerce or Revenue to the Ports of one State over those of another: nor shall Vessels bound to, or from, one State be obliged to enter, clear, or pay Duties in another.

No money shall be drawn from the Treasury, but in Consequence of Appropriations made by Law; and a regular Statement and Account of the Receipts and Expenditures of all public Money shall be published from time to time.

No title of Nobility shall be granted by the United States: And no Person holding any Office of Profit or Trust under them, shall, without the Consent of the Congress, accept of any present, Emolument, Office, or Title, of any kind whatever, from any King, Prince, or foreign State.

SECTION 10. No State shall enter into any Treaty, Alliance, or Confederation; grant Letters of Marque and Reprisal; coin money; emit Bills of Credit; make any Thing but gold and silver Coin a Tender in Payment of Debts; pass any Bill of Attainder, ex post facto Law, or Law impairing the Obligation

[5] See also amendment XVI.

of Contracts, or grant any Title of Nobility.

No State shall, without the Consent of the Congress, lay any Imposts or Duties on Imports or Exports, except what may be absolutely necessary for executing its inspection Laws; and the net Produce of all Duties and Imposts, laid by any State on Imports or Exports, shall be for the Use of the Treasury of the United States; and all such Laws shall be subject to the Revision and Control of the Congress.

No State shall, without the Consent of Congress, lay any duty of Tonnage, keep Troops, or Ships of War in time of Peace, enter into any Agreement or Compact with another State, or with a foreign Power, or engage in War, unless actually invaded, or in such imminent Danger as will not admit of delay.

ARTICLE II

SECTION 1. The executive Power shall be vested in a President of the United States of America. He shall hold his Office during the Term of four Years, and, together with the Vice-President, chosen for the same Term, be elected, as follows:

Each State shall appoint, in such Manner as the Legislature thereof may direct, a Number of Electors, equal to the whole Number of Senators and Representatives to which the State may be entitled in the Congress: but no Senator or Representative, or Person holding an Office of Trust or Profit under the United States, shall be appointed an Elector.

[The Electors shall meet in their respective States, and vote by Ballot for two persons of whom one at least shall not be an Inhabitant of the same State with themselves. And they shall make a list of all the Persons voted for, and of the Number of Votes for each; which List they shall sign and certify, and transmit sealed to the Seat of the Government of the United States, directed to the President of the Senate. The President of the Senate shall, in the Presence of the Senate and House of Representatives, open all the Certificates, and the Votes shall then be counted. The Person having the greatest Number of votes shall be the President, if such Number by a Majority of the whole Number of Electors appointed; and if there be more than one who have such Majority, and have an equal Number of Votes, then the House of Representatives shall immediately chuse by Ballot one of them for President; and if no Person have a Majority, then from the five highest on the List the said House shall in like Manner chuse the President. But in chusing the President, the Votes shall be taken by States, the Representation from each State having one Vote; A quorum for this Purpose shall consist of a Member or Members from two-thirds of the States, and a Majority of all the States shall be necessary to a Choice. In every Case, after the Choice of the President the Person having the greatest Number of Votes of the Electors shall be the Vice President. But if there should remain two or more who have equal Votes, the Senate shall chuse from them by Ballot the Vice-President.][6]

The Congress may determine the Time of chusing the Electors and the Day on which they shall give their Votes; which Day shall be the same throughout the United States.

No person except a natural born Citizen, or a Citizen of the United States, at the time of the Adoption of this Constitution, shall be eligible to the Office of President; neither shall any Person be eligible to that Office who shall not have attained to the Age of thirty-five Years, and been fourteen Years a Resident within the United States.

In case of the removal of the President from Office, or of his Death, Resignation or Inability to discharge the Powers and Duties of the said Office, the same shall devolve on the Vice President, and the Congress may by Law provide for the Case of Removal, Death, Resignation or Inability, both of the President, and Vice President, declaring what Officer shall then act as President, and such Officer shall act accordingly, until the Disability be removed, or a President shall be elected.

The President shall, at stated Times, receive for his Services, a Compensation, which shall neither be encreased nor diminished during the Period for which he shall have been elected, and he shall not receive within that Period any other Emolument from the United States, or any of them.

Before he enter on the Execution of his Office, he shall take the following Oath or Affirmation:—"I do solemnly swear (or affirm) that I will faithfully execute the Office of President of the United States, and will to the best of my Ability, preserve, protect and defend the Constitution of the United States."

SECTION 2. The President shall be Commander in Chief of the Army and Navy of the United States, and of the Militia of the several States, when called into the actual Service of the United States; he may require the Opinion, in writing, of the principal Officer in each of the executive Departments, upon any subject relating to the Duties of their respective Offices, and he shall have Power to grant Reprieves and Pardons for Offences against the United States, except in Cases of Impeachment.

He shall have Power, by and with the Advice and Consent of the Senate, to make Treaties, provided two-thirds of the Senators present concur; and he shall nominate, and by and with the Advice and Consent of the Senate, shall appoint Ambassadors, other public Ministers and Consuls, Judges of the supreme Court, and all other Officers of the United States, whose Appointments are not herein otherwise provided for, and which shall be established by Law; but the Congress may by Law vest the Appointment of such inferior Officers, as they think proper, in the President alone, in the Courts of Law, or in the Heads of Departments.

The President shall have power to fill up all Vacancies that may happen during the Recess of the Senate, by granting Commissions which shall expire at the End of their next Session.

SECTION 3. He shall from time to time give to the Congress Information of the State of the Union, and recommend to their Consideration such Measures as he shall judge necessary and expedient; he may, on extraordinary Occasions, convene both Houses, or either of them, and in Case of Disagreement between them, with Respect to the Time of Adjournment, he may adjourn them to such Time as he shall think proper; he shall receive Ambassadors and other public Ministers; he shall take Care that the Laws be faithfully executed, and shall Commission all the Officers of the United States.

SECTION 4. The President, Vice President and all civil Officers of the United States, shall be removed from Office on Impeachment for, and Conviction of, Treason, Bribery, or other high Crimes and Misdemeanors.

ARTICLE III

SECTION 1. The judicial Power of the United States, shall be vested in one supreme Court, and in such inferior Courts as the Congress may from time to time ordain and establish. The Judges, both of the supreme and inferior Courts, shall

---

[6] *This paragraph has been superseded by amendment XII.*

hold their Offices during good Behavior, and shall, at stated Times, receive for their Services a Compensation which shall not be diminished during their Continuance in Office.

SECTION 2. The judicial Power shall extend to all Cases, in Law and Equity, arising under this Constitution, the Laws of the United States, and Treaties made, or which shall be made, under their Authority;—to all Cases affecting Ambassadors, other public Ministers and Consuls;—to all Cases of admiralty and maritime Jurisdiction;—to Controversies to which the United States shall be a Party;—to Controversies between two or more States;—between a State and Citizens of another State;[7]—between Citizens of different States;—between Citizens of the same State claiming Lands under Grants of different States, and between a State, or the Citizens thereof, and foreign States, Citizens or Subjects.

In all Cases affecting Ambassadors, other public Ministers and Consuls, and those in which a State shall be Party, the supreme Court shall have original Jurisdiction. In all the other Cases before mentioned, the supreme Court shall have appellate Jurisdiction, both as to Law and Fact, with such Exceptions, and under such Regulations as the Congress shall make.

The trial of all Crimes except in Cases of Impeachment shall be by Jury; and such Trial shall be held in the State where the said Crimes shall have been committed; but when not committed within any State, the Trial shall be at such Place or Places as the Congress may by Law have directed.

SECTION 3. Treason against the United States shall consist only in levying War against them, or, in adhering to their Enemies, giving them Aid and Comfort. No Person shall be convicted of Treason unless on the Testimony of two Witnesses to the same overt Act, or on Confession in open Court.

The Congress shall have power to declare the Punishment of Treason, but no Attainder of Treason shall work Corruption of Blood, or Forfeiture except during the Life of the Person attainted.

ARTICLE IV

SECTION 1. Full Faith and Credit shall be given in each State to the public Acts, Records, and judicial Proceedings of every other State. And the Congress may by general Laws prescribe the Manner in which such Acts, Records and Proceedings shall be proved, and the Effect thereof.

SECTION 2. The Citizens of each State shall be entitled to all Privileges and Immunities of Citizens in the several States.

A Person charged in any State with Treason, Felony, or other Crime, who shall flee from Justice, and be found in another State, shall on demand of the executive Authority of the State from which he fled, be delivered up, to be removed to the State having Jurisdiction of the Crime.

[No person held to Service or Labour in one State, under the Laws thereof, escaping into another, shall, in Consequence of any Law or Regulation therein, be discharged from such Service or Labour, but shall be delivered up on Claim of the Party to whom such Service or Labour may be due.][8]

SECTION 3. New States may be admitted by the Congress into this Union; but no new State shall be formed or erected within the Jurisdiction of any other State; nor any State be formed by the Junction of two or more States, or parts of States, without the Consent of the Legislatures of the States concerned as well as of the Congress.

The Congress shall have Power to dispose of and make all needful Rules and Regulations respecting the Territory or other Property belonging to the United States; and nothing in this Constitution shall be so construed as to Prejudice any Claims of the United States, or of any particular State.

SECTION 4. The United States shall guarantee to every State in this Union a Republican Form of Government, and shall protect each of them against Invasion; and on Application of the Legislature, or of the Executive (when the Legislature cannot be convened) against domestic Violence.

ARTICLE V

The Congress, whenever two-thirds of both Houses shall deem it necessary, shall propose Amendments to this Constitution, or, on the Application of the Legislatures of two-thirds of the several States, shall call a Convention for proposing Amendments, which, in either Case, shall be valid to all Intents and Purposes, as part of this Constitution when ratified by the Legislatures of three-fourths of the several States, or by Conventions in three-fourths thereof, as the one or the other Mode of Ratification may be proposed by the Congress; Provided that no Amendment which may be made prior to the Year One thousand eight hundred and eight shall in any Manner affect the first and fourth Clauses in the Ninth Section of the first Article; and that no State, without its Consent, shall be deprived of its equal Suffrage in the Senate.

ARTICLE VI

All Debts contracted and Engagements entered into, before the Adoption of this Constitution shall be as valid against the United States under this Constitution, as under the Confederation.

This Constitution, and the Laws of the United States which shall be made in Pursuance thereof; and all Treaties made, or which shall be made, under the Authority of the United States, shall be the supreme Law of the Land; and the Judges in every State shall be bound thereby, any Thing in the Constitution or Laws of any State to the Contrary notwithstanding.

The Senators and Representatives before mentioned, and the Members of the several State Legislatures, and all executive and judicial Officers, both of the United States and of the several States, shall be bound by Oath or Affirmation, to support this Constitution; but no religious Test shall ever be required as a Qualification to any Office or public Trust under the United States.

ARTICLE VII

The Ratification of the Conventions of nine States, shall be sufficient for the Establishment of this Constitution between the States so ratifying the Same.

DONE in Convention by the Unanimous Consent of the States present the Seventeenth Day of September in the Year of our Lord one thousand seven hundred and Eighty seven and of the Independence of the United States of America the Twelfth. IN WITNESS whereof We have hereto subscribed our Names,

Declared in operation September 13, 1788, by resolution of the Continental Congress after ratification by eleven states.

AMENDMENT I

Congress shall make no law respecting an establishment of religion, or prohibiting the free exercise thereof; or abridging the freedom of speech, or of the press; or the right of the people peaceably to assemble and to petition the Government for a redress of grievances.

[7] This clause has been affected by amendment XI.
[8] This paragraph has been superseded by amendment XIII.

AMENDMENT II

A well regulated Militia, being necessary to the security of a free State, the right of the people to keep and bear Arms, shall not be infringed.

AMENDMENT III

No Soldier shall, in time of peace be quartered in any house, without the consent of the Owner, not in time of war, but in a manner to be prescribed by law.

AMENDMENT IV

The right of the people to be secure in their persons, houses, papers, and effects, against unreasonable searches and seizures, shall not be violated, and no Warrants shall issue, but upon probable cause, supported by Oath or affirmation and particularly describing the place to be searched, and the persons or things to be seized.

AMENDMENT V

No person shall be held to answer for a capital, or otherwise infamous crime, unless on a presentment or indictment of a Grand Jury, except in cases arising in the land or naval forces, or in the Militia, when in actual service in time of War or public danger; nor shall any person be subject for the same offence to be twice put in jeopardy of life of limb; nor shall be compelled in any criminal case to be a witness against himself, nor be deprived of life, liberty, or property, without due process of law; nor shall private property be taken for public use, without just compensation.

AMENDMENT VI

In all criminal prosecutions, the accused shall enjoy the right to a speedy and public trial, by an impartial jury of the State and district wherein the crime shall have been committed, which district shall have been previously ascertained by law, and to be informed of the nature and cause of the accusation: to be confronted with the witnesses against him; to have compulsory process for obtaining witnesses in his favor, and to have the Assistance of Counsel for his defence.

AMENDMENT VII

In suits at common law, where the value in controversy shall exceed twenty dollars, the right of trial by jury shall be preserved, and no fact tried by jury, shall be otherwise reexamined in any Court of the United States, than according to the rules of the common law.

AMENDMENT VIII

Excessive bail shall not be required, nor excessive fines imposed, nor cruel and unusual punishments inflicted.

AMENDMENT IX

The enumeration in the Constitution, of certain rights, shall not be construed to deny or disparage others retained by the people.

AMENDMENT X

The powers not delegated to the United States by the Constitution, nor prohibited by it to the States, are reserved to the States respectively, or to the people.

Ratification of first ten amendments—the Bill of Rights— completed December 15, 1791.

AMENDMENT XI

The Judicial power of the United States shall not be construed to extend to any suit in law or equity, commenced or prosecuted against one of the United States by Citizens of another State, or by Citizens or Subjects of any Foreign State.

Declared ratified January 8, 1798.

AMENDMENT XII

The electors shall meet in their respective states and vote by ballot for President and Vice-President, one of whom, at least, shall not be an inhabitant of the same state with themselves; they shall name in their ballots the person voted for as President, and in distinct ballots the person voted for as Vice-President, and they shall make distinct lists of all persons voted for as President, and of all persons voted for as Vice-President, and of the number of votes for each, which lists they shall sign and certify, and transmit sealed to the seat of the government of the United States, directed to the President of the Senate;—The President of the Senate shall, in presence of the Senate and House of Representatives, open all the certificates and the votes shall then be counted;— The person having the greatest number of votes for President, shall be the President, if such number be a majority of the whole number of Electors appointed; and if no person have such majority, then from the persons having the highest numbers not exceeding three on the list of those voted for as President, the House of Representatives shall choose immediately, by ballot, the President. But in choosing the President, the votes shall be taken by states, the representation from each state having one vote; a quorum for this purpose shall consist of a member or members from two-thirds of the states, and a majority of all the states shall be necessary to a choice. [And if the House of Representatives shall not choose a President whenever the right of choice shall devolve upon them, before the fourth day of March next following, then the Vice-President shall act as President, as in the case of the death or other constitutional disability of the President.][9]—The person having the greatest number of votes as Vice-President, shall be the Vice-President, if such number be a majority of the whole number of Electors appointed, and if no person have a majority, then from the two highest numbers on the list, the Senate shall choose the Vice-President; a quorum for the purpose shall consist of two-thirds of the whole number of Senators, and a majority of the whole number shall be necessary to a choice. But no person constitutionally ineligible to the office of President shall be eligible to that of Vice-President of the United States.

Declared ratified September 25, 1804.

AMENDMENT XIII

SECTION 1. Neither slavery nor involuntary servitude, except as a punishment for crime whereof the party shall have been duly convicted, shall exist within the United States, or any place subject to their jurisdiction.

SECTION 2. Congress shall have power to enforce this article by appropriate legislation.

Declared ratified December 18, 1865.

AMENDMENT XIV

SECTION 1. All persons born or naturalized in the United States, and subject to the jurisdiction thereof, are citizens of the United States and of the State wherein they reside. No State shall make or enforce any law which shall abridge the privileges or immunities of citizens of the United States; nor shall any State deprive any person of life, liberty, or property, without due process of law; nor deny to any person within its jurisdiction the equal protection of the laws.

SECTION 2. Representatives shall be apportioned among the several States according to their respective numbers, counting the whole number of persons in each State, excluding Indians not taxed. But when the right to vote at any election for the choice of electors for President and Vice-President of the United States, Representatives in Congress, the Executive and Judicial officers of a State, or the members of the Legislature thereof, is denied to any of the male inhabitants of such State, being twenty-one years of age, and citizens of the United States, or in any way abridged, except for participation in rebellion, or other crime, the basis of representation therein shall be reduced in the proportion which the number of such male citizens shall bear to the whole number of male citizens twenty-one years of age in such State.

SECTION 3. No person shall be a Senator or Representative in Congress, or elector of President and Vice-President, or

---

[9] *The part in brackets has been superseded by section 3 of amendment XX.*

hold any office, civil or military, under the United States, or under any State, who, having previously taken an oath, as a member of Congress, or as an officer of the United States, or as a member of any State legislature, or as an executive or judicial officer of any State, to support the Constitution of the United States, shall have engaged in insurrection or rebellion against the same, or given aid or comfort to the enemies thereof. But Congress may by a vote of two-thirds of each House, remove such disability.

SECTION 4. The validity of the public debt of the United States, authorized by law, including debts incurred for payment of pensions and bounties for services in suppressing insurrection or rebellion, shall not be questioned. But neither the United States nor any State shall assume or pay any debt or obligation incurred in aid of insurrection or rebellion against the United States, or any claim for the loss or emancipation of any slave; but all such debts, obligations and claims shall be held illegal and void.

SECTION 5. The Congress shall have power to enforce, by appropriate legislation, the provisions of this article.

Declared ratified July 28, 1868.

AMENDMENT XV

SECTION 1. The right of citizens of the United States to vote shall not be denied or abridged by the United States or by any State on account of race, color, or previous condition of servitude—

SECTION 2. The Congress shall have power to enforce this article by appropriate legislation.

Declared ratified March 30, 1870.

AMENDMENT XVI

The Congress shall have power to lay and collect taxes on incomes, from whatever source derived, without apportionment among the several States, and without regard to any census or enumeration.

Declared ratified February 25, 1913.

AMENDMENT XVII

The Senate of the United States shall be composed of two Senators from each State, elected by the people thereof, for six years; and each Senator shall have one vote. The electors in each State shall have the qualifications requisite for electors of the most numerous branch of the State legislatures.

When vacancies happen in the representation of any State in the Senate, the executive authority of such State shall issue writs of election to fill such vacancies: *Provided,* That the legislature of any State may empower the executive thereof to make temporary appointments until the people fill the vacancies by election as the legislature may direct.

This amendment shall not be so construed as to affect the election or term of any Senator chosen before it becomes valid as part of the Constitution.

Declared ratified May 31, 1913.

AMENDMENT XVIII

[SECTION 1. After one year from the ratification of this article the manufacture, sale, or transportation of intoxicating liquors within, the importation thereof into, or the exportation thereof from the United States and all territory subject to the jurisdiction thereof for beverage purposes is hereby prohibited.

[SECTION 2. The Congress and the several States shall have concurrent power to enforce this article by appropriate legislation.

[SECTION 3. This article shall be inoperative unless it shall have been ratified as an amendment to the Constitution by the legislatures of the several States, as provided in the Constitution, within seven years from the date of the submission hereof to the States by the Congress.][10]

Declared ratified January 29, 1919.

AMENDMENT XIX

The right of citizens of the United States to vote shall not be denied or abridged by the United States or by any State on account of sex.

Congress shall have power to enforce this article by appropriate legislation.

Declared ratified August 26, 1920.

AMENDMENT XX

SECTION 1. The terms of the President and Vice-President shall end at noon on the 20th day of January, and the terms of Senators and Representatives at noon on the 3d day of January, of the years in which such terms would have ended if this article had not been ratified; and the terms of their successors shall then begin.

SECTION 2. The Congress shall assemble at least once in every year, and such meeting shall begin at noon on the 3d day of January, unless they shall by law appoint a different day.

SECTION 3. If, at the time for the beginning of the term of the President, the President elect shall have died, the Vice-President elect shall become President. If a President shall not have been chosen before the time fixed for the beginning of his term, or if the President elect shall have failed to qualify, then the Vice-President elect shall act as President until a President shall have qualified; and the Congress may by law provide for the case wherein neither a President elect nor a Vice-President elect shall have qualified, declaring who shall then act as President, or the manner in which one who is to act shall be selected, and such person shall act accordingly until a President or Vice-President shall have qualified.

SECTION 4. The Congress may by law provide for the case of the death of any of the persons from whom the House of Representatives may choose a President whenever the right of choice shall have devolved upon them and for the case of the death of any of the persons from whom the Senate may choose a Vice-President whenever the right of choice shall have devolved upon them.

SECTION 5. Sections 1 and 2 shall take effect on the 15th day of October following the ratification of this article.

SECTION 6. This article shall be inoperative unless it shall have been ratified as an amendment to the Constitution by the legislatures of three-fourths of the several States within seven years from the date of its submission.

Declared ratified February 6, 1933.

AMENDMENT XXI

SECTION 1. The eighteenth article of amendment to the Constitution of the United States is hereby repealed.

SECTION 2. The transportation or importation into any State, Territory, or possession of the United States for delivery or use therein of intoxicating liquors, in violation of the laws thereof, is hereby prohibited.

SECTION 3. This article shall be inoperative unless it shall have been ratified as an amendment to the Constitution by conventions in the several States, as provided in the Constitution, within seven years from the date of the submission hereof to the States by the Congress.

Declared ratified December 5, 1933.

AMENDMENT XXII

SECTION 1. No person shall be elected to the office of the President more than twice, and no person who has held the office of President, or acted as President, for more than two years of a term to which some other person was elected President shall be elected to the office of the President more than once. But this article shall not apply to any person holding the office of President when this Article was proposed by the Congress, and shall not prevent any person who may be

---

[10] *Amendment XVIII was repealed by section 1 of amendment XXI.*

holding the office of President, or acting as President, during the term within which this Article becomes operative from holding the office of President or acting as President during the remainder of such term.

SECTION 2. This article shall be inoperative unless it shall have been ratified as an amendment to the Constitution by the legislatures of three-fourths of the several States within seven years from the date of its submission to the States by the Congress.

Declared ratified March 1, 1951.

AMENDMENT XXIII

SECTION 1. The District constituting the seat of Government of the United States shall appoint in such manner as the Congress may direct:

A number of electors of President and Vice President equal to the whole number of Senators and Representatives in Congress to which the District would be entitled if it were a State, but in no event more than the least populous State; they shall be in addition to those appointed by the States, but they shall be considered, for the purposes of the election of President and Vice President, to be electors appointed by a State; and they shall meet in the District and perform such duties as provided by the twelfth article of amendment.

SECTION 2. The Congress shall have power to enforce this article by appropriate legislation.

Declared ratified April 3, 1961.

AMENDMENT XXIV

SECTION 1. The right of citizens of the United States to vote in any primary or other election for President or Vice President, for electors for President or Vice President, or for Senator or Representative in Congress, shall not be denied or abridged by the United States or any State by reason of failure to pay any poll tax or other tax.

SECTION 2. The Congress shall have power to enforce this article by appropriate legislation.

Declared ratified February 4, 1962.

AMENDMENT XXV

SECTION 1. In case of the removal of the President from office or of his death or resignation, the Vice President shall become President.

SECTION 2. Whenever there is a vacancy in the office of the Vice President, the President shall nominate a Vice President who shall take office upon confirmation by a majority vote of both Houses of Congress.

SECTION 3. Whenever the President transmits to the President pro tempore of the Senate and the Speaker of the House of Representatives his written declaration that he is unable to discharge the powers and duties of his office, and until

he transmits to them a written declaration to the contrary, such powers and duties shall be discharged by the Vice President as Acting President.

SECTION 4. Whenever the Vice President and a majority of either the principal officers of the executive departments or of such other body as Congress may by law provide, transmit to the President pro tempore of the Senate and the Speaker of the House of Representatives their written declaration that the President is unable to discharge the powers and duties of his office, the Vice President shall immediately assume the powers and the duties of the office as Acting President.

Thereafter, when the President transmits to the President pro tempore of the Senate and the Speaker of the House of Representatives his written declaration that no inability exists, he shall resume the powers and duties of his office unless the Vice President and a majority of either the principal officers of the executive department or of such other body as Congress may by law provide, transmit within four days to the President pro tempore of the Senate and the Speaker of the House of Representatives their written declaration that the President is unable to discharge the powers and duties of his office. Thereupon Congress shall decide the issue, assembling within forty-eight hours for that purpose if not in session. If the Congress, within twenty-one days after receipt of the latter written declaration, or, if Congress is not in session, within twenty-one days after Congress is required to assemble, determines by two-thirds vote of both Houses that the President is unable to discharge the powers and duties of his office, the Vice President shall continue to discharge the same as Acting President; otherwise, the President shall resume the powers and duties of his office.

Declared ratified February 10, 1967.

AMENDMENT XXVI

SECTION 1. The right of citizens of the United States, who are eighteen years of age or older, to vote shall not be denied or abridged by the United States or by any State on account of age.

SECTION 2. The Congress shall have power to enforce this article by appropriate legislation.

Declared ratified July 1, 1971.

PROPOSED AMENDMENT XXVII

SECTION 1. Equality of rights under the law shall not be denied or abridged by the United States or by any State on account of sex.

SECTION 2. The Congress shall have the power to enforce, by appropriate legislation, the provisions of this Article.

Passed Congress March 24, 1972.

Justices of the United States Supreme Court

(Chief Justices are set in capital letters.)

NAME AND STATE	SERVICE TERM	YEARS	BORN	DIED	APPOINTED BY
JOHN JAY, N.Y.	1789-1795	5	1745	1829	Washington
John Rutledge, S.C.	1789-1791	1	1739	1800	Washington
(REJECTED AS CHIEF JUSTICE, 1795)					
William Cushing, Mass.	1789-1810	20	1732	1810	Washington
James Wilson, Pa.	1789-1798	8	1742	1798	Washington
John Blair, Va.	1789-1796	6	1732	1800	Washington
James Iredell, N.C.	1790-1799	9	1751	1799	Washington
Thomas Johnson, Md.	1791-1793	1	1732	1819	Washington
William Paterson, N.J.	1793-1806	13	1745	1806	Washington
Samuel Chase, Md.	1796-1811	15	1741	1811	Washington
OLIVER ELLSWORTH, Conn.	1796-1799	4	1745	1807	Washington
Bushrod Washington, Va.	1798-1829	31	1762	1829	J. Adams
Alfred Moore, N.C.	1799-1804	4	1755	1810	J. Adams
JOHN MARSHALL, Va.	1801-1835	34	1755	1835	J. Adams
William Johnson, S.C.	1804-1834	30	1771	1834	Jefferson
Brockholst Livingston, N.Y.	1806-1823	16	1757	1823	Jefferson
Thomas Todd, Ky.	1807-1826	18	1765	1826	Jefferson
Joseph Story, Mass.	1811-1845	33	1779	1845	Madison
Gabriel Duval, Md.	1812-1835	22	1752	1844	Madison
Smith Thompson, N.Y.	1823-1843	20	1768	1843	Monroe
Robert Trimble, Ky.	1826-1828	2	1777	1828	J. Q. Adams
John McLean, Ohio	1829-1861	32	1785	1861	Jackson
Henry Baldwin, Pa.	1830-1844	14	1780	1844	Jackson
James M. Wayne, Ga.	1835-1867	32	1790	1867	Jackson
ROGER B. TANEY, Md.	1836-1864	28	1777	1864	Jackson
Philip P. Barbour, Va.	1836-1841	4	1783	1841	Jackson
John Catron, Tenn.	1837-1865	28	1786	1865	Jackson
John McKinley, Ala.	1837-1852	15	1780	1852	Van Buren
Peter V. Daniel, Va.	1841-1860	19	1784	1860	Van Buren
Samuel Nelson, N.Y.	1845-1872	27	1792	1873	Tyler
Levi Woodbury, N.H.	1845-1851	5	1789	1851	Polk
Robert C. Grier, Pa.	1846-1870	23	1794	1870	Polk
Benj. R. Curtis, Mass.	1851-1857	6	1809	1874	Fillmore
John A. Campbell, Ala.	1853-1861	8	1811	1889	Pierce
Nathan Clifford, Me.	1858-1881	23	1803	1881	Buchanan
Noah H. Swayne, Ohio	1862-1881	18	1804	1884	Lincoln
Samuel F. Miller, Iowa	1862-1890	28	1816	1890	Lincoln
David Davis, Ill.	1862-1877	14	1815	1886	Lincoln
Stephen J. Field, Calif.	1863-1897	34	1816	1899	Lincoln
SALMON P. CHASE, Ohio	1864-1873	8	1808	1873	Lincoln
William Strong, Pa.	1870-1880	10	1808	1895	Grant
Joseph P. Bradley, N.J.	1870-1892	21	1813	1892	Grant
Ward Hunt, N.Y.	1873-1882	9	1810	1886	Grant
MORRISON R. WAITE, Ohio	1874-1888	14	1816	1888	Grant
John M. Harlan, Ky.	1877-1911	34	1833	1911	Hayes
William B. Woods, Ga.	1881-1887	6	1824	1887	Hayes
Stanley Matthews, Ohio	1881-1889	7	1824	1889	Garfield
Horace Gray, Mass.	1882-1902	20	1828	1902	Arthur
Samuel Blatchford, N.Y.	1882-1893	11	1820	1893	Arthur
Lucius Q. C. Lamar, Miss.	1888-1893	5	1825	1893	Cleveland
MELVILLE W. FULLER, Ill.	1888-1910	21	1833	1910	Cleveland
David J. Brewer, Kan.	1890-1910	20	1837	1910	Harrison
Henry B. Brown, Mich.	1891-1906	15	1836	1913	Harrison
George Shiras, Jr., Pa.	1892-1903	10	1832	1924	Harrison
Howell E. Jackson, Tenn.	1893-1895	2	1832	1895	Harrison
Edward D. White, La.	1894-1921	27	1845	1921	Cleveland
(CHIEF JUSTICE, 1910-1921)					
Rufus W. Peckham, N.Y.	1896-1909	13	1838	1909	Cleveland
Joseph McKenna, Calif.	1898-1925	26	1843	1926	McKinley
Oliver W. Holmes, Mass.	1902-1932	29	1841	1935	T. Roosevelt
William R. Day, Ohio	1903-1922	19	1849	1923	T. Roosevelt
William H. Moody, Mass.	1906-1910	3	1853	1917	T. Roosevelt
Horace H. Lurton, Tenn.	1910-1914	4	1844	1914	Taft
Charles E. Hughes, N.Y.	1910-1916	5	1862	1948	Taft
Willis Van Devanter, Wyo.	1911-1937	26	1859	1941	Taft
Joseph R. Lamar, Ga.	1911-1916	5	1857	1916	Taft
Mahlon Pitney, N.J.	1912-1922	10	1858	1924	Taft
Jas. C. McReynolds, Tenn.	1914-1941	26	1862	1946	Wilson
Louis D. Brandeis, Mass.	1916-1939	22	1856	1941	Wilson
John H. Clarke, Ohio	1916-1922	5	1857	1945	Wilson
WILLIAM H. TAFT, Conn.	1921-1930	8	1857	1930	Harding
George Sutherland, Utah	1922-1938	15	1862	1942	Harding
Pierce Butler, Minn.	1922-1939	16	1866	1939	Harding
Edward T. Sanford, Tenn.	1923-1930	7	1865	1930	Harding
Harlan F. Stone, N.Y.	1925-1946	21	1872	1946	Coolidge
(CHIEF JUSTICE, 1941-1946)					
CHARLES E. HUGHES, N.Y.	1930-1941	11	1862	1948	Hoover
Owen J. Roberts, Penn.	1930-1945	15	1875	1955	Hoover
Benjamin N. Cardozo, N.Y.	1932-1938	6	1870	1938	Hoover
Hugo L. Black, Ala.	1937-1971	34	1886	1971	F. Roosevelt
Stanley F. Reed, Ky.	1938-1957	19	1884	.....	F. Roosevelt
Felix Frankfurter, Mass.	1939-1962	23	1882	1965	F. Roosevelt
William O. Douglas, Conn.	1939-....	...	1898	.....	F. Roosevelt
Frank Murphy, Mich.	1940-1949	9	1890	1949	F. Roosevelt
James F. Byrnes, S.C.	1941-1942	1	1879	1972	F. Roosevelt
Robert H. Jackson, N.Y.	1941-1954	12	1892	1954	F. Roosevelt
Wiley B. Rutledge, Iowa	1943-1949	6	1894	1949	F. Roosevelt
Harold H. Burton, Ohio	1945-1958	13	1888	1964	Truman
FRED M. VINSON, Kentucky	1946-1953	7	1890	1953	Truman
Tom C. Clark, Texas	1949-1967	18	1899	.....	Truman
Sherman Minton, Indiana	1949-1956	7	1890	1965	Truman
EARL WARREN, Calif.	1953-1969	16	1891	1974	Eisenhower
John Marshall Harlan, N.Y.	1955-1971	16	1899	1971	Eisenhower
William J. Brennan, Jr., N.J.	1956-....	...	1906	.....	Eisenhower
Charles E. Whittaker, Mo.	1957-1962	5	1901	.....	Eisenhower
Potter Stewart, Ohio	1958-....	...	1917	.....	Eisenhower
Byron R. White, Colo.	1962-....	...	1917	.....	Kennedy
Arthur J. Goldberg, Ill.	1962-1965	3	1908	.....	Kennedy
Abe Fortas, Tenn.	1965-1969	4	1910	.....	Johnson
Thurgood Marshall, N.Y.	1967-....	...	1908	.....	Johnson
WARREN E. BURGER, Va.	1969-....	...	1907	.....	Nixon
Harry A. Blackmun, Minn.	1970-....	...	1908	.....	Nixon
Lewis F. Powell, Jr., Va.	1971-....	...	1907	.....	Nixon
William H. Rehnquist, Ariz.	1971-....	...	1924	.....	Nixon

Important Law Cases in American History

(With references to the pages on which they are mentioned)

Abrams v. United States, 250 U.S. 616 (1919).
Anarchists who had distributed leaflets urging workers not to produce munitions for American intervention in Russia were convicted for publishing language inciting resistance to the war effort. The conviction was affirmed over the dissent by Justice Holmes urging that there was no clear and present danger that the leaflets would hinder the war effort. (See page 214.)

Adamson v. California, 332 U.S. 46 (1947).
A state conviction was upheld against the claim that it violated the privilege against self-incrimination. The case is noted for Justice Hugo Black's dissent, urging that the Fourteenth Amendment makes the entire Bill of Rights binding upon the states. (See page 212.)

Allgeyer v. Louisiana, 165 U.S. 578 (1897).
A state law which prohibited an individual from contracting with an out-of-state insurance company for insurance of property within the state was held violative of due process. The right to contract outside the state is part of the liberty protected by due process. This decision marked the acceptance by the Supreme Court of the doctrine of substantive due process. (See pages 135 and 149.)

Baker v. Carr, 369 U.S. 186 (1962).
An action attacking the apportionment of a state legislature as violative of equal protection was held within the jurisdiction of federal courts. Under this decision, the question of the validity of legislative apportionments is no longer treated as a political question beyond judicial cognizance. (See page 291.)

Bank of Augusta v. Earle, 13 Pet. 519 (U.S. 1839).
An action in federal court in Alabama on bills of exchange by out-of-state corporations was held maintainable. The decision reversed a lower court ruling that corporations could do business only in states in which they were chartered. (See page 87.)

Barron v. Mayor of Baltimore, 7 Pet. 243 (U.S. 1833).
An action to recover compensation for the taking of property under the Fifth Amendment was held not maintainable against a state. The Fifth Amendment, as part of the Bill of Rights, is a limitation solely upon the federal government, not the states. (See page 121.)

Bell v. Maryland, 378 U.S. 226 (1964).
The conviction of Negro students who participated in a "sit-in" protest at a restaurant for violating trespass law was reversed because of the enactment of a later state law making it unlawful to refuse restaurant service because of race. Justice Douglas's concurring opinion would extend Fourteenth Amendment requirements to corporations. (See page 336.)

Brown v. Board of Education, 347 U.S. 483 (1954).
Action by Negroes to secure admission to public schools on a nonsegregated basis was held maintainable under the Fourteenth Amendment. Segregation is inherently discriminatory and hence violative of the guaranty of equal protection. (See page 289.)

Brown v. Kendall, 6 Cush. 292 (Mass. 1850).
An action of trespass for assault and battery where a verdict for a plaintiff was set aside. If a defendant can show he exercised due care, he should prevail. (See page 78.)

Camara v. Municipal Court, 387 U.S. 523 (1967).
A conviction for refusing to permit the warrantless inspection of a house by a housing inspector was reversed. Inspection of a home is a search within the Fourth Amendment and may not be conducted without a warrant. (See page 319.)

Charles River Bridge v. Warren Bridge, 11 Pet. 420 (U.S. 1837).
The grant of a charter to build and operate a bridge near another bridge for which a charter had previously been granted was held not to impair an obligation of contract in the first charter. This was the first important case laying down the rule that public contracts are are to be strictly construed in favor of states. (See pages 58 and 66.)

Civil Rights Cases, 109 U.S. 3 (1883).
The Civil Rights Act of 1875 prohibiting racial discrimination in hotels, theaters, and other public accommodations was held not authorized by the Fourteenth Amendment. The amendment bars only state action and has no application to discrimination by private individuals. (See page 129.)

Colonnade Catering Corp. v. United States, 397 U.S. 72 (1970).
A petition for the return of liquor seized by federal agents as a result of a forcible warrantless inspection was granted. Congress could authorize warrantless inspections in a closely regulated field such as liquor, but had not done so. (See page 319.)

Commonwealth v. Alger, 7 Cush. 53 (Mass. 1851).
A state law fixing lines in a harbor beyond which wharfs may not be built was upheld. The opinion contains one of the first definitions of the police power. (See page 66.)

Dartmouth College Case (Dartmouth College v. Woodward), 4 Wheat. 518 (U.S. 1819).
A state law which infringed upon a corporate charter was held invalid. A corporate charter is a contract which comes within the constitutional prohibition against impairing the obligation of contracts. (See pages 58 and 86.)

Dennis v. United States, 341 U.S. 494 (1951).
The conviction of Communist leaders for violating the Smith Act prohibition against teaching and advocating forcible overthrow of the government was affirmed. The decision involved the most important application of the Clear and Present Danger Test first enunciated by Justice Holmes. (See page 210.)

Dred Scott Case (Dred Scott v. Sandford), 19 How. 393 (U.S. 1857).
A Negro, a slave under Missouri law, was held unable to sue

for his freedom in a federal court in Missouri. The decision involved two main holdings: (1) A Negro is not a citizen within the Constitution; (2) a slave could not become free by residence in territory covered by the Missouri Compromise, since Congress violated due process in enacting the Compromise. The latter holding involved the first use of the doctrine of substantive due process by the Supreme Court. (See page 70.)

Endo Case (Ex parte Endo), 323 U.S. 283 (1944).
An emergency which may have justified the exclusion of persons of Japanese ancestry from the West Coast after Pearl Harbor did not justify the continued detention of a concededly loyal citizen after her loyalty was established, and her unconditional release was ordered. (See page 209.)

Farwell v. Boston and Worcester Rail Road, 4 Metc. 49 (Mass. 1842).
An action by an employee for injuries received in consequence of the carelessness of a fellow employee was held not maintainable. The decision lays down the fellow-servant rule, that an employer is not liable for injuries caused by the negligence of a fellow employee. (See page 82.)

Genesee Chief (Genesee Chief v. Fitzhugh), 12 How. 443 (U.S. 1851).
An act of Congress extending admiralty jurisdiction of federal courts to inland waterways, such as Lake Ontario, was upheld. The Court refused to follow English rule confining admiralty jurisdiction to high seas and rivers only as far as tidal flow extended. (See page 29.)

Gibbons v. Ogden, 9 Wheat. 1 (U.S. 1824).
A New York grant of a monopoly to operate steamboats between New York and New Jersey was held invalid as it was in conflict with an act of Congress regulating coasting trade. The case was noted for its broad opinion on the scope of the congressional commerce power. (See pages 53 and 55.)

Gideon v. Wainwright, 372 U.S. 335 (1963).
A state conviction was reversed because of a court's failure to furnish counsel for an indigent defendant. The decision holds the states to the requirements laid down by the Sixth Amendment with regard to the right to counsel. (See page 286.)

Goldberg v. Kelly, 397 U.S. 254 (1970).
A state's termination of welfare grants without a prior hearing was held violative of due process. Welfare payments may no longer be considered a mere "privilege" subject only to whatever procedural requirements are imposed by the legislature. (See page 303.)

Granger Cases (Munn v. Illinois), 94 U.S. 113 (1877).
State laws fixing the rates of grain elevators and railroads were held constitutional. When one devotes his property to a business in which the public is directly interested, he is subject to regulation for the common good to the extent of the interest he has thus created. (See pages 134 and 178.)

Griswold v. Connecticut, 381 U.S. 479 (1965).
A state law prohibiting the use of contraceptives and the giving of medical advice in such use was ruled unconstitutional as it applied to married couples. The law constituted an invalid intrusion upon marital privacy. (See page 304.)

Income Tax Case (Pollock v. Farmers' Loan & Trust Co.), 157 U.S. 429 (1895).
The federal income tax law was held unconstitutional. This was later overruled by passage of the Sixteenth Amendment. The case was noted for the extreme individualist argument of Joseph H. Choate and the concurring opinion of Justice Field. (See page 140.)

Ives v. South Buffalo Ry. Co., 201 N.Y. 271 (1911).
New York's workmen's compensation law was held violative of due process. The law imposes liability upon an employer who has done no wrong and involves an unconstitutional state interference with the relations between employer and employee. (See page 193.)

Jones v. Alfred H. Mayer Co., 392 U.S. 409 (1968).
An action for refusal to sell a home in a housing development because of race was held maintainable under a federal law providing that all citizens shall have the same right to purchase property as is enjoyed by white citizens. The statute is a valid exercise of congressional power under the Thirteenth Amendment to prohibit incidents of slavery. (See page 125.)

King v. Smith, 392 U.S. 302 (1968).
An Alabama "substitute father" regulation, requiring the disqualification of children from aid to dependent children if their mother cohabits with a man not obligated to provide support, was held invalid. The decision strikes down the "man in the house" rule which had been followed in welfare cases. (See page 313.)

Korematsu v. United States, 323 U.S. 214 (1944).
The exclusion of persons of Japanese ancestry from the West Coast after Pearl Harbor was upheld. Such exclusion orders could validly be issued by military authorities to deal with the danger of a threatened Japanese attack. (See page 208.)

License Cases, 5 How. 504 (U.S. 1847).
State laws forbidding the unlicensed sale of liquor were held invalid as conflicting with federal laws and treaties providing for the importation of liquor. The case was noted for the use of the term "police power" in Chief Justice Taney's opinion. (See page 57.)

Loan Association v. Topeka, 20 Wall. 655 (U.S. 1875).
A state law which authorized a grant by the city to a manufacturing company to induce the latter to locate a factory in the city was held unconstitutional. The use of the taxing power must be for a public, not a private, purpose. (See page 165.)

Lochner v. New York, 198 U.S. 45 (1905).
A state law prescribing maximum hours for bakers was held violative of due process. Such a law must fall as an arbitrary interference with freedom of contract. (See pages 137 and 140.)

McCulloch v. Maryland, 4 Wheat. 316 (U.S. 1819).
A Maryland tax on notes issued by the Bank of the United States was held invalid as a tax on a federal instrumentality. The court upheld the congressional power to create a bank, even though it was not expressly given in the Constitution, thus accepting the doctrine of implied powers stated by

Hamilton. It also gave effect to the Supremacy Clause, holding that federal instrumentalities are immune from state taxation or other interferences with their operation. (See pages 52 and 55.)

Mapp v. Ohio, 367 U.S. 643 (1961).
A state conviction was reversed because illegally seized evidence had been admitted at the trial. The decision holds the states to the standards laid down for searches and seizures by the Fourth Amendment. (See page 286.)

Marbury v. Madison, 1 Cranch 137 (U.S. 1803).
An original action in the Supreme Court for a writ of mandamus to compel the delivery of a commission to a justice of the peace in the District of Columbia. Relief was denied on the ground that the act of Congress granting the Supreme Court original jurisdiction in mandamus cases was contrary to Article III of the Constitution. This was the first Supreme Court decision holding an act of Congress unconstitutional. (See pages 49 and 54.)

Miranda v. Arizona, 384 U.S. 436 (1966).
A state conviction was reversed because of the use of statements given to the police during an interrogation. During such police interrogation, the individual has the right to the presence of an attorney, retained or appointed. He may be questioned without an attorney only if he has knowingly waived his right to have counsel at his side. (See page 288.)

Munn v. Illinois. See Granger Cases.

National Labor Relations Board v. Jones & Laughlin Steel Co., 301 U.S. 1 (1937).
The National Labor Relations Act was upheld as a valid exercise of federal power to regulate commerce. The decision marks the beginning of the recent broad interpretation of the Commerce Clause. (See page 200.)

Northern Securities Case (Northern Securities Co. v. United States), 193 U.S. 197 (1904).
The Sherman Anti-Trust Act was held applicable to a combination by stockholders in two competing railway companies to form a holding corporation to acquire a controlling interest in the railway companies. (See page 191.)

Plessy v. Ferguson, 163 U.S. 537 (1896).
A state law requiring racial segregation in railroad facilities was held constitutional. The decision laid down the "separate but equal" doctrine—that segregation as such does not violate the equal protection guaranty, provided the separate facilities are substantially equal. (See pages 129, 130, and 217.)

Reapportionment Cases (Reynolds v. Sims), 377 U.S. 533 (1964).
This decision rules that seats in state legislatures must be apportioned on the basis of an "equal population" principle. Equal protection demands substantially equal legislative representation for all citizens. (See page 291.)

Roberson v. Rochester Folding Box Co., 171 N.Y. 538 (1902).
An action to recover damages for violation of the right of privacy by the unauthorized use of the plaintiff's photo was held not maintainable on the ground that, without a statute, the law does not recognize any right of privacy. (See page 244.)

Roth Case (Roth v. United States), 354 U.S. 476 (1957).
This decision holds that obscene speech is not protected by the First Amendment. The opinion lays down a test to determine whether particular material is obscene, in terms of whether, to the average person, applying contemporary community standards, the dominant theme of the material appeals to prurient interest. (See page 306.)

Rylands v. Fletcher, L.R. 3 H.L. 330 (1868).
The defendants were held liable for flooding caused by a reservoir built by them on their land. The decision lays down the rule of absolute liability upon a landowner who brought on his land anything likely to do mischief if it escaped. (See page 157.)

Santa Clara County v. Southern Pac. R. Co., 118 U.S. 394 (1886).
An action to recover taxes, in which the defendant corporation could attack the laws on the ground that they violated the equal protection guaranty. This was the first decision holding that corporations are "persons" within the protection of the Fourteenth Amendment. (See page 131.)

Scenic Hudson Case (Scenic Hudson Preservation Conference v. Federal Power Commission), 354 F. 2d 608 (2d Cir. 1965).
An FPC order granting a license to construct a hydroelectric plant in the Hudson Valley was set aside because of the commission's failure adequately to consider the environmental impact of the plant. (See page 319.)

See v. Seattle, 387 U.S. 541 (1967).
A conviction for refusing to permit a fire inspector to examine a commercial warehouse without a warrant was reversed. The rule laid down in *Camara v. Municipal Court*, barring warrantless inspections, applied to business as well as residential premises. (See page 319.)

Slaughter-House Cases, 16 Wall. 36 (U.S. 1873).
A Louisiana law conferring a monopoly to slaughter livestock in New Orleans was held not violative of the Fourteenth Amendment. Privileges and immunities protected by the amendment do not include the right to earn a livelihood. Nor is due process violated, since the law does not involve deprivation of property. This case is noted for its narrow interpretation of the Fourteenth Amendment. (See pages 121, 124, and 133.)

Social Security Act Cases (Carmichael v. Southern Coal Co.), 301 U.S. 495 (1937), (Steward Machine Co. v. Davis), 301 U.S. 548 (1937).
Unemployment insurance and old-age insurance programs set up by the Social Security Act were held constitutional as valid exercises of the congressional power to tax and spend to provide for the general welfare. (See page 204.)

Sugar Trust Case (United States v. E. C. Knight Co.), 156 U.S. 1 (1895).
An action to enjoin the acquisition of sugar refineries as violative of the Sherman Anti-Trust Act was held not main-

tainable on the ground that the activities involved concerned manufacturing, not commerce, and hence did not come within the federal commerce power. (See page 172.)

Tenement House Cigar Case (Matter of Application of Jacobs), 98 N.Y. 98 (1885).
A New York law prohibiting cigar manufacture in tenements was held violative of due process. The law is an invalid denial of the right to carry on a lawful trade and, as such, is an arbitrary deprivation of property and liberty. (See page 135.)

Trevett v. Weeden (R.I. 1786).
One of the first cases in which a law was held unconstitutional. A Rhode Island statute was held invalid on the ground that it involved a violation of the right to a jury trial. (See page 91.)

Wabash Case (Wabash, St. Louis & Pacific Railway v. Illinois), 118 U.S. 557 (1886).
A state law regulating railroad rates was held unconstitutional as it applied to transportation whose origin or destination was beyond the boundaries of the state. Only Congress may regulate such interstate rates. (See page 179.)

Writs of Assistance Case (Mass. 1761).
A case in the Massachusetts Superior Court on the validity of general warrants sought by Crown officials in Boston. The case was noted for James Otis's argument against the legality of writs of assistance, perhaps the first American statement of the doctrine that legislation must comply with fundamental constitutional principles. (See page 18.)

Wynehamer v. People, 13 N.Y. 378 (1856).
A New York law prohibiting the sale of liquor was held violative of due process. This was one of the first decisions to be based upon due process as a substantive, as well as procedural, concept. (See page 69.)

Glossary of Legal Terms

agency That branch of the law which governs the relationship of principal and agent, where the latter acts for or represents the former by his authority.

allodial tenure The holding of land in absolute ownership, without obligation of service to an overlord.

attainder A legislative act directed against a specified person finding him guilty of some offense and imposing a penalty upon him.

attornment In old English law, the transfer by a lord of the services of his tenant to a new lord; more recently, the act by which a tenant acknowledges his obligation to a new landlord.

baron and feme The law governing the relations between husband and wife.

case law Law made through court decisions, rather than by statutes enacted by the legislature.

certiorari A writ commanding inferior courts to certify proceedings for review by higher courts, now used as the normal method of obtaining review by the U.S. Supreme Court.

chancery The court which developed the law of equity, as distinguished from the common-law courts.

civil law The system of law in countries deriving their law from Roman law, emphasizing statute law as opposed to case law.

common law The body of law developed by the English courts emphasizing case law, as opposed to civil law which emphasizes enacted law.

confession of judgment The act of a debtor in waiving defenses and permitting judgment by default to be entered against him.

contract of adhesion A standardized contract of the type used by large companies, such as insurance companies and banks.

deficiency judgment The amount due after a judgment has been partially satisfied, as through sale of mortgaged property.

double jeopardy The prosecution of an individual more than once for the same offense.

eminent domain The power to take private property for a public use or purpose.

entail Property restricted in succession to the owner's lineal descendants or a restricted class of them.

equity The system of law developed by the Court of Chancery, as distinguished from that developed by the common-law courts.

estate tail Property which descends to the owner's lineal descendants (children, grandchildren, etc.) so long as his posterity endures in a direct line.

evidence Proof legally presented at a trial and the law governing the manner in which it may be presented.

factor A commercial agent employed to sell merchandise consigned to him.

fee simple Property owned absolutely, with unconditional power of disposition during the owner's life and which descends to his heirs at his death.

fee tail   Property with a fixed line of succession to the owner's lineal descendants.

feoffment   The deed or conveyance by which property is transferred; originally the grant of land under feudal law.

garnishment   A proceeding whereby a person's property, money, or credits in the possession of another are applied to the former's debt to a third person.

habeas corpus   The writ used to challenge the legality of imprisonment or detention.

holder in due course doctrine   Under it, defenses available against one to whom a note, check, or bill of exchange is issued are not available against a holder in due course who took it in good faith and for value.

impeachment   A legislative proceeding to remove an executive or judicial officer for specified misconduct.

indictment   Accusation by a grand jury formally charging the person named with a specified crime.

jus disponendi   The power to dispose of property.

jus utendi et abutendi re   The right to use and to do exactly as one likes with property.

law merchant   Commercial law, originally based upon the rules, customs, and usages recognized by merchants and traders.

negotiable instrument   Any written promise or order to pay money which may be transferred by endorsement and delivery.

nolo contendere   A criminal plea of no contest, which has the effect of a guilty plea, but may not be used elsewhere as an admission.

person sui juris   A person having full legal capacity to manage his own affairs.

primogeniture   The exclusive right of inheritance belonging to the eldest son, to the exclusion of younger children.

procedural law   The branch of the law governing the way in which legal rights are vindicated, particularly the procedure in cases in court.

remainder   The remnant of an estate in land depending on any prior estate created, as where A is given the land for life, the remainder to B, which B receives after A dies.

reversion   The interest left in grantors of land and their heirs which comes back to them after the interests granted come to an end.

seignory   The right of a lord in land under feudal law.

seisin   The investiture of title by possession under feudal law.

settlor   The one who creates a trust.

sovereign immunity doctrine   The doctrine which bars suits against a government without its consent.

spendrift trust   A trust which is secured against the beneficiary's improvidence by restrictions against alienations by the beneficiary or his creditors.

stare decisis   The doctrine of adherence to the precedents laid down in decided cases.

statute law   The law laid down in legislative enactments.

substantive due process   Due process as a restraint upon the substance of laws, essentially a restraint against arbitrary laws.

substantive law   That part of the law which creates, defines, and regulates rights, as opposed to procedural law, which prescribes the procedures by which rights are vindicated.

sumptuary law   A law regulating conduct on moral grounds, such as a law against gambling or prostitution.

tenure   The method or system of holding land.

tort   A civil wrong; the wrong committed by a noncontractual breach of duties which causes injuries for which the law gives redress.

uses   The rights to the profits of land to which another has legal title and possession.

venue   The district in which an action is or may be brought.

Acknowledgments

Chicago Historical Society
   Mary Frances Rhymer
Bradley Barton Davis, New York
Meryle Evans, New York
The Free Library of Philadelphia
   Howell J. Heaney
   Frank Halperin
Shirley Green, Washington, D.C.
Harvard University Law School
   Mary L. Fisher

Elton M. Hyder, Jr., Fort Worth, Texas
Daniel W. Jones, New York
The Legal Aid Society, New York
   Susan Marx
Library of Congress
   Jerry Kearns
Harold Medina, Jr., New York
National Gallery of Art, Washington
   Caroline Backlund
The New-York Historical Society

Wilson G. Duprey
New York State Historical Association
   M. W. Thomas, Jr.
Northwestern University School of Law
   Kurt Schwerin
Christine Sutherland, London
University of Texas Law School
   Helen Hargrave
   Roy Mirsky
Larry Warner, Amarillo, Texas

Bibliography

Association of American Law Schools, *Select Essays in Anglo-American Legal History*, Boston, Little, Brown (1907–1909)

Berle, Adolph Augustus, and Means, Gardiner C., *The Modern Corporation and Private Property*, New York, Chicago, Commerce Clearing House (1932)

Beveridge, Albert Jeremiah, *The Life of John Marshall*, Boston, Houghton Mifflin (4 vols., 1919)

Bryce, James, *The American Commonwealth*, London, Macmillan (2 vols., 1888)

Carter, James Coolidge, *Law: its Origin, Growth and Function*, New York, G. P. Putnam's Sons (1907)

Chroust, Anton Hermann, *The Rise of the Legal Profession in America*, Norman, University of Oklahoma (2 vols., 1965)

Cooley, Thomas M., *A Treatise on the Constitutional Limitations, Which Rest upon the legislative power of the States of the American union*, Boston, Little, Brown (1868)

Corwin, Edward Samuel, *Constitutional revolution, ltd.*, Claremont, Calif., Pomono, Scripps, and Claremont Colleges (1941)

Cushman, Robert Eugene, *The Independent Regulatory Commissions*, New York, Oxford University (1941)

Dunne, Gerald T., *Justice Story and the Rise of the Supreme Court*, New York, Simon and Schuster (1971)

Fairman, Charles, *Mr. Justice Miller and the Supreme Court, 1862–1890*, Cambridge, Harvard University (1939)

Fairman, Charles, *Reconstruction and Reunion, 1864–1888 (History of the U.S. Supreme Court, Vol. 6)* New York, Macmillan (1971)

Fleming, Donald, and Bailyn, Bernard, eds., *Law in American History*, Cambridge, Harvard University (1971)

Frankfurter, Felix, *Mr. Justice Holmes and the Supreme Court*, Cambridge, Harvard University (1938)

Frankfurter, Felix, *Of Law and Men; papers and addresses, 1939–1956*, New York, Harcourt, Brace (1956)

Frankfurter, Felix, *The Commerce Clause Under Marshall, Taney and Waite*, Chapel Hill, North Carolina University (1937)

Friedman, Lawrence Meir, *A History of American Law*, New York, Simon and Schuster (1973)

Goebel, Julius, *Antecedents and Beginnings to 1801 (History of the U.S. Supreme Court, Volume 1)*, New York, Macmillan (1971)

Haar, Charles Monroe, ed., *The Golden Age of American Law*, New York, George Braziller (1965)

Hoffman, Paul, *Lions in the Street: The Inside Story of the Great Wall Street Law Firms*, New York, Saturday Review (1973)

Holmes, Oliver Wendell, *The Common Law*, Boston, Little, Brown (1881)

Horton, John Theodore, *James Kent, A Study in Conservatism, 1763–1847*, New York, Appleton-Century (1939)

Howe, Mark DeWolfe, *Justice Oliver Wendell Holmes*, Cambridge, Harvard University (2 vols., 1957–1963)

Howe, Mark DeWolfe, *Readings in American Legal History*, Cambridge, Harvard University (1949)

Hurst, James Willard, *The Growth of American Law: The Law Makers*, Boston, Little, Brown (1950)

Hurst, James Willard, *Law and Social Process in United States History*, Ann Arbor, University of Michigan Law School (1960)

Hurst, James Willard, *Law and the Conditions of Freedom in the Nineteenth-century United States*, Madison, University of Wisconsin (1956)

Hurst, James Willard, *The Legitimacy of the Business Corporation in the United States*, Charlottesville, University of Virginia (1970)

Jackson, Robert H., *The Struggle for Judicial Supremacy*, New York, Knopf (1941)

Kent, William, *Memoirs and Letters of James Kent*, Boston, Little, Brown (1898)

Kutler, Stanley I., ed., *The Dred Scott Decision: Law or Politics?*, Boston, Houghton Mifflin (1967)

Kutler, Stanley I., ed., *Judicial Power and Reconstruction Politics*, Chicago, University of Chicago (1968)

Kutler, Stanley I., *Privilege and Creative Destruction, The Charles River Bridge Case*, Philadelphia, Lippincott (1971)

Levy, Leonard W., *The Law of the Commonwealth and Chief Justice Shaw*, Cambridge, Harvard University (1957)

Lewis, Walker, *Without Fear or Favor, a biography of Chief Justice Taney*, Boston, Houghton Mifflin (1965)

Lewis, William Draper, ed., *Great American Lawyers*, Philadephia, John C. Winston Co. (8 vols., 1907–1909).

Magrath, C. Peter, *Morrison R. Waite: The Triumph of Character*, New York, Macmillan (1963)

Marke, Julius J., *Vignettes of Legal History*, South Hackensack, N.J., F. B. Rothman (1965)

McCloskey, Robert Green, *The Modern Supreme Court*, Cambridge, Harvard University (1972)

Means, Gardiner C., *The Corporate Revolution in America*, New York, Crowell-Collier (1962)

Miller, Perry, *The Legal Mind in America*, New York, Doubleday (1962)

Miller, Perry, *The Life of the Mind in America*, New York, Harcourt, Brace & World (1965)

Pound, Roscoe, *The Formative Era of American Law*, Boston, Little, Brown (1938)

Pound, Roscoe, *Interpretations of Legal History*, New York, Macmillan (1923)

Pound, Roscoe, *The Lawyer from Antiquity to Modern Times*, St. Paul, West (1953)

Pound, Roscoe, *The Spirit of the Common Law*, Boston, Beacon Press (reprint of 1921 ed.) (1963)

Pusey, Merlo J., *Charles Evans Hughes*, New York, Macmillan (2 vols., 1951)

Radin, Max, *Handbook of Anglo-American Legal History*, St. Paul, West (1936)

Reid, John P., *Chief Justice, the Judicial World of Charles Doe*, Cambridge, Harvard University (1967)

Reppy, Alison, ed., *David Dudley Field: Centenary Essays*, New York, New York University (1949)

Reppy, Alison, ed., *Law: A Century of Progress*, New York, New York University (3 vols., 1937)

Rogers, James Grafton, *American Bar Leaders*, Chicago, American Bar Association (1932)

Rostow, Eugene Victor, ed., *Is Law Dead?*, New York, Simon and Schuster (1971)

Schwartz, Bernard, *A Basic History of the U.S. Supreme Court*, Princeton, Van Nostrand (1968)

Schwartz, Bernard, *The Bill of Rights: A Documentary History*, New York, Chelsea House-McGraw-Hill (2 vols., 1971)

Schwartz, Bernard, *The Fourteenth Amendment Centennial*, New York, New York University (1970)

Schwartz, Bernard, *From Confederation to Nation: The American Constitution, 1835–1877*, Baltimore, Johns Hopkins (1973)

Schwartz, Bernard, *The Reins of Power*, New York, Hill and Wang (1963)

Schwartz, Mortimer D., and Hogan, John C., eds., *Joseph Story*, New York, Oceana (1959)

Story, William Wetmore, *Life and Letters of Joseph Story*, Boston, Little, Brown (2 vols., 1851)

Sunderland, Edson R., *History of the American Bar Association*, Ann Arbor, American Bar Association (1953)

Swaine, Robert Taylor, *The Cravath Firm and its Predecessors, 1819–1947*, New York, Ad Press (3 vols., 1946–1948)

Swisher, Carl B., *Roger B. Taney*, New York, Macmillan (1935)

Swisher, Carl B., *Stephen J. Field Craftsman of the Law*, Washington, Brookings Institution (1930)

Twiss, Benjamin R., *Lawyers and the Constitution, How Laissez Faire Came to the Supreme Court*, Princeton University (1942)

Tyler, Samuel, *Memoir of Roger Brooke Taney*, Baltimore, J. Murphy and Co. (1872)

Umbreit, Kenneth Bernard, *Our Eleven Chief Justices*, New York, Harper (1938)

Vanderbilt, Arthur T., *The Challenge of Law Reform*, Princeton, Princeton University (1955)

Vanderbilt, Arthur T., *Men and Measures in the Law*, New York, Knopf (1949)

Warren, Charles, *A History of the American Bar*, Boston, Little, Brown (1913)

Warren, Charles, *History of the Harvard Law School and of Early Legal Conditions in America*, New York, Lewis Pub. Co. (3 vols., 1908)

Warren, Charles, *The Supreme Court in United States History*, Boston, Little, Brown (3 vols., 1922)

Index Page numbers in boldface type refer to illustrations.